Content Delivery Networks:
Web Switching for Security,
Availability, and Speed

About the Author

Scot Hull is a graduate of the University of Maryland where he went AWOL from the Ph.D. program in philosophy and artificial intelligence six years ago. Currently, he is working as a network architect with America Online, where is his job responsibilities include the design and implementation of a next-generation network infrastructure for all of AOL-Time Warner. With over six years of industry experience, he has managed to do just about everything, from help desk work that caused him to run screaming into the night, to professional consulting for Nortel Networks, where he first became irradiated by Content Networking. Way back when, for reasons still unknown to him, he was allowed to teach Windows OS seminars countrywide, and more surpassing still, managed to achieve critical acclaim doing so. Later certified as an MCT, he taught the entirety of the Microsoft Certified Systems Engineer track as well as a dozen elective courses for Orange Technologies. Certified by Cisco as both a CCNP and CCDP, he is currently leading a frontal assault on Mount CCIE, and plans to take down the Juniper JNCIE, cancer and world hunger immediately following. He still gives professional talks and seminars on a variety of networking topics, including the new field of Content Networking. You can find him at tradeshows, goofing off online (sthull01@aol.com), or feverishly devising clever plot twists for his first novel.

About the Contributors

Calvin Au is currently a senior network architect at IBM Canada Ltd. He is a graduate from the University of Waterloo with a bachelor's of mathematics, majoring in computer science. Although his academic background was in software development, he has had extensive experience in the networking field. His credentials include Cisco CCIE and Nortel Support Expert (formerly Bay Networks Router Expert). In his spare time, Calvin enjoys tennis, basketball, and cycling.

Erik Brandsberg is currently a senior sales engineer for NetScaler, Inc., a Silicon Valley startup networking company that provides advanced network products for Content Networking. Formerly, Erik had worked at Alteon WebSystems and Exodus Communications as a network engineer, and before that had owned his own ISP in Alabama. It was during this time that his interest in Content Networking started, with the integration of the IP Filter package in FreeBSD with Squid for transparent proxying. Since then, Erik has been working with many major websites in product evaluations and network deployments, including the WWF, Lycos, Google, Yahoo, Siebel, and others. Outside of work, Erik spends his time with his lovely wife Janel, and two kids, Sydnee and John, or spending far too much time working on their house in Morgan Hill, California.

Perry Jannette is a senior network engineer with extensive knowledge in network design and optimization. He holds advanced certifications from Cisco as CCIE 7632, from Checkpoint as a CCSE, and from Microsoft as an MCSE. In addition to technical writing, his expertise includes Content Networking, routing protocols, and security. A native of the frosty north, Perry now lives with his wife in balmy Atlanta, Georgia, where he spends most of his free time playing with the latest and greatest computer gadgets.

Shannon M. Lake Sr., is the founder and CEO of OMNIVERGENT Communications. He has been managing consultant for clients such as Cisco Systems, Nortel Networks, Lucent Technologies, Intel Corporation, Phillips, Hitachi, Sniffer/Network Associates, Fore, and Redback Networks. He has worked with over 15 of the largest service providers. He has more than ten years professional and teaching experience in the telecommunications and advanced network service industries. His lecture topics range from Optical Networks to Network Architectures and also include software-based voice and video over IP and Directory Services technologies. His teaching settings have included the military, technology industry, and academia including UC Berkeley, UC Santa Cruz, UC Irvine, and UC San Diego. He has published several articles and is a contributing author on topics ranging from microprocessor design to convergence technology, and is an involved member of the press. He is working on a book called *Advanced Voice and Video over Circuit Oriented Data Networks: Omnivergent Technologies*. You can find out more information about him at http://www.slakeinfo.com or http://www.shannonlake.tv.

Kent Schumann has been a director of various technology, manufacturing, marketing, and services-related organizations for companies such as Nortel Networks, Alteon WebSystems, GTE Internetworking, Network General, Harman International, and Seymour Duncan. Kent has lived on both sides of the technology fence—leading enterprise IT teams as well as running organizations that provide solutions to IT departments. His technology expertise encompasses data networking, security, web hosting, and ISP infrastructure as well as various other areas. Kent received a bachelor's degree in political science from UC Santa Barbara, an M.B.A in technology management from the University of Phoenix, and is currently pursuing a juris doctorate from Concord University. He is also a Certified Production and Inventory Management (CPIM) professional from APICS.

Steve Shah (Riverside, CA) has been a UNIX systems/network administrator since 1992 and a programmer since 1986. Currently, he is responsible for administering five variants of UNIX and three variants of Windows NT. He has been working with Linux since version 1.09 (1994) and has administered Linux workstations since 1996. Steve is the author of both editions of *Linux Administration: A Beginner's Guide* and has contributed as an author of several publications including *Unix Unleashed* (Editions 1-3), *Red Hat Linux Unleashed* (Editions 2-3), and *Using Unix, 2nd Edition*. He has a B.S. in computer science and creative writing and an M.S. in computer science from the University of California, Riverside.

Dick Sison has held various pre-sales, post-sales, and technical training positions in the internetworking industry for over 20 years. His most recent position is Solutions Architect for Nortel Networks, where his expertise includes designing server load balancing networks. Prior to that, he was a network architect for Unisys Corporation designing LAN/WAN solutions in a pre-sales role. He holds vendor certifications as Master CNE with Novell, CCDP and CCNP with Cisco, and CCSE with Checkpoint.

Steve Wright currently works as a network engineer for America Online. Steve has several years of extensive network experience in both systems and infrastructure as both an engineer and a technical instructor, and his credentials include Cisco CCNP, Nortel ACE, and Microsoft Certified Instructor/Professional.

Content Delivery Networks: Web Switching for Security, Availability, and Speed

SCOT **HULL**

McGraw-Hill/Osborne

New York   Chicago   San Francisco
Lisbon   London   Madrid   Mexico City
Milan   New Delhi   San Juan
Seoul   Singapore   Sydney   Toronto

McGraw-Hill/Osborne
2600 Tenth Street
Berkeley, California 94710
U.S.A.

To arrange bulk purchase discounts for sales promotions, premiums, or fund-raisers, please contact **McGraw-Hill**/Osborne at the above address. For information on translations or book distributors outside the U.S.A., please see the International Contact Information page immediately following the index of this book.

Content Delivery Networks: Web Switching for Security, Availability, and Speed

1234567890 CUS CUS 0198765432

ISBN 0-07-219046-9

Publisher	**Proofreader**
Brandon A. Nordin	John Gildersleeve
Vice President & Associate Publisher	**Indexer**
Scott Rogers	Claire Splan
Acquisitions Editor	**Computer Designers**
Francis Kelly	Carie Abrew, Mickey Galicia
Technical Editor	**Illustrators**
Mahmoud Harb	Mickey Galicia, Michael Mueller,
Copy Editor	Lyssa Wald
Marcia Baker	**Series Design**
	Peter F. Hancik

This book was composed with Corel VENTURA ™ Publisher.

To my wife Julia. With all my love, forever and always.
And to Gus and Buster, for teaching me that some of the best things in
life are barking, running around in circles, one's own behind, hotdogs,
a good ear-scratch, and six-hour naps.
Life is definitely full of surprises. Who knew?

AT A GLANCE

CONTENTS

FOREWORD

funny thing happened on the way to my Ph.D. in philosophy. I went broke! I suppose that that's a sad cliché, but that's the way of it. To earn enough money to continue going to school, I took a job at a helpdesk, answering installation and configuration questions for the then-new Metropolitan Regional Information System for regional realtors. I worked there for about three months, and decided that I'd rather stick a needle in my eye than continue working at a help desk. I hadn't any notion of where to go to next, so I went where all good wannabe techies go—to a recruiter.

Having led seminar groups and given talks and such in grad school, and also having had some personal experience troubleshooting my personal Windows PC, I was obviously qualified for teaching Windows NT. So, I began my first training experience, traveling countrywide, teaching the same two-day Windows seminar in two cities a week, every week, for nine months. At the end of that job, I was so desperately bored that I started going out of my way to do what I could to make the trips more fun. Just to keep from going nuts, I ended up spending more than I was earning. My next jobs were consulting-oriented and educational, if slow. While working as a consultant and waiting for something to happen, I started technical writing and wrote a column for *Windows NT Magazine* called "Ask the Answer Desk" in a feature called "Inside Active Directory". Shortly thereafter, I got the opportunity to go back to training, so I jumped at it. I got my MCSE while teaching others to do the same, and had a lot of fun. From the LAN, I branched out into internetworking and security, and got my CCNP, CCDP, and CCSE.

I went to Alteon with the hope of trying to catch the caboose of the IPO train, and with the Nortel Networks acquisition, things were looking up. I was learning a lot about CDN technology, as well as designing and implementing CDNs. Then the market went south, and all my daydreams of early retirement with untold wealth died an unpleasant death. It's sad, really. But then I got the opportunity to go to AOL to design and implement all sorts of fantastic technologies I had toyed with for previous six years, and to explore even more.

Currently, my job responsibilities include network design, review, and implementation as well as new technology vetting and implementation. In addition to technical writing, I have presented seminars on Internet technologies, Content Delivery Networking, and network design issues. I can be reached by email, at <sthull01@aol.com>.

ACKNOWLEDGMENTS

This book, like many, is the product of many minds, and was definitely a team effort from its inception. This book has undergone a significant number of changes since then, with material passing from and into the hands of numerous individuals, listed here. Without them, you wouldn't be reading this; so to them, all thanks.

Benedicto Sison was a colleague of mine at Alteon WebSystems and Nortel Networks. Dick was an early and enthusiastic participant in this project, and with frightening efficiency, truly kicked things off by creating Chapter 9, and then stepping in again with Chapter 14.

Steve Shah, an ex-Alteonite now with Array Networks, stepped in at the eleventh hour and helped bring the book to a successful conclusion. His contributions are Chapters 5 and 8. Steve was a lucky find for me, and it was in large part to his high-caliber work that this project could be finished at all.

Kent Schumann, the director of Professional Services at Alteon WebSystems, was the driving force behind this project. Without his support, this book wouldn't have been possible. Without his encouragement, advice, vision, and rigor, this book would be less than it is. He was a great boss, and such a pleasure to work for, that I'm here, a year after parting ways, still sucking up! Kent spent many, many long months writing a viable introduction into the complex world of Content Delivery Networking, and that work has become Chapter 1.

Erik Brandsberg, also an Alteon/Nortel refugee, was the brains behind the DNS esoterica and the complexities of global networking, and was hunted, harried, and browbeaten into contributing heavily to Chapters 6 and 11. Erik now works for NetScaler, out of San Jose.

Perry Jannette is a CCIE whose greatest joy in life was writing Chapter 4 for this book. It was a pleasure, he has repeatedly told me, that could not be equaled. He is available for more writing assignments, and likes nothing better. All interested parties in Perry's writing services should contact him directly.

Calvin Au, a CCIE with IBM, was another last-minute addition to the team, stepping in for Chapter 3. Calvin, together with Steve Shah, truly helped bring it all together.

Steven Wright assisted with the technical detail of Chapter 12, but it was his continual needling and mockery that gave me the incentive, reason, and drive to finish, if for no other reason than to be able to thumb my nose at him. A colleague since 1996, Steve also worked for Alteon and Nortel Networks and currently is a network engineer for America Online.

I'd also like to thank Tom Ford, Shannon Lake, Meade Eggleston, Dev Roshan, Tom Porter, and Bryan Duvall for their comments and assistance with early drafts of various chapters. Each, at various points, helped to provide direction and organization for various chapters.

Finally, thanks to my editor, Francis Kelly. Your near-infinite patience made working with you a true pleasure, and your flexibility allowed the book to grow as you watched. I told you we'd get it done!

Thanks to all of them! My sincerest apologies to those I've overlooked.

INTRODUCTION

This book is about Content Delivery Networks (CDN), how to build them, why and when it's worth it (or not), and what you're doing to yourself when/if you do decide to build one. This book isn't a cookbook, it isn't a design guide, it isn't a technology review, but it's really all three. It's targeted at the technical manager, who has to make the decisions surrounding network design and optimization. It's targeted at the network engineer, who needs to implement the decisions that a manager will make. It's targeted at the curious, who are learning these problems and their technology solutions for the first time.

The technologies discussed here are both new and not so new. DNS, well, that's not new, but GSLB is. Since the beginning of this project, what has changed most isn't the solutions, it's number of players providing them. A year or so ago, very few vendors were aggressively marketing CDN solutions. Now, quite a few are, Array Networks and Extreme Networks being two of the newest entrants into the CDN market. On the other hand, the two largest internetworking equipment providers acquired two of the leading CDN vendors: Nortel Networks acquired Alteon and Cisco Systems got Arrowpoint. And in the last year, all of these vendors have seen their stock do something unexpected: collapse.

Perhaps as a direct result of the latter, a shift has emerged from the outsourcing model to the do-it-yourself model. Companies like Akamai and Digital Island have steadily lost ground to the corporate network architects who are willing to take on the design complexities themselves, with the vendors supplying them solutions. This book is especially for those architects, and the focus is on how to "do-it-yourself," as opposed to how to outsource it.

This is an interesting time, and these market changes mean crucial things for those interested in deploying Content Networking services to design and optimize their network infrastructures. First, with a sharp decline in investments following the stock market collapse in late 2000, very little truly new and innovative technologies have been created in the last year, making this book and the solutions herein still very timely. Second, Content Networking as a field, as well as the solutions that vendors are providing, have had another year to mature and stabilize, even if little in the way of advances has been in the offing. This means that current implementation decisions are still going to be relevant and sound, and will have significant beneficial technical impact. Finally, when the inevitable turnaround comes, corporations *will* look to start spending capital on infrastructure again, investments that have been forestalled by the slowing economy. Historically, the first types of investments made by such companies will not be in old technologies, but rather in the new, and nothing is newer than CDNs. The time for Content Networking is on the horizon, and the best solutions have yet to be invented.

This book is a discussion of solutions and the technologies that go into them and underlie them. The solutions vary across platforms, and this was partially deliberate and partially accidental. In relevant chapters, there are Case Studies that help illustrate some of the topics raised within the chapter. The hardware platforms vary and include Cisco, Alteon, Juniper, and others. As these design guides are included for illustrative purposes, the platforms mentioned are both relevant and convenient; no particular vendor bias is intended. When vendors are discussed in the text, the intention is to explore the best of breed solutions, knowing full well that as the state of the art changes, so too do the best possible targets for discussion. The intent was not to focus too deliberately on any one vendor's solution.

This book is a technology review and is an attempt to cover the breadth of the new and emerging field of Content Networking. The background technologies, such as Ethernet, HTTP, and SSL, are included for the sake of completeness and for those lacking such background. Some chapters, such as Chapters 6–8, cover material not likely to be well covered elsewhere, such as a discussion of DNS function (not just configuration), the impact of Network Access Point on network backbone design, and the latest solutions in web caching. The last five chapters focus specifically on how these underlying technologies are combined to create the old/new solutions that are Content Networking. Topics include Server Load Balancing, advanced SLB protocols, filtering and Firewall Load Balancing, Application Redirection, Bandwidth Management, and Global Server Load Balancing.

For those interested in exploring CDN technology, this book is a great first step. For those interested in taking it beyond that level, this book will be an invaluable resource.

CHAPTER 1

Introduction to Content Networking

OBJECTIVES

▼ Identify customer expectations for Content Networking

■ Define Content Networking

■ Describe the evolution to Content Networking

▲ Explain the technology fundamentals of Content Networking

In the old days, before the Internet revolution, companies ran their businesses on large, powerful, centralized systems, such as mini- and mainframe computers—AS/400, RS/6000, HP3000, HP9000, and many others. Intelligence and content were both contained within these systems. As the old economy grew at its stable rate, these systems would be expanded and upgraded to meet the slowly changing needs of its users.

In the mid-1990s everything changed. Internet-based infrastructures were expected to meet many different—and often conflicting—requirements, from both end users and content providers. From this radical change came many of the new concepts and technologies that make up Content Networking today. To understand how this technology works and where this industry is going, you need to understand where it came from and what's expected/required from it.

First, the players. *Users* can be defined as those clients who retrieve a given piece of content. That content could be an article from an online newspaper or a piece of financial information from an online banking institution, or receiving confirmation about a placed order for a selected item. *Content providers* can be divided into two categories: content owners and content delivery agents. As you might expect, the *content owners* own and control the content itself, whether that content is an audio file, a transaction providing a piece of inventory, or the latest election results. *Content delivery agents,* on the other hand, are those companies that provide the content owners with mechanisms to deliver their content more successfully to users around the globe at higher speeds and/or lower costs than they could otherwise do. These are traditionally the *xSPs*—service providers of various flavors.

Now that you know the *who*, it's important to understand the *what*—specifically, what these different parties expect from one another to address the issues properly that Content Networking infrastructures are built to handle.

USER EXPECTATIONS

When the new Internet economy was born in the 1990s, few people realized it would have so much impact on our culture, our economy, and our lives. The expectations by users of technology-based systems changed radically from what they'd been in the past. Seven major areas of user expectations shifted during this period and directly relate to the discussion of Content Delivery Networking (CDN). This isn't to say that the items on the following list weren't expected or required by users prior to the 1990s, of course. Instead, it's important to understand these expectations and requirements became pervasive throughout most demographics and user types in the 1990s, while they hadn't been present in a significant portion of the community a decade earlier. The list comprises the expectations and/or requirements users have of their computing- and content-based systems:

- ▼ Performance
- ■ Availability
- ■ Security
- ■ Anonymity
- ■ Ubiquity/Accessibility
- ■ Personalization/Relevancy
- ▲ Privacy

Each of these is addressed in turn.

Performance

No one ever enjoyed a slow computer system. Whether it's the user or the customer waiting on the phone for the rep to pull up the necessary data out of the computer, no one likes to wait. But, as the economy shifted to allow more direct access to computer systems by end customers, speed became an incredibly powerful tool because it directly related to customer satisfaction and retention—the so-called seven-second rule.[1] In this new economy, customer loyalty to a corporate web site isn't strong because switching to another site is easy. Suddenly, customers were demanding their vendors give them what they want—and it had better be quick.

Availability

Nothing better exemplifies the demand for availability than a television advertisement run by Internet pioneer Amazon.com in late 2000 and early 2001. The commercial shows a group of would-be shoppers at the locked entrance to their favorite shopping mall, attempting to do some late night shopping. The customers, staring blankly, appear to be baffled because the mall isn't open. This commercial underscores how Amazon.com and others changed the way customers shop. Just as customer expectations began to shift in the 1980s with 24-hour gas stations and super markets, in the 1990s customers began to expect high availability of their computer-based content—including all types of information and transaction data.

Security

Security is one of the most prevalent expectations in the user's conscious mind. Most studies indicate users continue to feel unsafe making purchases online because of fraud and theft. Unlike most of the other expectations, users currently have no way to evaluate a company's web security policy effectively and easily. The use of SSL is the only method to provide some hint of protection. But SSL only protects the data while in transit from client to server. Once the data is in the possession of the server or database, what assurances does a user have that their data will be secure?

Anonymity

Another huge distinction that can be made regarding customer expectations in the 1990s is the anonymity many people now take for granted. In the past, a computer/network client was part of a specific and well-defined community, such as a corporation, division, department, group, and so forth. Use could be controlled and monitored, if desired. Access to computer-based content could be restricted or delayed with relative ease because the impact of that restriction could be ascertained. As the Internet economy grew, and more unknown and undefined users began to access content, however, the impact of access (or lack thereof) to the content became much more complex and nearly impossible to measure accurately. Because many users of content aren't in a defined or subscribed grouping, it can be difficult, if not impossible, to notify them of downtime, slowdowns, or any type of change (even an improvement) that will affect their ability to access their desired content from where and when they want. Working hours and office location cannot be controlled by the content owners, unlike in the past when users were part of a corporation that could (and did) control time and location access to its content.

Personalization/Relevancy

Most users don't scream "I want more personalization!" Yet, personalization is a key factor to a user's satisfaction (or lack thereof) with a content site. Companies such as Yahoo! and Amazon.com have created powerful examples of this concept. Yahoo! created My.Yahoo. com as a user-configurable personalized content portal. By letting the user customize the content displayed to precisely represent their interests, users have strong encouragement to return to that site over and over again. Amazon uses a slightly different approach, by personalizing the content for the user, rather than making the user decide what content she wants to see. Amazon's system learns a user's interest by watching her shopping (and buying) patterns. This is akin to having a personal shopper at the local department store to help you find new and interesting items that match your personal taste. The simplest explanation is users require and respond to relevant content—and nothing is more relevant than content that's personalized for us.

Privacy

Telemarketers, junk mail, and door-to-door salesmen are only three prominent examples of why many users are outraged by the lack of solid privacy policies at many web sites. Users have learned the hard way that with only a little bit of information given out, the phone rings, the mailbox overflows, and the door is knocked on without their advance consent. Users want to be notified if their information will be shared with others. They want to be able to stop a transaction if this means someone will be tracking exactly what they buy and what they like. Whether it's to protect dirty little secrets or simply to guard one's right to privacy, users don't want their data indiscriminately used or distributed.

CONTENT PROVIDER EXPECTATIONS

Content and service providers also have certain expectations from the dramatic shift in computing paradigms over the past decade. These expectations include

▼ Security

■ Control

■ Manageability

■ Scalability

■ Flexibility

■ Diversity (devices and users)

■ Customer demographics/data

■ Differentiation

▲ Profitability

Security

Just as users expect their data to be protected by the content providers, the owners of the content want to keep data secure and inaccessible to unauthorized eyes. What good would it do to charge $4.95 per month for a subscription to a web site if any user could easily access the same content free? In addition, content providers owe their users secure systems that protect users' information, such as address, phone, social security, and credit cards.

True security is based on a multilayer approach, often given the analogy of peeling an onion. Layer after layer should be protected so, if one layer is comprised, the next layer still remains. Content networking doesn't address all layers of the onion—such as security policies and procedures—but it does address tools such as firewalls, virtual private networks (VPNs), intrusion detection systems, access control lists, filtering, and other such aspects of controlling unauthorized access.

Control

Content providers have only one true value on the Internet—the content they provide. So the capability to control that content becomes increasingly important. Whether it's controls that create different classes of service for different types of users (that is, bandwidth management) or the capability to select what types of content users access, content providers demand greater levels of control over their content to create a competitive advantage.

Manageability

As the complexity of Content Networking infrastructures increases, the capability to monitor and manage all the components becomes ever more crucial. Content providers need to have visibility into the performance of their systems to know if they're meeting the users' expectations of performance and availability. Even redundant systems are only truly useful if adequate monitoring and management is in place. If not, a redundant system might fail but go unnoticed, thus dramatically increasing the likelihood that a second failure might occur and cause an outage felt by users.

Scalability

Content providers must aim for the stars, yet keep a realistic perspective on their infrastructures. Because Internet-based infrastructures have the potential to reach the entire world (or at least the entire worldwide Internet community), a popular site can require incredible expansion over a short period of time. Yet, if a content provider intends to run a successful business, they must not overarchitect their infrastructure, lest the costs bankrupt them before ever seeing the dramatic expansion. So, content providers require the capability to expand their infrastructure easily, with minimal effort or disruption. This is the essence of *scalability*.

Flexibility

The entire Internet economy is a new, and essentially unknown, beast. Business models and fads rise and fall on a regular basis. It's critical for content providers to have flexibility in their infrastructures to adapt quickly to changing requirements from users and the Internet community. It might be years until a clearly successful approach exists to providing content on the Internet. Until that time, content providers need an infrastructure that enables them to take advantage of changing conditions and technologies easily without significant cost or disruption.

Diversity (Users and Devices)

With the expansion of Internet-enabled devices to include PDAs, wireless phones, and, eventually, our home appliances, it's critical that content and service providers are able to address the widest, most diverse groups of users to be successful. The delivery of content cannot be aimed at only one type of user. It needs to take into account the variety of users and devices that might request that content from anywhere at anytime.

Customer Demographics/Data

Content providers have a variety of different business value models to operate within. However, most models are most effective when the provider has accurate, detailed information about its users. Whether that data is used to target ads (that provide the revenue that pays for the content provided) or if the data is used to help target products to users based on their personal buying habits and interests, content providers must be able to make technical, networking decisions based on this type of information.

Differentiation

Although *differentiation* isn't something that can be specifically provided by technology, it's an important factor for service and content providers. Every company wants to be different. While a content networking solution provides serious differentiation if adopted earlier than competing firms, those competitors will likely adopt similar technology to survive. All significant differentiators are diminished and standardized over time. The most successful companies are constant innovators and always looking for a way to differentiate themselves for the 9 to 12 months that a new technology can exist without serious competition or emulation. Beyond that amount of time, companies would expect their competitors to copy their success and adopt similar technologies. The key factor for both content owners and service providers is to build infrastructures that are robust enough and scalable enough to allow them to innovate and differentiate themselves constantly as Content Networking systems continue to explode with new features and concepts. Companies that only implement the minimum structure to take advantage of today's technology might not have the right tools in place to take advantage of exciting new, incremental advancements of tomorrow.

Profitability

An old concept has reemerged in the new economy—profit. For many years in the late 1990s, Internet-based firms operated primarily on the basis of increasing revenue, market share, or mind share. Profitability was a long-term issue of little concern in the short run. As the new millennium got under way with recessionary tendencies, the frivolousness of the new economy quickly dissipated. Profitability once again is the key goal for all organizations. Content Networking solutions need to give content and service providers the capability to develop truly profitable businesses.

CONFLICTING EXPECTATIONS

The obvious challenge is how to provide users and content providers with tools, services, and infrastructures that meet or exceed their expectations. The even more devious challenge is how to do it simultaneously for both users and content providers because some of the expectations are in direct conflict with one another.

The most obvious conflict is between the user's expectation of privacy and the content provider's expectation of customer data. Users want to remain completely anonymous, while content providers want to know as much as possible about the users. Understanding the user is key to personalizing content. The situation surrounding the paranoia of privacy on the Internet is quite ironic. The irony is because many users and public user groups express serious concern over the protection of their privacy online, yet they completely ignore the reality of the non-Internet portion of their lives. Little has been done to control telemarketing, junk mail, and door-to-door salesmen that thrive on the demographic data gathered from many sources. The Internet is no different than any other medium: it can be most successful and provide useful content if it's allowed to understand its customers. The good news is, unlike those other intrusive methods of using (and sometimes abusing) collected data, the Internet allows for nonintrusive and constructive methods to personalize content for users. The amount of data that can be collected, analyzed, and used is far superior to the methods used with telemarketing or junk mail schemes. So users can get information relevant to them (and, thus, often desirable), while content providers can reach the most likely and relevant customer segments for their given product or service.

STRUCTURE OF THE INTERNET

While the design of the Internet was created to address one of the major expectations previously listed in terms of the network—availability—it does little to address other items, such as performance, security, and so forth. And, even with a highly available network, users aren't necessarily satisfied. Just as the Amazon.com commercial mall-goers are able to use the network of streets to reach the proper destination, if that destination is unavailable, a highly available network of streets and highways is wasted.

Problems of IP

Internet Protocol (IP) has won the protocol war against such rivals as Netbeui, IPX, DECnet, and many others. Yet IP isn't a perfect protocol. Because of the widespread adoption of the current version of IP, deficiencies, even if corrected, cannot be implemented easily or quickly.

The problem with IP is the simple fact that it's a nonintelligent delivery mechanism. The decisions it makes are based on a simple set of criteria to find the path to a given location. Using a delivery example, IP can find its way through multiple paths to get to a destination. Yet, when it arrives and rings the doorbell, if no one is home, it simply gives up. It doesn't peer through the window, it doesn't go through the gate and knock on the back door, and it doesn't go to the neighbor's house and try to deliver the package. It simply throws away the package. If someone is home, but tells the delivery person to go to another house, there's no problem. The problem arises only when no one answers the door—or at least the door isn't answered fast enough for the delivery person's patience.

The Internet is made up of thousands of different interconnected networks. Those connection points where a given network intersects another are usually referred to as *peering points,* which, public or private, can easily become congested and are often the cause of the many Internet traffic delays. In fact, three primary causes exist for poor Internet performance: peering point congestion, last-mile bottlenecks, and server constraints. These congestion points account for nearly all the delays users experience. In the future, congestion might also occur in the backbone network itself. But, today, so much overbuilt network backbone capacity exists that congestion is rarely an issue, except for a small number of older service providers. The *last-mile bottleneck* is an issue that can best be solved by enhanced access speeds using newer access topologies such as DSL, cable, two-way satellite, fixed wireless, and optical Ethernet. However, enterprises can remove some of the problem by implementing caching solutions. Consumers, for the most part, must rely on the service providers to offer high-speed access solutions to avoid the bottleneck.

Content Networking can alleviate many of the congestion problems caused by the other two common elements: peering points (by using caching and global load balancing) and server constraints (by using caching and local load balancing). Most of the following Content Networking discussions are aimed at solving these congestion dilemmas, while also trying to provide the many requirements discussed earlier. But it's important to remember that performance was the initial driving factor.

WHAT IS CONTENT NETWORKING?

To answer this question, another question must first be answered: What is content? *Content* can be any object that can be viewed, heard, purchased, sold, transmitted, or created. It can be a music file or video. It can be a piece of inventory—book, CD, flowers—or a used piece of equipment—computer, couch, or unfinished manuscript. It can be the latest news or the oldest novel.

Once you understand that content can be almost anything that's accessible via the Internet, you can begin to learn exactly what Content Networking is all about. Networking is quite well understood in its most basic concepts: it is the technical infrastructure that provides the conduit—the pathways—to interconnect different systems, so they can communicate with one another. Most people think of networking in terms of the 7-layer OSI model—focusing primarily on layer 2 (such as Ethernet switching) and layer 3 (such as IP routing). But content networking expands on this concept of a set of communication pathways. It creates powerful, yet complex, mechanisms to make communication path decisions based on more than simple technical labels (such as an IP address). Content Networking, as the name implies, makes networking decisions based on the content contained within the communication stream of help users and content providers to achieve their various expectations.

Living on the Edge

For today and the foreseeable future, content networking lives on the edges of the Internet—*both* edges. In user-initiated Internet networking (as opposed to system-to-system communication), the network traffic begins its life in some sort of Internet service provider (ISP) access point or point of presence (POP). This is the first edge of the Internet, called the *Subscriber Edge*. The traffic is most commonly directed across a network backbone (possibly multiple backbones through peering connections) and, eventually, ends at the other edge, in an Internet Data Center (IDC)—the *Content Edge*. Content networking has existed in the IDC for quite some time, while its prevalence in POPs is a relatively recent foray. Tremendous opportunities exist to use technology at *both* edges to meet user and content provider expectations.

CONTENT EDGE NETWORKING (CEN)—THE DATA CENTER

As previously mentioned, Content Networking has existed in the data center for quite some time. But its maturity and value-add have only recently become hot topics. We'll discuss some of the evolution that led us to where we are today, plus we'll look at some of the most fundamental technological concepts related to Content Networking in the data center, also referred to as *Content Edge Networking*.

CEN Evolution

As the Internet economy expanded rapidly in the mid-1990s, and as the list of expectations for both users and content providers began to grow into the long list mentioned previously, new approaches and technologies evolved to add new intelligence and value to traditional networking. The Internet economy required the capability to build a web infrastructure quickly, easily, and inexpensively yet, paradoxically, it also required the capability to grow massively without interrupting service. The first approach developed to address these conflicting requirements included two new concepts called server farms and round robin DNS.

Server Farms, RAIS, and DNS

The concept is fairly simple: create a set of similar servers with identical content to act as a unified and single entity. Similar to Redundant Array of Inexpensive Disks (RAID), the concept of low-cost, high-availability infrastructure expanded to the *server farm* or Redundant Array of Inexpensive Servers (RAIS). The initial challenge was how to make the servers appear as a single entity to the world. Because the Internet revolution, by its very nature, made client software and client configuration a thing of the past, the solution must be transparent to users. The existing Domain Name System (DNS) was a unique mechanism to mold this server farm into a single virtual system. By entering each IP address of the servers into the DNS records, clients would cycle through the various IP addresses and be evenly (roughly) spread across all the servers listed in the DNS records. These disparate servers could suddenly act as a single entity, without any client knowledge or need for reconfiguration.

Load Balancing Is Born

With this unique method of creating server farms, the concept of server load balancing (SLB) was born. Inexpensive servers can be added with relative ease. Traffic will spread among the various servers on a relatively equal basis, thus balancing the traffic among the servers. Although the term "load balancing" has always been used, this initial method (and a few other methods used later as well) was traffic balancing or session balancing. *Load*, which can be defined as not only the number of sessions but also the impact of those sessions on the servers, wasn't considered in the original equation. The term load balancing has been used consistently to describe all types of network traffic balancing whether or not true server "load" is ever considered.

DNS Is a Temporary Solution

As with many unique approaches and technologies, problems quickly arise that make old methods obsolete and create new opportunities for enhanced technology solutions. A group of engineers at Cisco Systems spearheaded an effort to overcome some serious limitations of the DNS-based load balancing solution. Cisco's Local Director was one of the first devices created for the explicit purpose of load balancing network traffic to a server farm.

The concept was simple: create a virtual IP address (VIP), which the DNS will point to. When traffic arrives at this VIP (which is contained on the load balancing device), the load balancer decides which of the servers in the server farm to send the traffic to. The Local Director product and the many products that quickly followed it—such as Alteon Networks, F5, and Arrowpoint—vastly improved on the DNS-based solution by enhancing two important areas of functionality: health checks and SLB Metrics.

Health Checks

The concept of the *health check* was quite possibly the single most important idea that allowed load balancing and content networking to be born. The fundamental flaw with round robin DNS-based load balancing was that it had no way of knowing whether the server to which it was directing traffic was functional. The foundational attribute of load balancers was that these devices could check to see if the server was, indeed, functioning properly. Health checks started out quite simple, at first testing only to see if ICMP packets could be received and responded to. This ensured the network, network interface card, operating system, and IP stack were functioning properly. Yet testing only those items still left a tremendous margin of error. Servers can be running, yet have the TCP stack no longer functioning properly. To address this, a TCP health check was soon added. This test attempts to open a TCP session to each server in the farm, and then close that session successfully. But, again, even with TCP running successfully, the specific application required by the user could be malfunctioning. So specific application-level health checks were developed, including POP, RADIUS, SMTP, and, of course, HTTP, where the device sends out a get request to a specific URL and checks to see if a 200 OK response is received.

Each type of health check follows the same process, regardless of type. At a set interval, the checks are sent out. If a check fails, the corresponding service on that server will be removed from rotation within the server farm. The health checks will continue to poll and, once they successfully achieve their results (usually three or four times in a row), the service on that server will be reengaged into the load balancing group.

Server Load Balancing Metrics

The concept of sending traffic to various servers in a farm might seem simple at first. And, in the beginning it was. The early load balancers provided a round robin approach to load balancing, similar to the original DNS method. This meant traffic would be sent equally to each server, one at a time. To this day, this method provides the most *equal* balancing of sessions between servers. The problem with this method is simple: not all servers are created equal!

One of the primary purposes and expectations of content providers from load balancing solutions is the capability to scale easily as traffic increases. The capability to start small, with minimal investment, and grow the infrastructure exponentially is a key reason why content networking solutions first evolved. Take the example of a web infrastructure that starts with only two servers but, a year and a half later, as demand and traffic have substantially increased, the site has expanded to 20 servers. If round robin is used to spread traffic among the servers, it's likely the load will be balanced, but far from optimized. This dilemma relates indirectly to Moore's Law, which says processing power doubles every 18 months. So, the servers purchased toward the end of the 18-month period are likely to have more memory, faster processors, faster disk drives, and many other improved efficiencies. Thus, server number 18 can probably handle many more sessions than server number 1. To address this dilemma, new metrics were created.

Weighted Round Robin   The first and most obvious solution to the problem of round robin's inefficient load balancing was simply to create a "weighting" per server. If a server were estimated to handle fives times as much traffic as another server, then a weight of 5 would be applied. Unfortunately, this approach is limited and impractical in most situations. First, it's difficult for most content providers to estimate accurately how much traffic a given server can handle in comparison to another server. Second, a server's capability to handle more or less traffic can change over time. As disk space fills or additional services are added, the system may slow down. Plus, certain servers might have routines that run at certain times (such as a backup routine), which would alter that machine's capability to handle as much traffic as normal; thus, the weight would be inaccurate for that period of time.

Dynamic Weighting—Least Connections   To compensate for the deficiencies of manually weighting servers during the load balancing process, a new method was developed. Because the load balancing device sees all traffic going to and from the servers, it has significant insight into how sessions are being handled. The Least Connections, or LeastConns, metric was developed based on the principle that, at any given moment, whichever server has the fewest connections should receive the next session. TCP sessions have a distinct start and finish. A device that sees these sessions open, and then close, can use this information to interpret server capability. At the beginning of the LeastConns process, sessions are balanced evenly to all servers in the farm. But immediately thereafter, the load balancing device watches to see which server has the fewest open sessions and directs the next request to that server. Each new session that arrives at the load balancing device is put through the same process. Interestingly, this provides a realistic and effective dynamic weighting for the servers.

The reason such a simple process works so effectively is quite basic. The purpose of a TCP session, in many cases, an HTTP session riding on top of TCP, is to open, pass data, and close. The faster those three steps can take place, the faster the end user can accomplish whatever she has set out to do. As servers become busy, their capability to pass data and close the session diminishes. The time from open to close begins to increase. Thus, the number of open sessions on a given server over a fixed period of time will be greater than on a similar, but faster, server. A faster server processes more open/close sequences than slower servers and, thus, receives a larger portion of the overall load from the load balancing device. LeastConns can be thought of as a dynamic weighting metric because it constantly adjusts itself based on the server's capability to open and close sessions, as compared to the other servers in the group. Take an example where server number two begins to run a backup routine late at night. Because of the extra workload on the CPU and disk subsystem while the backup program is executing, the server opens and closes sessions at a slower rate than an equivalent server that isn't running the extra routine. Because the other servers open and close sessions more rapidly, thus reducing the number of sessions currently open, they get proportionally more sessions. When the backup routing finishes, the server once again opens and closes sessions at a rate equal to that of the other servers, and receives equal traffic accordingly. More details are discussed about this and other metrics in later chapters.

Server Agents—the Myth

Many people—both content providers and equipment vendors—believed that by incorporating the use of software agents located on servers, load balancing could be vastly improved over the simple, yet effective, LeastConns metric. Most analysis of this approach has, instead, proven it to be only a myth—simply a high-tech urban legend. While on the surface this sounds feasible, some serious drawbacks reduce—if not totally eliminate—any possible benefits. The primary problem is attempting to define "load" for a given server. Each type of application has a different use, different traffic pattern, and different impact on server resources. Some types of transactions are processor-intensive; others are hard disk– or memory-intensive. Different brands of hardware and different types of operating systems react differently under the same set of load criteria. Determining whether 85 percent processor usage is good or bad on a Compaq or an IBM or a Sun machine, running Solaris or Linux or NT, with different amounts of memory and different speed of motherboard, becomes almost impossible. To determine the appropriate metrics proactively in advance and program them into the load-balancing device would truly be a marvel. Without a mathematical correlation that's the same for all servers and applications, the load-balancing device cannot consistently use those metrics in any meaningful way. Most vendors that have done so run the risk of hurting their customers by giving a false sense of load balancing that might not hold up under increased traffic. And, in many cases, server agents can cause performance degradation and even site failure if the metrics aren't tuned precisely to the specific server farm's environment. For content providers that have enough time and money to analyze their infrastructure accurately to determine relevant and consistent server data that correlates to end user performance, some improvement over LeastConns is definitely possible. But the benefit is small for most companies, compared to the cost involved with the type of detailed analysis and management required.

An additional problem with server agents is the simple fact that the agent program itself—because it runs on the target server—can interfere with the very results it's attempting to assess. LeastConns, on the other hand, doesn't require any type of agent running on the server. It simply measures the metric that's most important and most representative of an end user's requirements—the time it takes for a given server to open a session from a client, send or receive data, and close down that session.

In a perfect world, load balancing would incorporate all types of input to make the most intelligent load balancing decisions. Agents would be collected into a central repository that's cross-referenced against network-based metrics, such as LeastConns. Newer metrics have also been developed recently that perform tests for fastest response time and use that metric in a similar manner to LeastConns by tracking how quickly (not merely how many) packets are responded to.

Persistence

Although LeastConns made significant progress toward achieving Performance, Availability, Scalability, Manageability, and Flexibility for content providers and end users, new challenges arose to push the envelope much further. E-commerce became the buzzword of the mid- to late-1990s. As more and more people started making purchases over the web, site traffic for shopping began to accelerate quickly. Because all web-based Internet purchases are transacted using HTTP (or HTTPS) and because HTTP is a stateless protocol, the concept of the shopping cart became the load balancer's greatest puzzle. In an HTTP transaction, each web page is a distinct and separate TCP session. This concept works fine if each session reaches the same server every time, which was the "old" way of doing things before the invention of the server farm. But with the invention of the farm and load balancing, each subsequent web page might be served from a different server than the previous page—thus losing the knowledge of what was placed in that user's shopping cart.

Common Misunderstandings About Shopping Carts

Many people assume shopping cart persistence is a minor problem because they don't realize where or how transient data on web servers is stored. Three common misunderstandings exist regarding this subject:

▼ Shopping cart information is stored in the cookie. Fortunately, this isn't true. Cookies, as the analogy aptly describes, are small items that can be passed easily around and consumed quickly. If cookies were used to hold a user's shopping cart data, the cookie would continue to grow and grow, eventually becoming huge and too unwieldy to pass back and forth between client and server with each new TCP session (or every page).

■ Shopping cart information is replicated to all the servers in the farm. This, too, fortunately, is untrue. The easiest way to see the illogic in that approach would be not to look at the young, immature web site that only contains two or three servers but, instead, imagine that web site after a year of tremendous growth and expansion. Imagine 100 servers contained within the load-balanced farm. Each time a user places an item in her shopping cart, that server would need to communicate this information (along with a unique piece of data to be used as an identifier for that user) to 99 other servers. And each of the other 99 servers would communicate with each other whenever they have new shopping cart data to update. And each entry would need to be removed at some point in time when it was no longer deemed necessary. So, each of the 100 servers would need to constantly age out this data. It's easy to see how this doesn't scale.

▲ Shopping cart data stored in a backend database for all e-commerce web sites. This is, in fact, true for some of the larger sites, but it isn't at all assured for most sites. To use a database to store this transient data, many things must be considered. First, the data must be worthwhile to justify the cost. Because database write transactions impact server performance at 200 to 500 percent of a "read" transaction, architecting a site to handle a large amount of database writing can be costly for storing transient data such as shopping cart lists. Depending on the type of clientele, and the likelihood of purchase and the average value of each purchased item, different cost/benefit scenarios arise. Second, some way must exist to identify the user uniquely and to develop a plan to age out data from the database. Without an identifier and a plan to remove old data from the database, the database eventually becomes bloated and ineffective.

To combat this breakdown of shopping cart functionality, manufacturers of load balancing devices began to find new and unique ways to determine how to easily send a user back to the same server where he began his shopping cart session, thus preserving his information in the server's memory. To do this, load balancers began to go where network devices in the past had feared to tread: into the packet payload. By reading deep inside the packets, into the actual data payload of the session, the network device can use that information to identify and understand its user better. This formed the beginning of a whole new breed of network devices—Content Networking devices.

Firewall and VPN Load Balancing

Although not directly part of the technological evolution that created layer-seven persistence functions and other high-level functions, firewall and VPN load balancing gained substantial popularity around the same time—in the year 2000. Security is one of the few—if not the only—requirement end users have in common with content providers. Ironically, although security is such an important topic, it's one of the least understood and most improperly implemented aspects in most technology infrastructures. Remember the onion approach? Many individual security layers get wrapped together, so if one is peeled away, the next layer still exists. Many technologists who are new to security often assume one device or one tool will provide them with absolute security without any risk to their business. This is an obviously ignorant and dangerous way of thinking. A truly effective security program consists of many aspects: physical security combined with detailed policies and procedures, combined with proper user/staff education, combined with an array of tools and techniques to defend, combined with an array of tools and techniques to monitor.

With this in mind, firewalls, intrusion detection systems (IDSs), and virtual private networks (VPNs) are, indeed, important and common tools for providing part of a company's security program. Yet new problems are introduced when firewalls and VPNs are part of a company's infrastructure. Firewalls, by their very nature, usually are required to analyze all the traffic that passes through them to ensure the correct packets are being allowed, while the "bad" packets are being refused or dropped. But that analysis is a computing-intensive process that, at medium to high speeds, can dramatically affect a network's throughput and performance. Firewalls are one of the most likely performance bottlenecks and single points of failure in most infrastructures, especially web data center infrastructures. Similarly, VPNs have a relatively high incidence of failure. To address these issues of availability and performance for firewalls and VPNs, two basic approaches exist: built-in high availability (HA) versus load balancing (LB). Most firewalls and VPN solutions offer an HA option. They usually consist of a second identical platform that sits next to the original platform waiting for a failure. Normally, this second platform doesn't perform any functions until failure of the first unit—thus, it adds no performance benefit. The only way to get improved performance along with availability is to continually upgrade the hardware and software platforms to be optimized for the amount of peak traffic required. That process can be costly—in both time and money—as well as operationally difficult to maintain.

The other alternative is load balancing. This provides the same benefits discussed with server load balancing—the capability to maintain equipment easily (pulling it in and out of service), easy expansion for performance by adding additional boxes (even if only temporarily), and maximization of investment because all the units can be used to perform functions actively, rather than sitting idly by, waiting for a failure.

Of course, some downsides exist to using load balancing. First, the LB solution might be more costly at first, especially if the LB device is performing only that function. But as a company scales larger and peak traffic grows, that investment can easily be recouped. And, if the LB device is performing other functions at the same time, such as server load balancing, bandwidth management, or any number of other commonly used features of this class of devices, the price for adding FWLB or VPNLB is quite minimal. The type of FWLB/VPNLB solution chosen also affects the cost breakdown. Many vendors offer only a "sandwich" approach that requires two devices—one on either side of the FW or VPN. While this approach is widely accepted as the preferred security approach for FWLB, it adds significant cost. A single device approach for FWLB does run the risk of being misconfigured to allow unauthorized traffic to pass directly through the device acciden-tally, without being analyzed by the firewall. But this decision must be made by each company, based on its specific situation and risk factors including likelihood of breach, potential damage from breach, cost of protecting against breach, and staff capabilities and responsibilities for maintaining the equipment.

The one additional downside to an FWLB is complexity. An FWLB tends to be more complex to set up and maintain than built-in HA solutions. If properly set up, though, an FWLB can function without significant change or redesign for many years, even as new devices are added to be load balanced. And this extra complexity is normally far out-weighed by the operational benefits of load balancing because individual devices can be removed for upgrading or repair, without impacting the ongoing traffic flows at all.

FWLB and VPNLB became immensely popular in web infrastructures before beginning their adoption in enterprise network infrastructures and elsewhere. This early adoption inside the data center probably came from the technical awareness of load balancing in that area, while enterprise networks had little or no knowledge of load balancing until much more recently. In any case, FWLB and VPNLB are rapidly becoming popular within enterprise networks today.

Bandwidth Management

The concept of managing and altering network traffic (often called traffic *shaping* in the past) has been a popular concept in many customers' and vendors' minds for years. Yet few companies have deployed bandwidth management (BWM) solutions. Part of the reason revolves around the knowledge that the benefits aren't as easily defined as other technology solutions. Quite simply, BWM allows a company to provide differing levels of services within its infrastructure. An easy example is using BWM in a web infrastructure to pro-vide differing levels of network bandwidth to different customers. Assuming a standard 100 Mbps connection, the company might want to guarantee that the high-profile cus-tomers who access the financial section of the web site receive higher priority for band-width than do other customers. A BWM policy could be set to give 80 Mbps allocation for these high profile customers, while only 15 Mbps is guaranteed for all the other custom-ers. And, an additional 5 Mbps could be reserved for VPN traffic into the web infrastruc-ture to ensure the remote operational teams can always access the backend databases, servers, and devices—even during peak traffic times.

Bandwidth management is a tool to create effective Classes of Services (CoS). CoS is a component of Quality of Service (QoS). Typically, QoS refers to the entire life of a given data stream. Quality is assured at the required level based on the data type from end to end. CoS, on the other hand, only focuses on creating the various levels or classifications within the immediate environment, not necessarily covering the end-to-end path. Thus, if each segment of the data path had effective and equivalent CoS in place, it would effec-tively provide QoS for the entire path. CoS would be unnecessary in an unlimited band-width environment, but it becomes important in the reality of limited bandwidth and network bottlenecks we have today.

But placing a device in the path of traffic is a scary and costly proposition. BWM has received its biggest boost from vendors that have incorporated the functionality into existing devices already in the path of user traffic—such as load balancing devices. Performing BWM functions at close to wire speed, while also performing other functions such as LB, is a difficult challenge for vendors of these devices, and the impact of enabling the various services shouldn't be taken lightly.

Web Accelerators—Caching, SSL Acceleration, TCP Offload, and so forth

Web acceleration devices are an interesting new breed of technology solutions. They represent the epitome of what many feel will become the standard in the future—technology specialization. These devices don't technically do anything that isn't already done within the network—yet they provide tremendous improvement in common Internet traffic. The purpose of these devices is to remove as much processor burden from the servers as possible and handle that burden on the specialized (and optimized) device.

Secure Socket Layer (SSL) acceleration devices, as the name implies, remove the SSL process from web servers that need to provide secure HTTP (HTTPS) traffic to users. *SSL* is an encryption mechanism used to tunnel data back and forth between client and server, thus avoiding snooping on that data by others. However, the encryption and decryption function is processor-intensive—requiring significant mathematical calculations performed rapidly. By many estimates, a web server providing HTTPS was 70 to 90 percent *less* effective at delivering content compared to the same type of server providing standard nonencrypted HTTP traffic. In the beginning of the development of this technology, SSL was offloaded from the processor of the server to a specialized card inserted into the server. Because a web infrastructure scales beyond one or two servers, however, this approach rapidly becomes less desirable: it consumes valuable server space, provides more pieces of equipment to maintain and upgrade, and can be costly because a new card is needed in every server with an expensive certificate required for each one. And thus enters the SSL acceleration device. This device contains technology almost identical to the cards placed in the servers—they perform the encrypt and decrypt functions of SSL, thus passing only HTTP traffic to the server. With an SSL offload device, however, no server maintenance is required and, thus, it can be much more easily and cost-effectively scaled to handle increasing HTTPS traffic. The only significant downside of using this type of device is security. A security purist could argue that because this device decrypts the traffic from the client to the server, and then passes it to the server in clear, unencrypted format, the link between the SSL acceleration device and the server could be compromised and, thus, all user data would be visible. While the argument is technically valid, in practice it's of little concern. In almost all cases, the SSL acceleration devices coexist in the same cabinet or cage as the web servers. The only method that can be used to view the unencrypted data easily would require physical access to the wire connecting the servers and/or SSL devices to the switch. And, if physical access to the servers is possible, much larger and more significant security breaches need to be protected against. In the near future, SSL acceleration devices will solve this problem by creating a single encrypted tunnel between the device and the server. This reduces the burden on the server, by requiring it to maintain and encrypt/decrypt only one session (instead of hundreds), and it increases security by maintaining an encryption data stream all the way to the server.

Another type of acceleration device, although less common, is a TCP offload device, such as NetScaler's WebScaler product. This product is one of the only devices that seeks to relieve the burden of TCP from the web servers, much as SSL acceleration devices remove the HTTPS burden. The logic is simple: each TCP session has an inherent burden because it must negotiate a handshake between the client and server before passing any relevant data. Yet HTTP sessions (that ride on top of TCP) are usually brief, thus the burden of the handshake has a disproportional impact on web server performance. To combat this situation, the WebScaler device negotiates the TCP handshake directly with each individual client. Instead of passing each TCP session to the web server, the device creates only a few TCP sessions with each web server and makes all requests for data over those few, perpetual TCP connections. It then takes the data and parses it into the established client sessions, thus serving the required data without burdening the server with excessive TCP requests. This functionality is technically similar to how some load balancing devices provide a function called delayed bindings, which is discussed in Chapter 9. Thus, it's likely that many standard LB-type devices will adopt this TCP offload approach. In addition, products that provide TCP offload will rapidly add the entire set of standard load balancing features. Even without all the load balancing features, TCP offload devices are shown to have a positive return on investment (ROI). For a growing web site, the cost of the product is quickly covered by the reduced number of the servers needed. Typically, these products cost about as much as two or three well-equipped web servers. And it's not unreasonable to assume a company could avoid the purchase of dozens of servers if web site traffic is significant enough. TCP offload is definitely a complimentary function to standard load balancing.

Caching, which is also discussed in greater depth in relation to the topic of Content Distribution Networks, can also provide excellent web acceleration in the data center. By using caches in reverse proxy mode in front of the server farm, web traffic performance can be improved. Caches are optimized to serve large quantities of data quickly. They typically run on optimized hardware and operating systems as compared to web servers that use standard hardware and generic operating systems. Content Networking devices can point user traffic to web caches as part of the server farm to enhance the overall web experience.

Global Server Load Balancing

SLB is an effective and efficient way to increase performance and availability, while also improving operational and administrative control over the infrastructure. But limitations exist to the benefits that SLB (or, more specifically, "local" SLB) can provide. The most obvious limitation is the lack of guaranteed high availability with local SLB. Many events can occur to cause a loss of availability, such as core router failure, data center loss of network connectivity with the Internet, data center catastrophe (fire, power failure, and so forth) or even geographic catastrophes such as floods, earthquakes, and so forth. These events cannot always be predicted or protected against at a single location. Thus, the concept of globally distributing server farms is important.

Determining Site Location—Let's Race   Many large web sites have longed for the Holy Grail of always providing their users with the best path at each given moment from the users' location to the content they want to retrieve. The first part of the problem is that content is typically located in only one place. So, if a user requesting that content is located halfway around the world, the delays could be significant. Distributing data to various locations around the world is the first step to overcoming the problem. But, even as companies began to distribute their content to various web data centers around the world, it was still difficult to ensure the best path between that client and the content server. Why is this difficult, especially with so many ISPs offering service-level guarantees on both bandwidth and servers? The problem is caused by the very nature of how the Internet is constructed.

The Internet, as we all know, is constructed of many disparate networks connected to each other through peering and transit agreements. Many of these ISPs have invested tremendous amounts of money creating fast, enormous, backbone networks. Yet, when a web-hosting data center delivers content back to the user, it normally does so using a technique called *hot potato routing*, which simply means the web-hosting network will deliver the network traffic to the destination network (or the first hop in the path to get there) as quickly as possible. Even if the network of the web-hosting provider is vast and has plenty of available bandwidth, the traffic might be passed over a congested peering connection to a network with little available bandwidth.

Genuity's Hopscotch™ technology was one of the first attempts to solve the problem of finding a user's best path. From various collectors across Genuity's network, pings would be sent out and the round-trip time from various points would be gathered. Once the data was gathered (usually no more than two seconds), a decision on site selection was made and the user was redirected to the appropriate data center. Although not perfect, this was a valiant attempt to provide users with the best site selection for their request. More recently, Nortel Networks has developed a process called Footrace™ that seems to provide the best possible approach of any solution today. By simultaneously sending a response from all sites for a given piece of content, the first packet that arrives at the user determines the site to be used. This method provides a realistic view of the path between user and content, while requiring minimal overhead for the connection process.

In the future, better metrics might be available to enable you to determine not only which location but, specifically, which path is most efficient for the specific type of content and user combination at a given moment. As Content Networking technology works in conjunction with other emerging technologies, such as Multi-Protocol Label Switching (MPLS), the Holy Grail of best path might, indeed, come within your grasp.

Database Replication—The Ultimate Challenge   Because almost all robust web infrastructures rely on databases to some extent, they must be seriously considered when developing an effective infrastructure that meets all the previously mentioned requirements. The challenge can be described simply: databases cannot effectively do peer-to-peer transactions (also known as *bidirectional replication*) over slow or unreliable links, such as long distance Internet connections. But what does that really mean? And how does it affect the average web infrastructure?

Through load balancing, we discussed how many different types of systems such as servers, firewalls, routers, and other devices can be highly available, high performing, easily manageable, and extremely scalable. And global server load balancing extends those capabilities across multiple sites around the world. But databases don't fall into the same category. And, although database load balancing is just around the corner for many of the content networking vendors, limits exist to what load balancing can do. The problem is centered around the fact that databases often have their data changed. Typically, the reason for using a database is to easily store, organize, access, and update vast quantities of data. The last item—update—causes so many challenges. For the sake of this discussion, server clustering isn't mentioned because it only addresses a local site and doesn't provide geographic fault tolerance or location-based high performance. Essentially, two main types of database structures exist for highly available, distributed databases.

▼ **Master/Slave replication**   This is where a master database server and other "slave" database servers occur with identical information. The key is *all* changes are made to the master database, and then automatically *pushed* or replicated to the slave servers. This works well with web sites that use databases to generate pages dynamically, but the web site company controls all the data within the database. Most all of the major database vendors support this type of basic replication, which can work over fast, medium, or slow links.

▲ **Peer-to-peer replication**   This is where two or more database servers have identical information to start, but changes can be made to *any* of the databases and are then replicated to all the others. Most of the major database vendors support this type of replication with the following caveats: small number of replicated database servers and extremely fast links between databases. The problem arises when one (or both) of those conditions aren't met. To understand the problem, imagine a global server load-balancing example with three sites, all containing database servers that can be updated. A client could connect to one site and make a transaction that updates the database (let's say a password change or an e-commerce shipping terms modification). That database must replicate that change (along with all the other changes) to all the other databases around the world. The client then reconnects to a different site (per global server load balancing) and attempts to change the same item (password, shipping terms, and so forth). A high probability exists that the replication might not have taken place yet and the client might alter the same data on a different database server. Now, when the DB servers try to replicate, they'll have a replication conflict that can usually only be resolved by human intervention. On a small site, this isn't a huge problem. But, as you scale it up, the conflicts could become overwhelming.

Another common example of the problem is selling products with limited inventories. When you get down to the last "one" item in stock, many different people could potentially purchase the same "last" item because the database servers weren't synchronized quickly enough after the first person pressed the buy button. Many people will be falsely led to believe they purchased the last one when, in reality, a database conflict exists and the inventory isn't there.

There are good, though not widely used, hybrid approaches to deal with these issues. Of course, as with all technology designs, the right design approach varies substantially, depending on the business and technical objectives.

The following questionnaire can help to determine the better approach to take:

Data Distribution Questionnaire

1. Do you plan to have only a single DB server? If yes, no problem; stop here. If no, go to 1a.

1a. Are you using multiple database servers to increase availability or to increase performance, or both? (This answer might be used later.)

2. Will these database servers be connected by a high-speed network connection/ link such as ATM or fast Ethernet?

2a. Will only two database servers replicate to each other?

   If the answers to 2 & 2a are yes, stop here, no problem (though extremely high transaction systems still could have problems peer-to-peer replicating fast enough—but only a small number of companies would generate this much traffic). If the answer to either 2 or 2a is no, go to 3.

3. Will all data entry/modifications take place on a single database server? If yes, no problem, use master/slave replication with all the other nonprimary servers acting as slaves. If the answer is no, go to 4.

4. Will only add functions be performed on the distributed database servers (that is, no edit or modify to existing records)? If the answer is yes, replication should work okay, but go to question 4a, just in case. If the answer is no, definitely go to 5.

4a. Will all the added database records be completely independent of any database information that changes based on those additions (that is, the client can place an order for a product, regardless of whether it's in stock in the computer and that entry won't decrement the inventory in real time)?

   If the answer is yes, with proper programming and database development, it should work fine. If the answer is no, go to 5.

5. The customer will probably need to weigh a number of different options:

Option A   For many web infrastructures, designing a peer-to-peer style architecture on top of a master/slave architecture makes sense. This is done by allowing the slave databases to accept updates, which *aren't* applied directly in the slave database tables. Instead, the changes are stored in special tables for replication, which are sent back to the master and applied there first. If a conflict arises, this is known immediately and is communicated back to the slave, so it can communicate the information to the user. If no conflict exists at the master, the change is made to the master records, and then the master pushes the changes out to all slaves. This allows a peer-to-peer style architecture to help avoid problems in case the master fails and a new master must be elected, while controlling the conflict resolution in a central site. The drawback, of course, is extra latency involved for write transactions that require conflict validation. The bonus of this architecture is no extra latency exists for read transactions (obviously) or for write transactions that don't pose a conflict potential. Every transaction that requires conflict validation is run through a consistent process, so the outcome is repeatable and consistent. No two clients ever receive false success status.[2]

Option B   They could consider getting high-speed links (ATM, and so forth) between the database servers, hopefully, to overcome the replication limitations. Again, high-speed doesn't guarantee no conflicts will occur, but it makes conflicts much less likely than if they were traveling over the Internet. This option is *very* expensive, however, and can only be considered for those customers with plenty of cash to burn.

Option C   If question 1a was answered as "increase performance," the customer should consider simply buying faster hardware, building a cluster in one location, or looking at ways to optimize their database schema and programming. They should also consider factors such as reducing the number of database transactions (especially write transactions) done on the database per client visit. Write transactions have a much greater impact on performance than do read transactions.

Option D   If question 1a was answered as "increase availability" or "both," the customer needs to do a failure analysis and determine the likelihood of database failure and the impact to their business. Having a single point of failure for a DB server isn't necessarily the end of the world, if many other conditions are met. For example, if they have spare systems and components, 24/7 monitoring and management, and they have good static content distributed to multiple sites, they won't have as adverse an impact if their database fails. For example, for many years Cisco had a single point of failure with its backend database for its online ordering. Cisco sells billions of dollars of equipment online each year, yet realized it had no realistic, cost-effective mechanism to distribute its databases completely in a peer-to-peer manner. So, Cisco distributed its web servers and application servers all over the world. And Cisco built a bulletproof NOC in San Jose to protect its database—with a huge cluster, 24/7 monitoring, spare parts, great security, and so forth. If California falls into the ocean, however, Cisco online ordering will be offline. But users will still be able to access all the other features of Cisco's web site (without real-time order information). Cisco saw this as an unfortunate, but acceptable, business risk.

SUBSCRIBER EDGE NETWORKING— NETWORKING ON THE EDGE

Subscriber Edge Networking (SEN) is a relatively new term used to define the unique capabilities that can be used at the point the user first enters the Internet. In the past, the subscriber edge provided the least intelligent control over, or value-added service to, Internet traffic. In most cases, the decision was simply an allow/deny with bandwidth control based primarily on the size of the access pipe. Today, technology is rapidly changing the way traffic is managed at the subscriber edge.

This change is significant because the subscriber edge is where the most value can be discerned regarding the users. Access providers have the most accurate and robust set of data regarding the subscribers, their demographics, their location, and their preferences. Access providers know who we are, where we live, and even have some information about our credit worthiness (based on signing a service contract). If these pieces of data can be used to personalize the content provided to these users, the full benefits can only be imagined. In addition, the great potential exists to provide value-added services at the edge, such as personal firewall services, VPNs, and locally stored and streamed content.

SEN IP Services

Just as server load balancing devices, typically used in the data center, have evolved into multifunctional devices capable of load balancing many different devices and providing value-added features, such as bandwidth management, subscriber edge devices are also evolving. Shasta was a pioneer in developing a subscriber-aggregation platform that did more than simply authenticate users and aggregate them on to the provider's backbone. Universal aggregation is important for service providers to manage their subscribers easily. PPP, PPPoE, L2TP, and many other technologies are required at the aggregation point. Many of these technologies require some type of network authentication, such as via a RADIUS server. SEN IP services grew out of the foundation of subscriber aggregation.

Shasta engineers built a box capable of providing network-based services that traditionally required equipment located at the customer premises. By offering firewall, VPN, traffic steering, and many other functions in a device that also provides routing and subscriber aggregation, a whole new genre of products was born. SEN IP services are a boon to service providers—enabling them to offer valuable services, such as firewall and VPN, to their customers at a much lower cost than customer premise equipment (CPE)-based services. With a push of a button, a client can be configured for a personal firewall without the need of extra hardware, installation, or separate management. And, as devices such as this become MPLS-capable, they will be able to offer a quality of service never before thought possible.

Quality of service (QoS) can also be implemented.

Traffic steering is a relatively new concept that can be best applied at the subscriber edge. Traffic steering enables a service provider to control where users are directed when they access the Internet. Traffic steering could point them to a service provider portal web site, or it could simply provide relevant ad insertion in the delivered web pages. Because these decisions are controlled at the subscriber edge, much more user information is known and, thus, true personalization (and relevancy) is possible. Web traffic steering becomes important as service providers begin to incorporate it into Subscriber CDNs, discussed in the section "Subscriber CDN" later in this chapter. The subscriber edge holds tremendous potential that hasn't yet been completely harnessed.

CDNs and "Overlay" Networks

Content Distribution Networks (CDNs) are often confused with the concept of Content Networking, but the two terms are *not* interchangeable. CDNs are a subset of Content Networking. The purpose of a CDN is to distribute content across the vast Internet, so it's closer to the user, thus achieving two important user expectations—performance and availability—while also helping to achieve the content provider's expectations of scalability and flexibility. Companies such as Akamai and Digital Island first popularized the concept of CDNs. These companies created extensive networks of servers scattered across the Internet storing commonly used content for businesses that paid for the service. CDNs provide a service that's difficult for the average company to duplicate because they offer content distribution and storage across thousands of servers in hundreds of different locations.

Need for CDNs

The need for CDNs arises because the Internet is inherently latent and has no guarantees of service quality. The very nature of what made the Internet into the great enabling technology of our lifetime is the same thing that make it flawed in its capability to deliver content. Because the Internet is a collection of disparate networks linked together through public and private peering relationships, it has latency because of slow links, slow backbones, many network hops, and even distance (the speed of light is not really all that fast when you need a packet to travel around the globe and back).

Out of these challenges rose the CDN, but CDN is a new term. Only a few years ago, ISPs were deploying Web Cache Redirection systems, the precursor to today's CDN concept. In the late 1990s, many ISPs were coming to realize that providing Internet access was a low-margin commodity business. The costs to maintain access POPs and long-haul network backbones to carry the traffic across the country or around the world were increasing (or at least staying constant), while the cost of Internet subscriber access was declining. So, with costs increasing and margins decreasing, providers looked for ways to reduce their ongoing costs. While a significant portion of the cost was created by maintaining a high turnover (*churn*) subscriber service, a lot of money was being spent on network connectivity. Service providers wanted to reduce three main cost points:

▼ Network capacity from POP to backbone

■ Backbone network capacity itself

▲ Interconnection network capacity (peering points) with other networks

Understanding these three pieces of the service provider's network is important to understand fully the importance and impact of Content Networking for them. The POP is the location that people consider the entry to the service provider's network. This is the point at which the user (whether a consumer or business) is connected to the network over the last mile. *The last mile* is normally defined as the network connection between the user's premises and the POP. This last-mile connection could be copper, fiber, cable, or a variety of other physical media. The connection type could be a switched service, such as a telephone line, or a fixed service, such as DSL, cable, or even a T1. At the POP, the traffic needs to be routed or directed to its proper destination. The POPs are connected to each other via some sort of backbone network. This could be a dedicated fiber-optic network owned by the service provider or it could be a virtual network of ATM or frame-relay links purchased from a larger carrier. Either way, the backbone costs money to build (or lease) and to manage. In many cases, the backbone (at its full capacity) doesn't reach every POP. Thus, some POPs must be connected in the local metro area to a larger aggregation POP, sometimes called a *Super POP*. This Super POP would then be connected directly to the backbone network.

In most cases, the traffic is destined for somewhere on a completely different network. How does it get there? This is where peering points come into play. *Peering points* were developed in the earliest days of the Internet as a way to connect disparate networks together. The concept of the peering point is the foundation for the growth of the Internet as we know it today. Without peering, no interconnection and, thus, no Internet would exist—there would only be a large number of distinct networks that couldn't interact or communicate with each other. The earliest service providers such as CompuServe and Prodigy are excellent examples of this. So, to connect these various networks together, providers are needed to exchange traffic. Similar to the fence separating neighbors from one another, it begs the question of who owns and maintains this interconnection—and most importantly, who pays for it. The costs include the actual physical link, the equipment (such as routers), and the time to manage and monitor the connection. Peering points were originally intended as links between similar size networks—*peers*. With a roughly equal exchange of traffic, each party could pay for their half of the peering point and everything would be equitable. An extra challenge that arose (not discussed here) is the dilemma when one network doesn't consider the other an equal.

These costs could grow quite high, considering each network often had multiple peering points throughout a region or country and would connect to many peers at all these multiple locations.

Service providers realized if they could simply keep their users from leaving their network—or better yet, keep them from leaving the POP—costs could be significantly reduced. But, few, if any, service providers were in the content game. They didn't have the content people wanted to see. By using caches, though, service providers could bring the content users want closer. Caches were deployed in the POPs to force all cacheable traffic to stay within the POP. If a user requested data already stored in the cache, it would be served locally and would contribute to 30 to 40 percent reductions in traffic passing over the three points mentioned earlier. This significant reduction in traffic provided tremendous cost savings, even after factoring in the cost of the caching equipment.

An interesting by-product of these cache deployments was the user performance increased. So, service providers unknowingly increased customer satisfaction while achieving their initial goal to reduce costs. This concept soon spread. Innovative new companies, such as Akamai, realized many companies would be willing to pay a large amount of money to have their content locally accessible to users, thus providing their users with a better web experience. Taking the same concept of distributed caching, Akamai and others deployed servers around the world to store content of companies that paid for such a service, and the CDN was born.

Goals of a CDN

The purpose of a *CDN service* is to increase performance and availability. With distributed content around the world at hundreds of servers, failures would be less common and far less damaging than in a centralized content environment. The bandwidth fees charged for this content distribution service are two to three times (or more) the standard rate companies pay for Internet connectivity. But this is a small price to pay for better user performance and availability. This also provided the content providers with much greater scalability, and flexibility to grow and change over time. An additional benefit of CDN services is a reduction in infrastructure costs to the company purchasing the CDN service. The company simply pays for the ongoing service that offloads much of the traffic from its servers, thus reducing the amount of investment required in the related infrastructure. The infrastructure investment is made, instead, by the CDN provider and is shared among the many CDN customers.

While Akamai pioneered this type of service, by the end of 2000 dozens, if not hundreds, of companies were trying to get into the area. With the knowledge that both businesses and end users benefited from content distribution, many companies felt the opportunity for revenue generation was endless. Akamai's competitive advantage and long-term viability soon became suspect, as many new players attempted to build their own CDN.

Types of CDNs

While the basic concept and service provided by a CDN are essentially the same, regardless of type, a variety of different CDN types is discussed in the industry, relative to the way they're implemented. Three basic types of CDN implementations are Internet, Subscriber, and Enterprise.

Internet CDN *Internet CDN* is the generic name for the most commonly thought of Content Distribution Network scheme. It functions as described earlier, using a distribution of servers or caches at various points close to users. The service itself is sold to the content providers for them to ensure their web site and content will be readily accessible and perform well.

Three commonly discussed subtypes of Internet CDN also exist that, while serving identical purposes, differ slightly in their implementation and approach: Overlay CDN, Peering CDN, and Hosting CDN. Each one is briefly described here.

Overlay CDN   The term "overlay" network is commonly used to describe many of today's CDNs. Akamai is a prime example of an *overlay network* because it neither builds nor maintains layer 3 networks or data centers of its own. Instead, it has created a virtual network of servers scattered across many other providers' layer 3 network POPs and data centers. By overlaying this network of servers on top of the backbones of other companies, Akamai was able to create a new niche for CDN services without the extra expense of building networks or data centers. This can allow for an extensive network of servers and caches around the world.

Some downsides occur with this approach, however. First, as with any solution created through partnerships or outsourcing, overlay CDN providers must be cautious of the quality of the facilities they use. Because they don't control the networks, POPs, or data centers that house their equipment, they must be diligent in evaluating the quality and effectiveness. If they are unable to negotiate their requirements, they'll need to move elsewhere, which can be difficult and costly. In addition, overlay CDNs are narrowly focused. The breadth of services to offer customers isn't available because all services are CDN-based. Other implementations of CDNs allow service providers to create suites of services for their customers that can be useful in finding and keeping customers. Because CDNs are so new, this problem hasn't yet arisen. But, over time, pure play CDN providers, such as Akamai, will likely be acquired by a larger service provider that wants to enhance its services suite. Digital Island, another CDN pioneer, was acquired by Cable & Wireless in 2001 for that exact purpose.

Peering CDN   *Peering CDNs* provide the same service but, instead of positioning content at POPs or data centers, equipment is placed at the peering points between the service provider's network and its peers. This approach works well for service providers that have excess backbone speed and capacity, as well as substantial peering connections with other networks. Because backbone capacity isn't an issue, locating content at peering points is a more economical way to distribute content, as opposed to placing equipment in every POP. An obvious downside is content is only positioned on that provider's network and, thus, isn't as close to the user in all cases, as it would be in an extensive overlay network (which locates content on many different networks).

This approach could also be used by hosting service providers that don't have a substantial backbone. Thus, they want to offload content requests as soon as they enter the network at the peering points.

Hosting CDN   Another approach common for hosting service providers is to use their existing multiple data centers to house content for the CDN service. Although this won't have the reach of an overlay CDN, it will be much less expensive to build and maintain by using the existing investment in data center facilities. In many cases, hosting service providers will use a hybrid approach of both peering and hosting.

Subscriber CDN   Although technically similar to Internet CDNs, *subscriber CDNs* are targeted at a different market. An Internet access service provider can deploy content delivery infrastructure at POPs all over the network. Then, with that equipment in place, it can offer an enhanced service to access customers. Imagine being offered a service for five or ten dollars a month that would promise to improve your web surfing and content retrieval activities dramatically. Instead of simply offering it as a free piece of standard Internet access (as with the original caching deployments implemented as a cost-savings mechanism by service providers), providers can market this capability to their customers and reap more revenue. The primary target customers for a subscriber CDN are consumers and even some businesses. This CDN approach will commonly be coupled with the various enhanced IP-based subscriber services pioneered by Shasta, mentioned earlier in this chapter.

Enterprise CDN   The final type of CDN approach is the enterprise CDN (see Table 1–1). The obvious target customers are enterprises with distributed campuses in many different locations. The enterprise CDN places caching infrastructure in each major enterprise location and positions content for commonly used items such as files, training presentations, corporate audio or video announcements, and any other commonly used content objects. By implementing an enterprise CDN, companies can use more robust media, provide faster access to common files, and reduce wide area network (WAN) transport costs. Some service providers might offer a managed enterprise CDN that's essentially the same approach, but implemented and managed by the provider. This removes from the corporation the burden of learning the new technology and managing it appropriately and puts that burden on the service provider.

Elements of a CDN

Conceptually, a CDN isn't difficult to understand. Most CDNs don't rely on overly complex or intricate technology. Akamai's service was primarily based on homegrown applications

CDN Type	Paying Customer	Cache Locations
Internet—Overlay	Content Owners and Providers	Multiple data centers, POPs, peering points of various partners
Internet—Peering	Content Owners and Providers	Network provider's multiple peering points
Internet—Hosting	Content Owners and Providers	Hosting provider's multiple data centers
Subscriber	End Users	ISP's multiple POPs
Enterprise	Corporations	Corporation's central and branch offices, and possibly any of the previously mentioned locations

Table 1-1.   CDN Types

and technologies, while other providers' services were built using many standard products from companies such as Nortel, Cisco, and Inktomi.

A CDN has five essential elements. Some items overlap, depending on the specific technology selected. But, conceptually, these five elements are required to provide CDN services effectively. The elements are origin servers, caches, load balancers/redirectors, management, and accounting/billing.

Origin Servers   Quite obviously, content must originate from somewhere. A server, or set of servers, will contain the "master" content for that site. Copies of that content are then either pushed or pulled to the various locations around the globe. Changes to content are only made on the origin servers. In most cases, the origin server resides in a data center and, thus, won't be managed directly by the CDN service provider. The exception, of course, is in the case of a hosting CDN.

Caches   *Caches* act as the nonorigin content servers. These machines hold the content locally, waiting for users to request it. Essentially, two different models exist for distribution of content into caches: pull and push. In a *pull* model, caches start out empty and only store data as users request it. The benefits of a pull model are ease of deployment and management because, once the cache is configured, the service can begin functioning almost immediately. The primary disadvantage to the pull model is the first local user still must wait for the content to transfer across the public Internet in the normal manner. All local users after that point (within a given timeframe) benefit from the caching of that content because it's located locally for them to download. This first-user delay problem is quite significant for paid content services, such as video on demand or music downloads. Pull models are user-dependent and controlled. The content that's pulled is controlled almost totally by requests made from users. And users are all considered equal, in terms of retrieving and storing content. Of course, caches can be configured with many complex criteria to favor certain types of content over others and to have various expiration policies.

The *push* mechanism involves the selection of types of content or specific content predefined as desirable for users. That specific content is then pushed out from the origin servers and populated on the cache servers. The advantage to this approach is it avoids the first-user dilemma because the content is available even before the first user requests it. The downside to this approach is the complexity of identifying and managing content, so only the most useful is replicated to the caches. Determining, in advance, what users will want to access next is challenging, to say the least. The push style of content distribution is also referred to as *prepositioning* content.

Finally, there's a hybrid of both the pull and push models. This is becoming the most common method because it enables content owners to preposition selected items that are likely to be in high demand, while allowing the remaining items to be pulled when needed.

Load Balancers/Redirectors   A Content Distribution Network is only a viable solution if it's both scalable and available. In other words, if the service becomes less reliable or less able to grow and expand because content has been distributed, it defeats the purpose of the CDN in the first place. Load balancers and web cache redirection switches and appliances were created to address these issues.

Caches were originally built as regular computer systems running a special program to provide caching services. Because computers by their very nature aren't accessible 100 percent of time because of crashes, reboots, maintenance, and so forth, having a piece of equipment that would be highly available to direct traffic to those servers when they're available and to bypass those servers when they're down made sense. The WCCP specification was developed by Cisco to allow routers to use a pool of caches intelligently, thus allowing scalability. Unfortunately, as is discussed in Chapter 13, many flaws exist to this approach. And, instead, the more robust mechanism is a dedicated load balancer or cache redirection system. These systems perform continual health checks on the cache systems to ensure they're functioning, plus they offload a processing from the caches by sending noncacheable content directly to the Internet, rather than to the caches. By allowing the capability to add, remove, and maintain caches in a production environment, these systems provide the critical requirements of scalability and availability. As an added bonus, they might also help improve user performance.

Accounting and Billing   The most complex and least-developed aspect of a successful CDN is the accounting and billing piece. For the original purposes of distributing content (caching to save bandwidth costs), little or no accounting is necessary. Because the purpose of the original WCR concept was simply to save money on the reduction of bandwidth costs, the savings should become apparent in a short period of time.

As today's CDN services are built for the content owners, however, and not merely as a cost-saving mechanism for the service providers, accounting and billing become critically important. Remember, the direct customer of a CDN service is a corporation (big or small), while the direct benefits of the CDN are received by the individual web user (whether for business or personal use). The direct customer must be charged for the service provided. And that price can depend on various factors, including how many different distribution points were used, how much bandwidth was consumed at those different points, how much content was prepositioned, what class of service the customer chooses for users of its content, and over what period of time all these factors occurred. The systems to answer these questions easily for CDN service providers and their customers are still being integrated into CDN suites of tools. Many application providers have pieces that can be customized to address these needs, including companies such as HP (Smart Internet Usage) and Nortel Networks (Preside), to name two.

Management   As with many of today's technologies, to function effectively CDNs must be carefully managed and monitored. And, also like many of today's technologies, pieces of Content Distribution management are still in their infancy. Two important, yet distinct, types of management are involved with CDNs: operational and content.

Operational Management   Any piece of equipment, whether highly technical or not, must be properly monitored and managed proactively. CDNs are no exception. Management includes monitoring link saturation and cache server hit ratios, and expanding or condensing the cache server farm and network connections based on findings. Good management also includes verifying that the related equipment such as switches, routers, peering connections, and appliances are all working properly. This type of operation is quite standard for any piece of networking infrastructure. Tools for this type of management can range from homegrown SNMP-based tools to large-scale management tools such as OpenView, Tivoli, and UniCenter. In addition, standard network management tools are often incorporated into the suite of tools used for operational management, including RMON probes, distributed network analysis devices, and product specific management tools, such as Cisco's CiscoWorks and Nortel's Optivity and Preside tools.

Content Management   Managing content can be a troublesome and complex task. This involves making many of the decisions discussed earlier regarding pulling content or prepositioning it. Determining what types of content should be kept for long periods and what types shouldn't be cached at all is a perpetual question for the CDN provider. Content management decisions can change dramatically, depending on targeted user types and/or subscribing content owners. Tools for content management are being rapidly developed and released. Many traditional content management tools are designed for managing the content of the origin web infrastructure, but these aren't the same tools that provide for CDN content management. Tools are being developed by companies such as Volera, Nortel, Cisco, F5, and others. This area of the industry is still too new to say which products will truly meet the needs of tomorrow's CDNs.

WHO NEEDS A CONTENT NETWORKING SOLUTION?

Content Networking isn't yet seen as the air and water of technology infrastructures. But this is quickly changing. In a few years, people will look back and wonder how they ever functioned without load balancing, bandwidth management, caching, and all the other features of Content Networking solutions. Understanding who can benefit from Content Networking is the first step in the process of designing these solutions.

Enterprises

Enterprises do, indeed, have many uses for Content Networking solutions. In some cases, those benefits might come from services purchased from a provider that uses Content Networking technology. In other cases, certain companies will implement these technologies themselves. Load balancing for servers, gateways, firewalls, VPNs, IDSs, and caches is a definite "must have" technology for enterprises. The only way to achieve the necessary performance, scalability, operational effectiveness, and availability is through these advanced Content Networking functions. Enterprise CDNs will also be of interest to many companies as more and more content is required, and as multimedia becomes even more commonplace in the corporate setting.

Bandwidth management is still a long way off from being the killer app, but when it is an option on a required piece of infrastructure—such as a load balancer—BWM can provide great benefits to corporations in creating classes of service.

Obviously, any enterprises with a significant Internet web presence—whether e-commerce or content publishing—need to implement Content Networking immediately to use load balancing of web servers, SSL acceleration, and even reverse proxy caching. And, as the web presence becomes more business-critical, global load balancing and CDNs become crucial.

Service Providers

As many service providers struggle for their lives in the midst of the 2001 economic downturn, they need to continue offering more valuable services to their customers to move toward profitability. Basic services, such as data center collocation and Internet access, are commodity services with low (or even negative) margins. Content Networking solutions enable service providers to offer valuable new capabilities and functions to the services they sell today.

Data Center and Application Service Providers

The *data center* is the heart of Content Networking because this is where it all began. Service providers can offer services such as load balancing, bandwidth management, SSL acceleration, reverse proxy caching, high-availability firewalls and VPNs, and content delivery services to their customers, who currently only buy pipe, power, and ping in their data centers. These value-added services not only have the potential to bring in profitable revenue, they also create a much stronger hold on the customer. This is because the more complex and valuable the service, the more locked in the customers are. Application service providers might not sell these services directly to their customers, but they need to implement them just as much. The results from those services—availability, security, performance—are essential for the ASP model to succeed.

Managed Security Service Providers

A new breed of service provider is emerging to handle all things security-related. Offering highly available and manageable security services is essential when developing a business in this new area. Firewall, VPN, and IDS load balancing are far superior to built-in high availability solutions, especially for a provider focused on giving the best in security services.

Internet Service Providers

ISPs have been searching for value-added services for years. And, although a few of the largest ISPs have proven that Internet access can be profitable, much more profit can be gained. CDNs and SEN IP services are the two key areas on which ISPs should focus. ISPs must remember they control one of the most critical resources on the Internet—the user. As Subscriber Edge Networking begins to blossom, services and capabilities will expand at an incredible pace. ISPs also need to remember, though, that they—the ISPs—are easily replaced. Access isn't valuable. Content is. The easier, faster, and more secure ISPs can make it for users to access the content they desire, the sooner those ISPs will have increased revenues and profit margins—not to mention happy subscribers.

THE FUTURE OF CONTENT NETWORKING

As both edges of the network become more and more intelligent, the next logical step is to combine the intelligence from both edges simultaneously to make networking decisions. Decision factors could include location of user, location of content, type of content, priority of user, service level purchased, and many others. Also possible is that the backbones themselves will become more intelligent, but it's debatable whether there's significant value to that as long as decisions are made at both edges.

The challenge will be to find the way to communicate between the edges where disparate systems are used. Various attempts to create standards for content networking communication have already begun. The Content Alliance and Content Bridge groups have been formed by various vendors of products and services to attempt to create standards. In reality, these groups have only been used as marketing hype generators. As the content networking devices evolve and begin to talk from edge to edge, we will see more serious discussions about cross-platform communication and vendor interoperability.

REVIEW QUESTIONS

1. **What are the seven requirements of end users that relate to Content Networking?**

   The seven requirements of end users that relate to Content Networking are performance, availability, anonymity, ubiquity/accessibility, security, privacy, and personalization/relevancy.

2. **What are the nine requirements of service providers that relate to Content Networking?**

   The nine requirements of service providers that relate to Content Networking are security, control, manageability, scalability, flexibility, diversity, customer demographics/data, differentiation, and profitability.

3. **What was the original driving factor that led to today's concept of Content Networking?**

   The original driving factor that led to today's concept of Content Networking was performance requirements and to void peering congestion and server constraints.

4. **What is a "health check?"**

   A health check is a test connection of some type sent to a system—often a server, but not always—to ascertain if that service on that system is functioning as expected. A failure means that service on that system won't be used and a different healthy system must be used instead.

5. **What was the original load balancing metric used?**

   The original load balancing metric used was round robin.

6. **What is the most prevalent load balancing metric used?**

   The most prevalent load balancing metric used is Least Connections–LeastConns.

7. **Are server agents an effective tool to improve load balancing metrics?**

   Server agents are *not* an effective tool to improve load balancing metrics. The benefit is small for most companies, compared to the cost involved with the type of detailed analysis and management required to make them beneficial rather than useless or even detrimental.

8. **What are the most common functions performed by Content Networking devices?**

   The most common functions performed by Content Networking devices are load balancing, bandwidth management, caching, offload, redirection, and filtering.

9. **What is the best data replication method?**

   The best data replication method depends on the environment and the needs of the business. Many factors must be considered such as data update frequency, purpose of replication (performance vs. availability), and content types.

10. **What are the three major types of CDN service?**

    The three major types of CDN service are Internet CDN, subscriber CDN, and enterprise CDN.

11. **What are the three major types of Internet CDN implementation styles?**

    The three major types of Internet CDN implementation styles are overlay, peering, and hosting.

12. **What are the two main purposes of CDNs?**

    The two main purposes of CDNs are higher performance and availability.

END NOTES

1. Zona Research concluded that after seven seconds of waiting for a Web page, customer defection from the site rises rapidly from a 10 percent defection to a 30 percent abandonment rate.
2. Thanks to David Blessing for his input.

CHAPTER 2

Ethernet

OBJECTIVES

▼ Review basic Ethernet concepts

■ Differentiate the various Ethernet classes of service

■ Present Ethernet terminology

▲ Review some design guidelines for Ethernet networks

One of the keys to understanding and implementing a Content Networking solution successfully is to fully understand the elements that compose such a solution. In this chapter, we examine one of the most fundamental, and most generally ignored, technologies in Content Networks. Ethernet is the de facto standard for all local area network (LAN) implementations—hence, provider edge networking is forced to rely on the strengths and weaknesses of Ethernet. This chapter examines Ethernet and explores its origins, as well as its current common forms. The approach is to illuminate some of the more common and assumed technical specifications, and to attempt to address and clarify some of the more commonly misunderstood notions that attach to the technology.

Arguably, Ethernet isn't the ideal choice for implementation in a LAN. Some claim its survival is solely because of its flexibility and its simplicity to implement and understand. Others argue that success of Ethernet relies on one thing alone—its comparatively low cost. The point is somewhat moot: Ethernet is here, and it's here to stay.

Over the last few decades, Ethernet has evolved, with the technology supporting larger and faster connections. The term Ethernet refers to the family of LAN implementations that cover three primary categories: Ethernet, Fast Ethernet, and Gigabit Ethernet. This chapter provides an overview of each technology variant.

DIX AND IEEE 802.3

Ethernet is a base-band LAN specification invented by Xerox Corporation in the 1970s. Ethernet operates at 10 Mbps over coaxial cable with unshielded twisted-pair cable, a specification defined later. DEC, Intel, and Xerox jointly developed Ethernet Version 2.0, commonly called DIX. In 1980, the Institute of Electrical and Electronics Engineers (IEEE) 802.3 specification was adopted, based on the original Ethernet and, later DIX, technology.

DIX required the use of an outboard transceiver to attach a cable to the physical network medium. These transceivers performed many of the physical-layer functions, including media access and collision detection, and were physically separated from the interface itself. A transceiver cable would connect the end station to the transceiver. 802.3

provides for a variety of cabling options, one of which is a specification referred to as 10Base5, and this specification is the most similar to DIX. The connecting cable array was referred to as an attachment unit interface (AUI), and the network attachment device, the transceiver, was called a media attachment unit (MAU).

The various IEEE specifications were labeled as follows. The first element was a number, such as 10, which referred to the transmission speed—in this case, 10 Mbps. The next element was either BASE or BROAD to differentiate narrow from wide spectrum technologies. Finally, a letter or number would follow, to signify either the connection type or connection length. The letter *T* would represent twisted-pair cable, an *F* would represent fiber optics, and a 2 would refer to the coaxial cable segment length of 200 meters (actually it's 185 meters, but that doesn't round up well). See Table 2-1 for a break out of the various specifications.

Frame Formats

In Ethernet, data was packaged for delivery as a *frame*. Frames range in size from 64 to 1,518 bytes. Each frame contains a variety of information, including who sent it, where it's going, what protocol could read it once it arrives, and more. The elements were broken up into a header field, which carried the administrative information relevant to the frame, the actual data payload, and then a trailer, which usually included some simple method for verifying the frame didn't get garbled along the way.

The DIX and IEEE 802.3 frame fields are described here (see Figure 2-1).

Characteristic	DIX	10BASE-5	10BASE-2	10BASE-T	10ASE-FL
Data Rate (Mbps)	10	10	10	10	10
Signaling Method	Baseband	Baseband	Baseband	Baseband	Baseband
Maximum Segment length (m)	500	500	185	100	2,000
Cable Type	Copper coaxial	Copper coaxial	Copper coaxial	Unshielded twisted-pair	Fiber-optic

Table 2-1. Differences Between Ethernet Version 2 and the Various IEEE 802.3 Physical-Layer Specifications

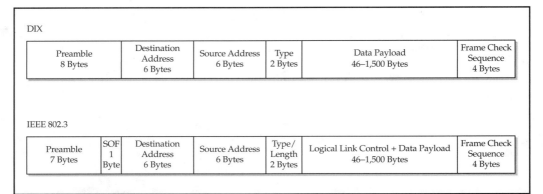

Figure 2-1. Frame fields associated with both DIX and IEEE 802.3 frames

▼ **Preamble** An alternating pattern of ones and zeros that indicate a frame is inbound to receiving stations. For DIX, the preamble was 64 bits in length and ended in a pair of ones, which indicated the frame was about to begin. 802.3 specified the length to be 56 bits and allowed for an additional Start-of-Frame delimiter.

■ **Start-of-Frame (SOF)** The 802.3 delimiter byte ends with two consecutive 1 bits, exactly like the DIX frame. In fact, the two frame types are indistinguishable at this point! The difference is this byte is called SOF by the IEEE and the end of the preamble by DIX.

■ **Destination Addresses** This is a 48-bit field. In DIX, the first bit of this address indicates whether the recipient is a multicast address. If it's set to 1, then the recipient isn't a single station, but rather a multicast group. The next bit, for either DIX or 802.3, will indicate a broadcast address if it's set to 1. Regardless, the IEEE will fix the first three bytes of the addresses to guarantee address uniqueness and the actual interface manufacturer will specify the last 3 bytes.

■ **Source Addresses** Another 48-bit field, with the address derived from the hardware generating the frame.

■ **Type/Length** This 16-bit field has two different meanings. For DIX, this field represents *type,* which specifies the upper-layer protocol to receive the data after Ethernet processing is completed. For example, IP would be indicated by a value of 2048. For a DIX frame, this value is always greater than 1536. On the other hand, for an 802.3 frame, this field can be less than that and, when the field is less, it indicates the *length* of the frame. What this field is used for is to discriminate actual data from padding. This is because minimum frame sizes exist and, occasionally, frames won't have sufficient data contained in them to meet the minimum requirements (64 bytes), so the interface needs to add junk data to pad out the frame to meet the minimum length requirements. The length field indicates where actual data ends and pad begins, so it can be discarded. When used this way, the duty of specifying the receiving higher-layer protocol falls to the IEEE 802.2 subheader that must be included in the data payload. More on this in the following.

- **VLAN Tag Header** This is part of a later standard called 802.1q, but we'll deal with this and Virtual LANs (VLAN) in the next chapter. (This is included here only for the sake of completeness and because a protocol trace using a sniffer program could turn up frames with these headers.) Unless the sniffer was sniffing a connection between two switches, these elements shouldn't appear. If they do, you have a problem directly tied to a misconfigured switch. Briefly, VLANs differentiate traffic based on some administrative criteria. The *tag* in the Ethernet header is simply a label and is one standardized way of identifying frames that belong on a particular VLAN. These tags are used only by and between switches, which commonly insert and remove them to keep their traffic flows straight. Standard end-stations have no idea what to do with this field, however. Further, because the tag, which is 4 bytes long, isn't part of the standard for either 802.3 or DIX, the tag is simply inserted into the frame and can cause the frame to exceed the max frame size of 1,518 bytes, and then cause the frame to be discarded as an error. Even if the frame isn't discarded, all data after the tag is pushed back 4 bytes. The end station, not expecting this, won't be able to make sense of the data in the field or any data that follows it. The data is also registered as an error, and then dropped.

- **Data** After header processing is complete, the data contained in the frame is sent to a higher-layer protocol, which for DIX is identified in the type field. In 802.3, this field can contain additional Logical Link Control (LLC) information in the 802.2 subheader, and this information can be used to drive the data to a particular higher-layer protocol. Data payloads will be from 46 to 1,500 bytes of information. If the amount of data the frame was formed to carry falls below the minimum threshold, 802.3 will pad the frame to fit the minimum. DIX relies on the network protocols to supply at least 46 bytes of information.

- **802.2 LLC PDU (802.3 Only)** Four fields are in the IEEE 802.2 subheader. The first is a 1-byte Destination Service Access Point (DSAP). This field provides the identification of the receiving higher-layer protocol. The next 1-byte field is the Source Service Access Point (SSAP), which identifies the sending higher-layer protocol. These two are generally the same. One to two bytes of control data follow this, with the rest of the data payload following that.

- ▲ **Frame Check Sequence (FCS)** This 32-bit sequence is the method by which a receiving station verifies the data contained within the frame has arrived intact. Also called the cyclic redundancy check (CRC), the FCS is generated by the sending device by running the values in the header and data fields, and then computing an original result. The receiving station recomputes the FCS on arrival and compares it to the FCS that arrived with the frame. If the two values were equal, the receiving station has a reasonable degree of confidence the data received was the data sent and nothing got lost or garbled along the way.

Inter-Frame Gap

The inter-frame gap (IFG) is a 96-bit time delay inserted between frames, where a bit time is equal to 100 nanoseconds (ns) for Ethernet, 10 ns for Fast Ethernet and 1 ns for Gig Ethernet. This delay has three functions. First, it allows end stations an opportunity to detect the carrier in an attempt to ensure that two or more stations don't transmit simultaneously. Second, it gives an Ethernet system time to prepare for the receipt of the next frame and time to move the current frame into a buffer or discard it. Third, it also provides a guaranteed dead period in which a station can determine whether a frame has ended. 96-bit times equals 9.6 μs for 10 megabits per second Ethernet. Fast Ethernet, being ten times faster, has a correspondingly shorter IFG, equal to 960 ns, and Gigabit Ethernet shortens this still further by a factor of 10, to 96 ns. In a CSMA/CD network, an end station will hesitate, listening to the carrier, for a period of time equal to the IFG before beginning to transmit.

Carrier Sense Multiple Access with Collision Detection (CSMA/CD)

In Ethernet's broadcast-based environment, all stations see all frames placed on the network. Following any transmission, each station must examine every frame to determine whether that station is a destination. Frames identified as intended for a given station are passed to a higher-layer protocol. Carrier Sense Multiple Access with Collision Detection (CSMA/CD) describes how the Ethernet protocol regulates communication among nodes. While the term might seem intimidating, if we break CSMA/CD apart into its component concepts, we'll see it describes rules similar to those people use in polite conversation.

When one Ethernet station transmits, all the stations on the medium receive and "hear" the transmission, just as when one person at the table talks, everyone present hears. CSMA/CD takes this a bit further and dictates that for anyone to hear, only one station can "talk" at a time. This is called *half-duplex* communication.

Things get more interesting when two stations try to transmit at the same time. If one station is already transmitting, another won't, provided it can detect the *carrier*, in other words, that a transmission is currently in progress. If it can detect data being transmitted on the line, the would-be transmitter will wait until a quiet moment occurs, and then transmit. If no data is currently being transmitted, however, or if it can't detect that data is currently being transmitted, two end-stations could end up transmitting across the same wires at the same time, and with considerably less success than the old party-line telephone systems. The sending station will continually monitor the data channel, even while transmitting. Manchester encoding specifies a regular voltage pattern for valid communication, but when two stations transmit simultaneously, the voltages can either cancel or add themselves together, resulting in invalid voltage fluctuations. Such irregularities indicate to the sender that a *collision* has occurred. On detection of a collision, the sending station (or stations) do one of two things. If the sender is tripped up early in the transmission—before the 8-byte preamble is completed—the sender will complete it. If the sender is tripped up at any point after the preamble is completed, the sender will simply stop at this point. Whichever happens, the sender then immediately follows with a 32-bit collision enforcement "jam" signal to indicate to all sending stations that an error has occurred.

The *Truncated Binary Exponential Back-Off Algorithm* governs retransmission after a collision has been detected. The rule specifies that stations interested in transmitting after a collision must wait a random period of time before trying again. Two stations can quite possibly be involved in multiple, successive collisions. After each successive collision, the delays double. After 16 consecutive attempts to transmit result in collisions, the would-be sender gives up and an error is sent up the protocol stack.

A collision on the wire can be an ugly thing. Data bits get concatenated on to other, perhaps unrelated, data bits, and this occurs randomly. So, not only does a line violation occur, but the resulting data frames can also be, well, garbled. The maximum frame size in Ethernet is fixed at 1,518 bytes, but frames much larger than this can result from collisions—these errors are called *giants*.

After a sender has successfully managed to transmit 512 bits of data (excluding a preamble) without a collision, a sender has successfully "acquired" the channel. This 512-bit time value is called the Ethernet *slot time* and, in 10 Mbps Ethernet, is equal to 51.2 μs. Any collisions that do occur, whenever they occur, must be communicated to every other end station within the slot time and, all things being equal, no collisions should occur in a collision domain *after* channel acquisition. This type of event is called a *late collision* and is usually an indication of a network diameter violation.

In Ethernet, a network diameter was defined by how long it took a signal to travel to one end of the network and back again. Intervening equipment, such as a bridge or repeating hub, adds a small amount of delay into the round-trip times. A 10BASE-5 Ethernet system could send a clear, 512-bit signal, round-trip, in approximately 2,800 meters. For 10BASE-T systems, this length was significantly shorter (100 meters), but had nothing to do with round-trip times. Instead, noncoaxial networks used lower-quality cabling than coaxial, and this led to severe signal attenuation problems. The round-trip times were more or less equal; however, the actual amount of signal that arrived was drastically reduced. Using twisted-pair cable with increasingly high numbers of twists per foot alleviated much of the noise issue, which contributed greatly to the signal attenuation problem. To further this, most twisted-pair circuitry implemented a squelch feature that simply eliminated signals below a certain level as noise or cross talk. Cable quality and noise reduction were the two primary factors in deciding the 100-meter segment length for 10BASE-T.

Collision Domains and Broadcast Domains

A *collision domain* is roughly defined as the area in which two transmitting stations are capable of having collisions. Intervening equipment, such as bridges and routers, can act to shorten a particular broadcast domain. A repeater or hub can act to lengthen one. Limits exist on how far a single collision domain can be extended, however, before it must be terminated. Typically, this has to do with the allowable length of a given network segment. If the segment is too long, round-trip times might exceed the slot time and, therefore, allow late collisions to occur. As mentioned, this would be bad. See the previous Table 2-1 for a list of segment length limitations by Ethernet type.

A *broadcast domain* is similar to a collision domain, but defined by the boundaries at which a single broadcast will be heard. Hubs, repeaters, bridges, and switches tend to extend broadcast boundaries because they operate at OSI layer 2 or lower. To terminate a broadcast domain, some layer 3 functionality must exist and, typically, this is defined at a router. The common wisdom is that routers don't forward broadcasts—and this is largely true, unless they're configured to do so. A typical instance of this is an IP Helper address configured to let DHCP clients reach a DHCP server that happens to reside on the far side of a router (or three). But again, this is neither common nor recommended.

Collision domains can be equal to broadcast domains in many simple LAN configurations. When a workgroup of computers is connected into a hub for basic connectivity to each other and, say, a printer, all the computers (and the printer) are said to be in the same broadcast domain. Hubs, being effectively layer 1 devices, don't do anything special to Ethernet communications—all they do is terminate cable runs. All devices communicating through a hub are communicating via CSMA/CD and, hence, all are in the same collision domain and in the same broadcast domain. In fact, any communication, broadcast or not, on hitting the hub, will be treated as a broadcast—the hub doesn't keep track of devices, all communications are flooded out of all active ports. The responsibility of the device is to drop and ignore information not expressly addressed to it. As you can see, this isn't the most secure approach to communications.

Replacing the hub with a simple layer 2 switch changes this picture considerably. Again, all devices are within the same broadcast domain (only layer 3 functionality serves to bound a broadcast) but, now, because of the characteristics of the switch, the collision domain becomes point to point—the only two devices in a given collision domain will be the end station and the switch itself. So, if five computers and one printer were all connected to a single switch, there would be one broadcast domain and six collision domains. Contrast this with the hub, which had one of each. Now, note that broadcasts are just as pervasive in a layer 2 switching solution as they were in a layer 1 hub solution. Communications between two stations on the same switch might well flood out all active ports on the switch, hence, swamping anyone connected. With a switch, however, this will only happen with broadcasts. Unlike hubs, switches do keep track of who is where and internally make temporary connections between ports to pass information—irrelevant ports aren't sent any data, unless it's a broadcast.

Replacing the switch with a router takes things a step further. Recall that broadcast domains are bounded by routers; with a router interconnecting all six devices, there would be six broadcast domains, and six collision domains. Because routers don't forward broadcasts (unless told to do so), any information that needs to traverse a router needs to have specific address information in it. Data is never flooded out the ports of a router.

As a rule of thumb, hubs are cheap, switches are fast, and routers are expensive. In Content Networking, a switch will typically be used to interconnect all the content servers in a data center for speed. Because most installations will use Full Duplex configurations to capitalize on the full-wire speed bidirectional flows, collision domains will be irrelevant because CSMA/CD won't be used. Virtual LANs (VLAN), covered in the next chapter, should be used to minimize the impact of broadcast domains.

Duplexing

Full-duplex communication provides the means of transmitting and receiving simultaneously on a single connection, instead of the party-line approach for which the half-duplex CSMA/CD provides. A full-duplex connection has only two endpoints and could be configured between two switches, between a switch and a server, between a switch and a router, and so on. Each transmitting station has its own transmission channel that isn't shared but, instead, is wired directly into the receiving channel on the other end of the connection. Because the connections are all point-to-point in this manner, collision detection is no longer an issue, so CSMA/CD isn't used. The standard that defines duplexing is IEEE 802.3x.

An interesting corollary to duplexing is a station can simultaneously transmit and receive at wire speed, so a 10 Mbps station could theoretically send a 10 Mbps data stream at the same time it receives one. Remember, the transmit and receive channels are completely separate in a full-duplex configuration. This has caused many to somewhat inaccurately ascribe an instant speed doubling effect to implementing a duplex connection, so a 10 Mbps Ethernet connection now is 20 Mbps or a Fast Ethernet link is now 200 Mbps. This is misleading to the point of being marketing propaganda because the station can't send *or* receive at twice the wire speed. It can simply send *and* receive at wire speed, a subtle but important distinction and good to remember when provisioning access. Finally, note, even in full-duplex operation, where carrier sense is ignored, the transmitting station will still insert a delay equal to the IFG between frames because this is what each Ethernet interface is designed to expect.

When the desired outcome is for two ends in a point-to-point connection to be in full-duplex, the two must agree on what the settings are. A great way to get mismatched errors is to have one end of a link set manually in full-duplex, while the other is set in half-duplex. Fast Ethernet provides an automatic method for handling this problem (see the following "Auto-Negotiation" section). For 10 Mbps Ethernet, this setting is usually handled manually, in the driver software itself. The options for managing the duplex setting are usually found under the configuration options for the adapter. Troubleshooting this problem is tricky because you may or may not see an error. Attach a sniffer on the line. If you see a significant number of FCS errors and/or an increasing number of runts, this could be an indication of a duplex mismatch. If the connection is between a pair of Cisco devices, an error could be reported to the console by the Cisco Discovery Protocol (CDP), which looks something like this:

```
%CDP-4-DUPLEXMISMATCH:Full/half duplex mismatch detected o1
```

Unfortunately, CDP only reports, it doesn't fix. You need to go to the line interface and reset the duplex setting to either half or full,

```
Switch-A> (enable) set port duplex 1/1 {half | full}
```

which should take care of the problem.

Flow Control

With a full-duplex connection, receiving traffic can quickly approach wire speed. At a network congestion point, such as a switch or a multi-interface router, where multiple streams of full-speed traffic intersect, oversubscribing a particularly desirable transit link is quite possible. Some servers being asked to perform intensive computations, such as those for SSL encryption (see Chapter 5 for a full description), could fall behind the upstream switch hurriedly, slamming traffic at it. For cases like these, IEEE 802.3x specifies an optional flow-control mechanism for use between the two stations on a point-to-point link.

If a receiving station becomes congested, it can send a MAC Control frame to the sender at the opposite end of the connection. MAC Control frames have a type code of 0x8808; any 802.3x-compliant device will single out these frames and scan the first two bytes of the data payload for an operational code. Otherwise, the frame will be standard, if fixed at the minimum frame size allowed. An operational code of 0x0001 indicates the frame is to be interpreted as a *pause* command. Pause frames can be singled out in sniffer traces by means of the destination MAC address—all pause frames are sent to a reserved local-only Ethernet multicast address of 01-80-C2-00-00-01 to facilitate processing. Following the operational code will be a 2-byte field, indicating the length of the pause requested. The actual period of the pause is calculated by multiplying this integer with 512-bit times.

Please note, flow control is only an option when coupled with a full-duplex connection.

Link Integrity Test and the Ethernet Heartbeat

In most Ethernet interfaces, there's at least one glowing LED, most probably green. Some will also have a red and/or an orange LED. Green LEDs on Ethernet interfaces are good things, they indicate "all is well" and traffic should be able to proceed—the interface is "up." Red, when found and lit, is an indication of a problem. Whatever the problem, the interface is "down" when this LED is lit. Orange indicates traffic, and this is the only one (if present) that should flicker, indicating traffic is being passed. Most manufacturers typically only implement a single LED and, again, that LED is typically green. This isn't to say it couldn't be, say, yellow. Whatever—when a single LED is found, it typically has to do with link; for the sake of argument, let's assume it's green.

Green LED = Good. This is pretty much the standard by which an operator will judge the connection between two Ethernet stations or between a station and its hub. The question of why and under what circumstances it would turn on is mostly ignored, which is bad. The green LED is tied to the Link Integrity Test, an unobtrusive background process designed into the interface, and starts operating almost as soon as the interface has power. What happens is an Ethernet transceiver transmits a normal link pulse (NLP) periodically to test the transmit path. All Ethernet devices transmit such NLPs during network idle times and do so 60 times a second. If the station receives NLPs, it turns on its green LED. Note, the receipt of inbound traffic also indicates to the receiver that the link is still up so, in the case of fiber systems where data is being continually transmitted in some form or other, this will suffice for link integrity tests. Also note, successfully lit link-light LEDs won't necessarily indicate data will successfully traverse the link or even that green LEDs on both sides indicate a good link. All this means is each station has received an NLP on its receive channel. Typically, a failure to communicate successfully over a connection that has a positive link-light on both ends indicates a wiring problem—most likely the cable isn't capable of discriminating signal from cross talk. It might be worth checking to see if you're using satin instead of a good Category 5 patch-cable.

The Ethernet Heartbeat is *not* another name for the link integrity test. This is a common error, and not sufficiently documented in introductory texts, so the mistake seems to refuse to die. While the term "heartbeat" seems to confuse the issue, it has less to do with simple link integrity than with CSMA/CD.

The Signal Quality Error (SQE) Test indicates that the collision detection circuits are working correctly. Implemented primarily in coaxial Ethernet systems where the transceiver is external to the interface, the SQE was first implemented in DIX as the Collision Presence Test (CPT). At this point, the unfortunate nickname of Heartbeat got attached. After each data transmission sent up the transceiver cable by the interface, the outboard transceiver sent a signal back down to the interface, testing the local circuit to verify the integrity of the collision detection circuitry. The test would never be sent out on the network proper, but only between the transceiver and the interface. The test would occur during the IFG, so the test accrued no overhead and was out of band. Successful receipt of the test indicated to the interface that the collision detection mechanism worked and, in the event of a collision, would be notified.

SQE is the IEEE 802.3 standardized version of the CPT, so while some minor differences exist in the timing and signal patterns, the functionality remains the same: an SQE Test after each transmission and, in the event of a collision, an SQE notification. Most modern systems have transceiver circuitry now integrated directly into the interface with the SQE Test disabled.

FAST ETHERNET

"Bigger, better, faster" applies equally well to the *Six Million Dollar Man* and to computer networking. New applications lead to higher resource demands and Fast Ethernet is one of the first attempts at taking the aging Ethernet technology to the next logical step. Fast Ethernet operates at 100 Mbps, ten times faster than Slow Ethernet. IEEE 802.3u defines the implementation of 100 Mbps Ethernet. The standard uses the existing IEEE 802.3 CSMA/CD specification for media access; therefore, Fast Ethernet retains the IEEE 802.3 frame format, size, and error-detection mechanism. Fast Ethernet supports both 10 and 100 Mbps using a sophisticated auto-negotiation protocol, described in the following, as well as full-duplex operation and flow control. One difference between 10BASE-T and 100BASE-T systems is that the IFG has been decreased tenfold, to 960 ns.

The other differences between the types of Fast Ethernet are due primarily to the different physical layer standards. 100BASE-TX specifies twisted-pair cabling, and 100BASE-FX specifies fiber-optic cabling. Note, other varieties exist, such as 100BASE-T2 and 100BASE-T4, but because these are effectively extinct, they won't be addressed here.

100BASE-FX is based on the Fiber Distributed Data Interface (FDDI) LAN specification. The media type specified is multimode fiber (MMF), where the cable that runs between nodes can be approximately 400 meters in length and, if full duplex is used, this can increase to 2 kilometers (km). Single-mode fiber (SMF), a far superior grade of fiber that also uses lasers instead of LEDs, wasn't included in the specification. Some vendors have designed SMF interfaces, however, and the cable runs between SMF nodes that can be up to 20km in length.

100BASE-TX is based on the copper derivation of the FDDI standard called, straightforwardly enough, the Copper Distributed Data Interface (CDDI), for physical layer control and access. 100BASE-TX supports shielded and unshielded twisted-pair (STP and UTP) cabling. Distance limitations between two nodes is still 100 meters, but the maximum size of a given collision domain shouldn't exceed 200 meters. This is because of the shortening of the bit-time interval to 10 ns. With data hitting the wire ten times faster than with its predecessor, the slot time also is shortened by a factor of 10. This means the network diameter is ten times shorter, or about 200 meters in total. To make a long story short, connecting two Fast Ethernet segments together via a hub is about all you can do: adding two hubs with a full 100 meters between them still only leaves 100 meters to get to both end stations. This doesn't leave much in the way of room for growth, but many ways exist around this. The most obvious is to use a full-duplex configuration and then break up a collision domain with an Ethernet switch or router.

Auto-Negotiation

Auto-negotiation enables devices to exchange Ethernet configuration information automatically. A connected device sends out periodic control messages on to the Ethernet segment. This information is interpreted by the peer at the other end of the link, and then is either used to help determine what settings would be required to communicate with the sender or to begin a negotiation process, whereby the two involved stations could settle on the most optimal configuration.

The requirements for auto-negotiation to succeed are relatively simple: both stations must have the auto-negotiation logic integrated into their Ethernet adapters. The standard that defines auto-negotiation is IEEE 802.3u and all adapters manufactured after 1996 will include this feature set. Most Fast Ethernet adapters will have dual-speed logic, enabling them to communicate at either 10 or 100 Mbps. These sophisticated adapters will have the settings for speed, flow control, and duplexing set to *automatic*, implying they'll use auto-negotiation to determine their settings on being introduced to the network.

Auto-Negotiation operates by a local device transmitting Fast Link Pulses (FLP) onto the network segment its directly connected link partner. A variation of the NLPs used in link integrity, FLPs are generated automatically at system startup, generated out of band,

and don't interfere with normal traffic. FLPs will perform the link integrity function, replacing the NLPs, and so are transmitted 60 times per second (16 ms, with a jitter of +/ -8 ms), with an additional pulse every 62.5 (+/- 7) μs. Each pulse contains a *link code word,* a 16-bit field that carries the system synchronization data.

The first five bits of the FLP is called the *selector field,* which identifies the IEEE 802.3 as the standard being used. The next eight bits is called the *technology ability field,* and defines the supported technologies relevant to the standard specified in the selector field. Following this is a single bit, the *remote fault* field, which indicates just that. Another single-bit field follows, the *acknowledgement* bit, which indicates to a local device that its link-partner has received its link code word. The last bit is the *next page* bit and, if set, indicates the link-partner has more link code words to exchange. This could occur if multiple messages don't fit into a single technology ability field. See Figure 2-2 for details.

These pulses work like advertisements, indicating which protocols their adapters support, at which speed, and whether full duplex is an option. A priority scheme is embedded into the advertisement, so 100BASE-TX full-duplex is preferred before half-duplex 100BASE-TX, which is then preferred before 10BASE-TX full-duplex, which is preferred before half-duplex 10BASE-TX. The two end stations, transmitting and acknowledging FLP information, match the highest priority setting received with the highest priority setting they can support. If no common technology is shared between the two partners, then the connection won't be made, and the LED won't light. If a link partner fails to receive any FLP information, but does detect the presence of NLPs, the connection will be made as half-duplex 10 Mbps Ethernet.

Note, auto-negotiation is primarily used in copper implementations of Fast Ethernet. This does *not* mean network devices linked over fiber segments cannot participate in auto-negotiation, but it does mean that if implemented, auto-negotiation simply decides parameters such as full-duplex or flow control, not rate of speed. The reasons for this are more pragmatic than anything else: fiber interfaces are built to support only 10 or 100 Mbps Ethernet.

The auto-negotiation feature is optional, and can be disabled. An entire school of thought adheres pretty rigidly to *Murphy's Law*—anything that can go wrong, will. With this in mind, the advice is, invariably, leave nothing to chance. If you want a particular connection to be 100 Mbps and full-duplex, configure it that way. Because auto-negotiation is always on by default and because the link will need to be renegotiated every time an interface goes down, plenty of opportunities occur for something to go awry in normal operations. So why take chances? This might be unnecessary, but you never know.

Selector Field 5 bits	Technology Ability Field 8 bits	RF 1 bit	ACK 1 bit	NP 1 bit

Figure 2-2. Fast Link Pulse frame format

GIGABIT ETHERNET

Gigabit Ethernet (GigE) is an extension of the IEEE 802.3 Ethernet standard, and is becoming a dominant player in high-speed LAN backbones and server connectivity. Standardized in 1998 as IEEE 802.3z, GigE operates at ten times the speed of Fast Ethernet. The actual differences between GigE and Fast Ethernet are pretty much reduced to multiplying or dividing by a factor of 10.

GigE seems a bit different at a physical layer perspective, at least on paper. The physical layer was entirely borrowed from the existing ANSI Fibre Channel standard and increased the speed to 1.25 Gbaud. Using a serial line-encoding scheme that inserts 25 percent overhead, the actual data throughput on the line is 1 Gbps, up from the 800 Mbps supported by Fibre Channel. 802.3z supports four different physical layer implementations, 1000BASE-LX, 1000BASE-SX, 1000BASE-CX, and later (with IEEE 802.3ad) 1000BASE-T.

1000BASE-SX specifies MMF as its medium, where the *S* specifies "short" as in "short wavelength" or "short run," and is intended for cable runs between 200 and 500 meters. 1000BASE-LX specifies either MMF or SMF as its medium, and—you guessed it—the *L* specifies "long wavelength" or "long run." The former spec is great for running fiber to the desktop, if you can get the cash to do this, or for wiring up a server farm, particularly useful in our current Content Networking context. The latter spec, as its name suggests, is better suited to long-haul backbone connections, as might be found in a campus or metropolitan area network (CAN or MAN, respectively). The benefit of using SMF on the long haul (for GigE, that is about 5km) is the theoretical bandwidth for SMF is pretty much infinite with respect to the current state of the art, so upgrading to a new technology later, such as 10 or 100 Gbps Ethernet (whenever those technologies become available) will simply require replacing nodes/interfaces instead of relaying fiber. 1000BASE-CX uses copper twinax cabling and is only implemented as a cheap method of providing interswitch cross connects, as might be found in a wiring closet. The maximum cable length supported for the CX specification is 25 meters for either full- or half-duplex configurations. Connectors are either High Speed Serial Data Connector (HSSC), also called the Fibre Channel Style 2 connector, or the 9-pin D-connector identical to that used in STP and Token Ring.

1000BASE-T is relatively new and, as previously mentioned, was codified in 802.3ad and introduced at the turn of the century. Like its slower speed 10- and 100BASE-T brethren, this physical layer spec allows for gigabit speeds over existing Category 5 twisted pairs. 1000BASE-T has a couple of interesting deviations from its predecessors, however. First is that it uses *all four wires* in the Cat 5 cable. What this means is 1000BASE-T simultaneously transmits *and* receives on all four wires. At the same time! This configuration is called *dual duplex* and, combined with a sophisticated signaling scheme and high-frequency transmission, will require heavy-duty digital signaling processors (DSP) to pull it all off. This variety of GigE is extremely intolerant of poor cable quality, and Cat 5 is the minimum recommended, with twists right up to the 8-pin RJ45 connector. Auto-Negotiation is included in the spec, allowing manufacturers to build 10/100/1000 Mbps interfaces and have the interface self-select the optimal connection type. Again, this is probably not *so* optimal in the sense that paying for a GigE interface isn't trivial. Paying for it and not using it seems criminal.

Worth noting is the MAC layer of Gigabit Ethernet is the same as that of Ethernet and Fast Ethernet, and exactly the same frame format as well as support for both full- and half-duplex transmission. In half-duplex mode, CSMA/CD presents some problems for straightforward acceleration to gigabit speeds. At speeds greater than 100 Mbps, packet sizes are smaller than the length of the slot-time in bits. To remedy the slot-time problem, the IEEE incorporated carrier extension into the Ethernet specification. Carrier extension adds nondata symbol bits to the frame until the frame meets the minimum slot-time required. In this way, the smaller packet sizes can coincide with the minimum slot-time and allow seamless operation with current Ethernet CSMA/CD. Specifically, the new slot time for GigE is 4,096 bit-times, up from 512 bit-times for Ethernet and Fast Ethernet (a factor of 8, for those of you keeping track). Carrier extension adds at most 448 extension bytes to the end of a frame, to increase the minimum frame size to 512 bytes and, therefore, equal to the new slot time. This extension adds a tremendous amount of overhead to the performance of GigE when using small frames, up to 88 percent! To get around this problem, the IEEE added another new feature to GigE, frame bursting.

Frame bursting allows an end station to transmit a series of frames over the wire without having to pause between frames, perhaps losing the carrier. The initial frame is sent normally, with carrier extension as needed. Then, the bursting station sends out the bursting stream, filling the interframe interval with carrier extension bits, so the wire never appears free to any other end station. Other stations on the wire then defer to the burst transmission because no idle time occurs on the wire. Frame bursts are limited in size to 65,536 bit times, plus the final frame. This burst mechanism is important for the use of small frame traffic and can improve efficiency significantly, potentially reducing the overhead to a much more acceptable 10 percent. Worth pointing out, however, is the issues and solutions just outlined are specific to a half-duplex implementation of Gigabit Ethernet, which isn't recommended.

DEPLOYING ETHERNET

We've spent the chapter examining Ethernet technologies, with an eye toward what a network administrator concerned about Content Networking should know. A preliminary examination of how these technologies fit together is something that should be explored before we can go farther. When you are deploying Ethernet, many concerns need to be addressed, including network segment diameters, maximum size of a collision or broadcast domain, what types of equipment are best used and where, and how to design a scalable system. Some of these concerns are relatively simple to address or even sidestep. Some require trial and error. For some, we can only point you in the correct direction and hope for the best.

Regarding network diameters and collision/broadcast domain sizes, this issue is best sidestepped completely. What you need to remember is copper implementations of Ethernet over twisted-pair cabling—far and away the most common and least expensive implementation—has a limit of 100 meters per segment. That's a lot, just over 320 feet. If your cable runs are longer than this, you have problems with your network design, not with Ethernet.

Ethernet switches are sufficiently inexpensive and available, so no good reason exists any more for not implementing them throughout a network. Repeating hubs, wherever they're found, should be removed and sold in some online auction posthaste. The comment that it's difficult to use a protocol analyzer with an Ethernet switch (but easy with an Ethernet hub) should be largely ignored. If sniffing is a requirement, most switches from reliable vendors, such as Nortel Networks and Cisco Systems, do incorporate some sort of port-snooping operation, so that objection should be easy to put to rest. The benefits of full-duplex connections (particularly the elimination of CSMA/CD) more than warrant the purchase of Ethernet switches. And, incidentally, the use of switches in a hierarchical manner enables the network planner to ignore some of the more inconvenient aspects of network diameters and collision/broadcast domains.

Cisco promotes an interesting three-layer network design model, where each layer has a specific goal and is physically separated from the other two in the ideal instance. The first layer, called the *access layer*, is where your clients and servers plug into the network. A *distribution layer* buffers one or many access layer devices from the *core layer*, and the primary responsibility for the distribution layer is policy enforcement. Core layer functions are entirely related to moving data and doing so fast. Access and distribution devices act as aggregation points in the network, with each providing successively higher bandwidth to the core, which is the fast, fat backbone to a network. This design lends itself most straightforwardly to the service provider network, where there are large networks to consider but, in a fractal sense, the design is also useful in smaller scales.

It works like this: in the Computer Science building at Miskatonic University, each floor's network needs are served by two or three Cisco Catalyst 2948XL Ethernet switches. Each has 48 10 Mbps Ethernet ports that are used to populate the drops in the offices on that floor. These switches would be considered the access layer. Each has a Fast Ethernet uplink that feeds into a single Cisco 3600 series router sitting in the wiring closet on that floor. All the other floors in the building have a similar configuration: Ethernet switch with 10 Mbps fan-outs to the offices and a Fast Ethernet uplink to the 3600. Each of these 3600s would be considered a distribution layer device. Each 3600 in each wiring closet has a Fast Ethernet run down to a wiring closet on the first floor, which terminates at a Cisco Catalyst 5000, which, in turn, has a connection to a fiber ring that runs throughout the campus. Every building on campus has a similar arrangement. These devices would be the core layer devices. See Figure 2-3 for an illustration. This design is flexible and easy to extend. Need more drops? No problem! Simply add another access layer device. Need to add another building? No problem! Run the fiber ring to the building and build out as described.

To some extent, this model applies to the data center, where we'll locate our Content Networking services. One element must be addressed before successfully designing any network, however, which is proper use and planning for bandwidth.

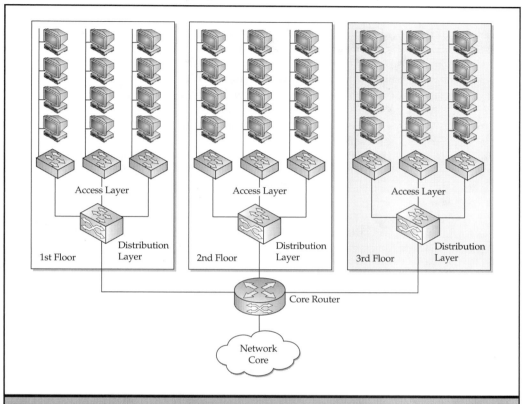

Figure 2-3. Three-Layer Network design model

The problem to avoid is called over-subscription; this occurs when more bandwidth is promised than is actually provided. We'll see how this works in a moment. While over-subscription is unavoidable to some extent, that is, unavoidable, without spending hideous amounts of money, it helps to remember it when you're trying to plan where to deploy Fast Ethernet and GigE. It works like this. If you have a farm of about ten servers providing the content for a web site and the farm is fed by a dual 10 Mbps feed, then equipping the servers with GigE adapters is probably a waste of money. 20 Gbps is never going to come out of a 20 Mbps feed. Upgrading everything to gigabit is a possibility, but not necessarily a cheap one, and now you've probably wandered well outside of your original project scope. Some caveats do need to be addressed. In many simple web server farms, the web servers themselves are the only element in the data center (aside from various pieces of networking hardware). As the complexity of a site grows, more elements can be introduced. It's becoming increasingly common for web sites to implement some sort of SQL database for storing complex, dynamic, or financial content. Application servers can be added to the repertoire of the site, such as streaming media servers, authentication servers, or online transaction servers, dedicated to the processing of orders and/or data. As these services are added, the bandwidth demand increases, but the traffic flows aren't always outwardly directed. Web servers might access database servers for content, application servers for specific applications, security servers for authentication information—none of which traverses the WAN link toward the client. In such cases, building out the bandwidth on the server farm might be wise, even though the ingressing feed might be significantly smaller, so there will be plenty of available bandwidth, and client requests won't have to compete with intrafarm traffic for service fulfillment.

You can design a complex data farm in several ways All are specific to the web technologies and applications that are being deployed. Security concerns also permeate such discussions, so a detailed examination of how to design such networks must wait until later.

Avoiding oversubscription in the network, at least to the extent possible, is still a design goal, however. In most circumstances, it makes little sense for each layer in a network to be successively slower than the layer below it. Access layer devices, generally speaking, are the slowest elements on the design, with the core at the highest speeds. The old 80/20 rule no longer applies, where 80 percent of all network traffic should be local and only 20 percent remote. With the rise of the Internet, that traffic pattern has reversed itself, where only 20 percent of traffic is local and 80 percent is remote. This isn't good news for network designers because this implies the majority of network traffic is bound for the WAN, the most expensive set of connections in any given network. Following the design goal of avoiding oversubscription and following the 20/80 rule, however, leads directly into the unfeasible solution of purchasing multigigabit WAN uplinks! Obviously, something has gone wrong here and, as to the state-of-the-art solution, that is, of course, Content Networking. Later chapters discuss the role and importance of *caching* to provide a way out of this mess.

Know that it will be almost impossible to design away both oversubscription and the 20/80 rule affordably. Still, steps exist that make good business sense. The first step is to estimate what levels of traffic will be needed at the edge of the network where the consumer is located. The next step is to determine where groups of these consumers will be aggregated together. The goal will be to provide enough access at this level to serve the majority of the consumers, the majority of the time. Think of it as an airline that continually oversells the seats on its planes, knowing not everyone booked will appear to claim a seat. The phone company does the same thing. If every single person in a single subdivision simultaneously picks up their telephone and attempts to place a call, quite a few will be mightily disappointed. The notion is somewhat simple—not everyone will need full access 100 percent of the time. What these approaches have done is to say that instead of simply avoiding oversubscription outright, some level of service below the optimal must be acceptable. Of course, no consensus exists as to what "acceptable" means, but in terms of a mission-critical web server/data farm, you can be reasonably certain this might mean something radically different from allowing corporate users to browse the Internet with impunity.

Oversimplifying, if the web servers are connected at 10 Mbps Ethernet, something faster should aggregate a set of them. Fast Ethernet is a likely choice, but saturation could occur at ten clients and, beyond that, oversubscription issues could occur. Biting the bullet, this is as good as it's going to get. Of course, you could use GigE, which would enable you to aggregate 100 clients before worrying about saturation. This doesn't leave much room to aggregate the aggregation, though. Remember, access feeds into distribution, which feeds into core. It might make more sense to leave GigE to the core instead. See Figure 2-4 for an illustration.

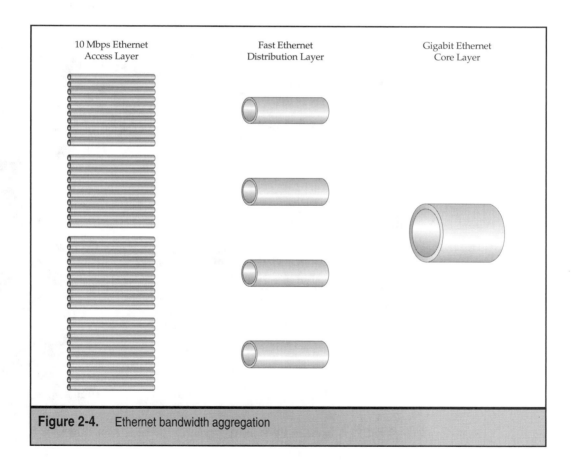

Figure 2-4. Ethernet bandwidth aggregation

SUMMARY

Ethernet is the primary networking technology found in the Content Network provider edge. It's fast, cheap, reliable, and ubiquitous. Ethernet is also taken pretty much for granted. However, Content Networking, in its currently implemented form, relies on Ethernet almost exclusively in the web data center and NOC. Most commercially available caches come with Ethernet interfaces of some sort and number, as do all web servers, switches and local area routers. The provisioning of an Ethernet link (or pair, for redundancy) is what most customers are paying for when they buy a network drop in an Internet Data Center or colocation facility. Ethernet is like American Express—it's everywhere you want to be (in Content Networking).

Further investigations into the technologies underlying Ethernet can be readily pursued by acquiring any one of a number of excellent books on the subject. The goal of this chapter was to provide a tour of the basics of Ethernet, and to familiarize the reader with some of the more interesting and pertinent Ethernet flora and fauna.

REVIEW QUESTIONS

1. **What is the IFG and what does it do?**

   The IFG provides a recognizable buffer between frames.

2. **What is the line encoding used in Fast Ethernet? In Ethernet? In Gigabit Ethernet?**

   The line encoding used in Fast Ethernet is 4B5B. In Ethernet, it's Manchester, and in Gigabit Ethernet, it's 8B10B.

3. **Where is the truncated exponential backoff algorithm used?**

   The truncated exponential backoff algorithm is used in CSMA/CD networks to define the amount of time an end station must wait after a collision has been detected before being able to retransmit.

4. **Which Ethernet technology uses Carrier Detection?**

   All Ethernet technology uses Carrier Detection!

5. **Which Ethernet technology uses Carrier Extension?**

   Gigabit Ethernet uses Carrier Extension.

6. **What technology is used to light up the green LED on a Fast Ethernet interface?**

   Fast Link Pulses (FLP) is used to light up the green LED on a Fast Ethernet interface.

CHAPTER 3

Advanced Ethernet Topics

OBJECTIVES

▼   Define Spanning-Tree Protocol

■   Describe the benefits and shortcomings of STP

■   Discuss what VLANs are and how they're used

■   Compare the differences between ISL and 802.1q trunking protocols

▲   Define and describe EtherChannel

Ethernet has come a long way since its inception in the early 1970s as a LAN protocol used to interconnect local PCs and printers. In 1979, Digital Equipment Corporation (DEC), Intel, and Xerox formed a committee for the purpose of standardizing an Ethernet system that any company could use. In September 1980, the three companies released Version 1.0 of the first Ethernet specification called the *Ethernet Blue Book,* or *DIX standard* (DIX stands for DEC, Intel, and Xerox).

Since then, Ethernet has enjoyed acceptance and much popularity because of its easy-to-understand technology. Because this technology is quite scalable and easy to work with, its widespread acceptance was inevitable. With such a large market share over other LAN technologies, Ethernet was able to use its clout in the market, and to evolve and improve over the years.

With any technology that has spanned three decades, shortcomings must be overcome with newer technology. One of the major stumbling blocks for Ethernet technology in terms of scalability comes in the form of loops in the network infrastructure. Because Ethernet doesn't incorporate any intelligence and, unlike Token Ring, no controlling workstation exists, a loop in the network can be rather catastrophic. Hence, STP was developed to eliminate such loops in the network.

The next challenge encountered by Ethernet was more of a metamorphosis of the existing specifications. People outgrew the expectation for this technology to move data between users and devices within the same building. Users soon wanted the capability to segment, privatize, and span segments over the WAN, as well as to do moves/adds/changes more easily and cost effectively. VLANs subsequently developed to address all these issues and more.

With ever-rising demands for additional bandwidth by new and larger applications, the Ethernet pipeline seemed more and more restricting. Even as Ethernet speeds increased by an order of magnitude each time, bandwidth always seemed to be at a premium for users. Perhaps this is a classic case of giving the users bandwidth and they'll find a way to use it all.

Over the years, Ethernet technology had to overcome many challenges and thrive in an environment that's both fast and furious. Ethernet has proven in the past to be fast, efficient, and flexible. With its massive market share, Ethernet can be found in most wiring closets and data centers worldwide. This investment by organizations on Ethernet infrastructure will ensure its existence for some time to come, much like the IBM mainframe. Inevitably, as long as the technology is used, enhancements and innovations will continue to be worked on and introduced.

SPANNING-TREE PROTOCOL

Spanning-Tree Protocol (STP) is a data-link layer protocol designed to run on 802.1d-compliant bridges and switches. STP was designed to eliminate loops in networks with redundant paths. Although you might question the need to have redundant links in a network in the first place, it's often important to maintain them as backups in case of a failover in the network. For an Ethernet network to function properly, however, only one active path can exist between any two nodes. Hence, STP was designed to manage the forwarding and blocking of passages in a redundant Ethernet infrastructure.

Currently, two forms of Spanning Tree formats exist in the networking world. The 802.1d flavor of Spanning Tree is the most popular and widely implemented, so we concentrate on it in this book. Although different in packet format, both types of Spanning Tree strive to achieve the same goal: to provide a loop-free environment. To provide nonlooping path redundancy, STP must first build a tree that spans all switches in an extended network. Once a topological tree has been established for the entire network, Spanning Tree will force certain redundant paths into standby (blocking) state. If a network segment with STP enabled becomes unreachable or if STP costs change, the Spanning-Tree algorithm recalculates the topology and reestablishes network connectivity by activating standby paths. This operation is totally transparent to end stations.

Spanning-Tree Protocol Port States

Switch ports running STP are always in one of the following five defined states at any given time:

▼ Blocking

■ Listening

■ Learning

■ Forwarding

▲ Disabled

A port can move from state to state as follows:

▼ From initialization to blocking

■ From blocking to listening or to disabled

■ From listening to learning or to disabled

■ From learning to forwarding or to disabled

▲ From forwarding to disabled

Figure 3-1 illustrates how a port moves through the five states.

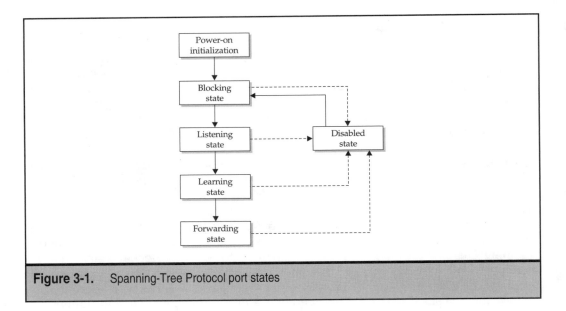

Figure 3-1. Spanning-Tree Protocol port states

Election of the Root Switch

All switches in a LAN environment with STP enabled communicate with one another though an exchange of messages. These messages are called bridge protocol data units (BPDUs). The switches need to maintain constant communication with each other to achieve the following:

▼ Elect a unique root switch from which a hierarchy can be established for the spanning-tree

■ Elect a designated switch for every LAN segment within the STP jurisdiction

▲ Eliminate loops in the LAN environment by placing ports in the path of a loop in standby state

The root switch in a Spanning-Tree topology is the highest node within the tree, with all other nodes being either a child or a descendent of its children. Only one possible path exists to the root switch from any node in the tree, and this path is generally the shortest path to the root switch. All other paths will be blocked. Hence, all possible loops are eliminated from the topology. A detailed description of how the root node is elected and the metrics used in the election process is discussed later in the chapter.

A need exists to present the metrics and key indicators that will be used in the election process of the root port switch.

Bridge Protocol Data Units

The Spanning-Tree topology works on BPDU message exchanges between participating switches, as you can see in Figure 3-2. BPDUs carry information about the transmitting switch,

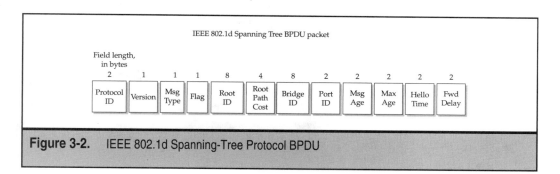

Figure 3-2.   IEEE 802.1d Spanning-Tree Protocol BPDU

including switch and port Media Access Control (MAC) addresses, switch priority, port priority, and port cost. Using this BPDU information exchange, STP running collectively on all the switches elects the root switch and root port for that switched network, as well as the root port and designated port for each switched segment. Initial BPDU messages sent between participating switches are called *configuration BPDUs*. Once a Spanning-Tree topology has been defined, then "topology-change" BPDUs are sent after a topology change has been detected to indicate that the spanning-tree algorithm should be initiated.

Configuration BPDU Fields

The following are fields that comprise an IEEE 802.1d Spanning-Tree BPDU packet.

- ▼ **Protocol Identifier**   Contains the value zero
- ■ **Version**   Contains the value zero
- ■ **Message Type**   Contains the value zero
- ■ **Flag**   A 1-byte field, in which only the first 2 bits are used. The first bit represents the Topology Change (TC) bit and is used to signal a topology change. The second bit represents the Topology Change Acknowledgement (TCA) bit and is used to acknowledge the receipt of a configuration message with the TC bit set.
- ■ **Topology Change Message Fields**
  - ■ **Protocol Identifier**   Contains the value zero
  - ■ **Version**   Contains the value zero
  - ■ **Message Type**   Contains the value 128
- ■ **Root ID**   Identifies the root bridge by listing its 2-byte priority followed by its unique 6-byte ID
- ■ **Root Path Cost**   Contains the cost of the path from the bridge sending the configuration message to the root bridge
- ■ **Bridge ID**   Identifies the ID and bridge priority of the bridge sending the message

- ■ **Port ID** Identifies the port from which the configuration message was sent. This field allows loops created by multiple attached bridges to be detected and handled

- ■ **Message Age** Specifies the amount of time elapsed since the root sent the configuration message on which the current configuration message is based

- ■ **Maximum Age** Indicates when the current configuration message should be deleted

- ■ **Hello Time** Indicates the time period between root bridge configuration messages

- ▲ **Forward Delay** Indicates the length of time participating switches should wait before transitioning to a new state after a topology change. If a switch transitions too soon, then not all network links will be ready to change state, and loops can result.

HOW THE STP ALGORITHM WORKS

The following is a breakdown of the Spanning-Tree Algorithm into individual steps taken by the switch when the algorithm is run.

1. Each participating switch is assigned an 8-byte unique switch identifier. The first two bytes of the address are derived from the priority given to the switch. The last six bytes are derived from a MAC address found on one of the switch ports. The lowest MAC address is usually chosen for this purpose; however, different manufacturers tend to have proprietary ways of choosing the MAC address.

2. After the configuration BPDUs are exchanged among all switches within the segment, the switch with the lowest switch identifier becomes the root bridge. The network administrator can control which bridge becomes the root bridge by assigning a lower priority value to the bridge desired to become the root bridge.

3. Each switch port is associated with a path cost. The path cost represents the cost of transmitting a frame out onto that switched segment though the port. The network administrator typically assigns a cost for each port based on the speed of the link (for example, the cost of a port connected to a 100-Mbps LAN would be lower than a port connected to a 10-Mbps LAN).

4. Each switch determines its root port and root path cost. The *root path* is the port that represents the shortest path from itself to the root switch. The root path cost is the total cost to the root switch.

5. For every LAN segment, all participating switches elect a designated switch from among the switches on that LAN segment. A *designated switch* is the switch on each LAN segment that provides the minimum root path cost. Only

the designated switch has a path to forward frames to and from that LAN segment toward the root switch.

6. All participating switches select ports for inclusion in the spanning tree. The selected ports will be the root port, as well as the designated ports for the designated switch. *Designated ports* are those where the designated bridge has the best path to reach the root. If two or more switches have the same root path cost, the switch with the lowest switch identifier becomes the designated switch.

7. By recursively following the previous steps for all switches from the root on down, all the switches directly connected to each LAN segment become blocked, thereby removing any loops in the topology.

Implications of STP in a LAN Environment

When a switch or a single port in a switch is brought online, there's an invocation of the STP calculation on the port(s). The result of the calculation will be the transition of the port into forwarding or blocking state, depending on the position of the port in the network and applicable STP parameters. The calculation and transition period typically takes 30–50 seconds (depending on the manufacturer). At this time, no user data is passed out of that port. This delay in allowing traffic to traverse the port can have an adverse effect on some applications. For example, clients using DHCP to obtain IP address information will time out during this delay.

Once a topology running STP is established and all elections have been completed for each segment, the frequency of STP recalculation is minimal. The STP algorithm should only be invoked if either a root switch or a designated switch is down. With this in mind, administrators should be aware that a constantly changing STP topology triggering frequent STP recalculations is an indication of a problematic network.

Note, the changes or frequent recalculation of STP is indicative of a problem on the network. Administrators should pay close attention to this value in their troubleshooting process.

The solution to this dilemma can be solved using a Cisco feature called portfast. Once *portfast* is enabled on a port, that port will always begin in the forwarding state. The port still participates in STP. If the port should be part of a loop, it will eventually transition into STP blocking state. Note, portfast should never be enabled on a port directly connected to another STP participating switch. Although portfast is a useful feature when used correctly, its incorrect use can mean almost certain disaster for any functional network.

The portfast option is dangerous if used improperly. LAN Administrators should be careful when implementing this option.

Although the STP is excellent at preventing loops, it has left the network exposed to malicious attacks. When a port is participating in STP on any given LAN segment, it's susceptible to other devices impersonating a switch, joining the same segment using a lower switch priority, and becoming the designated or root switch. This false device can wreak havoc by changing the STP topology, thus rendering the network suboptimal. Attackers can cause recalculations of the STP algorithm by the temporary introduction and subsequent removal of STP devices with low (zero) bridge priority. This can be considered a simple form of Denial of Service (DoS) attack on the network.

VIRTUAL LOCAL AREA NETWORKS—VLANS

Virtual Local Area Networks (VLANs) are essentially switched networks that are logically segmented-based on an organizational or functional grouping, instead of the traditional physical or geographical groupings. For example, all clients and servers belonging to the accounting department can be connected to the same VLAN, regardless of their physical connections to the network or because they might be intermingled with other departments. Reassignment of users from one VLAN segment to another can be done through software configuration instead of the physical unplugging and moving of devices or wires.

Benefits of VLANs

VLANs provide the following benefits:

▼ Reduced administration costs for moves, adds, and changes

■ Controlled broadcast activity

■ Workgroup and network security

▲ Leveraging of existing hub investment

Reduced Administration Costs

Almost as certain as taxes and death, organizations will reorganize. Management and administrators knew this from the onset; however, they never had a choice but to set up costly infrastructure that was, at best, a sunk cost. Each year, 20 to 40 percent of the workforce is physically moved. Not surprisingly, the greatest expense in managing a network is directly attributed to these moves, adds, and changes. Most changes require recabling, new station addressing, and hub or router configuration. Invariably, as soon as administrators stabilize the network, more changes are implemented and the network once again becomes unstable.

VLANs were introduced to address this cost and efficiency issue. VLANs provide an effective mechanism to control changes and to eliminate the cost of hub and router reconfiguration. This lack for a need to reconfigure network hardware is because VLANs allow network addresses to be free of geographical location restrictions. For example, users moving from one building to another building can assume their existing IP address at the new location with only minimal or no reconfiguration necessary.

InterVLAN communication always requires a layer 3 function, such as a router.

This isn't a true statement because routing can be done without a router. What I mean is this: a router would be needed for the first packet but, after that, the packets are switched and bypass the router. This is what's called *layer 3 switching*. Both routing and layer 3 switching are beyond the scope of this book.

Controlling Broadcast Activity

Broadcast traffic occurs in almost all networks, independent of how large or small and how busy or idle the network can be. Although this type of traffic is essential in the normal operation of a network, too much of it can be a hazard to the overall performance of infrastructure. Broadcast traffic can be attributed to one of the following factors:

▼ Types of applications running over network

■ Types of network protocols running over network

■ Types of servers residing on segment

■ Amount of logical segmentation within network

▲ Use of network resources

Although many applications are becoming more network-friendly and have made efforts to reduce broadcasts over the network, an increasing number of multimedia applications are both broadcast- and multicast-intensive. Apart from applications that broadcast traffic onto the network, faulty network devices, such as network interface cards, can also cause extensive broadcast errors. If these defective devices aren't found and removed from the network, serious degradation of network performance, as well as complete network outages, can result.

Fortunately, measures can be taken to prevent broadcast-related problems. One of the most effective measures is to use a router to segment the network properly into different broadcast domains. *Routers* isolate between different segments, so a problem in one area cannot damage other parts of the network. Thus, while one segment might experience a broadcast storm because of a faulty network device, the rest of the network is protected from this disaster because the router will never forward broadcasts. Routers provide a network with greater reliability, safeguard the network from inefficient bandwidth use, minimize broadcast traffic overhead, and enable greater application traffic throughput.

As network engineers migrate their existing networks to switched architectures, the functionality of the router is forgotten and, in turn, is used solely for the purpose of routing data. By not placing routers between switches, broadcasts have a larger domain to wreak havoc. This new type of architecture is called a *flat network*—one broadcast domain across the entire network. The advantage of a flat network is it can provide both low latency and high throughput performance because all data is switched by hardware and never needs to be routed in layer 3. The disadvantage is that a flat network increases the network's vulnerability to broadcast storms.

One major advantage of a VLAN is its capability to create different broadcast domains effectively, without the use of a costly router. Segmentation can be achieved by assigning ports or users to specific VLANs on a single switch or over multiple connected switches. Broadcast traffic in one VLAN is never transmitted outside that VLAN. This solution substantially reduces overall broadcast traffic, frees bandwidth for user traffic, and lowers the overall vulnerability of the network to broadcast storms. In essence, VLANs afford the network higher throughput by freeing up overhead otherwise used by broadcast traffic. The result of this reduction in overhead, in turn, greatly increases the performance of the network.

The assumption is valid only if the LAN segmentation is implemented with the intention that no interVLAN communication is required. Otherwise, layer 3 devices, such as a router, are needed to perform this task. One major benefit of creating a different broadcast domain is performance enhancement. This happens by gaining bandwidth that would normally be consumed by the broadcast packets, which is directly dependent on the number of devices and the type application running.

Better Network Security

The dependency of companies on conducting business over the Internet and intranet has grown exponentially in the last three years. As a result, network infrastructures are carrying an increasing volume of confidential mission-critical data. This data requires security through restricted access. An inherent flaw in current LAN technology is it's difficult to restrict access to the media. By plugging a simple monitoring tool into a live port on a shared LAN, an unauthorized user has access to all media traversing the LAN.

The introduction of VLANs solved many security issues without compromising functionality. VLANs, however, weren't intended as a security measure. A VLAN must be implemented with security in mind to make it an effective security tool. To take full advantage of VLAN security, add the following procedures to the network policy:

▼ Restrict the number of users on any VLAN to only those who are authorized

■ Prevent users from joining a VLAN without first receiving approval from the network management

▲ Configure all unused ports to a default low-service VLAN

VLANs can, therefore, be used to provide segmentation, restrict individual user access, flag unwanted intrusion into the network, and control the size and reach of the broadcast domain. Segmentation can be achieved by grouping switch ports based on the type of applications and access privilege, or by placing restricted applications and resources on a secured VLAN.

Further security measures can be added by the use of router access lists. Access lists are effective in restricting communication between VLANs. These restrictions can be placed on criteria such as station addresses, application types, protocol types, and even time of day.

Another added security feature is dependent on the switch hardware in use, for example, using Cisco switch 4000,5000,6000. Administrators can restrict the switch port to be used with a certain unique MAC address programmed into the switch. Thus, they can prevent access to the network even when physical access to the switch is breached.

Leveraging Existing LAN Hub Investments

Hub devices are considered the most common networking device and can be found in almost any wiring closet. Because the initial investment for hubs is rather high, many businesses are reluctant to replace them with even more costly switches. By leveraging the existing infrastructure of the hubs, a significant cost reduction can be obtained and a way to ease in the technology can be provided. A common method of leveraging this investment involves cascading existing hubs from newly installed switches, as shown in Figure 3-3.

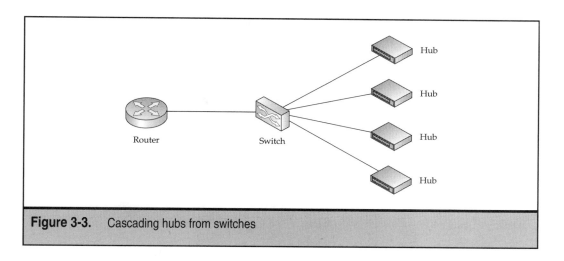

Figure 3-3.   Cascading hubs from switches

In the previous diagram, all users connected to each hub belong to the same VLAN. The VLANs in this configuration are defined at the switch port level, so the hub connected to the port will inherit the same VLAN. All the stations that share a hub segment are assigned to the same VLAN. If an individual station must be reassigned to another VLAN, that station must relocate to the appropriate hub module. As more users and devices are moved off the shared hubs and onto switch ports, the architecture is slowly migrated to a high-performance platform.

VLAN TRUNK PROTOCOL

The VLAN Trunk Protocol (VTP) is a Cisco proprietary management protocol that helps to reduce the administration in a multiswitch LAN environment. The first step in setting up VTP is to choose a VTP server and define a VTP domain on that server. Second, set all other switches as client or transparent switches. Third, and last, define a VTP domain for all server and transparent switches to be interconnected. Once this is done, all new VLANs created on the VTP server will be distributed to all switches in the same domain. The recommendation is that more than one switch should *not* be configured in server mode for any given VTP domain. This is to ensure that control is centralized and that conflicting changes cannot be made on both switches at the same time.

Each switch running VTP advertises its management domain, a configuration revision number, and its known VLANs and their specific parameter on its trunk ports. A *VTP domain* is made up of one or more interconnected devices that share the same VTP domain name. Each switch can be configured in one VTP domain only.

VTP servers and clients maintain all VLANs everywhere within the VTP domain. The VTP domain is used to define the boundary for a specific VLAN. VTP servers maintain configuration information either in nonvolatile random access memory (RAM) or acquire it via the Trivial File Transfer Protocol (TFTP).

The VTP server can be used to modify global VLAN information using the VTP Management Information Base (MIB) or the command-line interface (CLI). When VLANs are added, an advertisement is sent out to all servers and clients in the domain. This advertisement essentially updates all switches with information on the newly added VLAN. The VTP server can also be used to instruct all switches in the domain to delete a VLAN and disable all ports assigned to it.

The advertisement updates sent out by VTP servers are sent to a multicast address, so all neighboring devices will receive it. These advertisements aren't forwarded by normal bridging processes, however, so they'll never be propagated past the neighboring device. All devices on the same management domain will learn of any new VLANs configured on the VTP server. Hence, this feature allows centralized access and configuration capabilities.

In a campus or enterprise environment, it's important to note that the configuration of the VTP domain on the switch is well planned. You need to configure two modes: The first is server mode, which maintains the overall VLAN information across the network, and the second is transparent mode, which, can only learn about other VLANs advertised by the VTP domain server. If you have two switches configured as a VTP server mode, any changes on one or the other could easily propagate across the network and could create a problem.

How VTP Works

When a new VLAN is added to a VTP server, an advertisement is sent out as a broadcast. Neighboring devices running VTP receive the advertisement. If the advertisement is intended for the domain on the switch, then the switch accepts the traffic of the new VLAN. It then propagates the advertisement to all its trunks after adding the VTP-learned VLANs to their trunks. The VTP-pruning protocol limits the reach of this forwarding to the boundary of the network where the VLAN extends, based on VLAN membership resident within the switch.

Periodic advertisements are used to track configuration changes and communicate them among all participating switches in the network. When a new switch is added to the network, the new device receives a series of updates and information from the VTP. Using that information, it automatically configures itself with all existing VLANs and begins to participate as an active member of the network.

VLAN Trunking

A *trunk* is a point-to-point link carrying several VLANs. The purpose of a trunk is to save ports when creating a link between two devices that implement more than one VLAN, typically two switches. Trunks also allows the extension of those VLANs across the entire network.

To send the traffic of multiple VLANs over a single link, the switch must first encapsulate all data to be sent out. Two trunking encapsulations available for the Ethernet trunk ports are

▼ **Inter-Switch Link (ISL)**   A Cisco proprietary trunking encapsulation

▲ **IEEE 802.1q**   An industry standard trunking encapsulation recognized by multivendors. One of the reasons this standard is often favored over the ISL flavor is because it isn't vendor-dependent and is, therefore, more scalable and flexible to implement.

The benefit of using 802.1q as a trunking mode is the elimination of proprietary protocol that's vendor-dependent.

INTER-SWITCH LINK (ISL) ENCAPSULATION

Inter-Switch Link (ISL) encapsulation was developed and patented by Cisco Systems to deliver interconnection between two proprietary Cisco VLAN-capable Ethernet devices using the Ethernet MAC and Ethernet Media. The packets on the ISL link contain a standard Ethernet, FDDI, or Token Ring frame, and the VLAN information associated with that frame.

The ISL frame contains three primary fields: the header, the original packet, and the FCS at the end. The ISL frame is displayed in Figure 3-4.

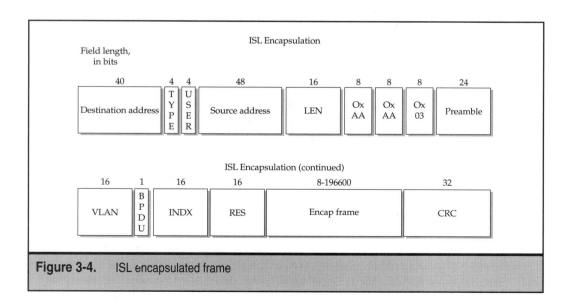

Figure 3-4.   ISL encapsulated frame

The following describes fields found in a Cisco Inter-Switch Link (ISL) encapsulated frame.

▼ **Destination Address**   The Destination Address or DA field is a 40-bit field that is set to 0x01-00-0c-00-00. This address is a multicast address destined for all ISL listeners.

■ **TYPE**   The TYPE field indicates the type of frame encapsulated and could be used in the future to indicate alternative encapsulations. The following TYPES have been defined.

Value	TYPE
0000	Ethernet
0001	Token-Ring
0010	FDDI
0011	ATM

■ **USER**   This field is used as an extension of the TYPE field.

■ **Source Address**   The Source Address or SA field is a 48-bit field that includes the source address of the ISL packet. The format of the address should be the 802.3 MAC address of the switch port transmitting the frame.

■ **LEN**   The LEN field is a 16-bit field that describes the length of the packet in bytes excluding the DA, T, U, SA, LEN, and CRC fields. The total length of all excluded fields is 18-bits long, so the LEN field is always the total length of the ISL packet minus 18 bytes.

■ **AAAA03**   The AAAA03 field is an 18-bit constant value of 0xAAAA03.

■ **HSA**   The High Bits of Source Address is the upper 3 bytes or the manufacturer's ID portion of the Source Address field. Because ISL is Cisco proprietary, this field must read 0x00-00-0c for ISL to work.

■ **VLAN**   The VLAN field is the virtual LAN ID of the packet. The field is a 15-bit value used to distinguish frames from different VLANs. This field is often referred to as the color of the packet.

■ **BPDU**   The BPDU field is a 1-bit flag that indicates if the packet contains a BPDU. BPDUs are used by the STP to create and maintain the Spanning Tree.

■ **INDX**   The INDX field indicates the port index of the source of the packet as it exits the switch. This is used for diagnostic purposes only and is often discarded by the receiving switch.

■ **RES**   The RES field is used only when the Token Ring or FDDI packets are encapsulated within the ISL packet. When a Token Ring frame is encapsulated, the AC and FC fields are placed here. If an FDDI frame is encapsulated within the ISL packet, the FC field is placed in the least significant byte of this field. For any other frame types, such as Ethernet, the RES field should be set to all zeros.

- **ENCAP Frame** This field contains the encapsulated frame, including its own CRC value. The CRC included within this field must be valid once the ISL header and CRC fields have been removed. The length of the field can vary from 1 to 24,575 bytes long to accommodate Ethernet, Token Ring, and FDDI frames.

- ▲ **CRC** This field contains a standard 32-bit CRC value calculated on the entire encapsulated frame from the DA field to the ENCAP Frame field. The destination port will check this CRC and can discard packets that don't have a valid CRC. Note, this CRC is an additional CRC to the one inside the ENCAP Frame field.

IEEE 802.1q TRUNKING

The IEEE 802.1q standard specifies that an internal mechanism is used when trunking VLANs. This essentially means a tag is inserted within the frame, instead of encapsulating the entire frame, as in ISL.

Trunks that comply to 802.1q standards contain a unique VLAN called the *native VLAN*, which is never tagged. The native VLAN is configured to be the same on each side of a link, so network devices on either side can deduce to which VLAN a frame belongs if it receives a frame without tagging. The tagging process is simply a modification to an existing frame. The trunking device inserts a 4-byte tag, discards the existing FCS, and recomputes a new FCS, as shown in Figure 3-5.

The following describes the fields found in an IEEE 802.1q frame and fields that are carried forward from a transition from an IEEE 802.3 frame.

- ▼ **Destination Address** Destination MAC address of the packet.

- **Source Address** Source MAC address of the packet.

- **Etype** The EtherType field identifies the frame as a compliant 802.1q frame and is equal to the value 0x8100.

- **Pri** This is a 3-bit field that specifies 802.1q priority tagging.

- **VLAN-ID** This is a 12-bit VLAN-ID field that's used to distinguish frames from different VLANs.

- **Len/Etype** This is a 16-bit field that's carried forward from the original frame and is used to identify the upper-layer protocol to receive the data (Ethernet). This field indicates the number of bytes of data to follow it in an IEEE 802.3 frame.

- **Data** After physical-layer and link-layer processing is complete, the data contained in the frame is sent to an upper-layer protocol, which is identified in the Type field for Ethernet frames. Although Ethernet Version 2 doesn't specify any padding, it expects at least 46 bytes of data, and IEEE 802.3 frames require a minimum 64 bytes of data (this can be achieved through padding).

- ▲ **FCS** This sequence includes a 32-bit field cyclic redundancy check (CRC) value, which is recalculated after the VLAN tag has been added.

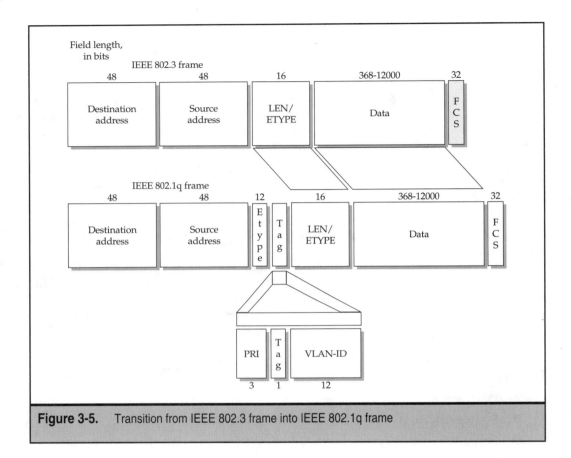

Figure 3-5. Transition from IEEE 802.3 frame into IEEE 802.1q frame

THE ROLE OF VLANS IN MODERN DATA CENTERS

The role that VLANs play in today's data centers is far more significant than those in the past. This is mainly due to its ability to become so flexible and scalable all at the same time. A large part of this scalability and flexibility comes from an emerging technology called EtherChannel.

EtherChannel

EtherChannel is a complementary technology to Fast Ethernet and Gigabit Ethernet that enables the combination of multiple Fast or Gigabit Ethernet lines into an extended trunk. Speeds of up to 800 Mbps or up to 8 Gbps are achieved when combining multiple Fast Ethernet or Gigabit Ethernet, respectively. For the purpose of simplicity, EtherChannel can be thought of as a sophisticated way of port grouping that enables more functionality and efficiency. EtherChannel technology provides fault-tolerant, high-speed links among switches, routers, and servers. By building on the existing IEEE 802.3 Ethernet standard, EtherChannel has the benefits of being highly scalable, transparent to networked applications, and capable of load balancing over multiple links with redundancy.

Scalable

EtherChannel allows bundled segments to be associated in groups of two or four. Groups of two links provide twice the aggregate bandwidth of a single link, while bundles of four links provide four times the aggregate bandwidth. These combinations provide aggregate bandwidth rates between Fast Ethernet and Gigabit Ethernet.

EtherChannels scalability allows the technology to be deployed across a broad spectrum of network infrastructures. For example, EtherChannel can be deployed between the wiring closet and the data center using a pair of full-duplex Fast Ethernet links providing 400+ Mbps. In the data centers, EtherChannel can be used to link up to four pairs of Fast Ethernet to provide 800 Mbps of bandwidth between high-speed servers and the backbone. Last, up to 8 Gbps of total bandwidth can be achieved with the aggregation of multiple Gigabit Ethernet links to provide a backbone network infrastructure capable of handling the most demanding traffic loads.

Transparent to Network Applications

Because EtherChannel is a complementary technology to Fast Ethernet and Gigabit Ethernet, its deployment is transparent to networked applications. Each Fast Ethernet or Gigabit Ethernet link in the EtherChannel bundle is IEEE 802.3- (802.3z for Gigabit Ethernet) compliant and is clocked at 100 Mbps or 1,000 Mbps (200 Mbps and 2,000 Mbps full-duplex), respectively. A standard is being developed by various vendors to bundle Ethernet to provide the benefits of this technology on a smaller scale. This technology is currently deployed among switches, routers, and servers with minimal overhead on the hardware.

Load Sharing and Redundancy

In addition to providing scalable bandwidth and seamless integration, EtherChannel also provides load sharing and redundancy. The technology provides load-balancing capabilities and management of links in a bundle by distributing traffic across the multiple links in the channel and monitoring the performance of these links. Redundancy is incorporated into the technology by automatically rerouting traffic onto an alternative link if any given link is cut. This rerouting of traffic is done in a matter of milliseconds and is transparent to the end user.

Currently, two load-sharing algorithms are being implemented by vendors: destination MAC address-based, and round robin-based. Using the destination MAC address-based method, the transmission port selected is determined by the one or two low-order bits of the destination MAC address. This method ensures all packets arrive in order, but doesn't always result in equal loading. This is because an uneven distribution of MAC addresses would result in an unbalanced distribution over the links. The round-robin method of load sharing provides a better spread of bandwidth across all links in the EtherChannel; however, this method is prone to out-of-order packets. The implications of out-of-order packets are great in a network where timing is critical, so this method is slowly being phased out by vendors.

EtherChannel and VLANs

EtherChannel's high-bandwidth output can be leveraged in the implementation of VLANs to yield a scalable solution that has excellent management capabilities. EtherChannel bundles can be configured to function as either ISL or IEEE 802.1q trunks to carry multiple VLANs from point-to-point devices across a high-speed medium. The only restriction placed on this implementation is that all VLAN trunks belonging to an EtherChannel must be in the same mode (either ISL or IEEE 802.1q).

SUMMARY

The evolution of Ethernet technology has been a rapid and innovative endeavor since its inception more than two decades ago. Over the years, many individuals and conglomerates have invested time, energy, and resources into the research and development of this technology. In return, the users of this media have gained a reliable and versatile infrastructure that continues to evolve as business and technological needs change.

What we see for this technology in the future is continued scalable bandwidth integrated into flexible and secure media. As more applications are developed and deployed over networks, demand for bandwidth will naturally grow proportionally. At the same time, security must be heightened to keep up with demands for secure transactions over shared media, such as Ethernet.

With the recent boom in wireless technology, traditional Ethernet has to contend with competition in a whole new arena. Currently, wireless technology is still in its infancy stages. Once the technology matures and the costs begin to fall, however, Ethernet will have to stop resting on its laurels and begin to defend its territory. Either way, Ethernet will continue to be deployed and maintained for years to come.

REVIEW QUESTIONS

1. **What IEEE standard covers the specifications for the Spanning-Tree Algorithm?**

   IEEE 802.1d

2. **Name the five states that a port can be in when participating in Spanning Tree?**

   Blocking, Listening, Learning, Forwarding, and Disabled

3. **What packets are used in a LAN environment by participating Spanning-Tree devices to communicate?**

   Bridge Protocol Data Units (BPDU) messages

4. **What Cisco proprietary management protocol is used to manage VLANs in a multi-switch LAN environment?**

   Cisco VLAN Trunk Protocol (VTP)

5. **Name the two trunking encapsulations available for encapsulating traffic over a VLAN trunk.**

   Inter-Switch Link (ISL) encapsulation and IEEE 802.1Q

6. **What is the fundamental technology behind EtherChannel?**

   EtherChannel is essentially a high-speed bundled version of Ethernet or IEEE 802.3.

CHAPTER 4

HTTP and the World Wide Web

OBJECTIVES

▼ Review the history and evolution of HTTP

■ Discriminate among various versions of HTTP

■ Become familiar with the operation of HTTP

■ Discuss packet-level dynamics of HTTP

▲ Review basic HTTP security

Imagine a little schoolgirl in a remote town in Alaska is doing research for a school project. This child is sitting in front of a computer at her school, surfing the Web. She is able to find extensive information with one simple search and she works to complete her project on time. The information she retrieves is intact and arranged "just so." And that information carries with it links to other sets of related information. The information includes text she can study and pictures she can embed in her reports, and, perhaps, a short movie clip or clever animation. Given the structure of the information she retrieves, she can spend her time productively, while she chases down facts and clues to other information she can use on her report.

Content Networking is entirely consumed with this entire process—from creating and formatting information to the successful delivery of that information. As you learned in the last chapter, many components make this kind of communication possible. In this chapter, two of the primary vehicles underlying Content Networking on the World Wide Web are discussed: HTML and HTTP. Hypertext Markup Language (HTML) is the standard programming language used on the Web for formatting text and images so they're readable by a user application, typically a browser. Hypertext Transfer Protocol (HTTP) is used to transfer the HTML pages from a server down to a client, so the client can view the document. This chapter outlines the history of HTTP and the functionality of HTTP. The focus here is on HTTP, but for more information on HTML, see the reference section at the end of this chapter.

HISTORY

The World Wide Web (WWW) was created in the early 1990s by researchers at Conseil Européen pour la Recherche Nucléaire (CERN)—specifically Tim Berners-Lee—all of whom were interested in sharing information. The information needed to be in a format that enabled each researcher to view the document and make additions or corrections, if necessary. The system also needed to have hyperlinks, or embedded objects, within the document, which took you to a new document when the object was accessed. Tim Berners-Lee wrote the first browser and server software, and he needed a protocol that would facilitate connections from the browser to the server.

The original design requirements for HTTP were simple: the protocol needed to be able to issue a request and have the server generate a response. Thus, the protocol was operating in a client/server environment and needed to use the existing infrastructure. The client and the server needed to use a common language for this request/response sequence, so HTTP was developed.

The first release of HTTP—HTTP 0.9—was released in 1991. Since then, two other versions have been released: version 1.0 in 1996 and version 1.1 in 1998. Each version has included major enhancements from the previous version. These versions are outlined in the following sections, and further reading can be found in the suggested reading section at the end of this chapter.

How It Works

HTTP is built on the client/server model, where the client makes a request of the server. The server processes that request and sends a response back to the client. HTTP was designed to take advantage of the existing Internet infrastructure, and it uses Transmission Control Protocol (TCP) as its transport mechanism. HTTP is built on top of TCP, which means HTTP is a connection-oriented protocol, but that's the extent of our discussion about it. A discussion of TCP/IP is outside the scope of this book, and we assume the reader already has this knowledge.

The HTTP client request contains a method, a version, and a set of headers. A given HTTP response contains a status code, response headers, and the content requested. The following contains an in-depth look at these methods, headers, and status codes.

The Uniform Resource Locator (URL) gives a lot of information about resources. The URL specifies the name of the resource (perhaps a document of some kind), it defines the location of the resource (usually a server located on an intranet or, perhaps, on the Internet) and what protocol to use to access that resource successfully. The following URL specifies that the resource is located at www.alteonwebsystems.com and is a document called index.html. The URL further specifies that HTTP should be used to retrieve this document:

```
http://www.alteonwebsystems.com/index.html
```

The port hasn't been defined, so a default TCP port of 80 is assumed. To specify a different port, the port number would follow immediately after the domain name.

```
http://www.alteonwebsystems.com:8080/index.html
```

The Uniform Resource Identifier (URI) refers to the location and resource within the URL. In the previous example, the URI would be www.alteonwebsystems.com /index.html.

HTML

HTML is the standard programming language for the WWW. HTML is comprised of a set of *tags,* which define how the document should be formatted by the client application. These tags also define the start and the end of the document. In the following example, you can see the use of tags (brackets surround them) and the preceding forward slash that denotes the end of a particular tag. The document is transferred from the server to the client in ASCII format. The client is responsible both for parsing the document and formatting it for the user application. The browser parses the documents and, in turn, requests any imbedded objects indicated by the HTML code.

```
<HTML>
<title>Hello World</title>
<a href="http://www.alteonwebsytems/hello.html"> Hello World!</a>
</HTML>
```

HTTP/0.9

The functionality of the first release of HTTP was limited; the protocol was designed for simplicity. In its original form, the protocol didn't have provisions for status messages, different types of headers, or embedded graphics (the actual specification itself only filled a single page!). A description of its functionality follows:

▼ **Connection**   The client attempts a TCP/IP-based connection to the server using the fully qualified name or the IP address and the TCP port number. if the client doesn't request a specific TCP port, port 80 is assumed. The server either accepts or denies the connection. If the server accepts the connection, then the request is parsed.

■ **Request**   The request contains a single request method: GET. The GET request contains the document address.

■ **Response**   The server processes the request and responds to the client with a byte stream of ASCII text. No way exists to send status messages on whether the transaction was successful.

▲ **Disconnect**   Once the response is complete, the server issues a disconnect request to terminate the TCP/IP session. (Note: some servers may impose a timeout period before closing the connection, such as 30 seconds.)

The goal was to get a functional protocol that allowed a simple request to be fulfilled. This design was flexible and allowed for enhancements in the next version.

HTTP/1.0

HTTP/1.0 implemented large-scale improvements over HTTP/0.9, and it addressed the need to be backward-compatible. The revised protocol, which was worked on by several people, was the first actual standard. Its features were significantly more refined than its immediate predecessor and included a variety of different header types, including those error codes we know and love, as well as the capability to post data and not simply *get* data. HTTP/1.0 also includes the capability to authenticate a client using basic, or clear-text, authentication. HTTP/1.0 added more methods, listed in Table 4-1, as well as status codes, shown in Table 4-2, and headers, listed in Table 4-3. All of these are defined in the following.

HTTP/1.1

As in HTTP/1.0, HTTP/1.1 had to be backward-compatible with previous versions of HTTP. The rapid growth of the Internet stipulated robust requirements for HTTP/1.1—more so than previous versions—and also added various new functions.

Perhaps the most important enhancement was the use of persistent connections. *Persistent connections* were important because they enabled the client to submit multiple requests over a single TCP/IP connection using the Keep-Alive value in the connection header. Prior to this, HTTP had to open a separate TCP/IP connection for each new request. This meant each embedded object would require a separate request and, therefore, a distinct and separate TCP/IP connection. In addition, a new session couldn't be initiated until and unless the prior session had either completed or timed out. As you can see, having to open multiple TCP sessions to transfer a relatively small amount of data was extremely cumbersome, and the network overhead associated with all these sessions could well exceed the actual data attempting to be transferred. Persistent connections were, therefore, a vast improvement and dramatically increased the performance of the protocol. HTTP/1.1 made persistent connections the default. In HTTP/1.0, the Keep-Alive had to be specified to keep the connection persistent.

Another major improvement from HTTP/1.0 is the use of *request pipelining,* which enables the client to perform multiple requests before it receives a response from a previous request. Coupling this feature with multiple persistent connections dramatically increased the potential speed and efficiency of any given data transfer.

Let's see how these two features work together. A client opens a persistent connection to a resource and issues a request. When the document is received, the connection is closed and the client starts to parse the document for embedded objects. If the client finds any embedded objects, it opens another persistent connection and issues multiple requests over this connection. The client then receives the embedded objects and displays them in the application. The net result is the application is able to load data into the browser-displayed document at a greater rate than ever before.

HTTP/1.1 also provided several other benefits, including the following: a method of debugging HTTP requests by using the TRACE method; the addition of cache control mechanisms, whereby HTTP/1.1 could include information to tell proxy servers and clients what data can be or shouldn't be cached, thus increasing the efficiency of data retrieval; authentication could be performed using the message digest format; and HTTP/1.1 included increased methods, headers, and status messages (displayed in Tables 4-1 through 4-3).

Method	HTTP/0.9	HTTP/1.0	HTTP/1.1
GET	*	*	*
HEAD		*	*
POST		*	*
PUT			*
DELETE			*
TRACE			*

Table 4-1. HTTP Methods

Status Code	HTTP/0.9	HTTP/1.0	HTTP/1.1
100			*
101			*
200		*	*
201		*	*
202		*	*
203			*
204		*	*
205			*
206			*
300			*
301		*	*
302		*	*
303			*
304		*	*

Table 4-2. Status Codes

Status Code	HTTP/0.9	HTTP/1.0	HTTP/1.1
305			*
306			*
307			*
400		*	*
401		*	*
402			*
403		*	*
404		*	*
405			*
406			*
407			*
408			*
409			*
410			*
411			*
412			*
413			*
414			*
415			*
416			*
417			*
500		*	*
501		*	*
502		*	*
503		*	*
504			*
505			*

Table 4-2.   Status Codes *(continued)*

Header	HTTP/0.9	HTTP/1.0	HTTP/1.1
Accept			*
Accept-Charset			*
Accept-Encoding			*
Accept-Language			*
Accept-Ranges			*
Age			*
Allow		*	*
Authorization		*	*
Cache-Control			*
Connection			*
Content-Encoding		*	*
Content-Language			*
Content-Length		*	*
Content-Location			*
Content-MD5			*
Content-Range			*
Content-Type		*	*
Date		*	*
ETag			*
Expect			*
Expires		*	*
From		*	*
Host			*
If-Match			*
If-Modified-Since		*	*
If-None-Match			*
If-Range			*
If-Unmodified-Since			*
Last-Modified		*	*
Location		*	*
Max-Forwards			*

Table 4-3.   Headers

Header	HTTP/0.9	HTTP/1.0	HTTP/1.1
Pragma		*	*
Proxy-Authenticate			*
Proxy-Authorization			*
Range			*
Referer		*	*
Retry-After			*
Server		*	*
TE			*
Trailer			*
Transfer-Encoding			*
Upgrade			*
User-Agent		*	*
Vary			*
Via			*
Warning			*
WWW-Authenticate		*	*

Table 4-3.   Headers *(continued)*

Request Methods

Request methods are used in the initial client communication. The client makes a request to the server for a specified resource. The following is a discussion of the various request methods.

GET

The *GET* method is the basis for most client requests. The GET method specifies the resource to request and the HTTP version to use in the session. The GET method can be conditional when combined with the appropriate headers. In the following example, the client requests the / resource and tells the server to use HTTP 1.1. The / resource is the default resource for the server, and the server should respond with the default document. Example:

```
GET: / HTTP/1.1
```

HEAD

The *HEAD* method is identical to the GET method, except the entity body isn't returned with the response. The HEAD method can be used to test the validity of hypertext links.

POST

The *POST* method is used to provide the client with the capability to update an existing resource. The update won't change the existing resource, but it does add content to support the resource. A common use of the POST header is a newsgroup. The resource—the newsgroup—already exists. The information posted becomes a subset of the resource.

PUT

The *PUT* method either creates a new entity or updates the existing entity. If the entity exists and new information is PUT, it overwrites the existing data. The difference in the PUT and POST methods deals with the Request-URI. The URI in the POST method specifies the resource, while the user agent in the PUT method specifies the resource.

DELETE

The *DELETE* method specifies the resource to be deleted. The server must reply with a status message, but doesn't necessarily have to complete the operation.

TRACE

The *TRACE* method is generally used for troubleshooting purposes. This method is usually combined with the Via header and the Max-Forwards header to see the path the request/response traversed. The response won't include an entity.

OPTIONS

The *OPTIONS* method is used to gather communication options about a particular resource or server. An example would be a request to see if the server supports HTTP/1.1 without making a request to a specific resource.

Response Status Code Definitions

The Response status code messages act as a kind of acknowledgement to the user agent that they can continue or that some action needs to be taken to fulfill their request.

1xx Informational

The Informational status codes were introduced in HTTP 1.1 and won't be sent to a client using HTTP 1.0. The following is a list of informational messages and what they mean.

▼ *100 Continue*   This status message tells the client to continue sending its request. If the client has finished sending the request, this status message should be ignored.

▲ *101 Switching protocols*   This message is a reply to the UPGRADE header received from the client. The server switches to the appropriate protocol after the termination of the 101 response.

2xx Successful

The server responds with this type of status message when the request has been received and accepted.

- ▼ *200 OK*   This status message is the most common Successful message. The data returned with the message depends on the method that submitted it.

- ■ *201 Created*   This status message indicates the request has been accepted and a new resource is being created. The newly created URI is returned to the client for further action.

- ■ *202 Accepted*   This status message indicates the request has been accepted, but the processing hasn't yet taken place.

- ■ *203 Non-Authoritative Information*   This status message indicates the information returned isn't the definitive set. This may be a subset or a superset of the original information.

- ■ *204 No Content*   This status message indicates the request has been fulfilled, but no information needs to be returned to the client.

- ■ *205 Reset Content*   This status message indicates the user agent should reset the content. This is usually used when the user agent needs to enter data.

- ▲ *206 Partial Content*   This status message indicates the request included a Range header and it has been fulfilled.

3xx Redirection

This type of status code indicates to the client that something else must be done to fulfill the request. The message could indicate that the content has been moved, and to get to the new location, the user agent will need to take further action.

- ▼ *300 Multiple Choices*   This status message indicates the user agent needs to choose from a set of available resources.

- ■ *301 Moved Permanently*   This status message indicates the URI has permanently moved to another location. The user agent should see the message and automatically move to that location.

- ■ *302 Found*   This status message indicates the requested URI has temporarily been moved to another location. The user agent should continue to use the original URI unless otherwise specified.

- ■ *303 See Other*   This status message indicates the requested information can be found at another location. This is different than the 302 message, which is a temporary move, and the 303 message is usually used as a response to POST script.

- ■ *304 Not Modified*   This status message indicates the content hasn't changed and the user agent should use the existing content.

- *305 Use Proxy* This status message indicates the request should be submitted to the proxy instead of the actual server.

- *306 Unused* This status message is reserved.

▲ *307 Temporary Redirect* This status message indicates the requested URI has temporarily been moved to another location. The user agent should continue to use the original URI unless otherwise specified.

4xx Client Error

This type of status message indicates a problem exists on the client side of the connection.

▼ *400 Bad Request* This status message indicates the server received the request, but the request was malformed. The client shouldn't resend the request unless modifications to the request are made.

- *401 Unauthorized* This status message indicates authentication is needed for the particular request. The server will return a WWW-Authenticate header field to initiate the challenge/response authentication sequence.

- *402 Payment Required* This status message is reserved for future use.

- *403 Forbidden* This status message indicates the request was received, but the request won't be fulfilled. Authentication won't help the request and the request shouldn't be resubmitted.

- *404 Not Found* This status message indicates the server couldn't find the requested resource.

- *405 Method Not Allowed* This status message indicates the client would like a list of valid methods for the requested resource.

- *406 Not Acceptable* This status message indicates the requested resource isn't capable of responding with the information specified in the request header.

- *407 Proxy Authentication Required* This status message indicates the client must first authenticate to the proxy before the request can be fulfilled.

- *408 Request Timeout* This status message indicates the server reached its timeout period before the client produced its request.

- *409 Conflict* This status message indicates the resource in its current state had a conflict with the request. The request should be reformed and resubmitted.

- *410 Gone* This status message indicates the requested resource is no longer available at the location specified in the header. This is a permanent condition, and future requests shouldn't be made to this resource at the specified location.

- *411 Length Required* This status message indicates the server requires a Content-Length header in the request. The client may resubmit the request if it includes the Content-Length header.

- *412 Precondition Failed*   This status message indicates the precondition specified in the request failed and, therefore, the request wasn't processed.

- *413 Request Entity Too Large*   This status message indicates the server refuses to process the request because the request entity is larger than the server can handle.

- *414 Request-URI Too Long*   This status message indicates the server won't process the request because the Request-URI is too long.

- *415 Unsupported Media Type*   This status message indicates the server won't service this request because the requested resource isn't in a format supported by the client request.

- *416 Requested Range Not Satisfiable*   This status message indicates the requested range doesn't fall within the current resource entity.

- *417 Expectation Failed*   This status message indicates the server couldn't meet the Expect header information.

5xx Server Error

These status messages indicate the server has erred and might not be capable of performing the request.

- *500 Internal Server Error*   This status message indicates the server couldn't fulfill the request because of an unexpected error.

- *501 Not Implemented*   This status message indicates the server doesn't support the requested method and, therefore, the server cannot fulfill the request.

- *502 Bad Gateway*   This status message indicates the server received an invalid response from an upstream server while it was acting as a gateway.

- *503 Service Unavailable*   This status message indicates the requested resource is temporarily unavailable. This error usually occurs when the Web server is offline or overloaded.

- *504 Gateway Timeout*   This status message indicates that while acting as a gateway, the server didn't receive a response from the request upstream resource.

- *505 HTTP Version Not Supported*   This status message indicates the server doesn't support the version of HTTP the client is trying to use.

Message Headers

The following is a brief description of the message headers. The goal here is to simply introduce some of the common elements and their roles. For a painfully complete discussion, don't forget to see the RFC.

General-header Fields

The following are a list of the fields that could be found in the general-header. The examples used are illustrative, but certainly not exhaustive. Again, refer to the RFC if you seek a more complete review.

Cache-Control   This header specifies directives in the request/response sequence, which must be followed by all caching mechanisms. Example:

```
Cache-Control: private
```

If a cache mechanism is in the path, this particular directive tells the cache mechanism it cannot cache this content in a general pool. This content is intended for a particular client. The example directive used—private—could be used when setting a cookie or when communicating sensitive information to a particular client.

Connection   This header enables the client to specify options that should be used for this session. Example:

```
Connection: Keep-Alive
```

Date   This header specifies the date and time at which the response was sent. Example:

```
Date: Mon, 12 Mar 2001 18:13:18 GMT
```

Pragma   This header specifies directives that must be followed along the session path. Example:

```
Pragma: no-cache
```

Transfer-Encoding   This header indicates whether anything has been done to the packet to change the encoding. Example:

```
Transfer-Encoding: chunked
```

Upgrade   This header indicates the client also supports other protocols and the server can switch to one of these if it chooses. Example:

```
Upgrade - HTTP/2.0
```

Via   This header indicates the connection has been formed through a proxy or gateway. The proxy or gateway adds the header to indicate it exists along the path. Example:

```
Via: 1.1 kader
```

1.1 is the HTTP version and *kader* is the name of the proxy.

Request-Header Fields

The following list are fields.

Accept   This header indicates the client will accept certain media types in the response. Example:

```
Accept: images/jpeg, images/gif, */*
```

The */* is the wildcard expression to accept any media type.

Accept-Charset   This header defines the character set valid for the response. Example:

```
Accept-Charset: iso-8859-5, *
```

The * is a wildcard and is viewed as accepting any character set.

Accept-Encoding   This header defines what type of encoding the client will expect in the response from the server. If the server cannot support the encoding, it should send a status message indicating this condition. Example:

```
Accept-Encoding: gzip, compress
```

Accept-Language   This header defines what type of language the client will expect in the response from the server. Example:

```
Accept-Language: en-us, *
```

The * is used for wildcard cases and accepts any language.

Authorization   This header indicates the user-agent wants to authenticate to the server, usually after receiving a 401 status message. Example:

```
Authorization: credentials
```

From   This header indicates the user-agent has included an e-mail address in the request. Example:

```
From: someuser@alteon.com
```

Host   This header defines the host and the port number of the requested resource. Example:

```
Host: www.alteonwebsystems.com
```

If-Modified-Since   This header indicates that if the entity hasn't been modified since the date given, the entity shouldn't be returned. If the entity isn't returned, a status message 304 should be returned. Example:

```
If-Modified-Since: Tue, 30 Jan 2001 06:56:43 GMT
```

If-Match   This header is used with a method to make it conditional, to determine if the entity the user-agent has already obtained is current. Example:

```
If-Match: "test"
```

If-None-Match   This header is used with a method to make it conditional, to determine if none of the entities the user-agent has already obtained is current. Example:

```
If-None-Match: *
```

If-Range   This header indicates the client may have a partial copy of an entity, and this request is asking for the remaining portion of the entity. If the entity has changed, the server should send the entire entity. This header must be used in conjunction with the *Range* header. Example:

```
If-Range: entity-tag or date
```

If-Unmodified-Since   This header is used with a method to make it conditional, to determine if the entity has been modified since the date provided. If the entity hasn't been modified, the server should continue with the request as if the *If-Unmodified-Since* header didn't exist. If the entity has been modified, the server should return the 412-status message. Example:

```
If-Unmodified-Since: Tue, 30 Jan 2001 06:56:43 GMT
```

Max-Forwards   This header is used with the *Trace* and *Options* methods to provide a mechanism to set a limit on the number of proxies that can forward this request. This is useful for troubleshooting a connection that appears to be failing somewhere in the path. Example:

```
Max-Forwards: 5
```

Proxy-Authorization   This header indicates the client is attempting to identify itself to a proxy that requires authentication. This header will be in response to a *Proxy-Authenticate* header received from the proxy. Example:

```
Proxy-Authorization: credentials
```

Range   This header specifies a byte range in the entity-body, which the client would like to request, instead of requesting the entire entity. This header can request a single byte range or a set of ranges. Example:

```
Range: range-specifier
```

Referer   This header defines the address obtained from the URI-Request. This header is included for the server's benefit only. The client doesn't make use of it. (Yes, this is spelled incorrectly, but that's the way it's defined.) Example:

```
Referer: http://www.alteonwebsystems.com
```

TE   This header indicates what extension transfer headings it's willing to accept and if it will accept trailer fields in chunked encoding. Example:

```
TE: deflate
```

Trailer   This header indicates header fields are contained in chunked transfer-encoding. Example:

```
Trailer: fieldname
```

User-Agent   This header defines the user-agent making the request. The server can use this for statistical analysis or it can tailor responses based on the information contained in the header. Example:

```
User-Agent: Mozilla/4.0 (compatible; MSIE 5.5; Windows 98)
```

Response-Header Fields

What the server sends back will of course depend on the specific request that was made. Here follows a list of valid responses, with some brief examples.

Accept-Ranges   This header indicates to the client that the server will accept ranges for a request. Example:

```
Accept-Ranges: bytes
```

Age   This header is used with cache servers to represent the amount of time since the origin server responded. Example:

```
Age: A non-negative number
```

Location   This header indicates the server would like to redirect the client to a different location, so the request for the resource can be completed. For 201 status messages, the location contains the newly created location. For 3xx status messages, the server indicates the preferred URI for the requested resource. Example:

```
Location: http://www.alteonwebsystems.com/document.html
```

Proxy-Authenticate   This header must be included when the server responds with a 407 status message, indicating a proxy server in the path requires authentication. Example:

```
Proxy-Authentication: challenge
```

Retry-After   This header indicates how long the requested service is predicted to be unavailable. When used with a 503 status message, this header indicates how long the requested service predicted to be unavailable. When used with a 3xx status message, it indicates how long the client should wait before issuing the redirected request. Example:

```
Retry-After: Tue, 30 Jan 2001 06:56:43 GMT
```

Server   This header defines the type of software running on the server. Example:

```
Server: Microsoft-IIS/5.0
```

Vary   This header indicates whether the cache server may use the content when replying to subsequent requests for the same content. Example:

```
Vary: field name
```

Warning   This header is used to carry additional information about a status message. Example:

```
Warning: [value]
```

WWW-Authenticate   This header is used in conjunction with the 401 status message to indicate authentication is needed. The response will contain a challenge. Example:

```
WWW-Authenticate: challenge
```

Entity-Header Fields

Entity-header fields are a specification of the type and formatting of data being requested. The following is a list of the headers that might be good to keep track of.

Allow   This header indicates the supported methods. Example:

```
Allow: GET, HEAD
```

Content-Encoding   This header indicates the media-type applied to the entity-body. Example:

```
Content-Encoding: gzip
```

Content-Language   This header indicates the language used within the entity. Example:

```
Content-Language: en-us
```

Content-Length   This header indicates the size of the entity-body in octets. Example:

```
Content-Length: 15736
```

Content-Location   This header indicates the entity may also be available from the specified location. Example:

```
Content-Location: http://www.alteonwebsystems.com/test.html
```

Content-MD5   This header indicates an enclosed MD5 digest exists of the entity. Example:

```
Content-MD5: md5-digest
```

Content-Range   This header indicates the location in the entity body where this range fits. Example:

```
Content-Range: bytes 2100-4532
```

Content-Type   This header indicates the media type the server is using for the entity-body. Example:

```
Content-Type: text/html
```

ETag   This header indicates a unique value derived by the Web server for this specific entity. Example:

```
Etag: "2043d8cd898ac01:8ef"
```

This ETag is associated with a specific graphics file.

Expires   This header defines when the content in the response becomes stale. This doesn't mean the content isn't good if it expired. This header works in conjunction with the Cache-Control header to deliver the most current content. Example:

```
Expires: Tue, 30 Jan 2001 06:56:43 GMT
```

Last-Modified   This header indicates when the entity was last modified. If the entity is a file, it could be the operating system's last modified date and time. Example:

```
Last-Modified: Tue, 30 Jan 2001 06:56:43 GMT
```

HTTP SECURITY

The need for secure transactions has been around since the inception of computing. Many ways exist to handle that security: authentication, encryption, private communication lines—and the list goes on. The challenge faced by HTTP is it would have to cross a public infrastructure to complete any transaction. Protecting data that traverses a public infrastructure has many pitfalls: you not only have to protect the data itself, you have to protect the session. To protect the data and the session, the Internet community has implemented encryption methods and data authentication. By encrypting the data, capturing packets and deciphering what they say is nearly impossible. This is because doing so would require a hacker to break the encryption algorithm. Even if hackers managed to break the encryption algorithm, however, they would still need more than one packet to learn something about the data. The hacker can attempt to hijack a user's connection by capturing the packet, changing the source address, and then sending it to the target destination, and hope that the target will simply send all further data to the new source; however, this is where data/session authentication comes in. One interesting method of authentication uses digital signatures. Before the client sends the packet, it is digitally signed. This signing process uniquely identifies the contents of the packet. If any data is altered in transit, say, a new source IP address embedded, the signature will no longer correspond exactly to the data. When the packet reaches its destination, the server simply compares the digital signature that came with the data with a recomputation of what that signature should have been if it were derived from the current data. If they match, the data is accepted as genuine. So, if a hacker were to intercept this packet and substitute an address, the server would know immediately upon verification of the signature that the data had been compromised.

Three security methods can be used with HTTP: authentication, HTTPS, and S-HTTP. These are all described in the following sections. Another widely deployed method, Secure Sockets Layer (SSL), is discussed in the next chapter.

Authentication

Authentication in HTTP can happen in two different ways. The first method, *Basic*, uses clear text to exchange the user name and password. There isn't anything else to this. The server sends an authentication challenge to the client and a little box opens in the client's browser. The user enters the user name and password, and off they go—as plain old text. This isn't terribly secure. If the session was authenticated using Basic authentication, the user name and password are easily obtained by using a protocol analyzer to capture the packet flow. Once someone has captured this information, that person has access to resource.

Message Digest is a second, more rigorous, method of HTTP. This method uses a one-way hashing algorithm to mask the data you want hidden. RSA Data Security markets a series of message digest algorithms, the most popular because of its strength, being Message Digest #5 (MD5). The way MD5 works is like a paper shredder: data goes in, a hash comes out. The interesting thing with a one-way hash is a password so hashed produces a unique result, that is, no matter who hashes it or when, the hash is always the same. With a hash, however, reversing it is virtually impossible. Even with the hash and the algorithm, reverse engineering to try to get the original password is, for all intents and purposes, impossible. In authentication schemes, this hash is then sent off to the server, along with the user name, which is typically not hashed. The server then receives this hash and matches it against the hashes stored in its security database. If they match, access is granted. If not, the session is killed, and an error message is sent back to the client. (The server doesn't actually have the password—all it has is the hash, so someone snooping around won't actually see the passwords themselves, just the hash.)

Remember, a Message Digest algorithm is used to protect the password, but all the other information is unprotected.

While Message Digest offers a more secure authentication method than Basic, it isn't enough by itself. Recall that if the session was authenticated using MD5, the user name would still be sniffable. Even though the password may be unreadable to the person who intercepts it; that person still has the user name and can now start guessing passwords.

Another flaw with the HTTP authentication method is it requires the client to request a resource. If that resource requires authentication, the server sends a status message indicating this and the client then sends its credentials in the next message. This makes things even easier for the person who is capturing the session. That person knows exactly when to expect the user name and password.

Also, note that in using either of these methods, the data is still transmitted in its raw, unencrypted format. If the session is meant to be secure, encryption should always be used. By default, all HTTP sessions transfer data in clear text format.

More information about authentication can be found in RFC 2617.

HTTPS

HTTPS, which is HTTP traffic encrypted by an SSL session, is detailed in the following chapter. HTTPS can provide encryption, digital signatures, and secure authentication. It uses the authentication mechanisms already built into HTTP and encrypts the traffic for safe transport across the Internet. HTTPS and S-HTTP (see the following) take two different approaches to solve the same problem. They both use encryption and digital signatures, but they work at different layers in the OSI model. S-HTTP is used to encrypt only HTTP traffic. HTTPS can be used to encrypt other applications, such as S/MIME, for secure mail transactions.

S-HTTP

Secure-HTTP (S-HTTP) hasn't been extensively deployed. By the time it was developed, HTTPS had made significant inroads into becoming the de facto standard for securing HTTP traffic.

S-HTTP is an add-on to HTTP and is designed to provide much-needed security. Much like HTTPS, S-HTTP can be used to encrypt, digitally sign, and authenticate sessions. S-HTTP works by encrypting the HTTP session information only, unlike HTTPS, which encrypts more layers of the OSI model.

As previously mentioned, to use HTTP authentication, the client has to request a resource. Then, the user is prompted for credentials. S-HTTP makes provisions so the client resource request and authentication will be encrypted. More information about S-HTTP can be found in RFC 2660.

HTTP PROTOCOL ANALYSIS

This section looks at the HTTP protocol through the eyes of a protocol analyzer. The protocol analyzer, or *sniffer*, has the capability to look at all layers of the OSI model and can look at the entire session. This section focuses on the HTTP session, but not at the TCP/IP sessions surrounding the HTTP session.

The first analysis performed is a look at an HTTP 1.1 session. The format for this section is an image of the capture screen, followed by a description. The session information presented is a capture of a client making a request to the URL http://www.alteonwebsystems.com.

The client submits a HTTP 1.1 request to the server in Figure 4-1. The initial request specifies what the client expects from this transaction.

▼ **Line 1**   The client tells the server it wants to use protocol HTTP 1.1 during this session. The GET method describes the content the client is requesting. In this case, the client is requesting this document /. This tells the server it should send the default document back to the client.

■ **Line 2**   Defines what types of media the client will Accept. In this request, the client is specifying several media types, images, applications, and a wildcard media type.

■ **Line 3**   Defines the language the client will accept in the response from the server.

■ **Line 4**   Defines the encoding the client will accept in the response from the server.

■ **Line 5**   Defines what type of user-agent is making the request. This should be present in all requests. This header can be used by the server to tailor responses to the specific user-agent.

```
HTTP: ----- Hypertext Transfer Protocol -----
HTTP:
HTTP: Line  1:  GET / HTTP/1.1
HTTP: Line  2:  Accept: image/gif, image/x-xbitmap, image/jpeg, image/pjpeg,
HTTP:              application/vnd.ms-powerpoint, application/vnd.ms-excel, ap
HTTP:              plication/msword, */*
HTTP: Line  3:  Accept-Language: en-us
HTTP: Line  4:  Accept-Encoding: gzip, deflate
HTTP: Line  5:  User-Agent: Mozilla/4.0 (compatible; MSIE 5.5; Windows 98)
HTTP: Line  6:  Host: www.alteonwebsystems.com
HTTP: Line  7:  Connection: Keep-Alive
HTTP: Line  8:
HTTP:
```

Figure 4-1.   Client request

■ **Line 6**   Specifies where the requested resource can be found. This header may be used if multiple web sites are running on a web server.

■ **Line 7**   The Connection header specifies that Keep-Alive should be used for this session. If Keep-Alive isn't specified, the server closes the TCP/IP connection after it finishes with the response.

▲ **Line 8**   The empty line with the CRLF at the end signifies the request has completed.

In Figure 4-2, the server responds to the client with a series of headers and the HTML data.

▼ **Line 1**   The server responds with a status message that indicates the server has accepted the connection and agrees to the parameters specified in the client request.

■ **Line 2**   The server indicates the type of software running this particular web site.

■ **Line 3**   Specifies the date and time at which the response was sent.

■ **Line 4**   The Set-Cookie header specifies the cookie that should be written to the client. In this case, the server is writing several pieces of information to the client: SITESERVER ID, expiration date, the path, and the domain.

■ **Line 5**   The Expires header is used in conjunction with the Cache-Control header to let the cache server know when the data will become stale. The date in this capture is in the past, but this doesn't mean the date isn't good. It tells the cache server to see if this is the most current data.

■ **Line 6**   The Content-Length header indicates the size of the entity-body, indicated in octets.

■ **Line 7**   The Content-Type header specifies the media type in which the server is transmitting the entity-body. In this example, the server is responding with text/html.

■ **Line 8**   This line specifies more information that should be written to the cookie.

■ **Line 9**   The Cache-Control is set to use private. This indicates the content must be destined for a single client, not a cache server. The private directive is used in this case because the response also contains a cookie destined for this particular client.

■ **Line 10**   This line tells the client the header information has concluded.

■ **Lines 11–34**   These lines are the actual HTML data the server is sending the client.

▲ **Line 35**   This line specifies the end of this packet, but the HTML data continues in the next packet.

In Figure 4-3, the packet uses the header information transferred in the previous packet. This packet contains all HTML data. Figure 4-4 shows the HTML data download has concluded. Please note, only a subset of all the HTML data download screens were captured.

```
HTTP: ----- Hypertext Transfer Protocol -----
HTTP:
HTTP: Line   1:  HTTP/1.1 200 OK
HTTP: Line   2:  Server: Microsoft-IIS/5.0
HTTP: Line   3:  Date: Tue, 15 May 2001 21:27:02 GMT
HTTP: Line   4:  Set-Cookie: SITESERVER=ID=1af576746044f48460c2bd582b17b306;
HTTP:            expires=Monday, 01-Jan-2035 00:00:00 GMT; path=/; domain=.al
HTTP:            teonwebsystems.com
HTTP: Line   5:  Expires: Thu, 01 Dec 1994 16:00:00 GMT
HTTP: Line   6:  Content-Length: 19177
HTTP: Line   7:  Content-Type: text/html
HTTP: Line   8:  Set-Cookie: ASPSESSIONIDGGQGQNZG=CKBHKLMANKMNPPLFGJCPPKEP; p
HTTP:            ath=/
HTTP: Line   9:  Cache-control: private
HTTP: Line  10:
HTTP: Line  11:  <!-- Copyright (c) 2000, Nortel Networks, Inc. --><!-- pt 1.
HTTP:            0 -->
HTTP: Line  12:  <html>
HTTP: Line  13:  <head>
HTTP: Line  14:  <09><title>Nortel Networks: Personal Internet</title>
HTTP: Line  15:  </head>
HTTP: Line  16:
HTTP: Line  17:  <body bgcolor="#ffffff" leftmargin="5" topmargin="5" marginw
HTTP:            idth="5" marginheight="5" text="#000000" link="#330066" vlin
HTTP:            k="#666666" alink="#990000">
HTTP: Line  18:  <table width="600" cellpadding="0" cellspacing="0" border="0
HTTP:            ">
HTTP: Line  19:
HTTP: Line  20:  <!-- begin top banner -->
HTTP: Line  21:  <form target="_top" method="post" action="http://www.norteln
HTTP:            etworks.com/cgi-bin/dropgo.cgi">
HTTP: Line  22:  <tr>
HTTP: Line  23:  <09><td><img src="/images/clear.gif" width="127" height="1" bor
HTTP:            der="0" alt="" /></td>
HTTP: Line  24:  <09><td><img src="/images/clear.gif" width="30" height="1" bord
HTTP:            er="0" alt="" /></td>
HTTP: Line  25:  <09><td><img src="/images/clear.gif" width="400" height="1" bor
HTTP:            der="0" alt="" /></td>
HTTP: Line  26:  <09><td><img src="/images/clear.gif" width="32" height="1" bord
HTTP:            er="0" alt="" /></td>
HTTP: Line  27:  <09><td><img src="/images/clear.gif" width="11" height="1" bord
HTTP:            er="0" alt="" /></td>
HTTP: Line  28:  </tr>
HTTP: Line  29:  <tr valign="top">
HTTP: Line  30:  <09><td bgcolor="#18399C" colspan="5">
HTTP: Line  31:  <09>
HTTP: Line  32:  <09><table border="0" width="100%">
HTTP: Line  33:  <09><tr>
HTTP: Line  34:  <09><td><a href="/"><img
HTTP:
```

Figure 4-2. Server response

```
HTTP: ----- Hypertext Transfer Protocol -----
HTTP:
HTTP: Line   1:    src="/images/alteon_logo.gif" width="260" height="39" alt="
HTTP:              Alteon WebSystems" border="0" /></a></td>
HTTP: Line   2:    <09><!-- <td background="/images/back_bl.gif" bgcolor="#254bab"
HTTP:                width="30"><img src="/images/clear.gif" width="30" height="
HTTP:              1" border="0" alt="" /></td> -->
HTTP: Line   3:    <09><td align="right" bgcolor="#18399C" width="400">
HTTP: Line   4:    <0909><a href="http://www.nortelnetworks.com"><img src="/images/
HTTP:              logo.gif" width="127" height="39" alt="Nortel Networks" bord
HTTP:              er="0" /></a>
HTTP: Line   5:    <09></td>
HTTP: Line   6:    <09><td background="/images/back_bl3.gif" bgcolor="#254bab" wid
HTTP:              th="11"><img src="/images/clear.gif" width="11" height="1" b
HTTP:              order="0" alt="" /></td>
HTTP: Line   7:    </tr>
HTTP: Line   8:    </table></td>
HTTP: Line   9:    </tr>
HTTP: Line  10:    </form>
HTTP: Line  11:    <tr>
HTTP: Line  12:    <09><td valign="top" colspan="5" bgcolor="#ff9900"><img src="/i
HTTP:              mages/orange.gif" width="600" height="2" border="0" alt="" /
HTTP:              ></td>
HTTP: Line  13:    </tr>
HTTP: Line  14:
HTTP: Line  15:
HTTP: Line  16:    <tr>
HTTP: Line  17:    <09><td valign="top" align="right"><img src="/images/sideline_p
HTTP:              i.gif" width="127" height="54" border="0" alt="" /><br />
HTTP: Line  18:
HTTP: Line  19:    <09><!-- begin left sidebar -->
HTTP: Line  20:    <09><a href="http://www.nortelnetworks.com/corporate/leadership
HTTP:              /personal/index.html"><img src="/images/btn_vision.gif" widt
HTTP:              h="127" height="20" alt="Vision" border="0" /></a><br />
HTTP: Line  21:    <09><a href="/products/"><img src="/images/btn_products.gif" wi
HTTP:              dth="127" height="20" alt="Products" border="0" /></a><br />
HTTP:
HTTP: Line  22:    <09><a href="/services/"><img src="/images/btn_services.gif" wi
HTTP:              dth="127" height="20" alt="Services" border="0" /></a><br />
HTTP:
HTTP: Line  23:    <09><a href="/support/"><img src="/images/btn_support.gif" widt
HTTP:              h="127" height="2
HTTP:
```

Figure 4-3.   Server response with no header information and HTML data

```
⊟-🖳 HTTP: ----- Hypertext Transfer Protocol -----
   ┈🗋 HTTP:
   ┈🗋 HTTP: Line  1:   tworks.com/help/">Help</a> |<090909>
   ┈🗋 HTTP: Line  2:   <0909090909><a href="http://www.nortelnetworks.com/help/legal/index
   ┈🗋 HTTP:               .html">Legal</a> |
   ┈🗋 HTTP: Line  3:   <0909090909><a href="http://www.nortelnetworks.com/help/legal/index
   ┈🗋 HTTP:               .html#copyright">Copyright</a> |
   ┈🗋 HTTP: Line  4:   <0909090909><a href="http://www.nortelnetworks.com/help/legal/index
   ┈🗋 HTTP:               .html#privacy">Privacy Statement</a><br />
   ┈🗋 HTTP: Line  5:   <0909090909>Copyright &copy; Nortel Networks Limited 2001. All Righ
   ┈🗋 HTTP:               ts Reserved.
   ┈🗋 HTTP: Line  6:   <0909>
   ┈🗋 HTTP: Line  7:   <090909></font></td>
   ┈🗋 HTTP: Line  8:   <0909></tr>
   ┈🗋 HTTP: Line  9:   <09></table></td>
   ┈🗋 HTTP: Line 10:   </tr>
   ┈🗋 HTTP: Line 11:   </form>
   ┈🗋 HTTP: Line 12:   <tr>
   ┈🗋 HTTP: Line 13:   <09><td><img src="/images/clear.gif" width="127" height="1" bor
   ┈🗋 HTTP:               der="0" alt="" /></td>
   ┈🗋 HTTP: Line 14:   <09><td><img src="/images/clear.gif" width="30" height="1" bord
   ┈🗋 HTTP:               er="0" alt="" /></td>
   ┈🗋 HTTP: Line 15:   <09><td><img src="/images/clear.gif" width="400" height="1" bor
   ┈🗋 HTTP:               der="0" alt="" /></td>
   ┈🗋 HTTP: Line 16:   <09><td><img src="/images/clear.gif" width="32" height="1" bord
   ┈🗋 HTTP:               er="0" alt="" /></td>
   ┈🗋 HTTP: Line 17:   <09><td><img src="/images/clear.gif" width="11" height="1" bord
   ┈🗋 HTTP:               er="0" alt="" /></td>
   ┈🗋 HTTP: Line 18:   </tr>
   ┈🗋 HTTP: Line 19:
   ┈🗋 HTTP: Line 20:
   ┈🗋 HTTP: Line 21:   </table>
   ┈🗋 HTTP: Line 22:   </body>
   ┈🗋 HTTP: Line 23:   </html>
   ┈🗋 HTTP:
```

Figure 4-4.   Continuation of the server response with HTML data

Figure 4-5 shows that once the client has the HTML data, it parses this data looking for embedded objects. The client also formats this data for presentation in the appropriate application. This image shows the client has made a request for an image embedded in the HTML data.

▼ **Line 1**   The first line uses the GET header to request /images/clear.gif using HTTP/1.1.

■ **Line 2**   The Accept header tells the server it will accept any media types.

■ **Line 3**   The Referer header lets the client tell the server where it received this Request-URI. This particular Request-URI came from the original request submitted to http://www.alteonwebsystems.com.

```
HTTP: ----- Hypertext Transfer Protocol -----
   HTTP:
   HTTP: Line  1:   GET /images/clear.gif HTTP/1.1
   HTTP: Line  2:   Accept: */*
   HTTP: Line  3:   Referer: http://www.alteonwebsystems.com/
   HTTP: Line  4:   Accept-Language: en-us
   HTTP: Line  5:   Accept-Encoding: gzip, deflate
   HTTP: Line  6:   User-Agent: Mozilla/4.0 (compatible; MSIE 5.5; Windows 98)
   HTTP: Line  7:   Host: www.alteonwebsystems.com
   HTTP: Line  8:   Connection: Keep-Alive
   HTTP: Line  9:   Cookie: SITESERVER=ID=1af576746044f48460c2bd582b17b306; ASPS
   HTTP:            ESSIONIDGGQGQNZG=CKBHKLMANKMNPPLFGJCPPKEP
   HTTP: Line 10:
   HTTP:
```

Figure 4-5.   Client request for embedded objects

- **Lines 4–8**   These lines are the same as the original request. Please refer to the first figure/description for further information.

- **Line 9**   This line sends the cookie that was originally written by the server back to the server.

- ▲ **Line 10**   The empty line indicates the request has concluded.

In Figure 4-6, the server responds to the GET for the image file in the last figure with some response headers and the graphics data. Notice at the bottom of this figure, the graphics data is denoted without any headers.

- ▼ **Lines 1–3**   These lines are the same as the response for the HTML data.

- **Line 4**   The Content-Type is marked as image/gif. The client should expect to see graphics data following the header information.

- **Line 5**   Indicates to the client that the server will accept a request for ranges of data represented in bytes.

- **Line 6**   The Last-Modified header indicates the item was last modified on this date and time.

- **Line 7**   The ETag header is a unique value derived by the Web server for this specific entity. This ETag represents the graphics file requested by the client.

- **Line 8**   The Content-Length header indicates the size of the entity-body, indicated in octets. The 45 represents the amount of data the client should expect to see.

- ▲ **Line 9**   The empty line indicates the response has concluded.

```
HTTP: ----- Hypertext Transfer Protocol -----
   HTTP:
   HTTP: Line  1:   HTTP/1.1 200 OK
   HTTP: Line  2:   Server: Microsoft-IIS/5.0
   HTTP: Line  3:   Date: Tue, 15 May 2001 21:27:02 GMT
   HTTP: Line  4:   Content-Type: image/gif
   HTTP: Line  5:   Accept-Ranges: bytes
   HTTP: Line  6:   Last-Modified: Tue, 30 Jan 2001 06:56:43 GMT
   HTTP: Line  7:   ETag: "2043d8cd898ac01:8fc"
   HTTP: Line  8:   Content-Length: 45
   HTTP: Line  9:
   HTTP:
   HTTP: [45 bytes of Graphics Data]
   HTTP:
```

Figure 4-6.   Server response to the GET

Figure 4-7 shows a request for another graphics file. The difference is in the response because the graphics file is larger than a single packet, multiple packets will be sent from the server. In Figure 4-8, the server replies with the next image. This image is too large to fit in one packet, so it sends the maximum data that it can fit in this packet. Figure 4-9 shows the rest of the graphics data will be transmitted to the client in a separate packet without headers.

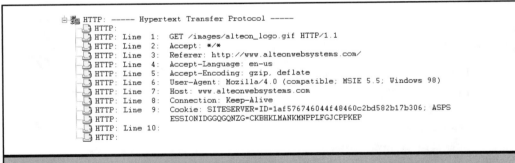

```
HTTP: ----- Hypertext Transfer Protocol -----
   HTTP:
   HTTP: Line  1:   GET /images/alteon_logo.gif HTTP/1.1
   HTTP: Line  2:   Accept: */*
   HTTP: Line  3:   Referer: http://www.alteonwebsystems.com/
   HTTP: Line  4:   Accept-Language: en-us
   HTTP: Line  5:   Accept-Encoding: gzip, deflate
   HTTP: Line  6:   User-Agent: Mozilla/4.0 (compatible; MSIE 5.5; Windows 98)
   HTTP: Line  7:   Host: www.alteonwebsystems.com
   HTTP: Line  8:   Connection: Keep-Alive
   HTTP: Line  9:   Cookie: SITESERVER=ID=1af576746044f48460c2bd582b17b306; ASPS
   HTTP:            ESSIONIDGGQGQNZG=CKBHKLMANKMNPPLFGJCPPKEP
   HTTP: Line 10:
   HTTP:
```

Figure 4-7.   Client request for embedded objects

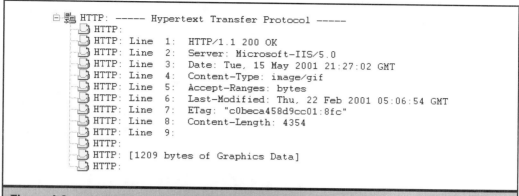

```
HTTP: ----- Hypertext Transfer Protocol -----
HTTP:
HTTP: Line  1:  HTTP/1.1 200 OK
HTTP: Line  2:  Server: Microsoft-IIS/5.0
HTTP: Line  3:  Date: Tue, 15 May 2001 21:27:02 GMT
HTTP: Line  4:  Content-Type: image/gif
HTTP: Line  5:  Accept-Ranges: bytes
HTTP: Line  6:  Last-Modified: Thu, 22 Feb 2001 05:06:54 GMT
HTTP: Line  7:  ETag: "c0beca458d9cc01:8fc"
HTTP: Line  8:  Content-Length: 4354
HTTP: Line  9:
HTTP:
HTTP: [1209 bytes of Graphics Data]
HTTP:
```

Figure 4-8.   Server response with the graphics data

Now, let's compare the HTTP 1.0 and the HTTP 1.1 request and response headers.

Figure 4-10 shows only two differences occur in this HTTP 1.0 request and the HTTP 1.1 request. The first difference is in Line 1: the GET specifies the HTTP version to use. The second difference is the Accept-Encoding header: this header wasn't available in HTTP 1.0.

Figure 4-11 shows the HTTP 1.1 client request. The differences between this and the HTTP 1.0 client request are listed in Figure 4-10.

Figures 4-12 and 4-13 compare an HTTP 1.0 server response to an HTTP 1.1 sever response. The only difference in the response is the Connection: Keep-Alive. This is present in the HTTP 1.0 response because Keep-Alive isn't the default state for connections. Notice the server uses HTTP 1.1 in the response.

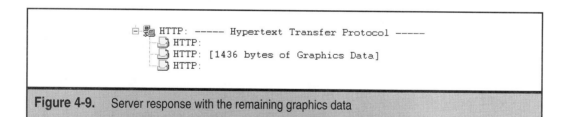

```
HTTP: ----- Hypertext Transfer Protocol -----
HTTP:
HTTP: [1436 bytes of Graphics Data]
HTTP:
```

Figure 4-9.   Server response with the remaining graphics data

```
⊟ 🖳 HTTP: ----- Hypertext Transfer Protocol -----
   └ 🗋 HTTP:
   └ 🗋 HTTP: Line  1:   GET / HTTP/1.0
   └ 🗋 HTTP: Line  2:   Accept: image/gif, image/x-xbitmap, image/jpeg, image/pjpeg,
   └ 🗋 HTTP:                 application/vnd.ms-powerpoint, application/vnd.ms-excel, ap
   └ 🗋 HTTP:                 plication/msword, */*
   └ 🗋 HTTP: Line  3:   Accept-Language: en-us
   └ 🗋 HTTP: Line  4:   User-Agent: Mozilla/4.0 (compatible; MSIE 5.5; Windows 98)
   └ 🗋 HTTP: Line  5:   Host: www.alteonwebsystems.com
   └ 🗋 HTTP: Line  6:   Connection: Keep-Alive
   └ 🗋 HTTP: Line  7:
   └ 🗋 HTTP:
```

Figure 4-10.   Client request using HTTP 1.0

Note, in Figure 4-13, a Connection header isn't present because the Keep-Alive connection state is the default in HTTP 1.1.

The analysis presented here is only a small part of the actual capture. To look at the entire capture, use a network analyzer and capture an HTTP session.

```
⊟ 🖳 HTTP: ----- Hypertext Transfer Protocol -----
   └ 🗋 HTTP:
   └ 🗋 HTTP: Line  1:   GET / HTTP/1.1
   └ 🗋 HTTP: Line  2:   Accept: image/gif, image/x-xbitmap, image/jpeg, image/pjpeg,
   └ 🗋 HTTP:                 application/vnd.ms-powerpoint, application/vnd.ms-excel, ap
   └ 🗋 HTTP:                 plication/msword, */*
   └ 🗋 HTTP: Line  3:   Accept-Language: en-us
   └ 🗋 HTTP: Line  4:   Accept-Encoding: gzip, deflate
   └ 🗋 HTTP: Line  5:   User-Agent: Mozilla/4.0 (compatible; MSIE 5.5; Windows 98)
   └ 🗋 HTTP: Line  6:   Host: www.alteonwebsystems.com
   └ 🗋 HTTP: Line  7:   Connection: Keep-Alive
   └ 🗋 HTTP: Line  8:
   └ 🗋 HTTP:
```

Figure 4-11.   Client request using HTTP 1.1

```
HTTP: ----- Hypertext Transfer Protocol -----
HTTP:
HTTP: Line  1:   HTTP/1.1 200 OK
HTTP: Line  2:   Server: Microsoft-IIS/5.0
HTTP: Line  3:   Date: Tue, 15 May 2001 21:09:21 GMT
HTTP: Line  4:   Connection: keep-alive
HTTP: Line  5:   Set-Cookie: SITESERVER=ID=415711ddd1f6a03d9309a929327fe6e5;
HTTP:            expires=Monday, 01-Jan-2035 00:00:00 GMT; path=/; domain=.al
HTTP:            teonwebsystems.com
HTTP: Line  6:   Expires: Thu, 01 Dec 1994 16:00:00 GMT
HTTP: Line  7:   Connection: Keep-Alive
HTTP: Line  8:   Content-Length: 19177
HTTP: Line  9:   Content-Type: text/html
HTTP: Line 10:   Set-Cookie: ASPSESSIONIDGGQGQNZG=OGBHKLMAAAHBLMNEHEDNGJLB; p
HTTP:            ath=/
HTTP: Line 11:   Cache-control: private
HTTP: Line 12:
HTTP: Line 13:   <!-- Copyright (c) 2000, Nortel Networks, Inc. --><!-- pt 1.
HTTP:            0 -->
HTTP: Line 14:   <html>
HTTP: Line 15:   <head>
HTTP: Line 16:   <09><title>Nortel Networks: Personal Internet</title>
HTTP: Line 17:   </head>
HTTP: Line 18:
HTTP: Line 19:   <body bgcolor="#ffffff" leftmargin="5" topmargin="5" marginw
HTTP:            idth="5" marginheight="5" text="#000000" link="#330066" vlin
HTTP:            k="#666666" alink="#990000">
HTTP: Line 20:   <table width="600" cellpadding="0" cellspacing="0" border="0
HTTP:            ">
HTTP: Line 21:
HTTP: Line 22:   <!-- begin top banner -->
HTTP: Line 23:   <form target="_top" method="post" action="http://www.norteln
HTTP:            etworks.com/cgi-bin/dropgo.cgi">
HTTP: Line 24:   <tr>
HTTP: Line 25:   <09><td><img src="/images/clear.gif" width="127" height="1" bor
HTTP:            der="0" alt="" /></td>
HTTP: Line 26:   <09><td><img src="/images/clear.gif" width="30" height="1" bord
HTTP:            er="0" alt="" /></td>
HTTP: Line 27:   <09><td><img src="/images/clear.gif" width="400" height="1" bor
HTTP:            der="0" alt="" /></td>
HTTP: Line 28:   <09><td><img src="/images/clear.gif" width="32" height="1" bord
HTTP:            er="0" alt="" /></td>
HTTP: Line 29:   <09><td><img src="/images/clear.gif" width="11" height="1" bord
HTTP:            er="0" alt="" /></td>
HTTP: Line 30:   </tr>
HTTP: Line 31:   <tr valign="top">
HTTP: Line 32:   <09><td bgcolor="#18399C" colspan="5">
HTTP: Line 33:   <09>
HTTP: Line 34:   <09><table border
HTTP:
```

Figure 4-12. HTTP 1.0 server response to the HTTP 1.1 client request

```
⊟ 🖳 HTTP: ----- Hypertext Transfer Protocol -----
  ┕─🗋 HTTP:
  ┕─🗋 HTTP: Line  1:   HTTP/1.1 200 OK
  ┕─🗋 HTTP: Line  2:   Server: Microsoft-IIS/5.0
  ┕─🗋 HTTP: Line  3:   Date: Tue, 15 May 2001 21:27:02 GMT
  ┕─🗋 HTTP: Line  4:   Set-Cookie: SITESERVER=ID=1af576746044f48460c2bd582b17b306;
  ┕─🗋 HTTP:              expires=Monday, 01-Jan-2035 00:00:00 GMT; path=/; domain=.al
  ┕─🗋 HTTP:              teonwebsystems.com
  ┕─🗋 HTTP: Line  5:   Expires: Thu, 01 Dec 1994 16:00:00 GMT
  ┕─🗋 HTTP: Line  6:   Content-Length: 19177
  ┕─🗋 HTTP: Line  7:   Content-Type: text/html
  ┕─🗋 HTTP: Line  8:   Set-Cookie: ASPSESSIONIDGGQGQNZG=CKBHKLMANKMNPPLFGJCPPKEP; p
  ┕─🗋 HTTP:              ath=/
  ┕─🗋 HTTP: Line  9:   Cache-control: private
  ┕─🗋 HTTP: Line 10:
  ┕─🗋 HTTP: Line 11:   <!-- Copyright (c) 2000, Nortel Networks, Inc. --><!-- pt 1.
  ┕─🗋 HTTP:              0 -->
  ┕─🗋 HTTP: Line 12:   <html>
  ┕─🗋 HTTP: Line 13:   <head>
  ┕─🗋 HTTP: Line 14:   <09><title>Nortel Networks: Personal Internet</title>
  ┕─🗋 HTTP: Line 15:   </head>
  ┕─🗋 HTTP: Line 16:
  ┕─🗋 HTTP: Line 17:   <body bgcolor="#ffffff" leftmargin="5" topmargin="5" marginw
  ┕─🗋 HTTP:              idth="5" marginheight="5" text="#000000" link="#330066" vlin
  ┕─🗋 HTTP:              k="#666666" alink="#990000">
  ┕─🗋 HTTP: Line 18:   <table width="600" cellpadding="0" cellspacing="0" border="0
  ┕─🗋 HTTP:              ">
  ┕─🗋 HTTP: Line 19:
  ┕─🗋 HTTP: Line 20:   <!-- begin top banner -->
  ┕─🗋 HTTP: Line 21:   <form target="_top" method="post" action="http://www.norteln
  ┕─🗋 HTTP:              etworks.com/cgi-bin/dropgo.cgi">
  ┕─🗋 HTTP: Line 22:   <tr>
  ┕─🗋 HTTP: Line 23:   <09><td><img src="/images/clear.gif" width="127" height="1" bor
  ┕─🗋 HTTP:              der="0" alt="" /></td>
  ┕─🗋 HTTP: Line 24:   <09><td><img src="/images/clear.gif" width="30" height="1" bord
  ┕─🗋 HTTP:              er="0" alt="" /></td>
  ┕─🗋 HTTP: Line 25:   <09><td><img src="/images/clear.gif" width="400" height="1" bor
  ┕─🗋 HTTP:              der="0" alt="" /></td>
  ┕─🗋 HTTP: Line 26:   <09><td><img src="/images/clear.gif" width="32" height="1" bord
  ┕─🗋 HTTP:              er="0" alt="" /></td>
  ┕─🗋 HTTP: Line 27:   <09><td><img src="/images/clear.gif" width="11" height="1" bord
  ┕─🗋 HTTP:              er="0" alt="" /></td>
  ┕─🗋 HTTP: Line 28:   </tr>
  ┕─🗋 HTTP: Line 29:   <tr valign="top">
  ┕─🗋 HTTP: Line 30:   <09><td bgcolor="#18399C" colspan="5">
  ┕─🗋 HTTP: Line 31:   <09>
  ┕─🗋 HTTP: Line 32:   <09><table border="0" width="100%">
  ┕─🗋 HTTP: Line 33:   <09><tr>
  ┕─🗋 HTTP: Line 34:   <09><td><a href="/"><img
  ┕─🗋 HTTP:
```

Figure 4-13.   HTTP 1.1 server response to the HTTP 1.1 client request

SUMMARY

HTTP has evolved from a way to share information by scientists to a way of life for most people. People are now using HTTP—and the World Wide Web it is built on—to shop, to communicate, and, perhaps, most important, to be part of an online community. As HTTP has continued to evolve, a multitude of features have been added, including security and the addition of many new types of applications that run on top of HTTP.

This chapter provided an overview of HTTP and how it works. HTTP versions .9 through 1.1 were discussed, and the functional differences, such as persistency and request pipelining between the protocols were illuminated. This chapter also looked at HTTP security issues, and discussed and took a prolonged look at a protocol analysis of an HTTP communication. As previously mentioned, please see the Suggested Reading for further discussion.

REVIEW QUESTIONS

1. **Name one primary advantage of HTTP/1.1 over HTTP 1.0.**

   Request pipelining or persistent connections, among others.

2. **Name two types of authentication mechanisms for HTTP.**

   Basic or clear text, and message digest.

3. **Are all the versions of HTTP backward-compatible?**

   Yes. All versions are designed to be backward-compatible.

4. **What is the difference between S-HTTP and HTTPS?**

   HTTPS can be used to encrypt applications other than HTTP.

SUGGESTED READING

RFC1945, Hypertext Transfer Protocol—HTTP/1.0
RFC 2616, Hypertext Transfer Protocol—HTTP/1.1
RFC 2617, HTTP Authentication: Basic and Digest Access Authentication
RFC 2660, The Secure Hypertext Transfer Protocol

CHAPTER 5

SSL

OBJECTIVES

▼ Understand the fundamental concepts behind the cryptography of SSL

■ Become familiar with the SSL protocol itself

■ See the SSL protocol in action on a Web server

▲ Understand the role of SSL accelerators

Nicely compartmentalized, protocol independent, and widely supported by both commercial and free implementations, the Secure Sockets Layer (SSL) has become the de facto standard for cryptography over the Internet. And rightfully so.

To see why you need SSL, you only have to look at the path of a packet scurrying across the Internet. A simple traceroute from a server I manage in San Jose, California to www.amazon.com shows my packets start in downtown San Jose, go across the street, pop out of Sacramento, California, turn north to Portland, Oregon, and, finally, end up at Amazon headquarters in Seattle, Washington. Over 14 hops are visible along the path—each one potentially watching and reading the contents of my packets, each one marking a point along the way where some evildoer could change the contents of my packets, adding items, changing delivery addresses, or what have you.

Realizing the need for secure transactions across the Internet, the folks at Netscape back in 1994 released the specifications to SSL 1.0. Despite having a patent on the technology, Netscape welcomed feedback from the Web community and encouraged the development of SSL as a joint project. By the end of 1995, SSL 3.0 was published. During its early days, it competed with Secure-HTTP, another solution to the security problem posed by the Internet. The key difference between Secure-HTTP and SSL, however, is SSL remained protocol-independent. In essence, any TCP-based protocol could use SSL as its underlying security mechanism without a lot of extra work. With flexibility and corporate sponsorship, SSL won the battle and became the cryptographic tool of choice for e-commerce on the Internet.

With all the feedback, help, and insight from the Internet community, Netscape felt SSL should belong to the community rather than to them. So, in May 1996, Netscape passed the control and responsibility for the upkeep of SSL to the Internet Engineering Task Force (IETF). The *IETF* is essentially responsible for the development of protocols and standards for the Internet, and all its work is shared with the public. In an effort to demonstrate the protocol was unbiased in any way, the name of SSL was changed to Transport Layer Security (TLS). The first official TLS specification was released in 1999.

TLS 1.0 has few differences from SSL 3.0. This is a testament to the solid work done on SSL from the start. Unless you're interested in implementing the protocol itself (or you're simply curious), you needn't worry about their differences. Most protocol implementations (such as that from the OpenSSL group, http://www.openssl.org) group SSL 3.0 with TLS 1.0 and can properly support both.

In this chapter, you begin by stepping back and getting a lesson on basic cryptography. Armed with the fundamentals, you tackle the SSL protocol itself, followed by a description of SSL's application in Web infrastructure.

CRYPTO 101

Let me begin by saying *cryptography is hard*. Don't expect to learn and become a cryptography expert quickly and most definitely don't expect to become an expert after reading this section. The purpose of this section is to provide a gentle introduction to the basics of cryptography (often referred to as simply *crypto*), the terms, and the basic ideas behind how they work. These nuggets of information should be enough for you to use an implementation of SSL to secure your network.

Let's start with the simplest form of crypto: secret key cryptography.

SECRET KEY CRYPTOGRAPHY

The idea behind secret key cryptography (more formally called *symmetric key cryptography*) is that both the sender and the receiver of a message have a preagreed on a "key" that can be used to "unlock" a message. In its simplest forms, a *key* can be as simple as a table of character mappings such as *b* means *a,* and *c* means *b,* and so forth. The recipient can then use the same table to decode a message.

To see this in action, let's go back to a simpler problem: passing a note in class. The goal: to send a message to your friend without getting caught. The method: tightly folding of paper. The problem: this is security through obscurity. You're relying on no one else bothering to unwrap the paper and peek inside at the message. Worse, if the teacher sees the note being passed, it could quite possibly be read aloud to the class.

Solving this problem requires some planning on both the sender and the receiver's part. Let's assume you plan in advance to use the Caesar's Algorithm for encoding. The algorithm is your cipher. In the case of the Caesar Algorithm, the *cipher* works by adding some constant value to each character being encoded. The value chosen for a particular message is the *key*.

For two friends to exchange an encoded message, they must first agree on using Caesar's Algorithm as the cipher. Then they must agree on using a particular value as a key. For this example, let's assume they pick a key of 5. With the agreement in place, one of them can encode the message "coffee" as "htkkjj." (The letter *h* is five letters after *c,* the letter *t* is five letters after *o,* and so forth.) One friend can then send the paper to the other friend without even having to worry about folding it. If others see it, all they'll see is garbage. When the intended recipient sees the message, he can use the preagreed upon cipher and key to decrypt it back into the original message.

Common symmetric key ciphers are 3DES (pronounced "triple-des") and RC4. *3DES* is a *block cipher*, meaning the algorithm encrypts and decrypts data in equal-sized blocks. If you want to send a message that's less than the size of a block, padding must be added to the end, so the block is filled out. 3DES is considered among the most secure symmetric ciphers, but this comes at the expense of requiring more computational power to work with.

In contrast to 3DES, *RC4* is a *stream cipher,* meaning it works with one character at a time when it performs its work. In addition to working with smaller units of data, RC4 is also a much simpler and, thus, faster algorithm. Some folks have made it a competition of sorts to come up with the smallest implementation!

Key Size

In the previous example, you saw how a student could use Caesar's algorithm with a key set to 5 to pass a note in class. In this case, the key size is short, making it potentially easier to decode the message without necessarily having the key.

By the very nature of Caesar's algorithm, the key must be small. To understand how key size can affect the quality of the encryption, let's extend Caesar's algorithm a bit. Instead of a single number affecting every number, you want a series of numbers to affect a string of input. For example, if you take 1, 3, and 7, and then apply Caesar's algorithm to one letter at a time rotating around those three numbers, you would see

String:	H	E	L	L	O	W	O	R	L	D
Key:	1	3	7	1	3	7	1	3	7	1
Result:	I	H	S	M	R	D	P	U	S	E

Because a single letter can be encoded up to three different ways (the letter *A* could be *B*, *D*, or *H*), it will take someone doing cryptanalysis a lot longer to break this code. In essence, you have a key length of 3.

This is where the strength of computers comes into play. Instead of small key sizes like 3, you could apply key sizes of 25 to Caesar's algorithm, thereby making it possible for every letter and symbol potentially to map to every other letter or symbol. The result would be an even more difficult code to break.

As you can see in this example, key size has a great influence in the ability for someone to break a scheme. The larger the key length, the more possibilities exist, and the more difficult it becomes to break a scheme by brute force, exhaustively testing every possible key until a match is found. The goal is to have so many possibilities that it would take years to iterate through all of them, at which point the information is unlikely to need securing anymore.

For a sense of perspective, 32 bits gives you 4,294,967,296 possible keys. 56 bits gives you 72,057,594,037,927,936 possible keys. As it turns out, a key length of 56 bits can be broken by a couple of Pentium class PCs in real time, that is, fast enough to make a difference. Each added bit doubles the number of possibilities, so 64 bits in the key means it's 256 times more difficult to crack, which might translate into a few months using those Pentiums. The current choice for key size in symmetric ciphers is 128 bits. For those of you curious types, 128 bits gives you 340,282,366,920,938,463,463,374,607,431,768,211,456 possible keys. If you could iterate through 100 trillion keys a second, you would need something like 100 million billion years to iterate through all the key combinations. By way of comparison, the Sun will burn out in 8 billion years.

Public Key Cryptography

Symmetric key cryptography works great when an opportunity exists for two parties to meet in advance, so they can agree on a key. In applications slightly more serious than that of passing notes in school, however, being able to meet in advance to exchange key information presents a Catch-22: if the two parties could meet in a secure place to exchange their keys, why can't they use that opportunity to exchange the secret information as well? This problem is especially apparent in e-commerce situations where the two parties are the customer with a credit card and a web server hiding in a server room thousands of miles away.

To solve this problem, asymmetric cryptography was created. The underlying principle of *asymmetric cryptography* is this: in mathematics, creating problems is much easier than solving them. Take, for instance, a simple math problem of multiplying two numbers: 374 and 874. A few clicks of the mouse button and you know their product is 326,876. However, factoring 326,876 to find the two numbers it took to create it is a much more difficult and time-consuming problem. This is the essence of asymmetric cryptography, better known as *public key cryptography*.

Two keys are created. The first key is the *public key* that can be shared with anyone by any means. You could even go so far as to publish this key on a billboard in the busiest part of town. The second key is the *private key*. This component must be kept secret from everyone else.

Once the keys are created, anyone can encrypt a message with the public key. Once encrypted, however, the only way to decrypt the message is with the private key. This ensures that messages destined for the owner of the private key cannot be read by anyone else.

Several public key encryption algorithms exist, but the one you want to focus on for SSL is the Rivest Shamir Adleman (RSA) algorithm. The RSA algorithm is particularly interesting because it can work in both directions, that is, what is encrypted with the private key can be decrypted with the public key and vice versa. This feature of the algorithm makes it useful in validating identity, as well as providing a method of secure information transport.

For example: Heidi wants to send a message to Steve. Heidi creates a public/private key pair and encrypts a message using her private key. She then advertises her public key and sends a message encrypted by her private key to Steve. By using the public key, Steve can validate that the encrypted message was, in fact, from Heidi because no other public key could decrypt it. Remember this example because proof of identity is important to certificates, which you learn about later in this chapter.

Putting It Together: Hybrid Encryption Schemes

Public key cryptography is an incredibly powerful way to provide encryption and decryption services but, unfortunately, it has a down side: from a computational standpoint, generating keys, as well as processing the encryption and decryption, takes a lot of work. Furthermore, because one of the keys is public, larger key sizes must be used to ensure the security of the messages being encrypted. Translated into CPU cycles, this means even the fastest of servers in 2001 can only handle 50–70 RSA exchanges a second. Unfortunately, this isn't as much progress as you might hope for. Taking a step back to 1994—the year SSL was created—Pentium-class machines from Intel were just becoming available. This meant the fastest PC class machine you could get was a Pentium running at 100 MHz. They could perform approximately ten 1,024-bit RSA operations per second. This isn't very many, especially for a server that might need to accept a lot of transactions.

To deal with this performance limitation, hybrid encryption schemes were developed to take advantage of the performance benefit offered by symmetric key encryption and the security offered by public key encryption.

Let's get back to Heidi and Steve. Heidi wants to send Steve a message over a public network, like the Internet, so Steve starts by generating a public/private key pair that are each 1,024 bits in length. Steve keeps his private key to himself, but advertises the public key on a billboard in Los Angeles where anyone interested in reading it, can. Heidi then takes the public key and uses it to encrypt a randomly generated 128-bit number for use as the symmetric key. She can now send this encrypted 128-bit number back to Steve because he's the only one who can decrypt it.

Once Steve receives the random number, he decrypts it with his private key. Now both Heidi and Steve have the same 128-bit random number. They can use this in conjunction with a symmetric cipher to start communicating with one another in a secure manner.

So how exactly did Heidi and Steve manage to secure a connection? They did so by not sending any private information over the network that could be used by a third party intercepting traffic. Looking at Figure 5-1, you see only two pieces of information crossing the network before the encrypted session begins: the public key and the encrypted random number. Anyone can have the public key, and the encrypted number is useless without the private key (which was never sent ov,er the network).

This is the cryptographic foundation necessary for SSL to work.

Certificates

When Heidi wanted to send a message to Steve, she looked for his public key to encrypt a random number. However, nothing prevents malcontents from intercepting or replacing Steve's public key with their own. When Heidi sends back the encrypted random number, it could be intercepted, the random number decrypted, and secured communication begun. Meanwhile, Heidi would think she was talking to Steve.

To keep this type of identity theft from occurring, public key certificates were created. *Public key certificates* serve as a form of identification for the holder of a public/private key pair and are issued by a trusted third party. These IDs vouch for the party identified, similar to the way a driver's license identifies a driver. Supposedly, to get a driver's license, a prospective driver needs to prove his identity. A Social Security card, credit cards, bills, another photo ID—something is required to identify the driver to the agency. Once proof of identity is confirmed (or confirmed enough), the agency will issue a license. This license is then good throughout the state and can be used to confirm the identity of the driver beyond his word that he is who he says he is. The guarantee that the ID is accurate is only as good as the check performed by the issuing agency, of course, but something is

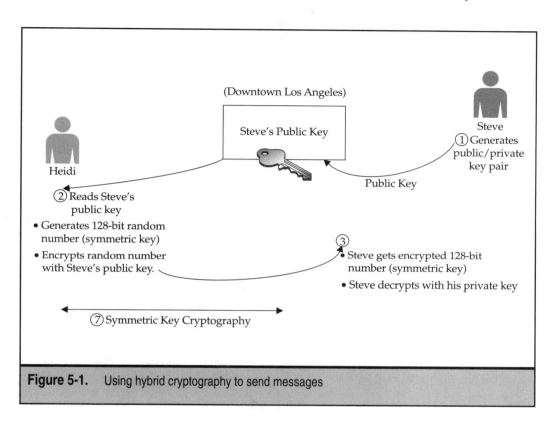

Figure 5-1.   Using hybrid cryptography to send messages

better than nothing. In the case of Heidi and Steve, Heidi doesn't have much in the way of verifying Steve is Steve and not some doppelganger.

Certificates work the same way. In the context of Content Networking, a web-based vendor might want to acquire a certificate issued by some credible agency, called a Certificate of Authority (CA), such as VeriSign. *VeriSign* is a real company, with a real web site, a physical office, and real employees, which offers real services. All of this can be verified. The goal is for customers to know and trust VeriSign, because VeriSign can verify that a company exists, is a business, has a real web site, and, perhaps, has a physical office, real employees, and offers real services—all before issuing that business a certificate. Customers, either knowing or at least intuiting this level of service, could then look for VeriSign's signature on a certificate, and then know VeriSign believes the company holding that certificate is who it says it is. If the signature is there, the customer knows she is truly connecting with the web site she intended to. In the earlier example, Heidi could use the certificate to verify further that she was talking to Steve—before she exchanges any messages with him.

Certificates contain all sorts of information, including the organization that issued the certificate, how long the certificate is good, what person or organization the certificate is being issued to, and the subject's public key. Also included is the issuer's digital signature.

Creating a *digital signature* takes two steps. The first step is to generate a hash of the certificate. *Hash functions* are mathematical meat grinders, which take some body of input (in this case, the certificate) and run it through some algorithmic functions. The output of a hash function is a small, fixed-sized number. Because the input is exactly the same, the output is also always be the same, and any changes to the input string results in a demonstrably different hash. The second step is to take the hash and encrypt it using the private key of the issuing company. The only way to decrypt this hash is by using the associated public key.

The result is a certificate, identifying the company, signed by another company that vouchsafes for the integrity of that company. Embedded in the certificate is a method for anyone to verify the contents are accurate—simply decrypt the signature using the public key of the issuer, run your own hash on the contents of the certificate, and compare it to the decrypted hash. If a perfect match occurs and you trust the issuer, then you can be reasonably confident the certificate user is who she says she is.

Of course, for this to work, the issuer must share its public key with everyone. This is done in licensing agreements with the makers of Web browsers, ensuring every browser ships with a copy of public keys from the major certificate authorities (such as VeriSign).

As a result, when a Web server sends its certificate to a browser, the browser does three things: first, it computes the hash of the certificate itself. Next, it decrypts the hash that came with the certificate—because only the certificate authority's public key can decrypt the hash, the browser is certain the issuer did issue the certificate, and, finally, it compares the two hashes. If they are the same, the Web browser knows the certificate is from the site it claims to be and the certificate authority has validated the site.

Who Watches the Watchmen: The CA's Certificates

So far, you have seen that browsers can trust certificates signed by CAs, but how do we know we can trust the CA?

It turns out that CAs also use certificates to identify themselves. These certificates are formatted in the same way any other certificate is, but the important part is the issuer and the subject are one and the same. Even the public keys in the certificate are identical. But, just because the issuer and subject are identical doesn't mean a browser should instantly trust the certificate! Instead, the browser checks its own list of trusted CAs and compares the public keys in the certificate with what it knows. If the two public keys (the browser's local copy and the certificate's) are identical, then the certificate is okay. The browser gets its list of public keys from the browser maker. The browser maker gets those public keys directly from the CAs.

Certificate Hierarchies

Anyone with a public/private key pair can sign a certificate. That's the easy part. The hard part is getting everyone else to trust you! To deal with this, certificate hierarchies exist. A *certificate hierarchy* is a chain of certificates with each certificate signing the next one down. The client asking for the certificate can walk this chain of certificates until it finds a certificate signed by someone known and trusted.

For example, assume a large, multinational company wants to set up its own CA. Every browser in the company knows about the *root authority*, that is, the certificate that signs all other certificates. As a result, every browser knows the root authority's public key. The problem with this company is so many departments exist, it's simply too cumbersome for the central systems administration group to provide certificates to everyone. Thus, departments are delegated the task of issuing their own certificates. Because all departments don't know about all other departments, it's important for each department to be issued a certificate signed by the root certificate. From this departmental certificate, other certificates are signed.

When a client in one department contacts a server in another department and asks for its certificate, it is given a chain of certificates. This *chain of certificates* starts with the certificate of the server itself as signed by the department certificate. The chain then also contains the certificate issued to the department as signed by the root authority. Walking up the chain, the browser can compute the hashes and validate that each certificate was in fact signed by the next certificate up the chain. When the browser finds the department certificate was signed by the root authority, the browser can stop checking because it knows about the root authority and already trusts it.

With web sites now needing hundreds of certificates for all their servers, CAs like Verisign have started issuing a single signed certificate for use by the site. The site can then sign all the certificates for their individual servers themselves. Each server then sends the chain of certificates to any requesting browser.

Certificate Signing Requests

The process of getting a certificate is relatively easy. You must begin by generating a certificate signing request (CSR). How the CSR is generated varies from web server to web server. In the following "Configuring Your Own SSL Sever" section, you step through the process of generating a CSR as an example.

A *CSR* embeds some basic information about you, your company, and contact information. It also embeds into it a public key. The Web server, when generating the CSR, will have also generated a private key to go along with the public key. Be sure the private key stays in a safe place.

Once you have the CSR in hand, you need to contact a CA such as Verisign (http://www.verisign.com) so it can sign the certificate. Typically, a minimal charge is involved for signing a certificate, and the resulting signed certificate is only valid for a fixed time (usually one year).

With a signed certificate in hand, you then need to install it on your Web server, making sure the server correctly associates the signed certificate with the appropriate private key.

Figure 5-2 shows the steps taken by CAs, web site owners, and browser makers, so users can easily validate whether a site's certificate is authentic and signed by a trusted CA.

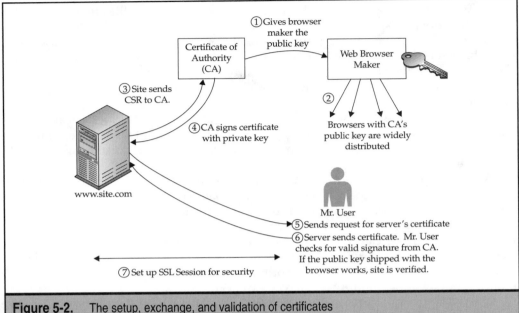

Figure 5-2. The setup, exchange, and validation of certificates

CONFIGURING AND INSTALLING YOUR OWN SSL SERVER

Of course, no better way exists to understand SSL than to install your own server and play with it. In this section, you step through the process of setting up the Apache web server with the mod_ssl toolkit and OpenSSL library. Please note, this process assumes you're using a Unix-based system (such as Linux, FreeBSD, or Solaris) and are comfortable with compiling/installing software on it. As with anything you do for the first time, avoid production servers during your initial experiments with SSL servers.

NOTE: Apache and OpenSSL prefer being compiled with the GNU C compiler (gcc). If your operating system doesn't ship with it (for example, Solaris), you might find it prudent to download and install it. Solaris users can find precompiled packages at http://www.sunfreeware.com.

Begin by downloading the following packages:

▼ Apache 1.3.20 (http://httpd.apache.org/dist/httpd)

■ OpenSSL 0.9.6b (http://www.openssl.org/source)

▲ mod_ssl-2.8.4-1.3.20 (http://www.modssl.org/source)

For this discussion, I assume you downloaded them to the /usr/local/src directory.

Unpacking the Packages

Begin by unpacking the tarballs like so:

```
[root@ford src]# tar -xvzf openssl-0.9.6b.tar.gz
[root@ford src]# tar -xvzf mod_ssl-2.8.4-1.3.20.tar.gz
```

This leaves you with three subdirectories: apache_1.3.20, openssl-0.9.6b, and mod_ssl-2.8.4-1.3.20. Let's begin with compiling OpenSSL.

Compiling OpenSSL

The folks who developed OpenSSL made it easy to configure. Begin by going into the directory where the source code is unpacked:

```
[root@ford src]# cd openssl-0.9.6b
```

Now, go through the configuration process. This has been completely automated via a shell script appropriately called config. To run this script, simply type

```
[root@ford openssl-0.9.6b]# ./config
```

You'll see a great deal of output stream by your screen. This is normal. At the end of the process, you should see a line stating "Configured for *system*" where *system* is the name of the operating system on which you're performing the configuration. If you get an error at this point, check to see if your development environment is properly configured and you have the necessary permissions to get to it. For additional information on handling errors, read the INSTALL file that comes with OpenSSL.

Now, you build OpenSSL with the make tool like so:

```
[root@ford openssl-0.9.6b]# make
```

This takes a few minutes to run, depending on the performance of your system and how busy it is. An unloaded Pentium III at 800 MHz running FreeBSD can compile OpenSSL in about two minutes.

With OpenSSL built, you'll want to test it before installing it. To test OpenSSL, simply run

```
[root@ford openssl-0.9.6b]# make test
```

This validates that your build is, in fact, working correctly. If any of the tests fail, do a **make distclean**, and then try configuring and compiling again. Make sure that, along each step of the way, you didn't miss any errors that occurred. You shouldn't use a build of OpenSSL if it can't pass its own tests.

The last step is to install OpenSSL. If you've been performing these steps as yourself, you must su to root at this time. By default, OpenSSL installs itself in /usr/local/ssl. You don't have to install OpenSSL, but it's recommended. The tools that come with OpenSSL are likely to be handy in the future because many other tools can be SSL-enabled with the OpenSSL package.

To install OpenSSL, type

```
[root@ford openssl-0.9.6b]# make install
```

Again, a great deal of output will be on the screen as OpenSSL is copied into the right place. Once this is done, back out of the current directory before you move on to the next step:

```
[root@ford openssl-0.9.6b]# cd ..
```

Configuring and Compiling Apache with mod_ssl

The mod_ssl package is a series of patches applied to the Apache web server source code. Thus, you don't compile mod_ssl directly. Instead, you apply the patch to Apache, and then compile Apache.

Thankfully, the developer of mod_ssl has done a terrific job of making this a painless task. Let's start with configuring mod_ssl. Begin by moving into the mod_ssl directory.

```
[root@ford src]# cd mod_ssl-2.8.4-1.3.20
```

Once there, you configure mod_ssl by telling it where the Apache source code is and where the OpenSSL libraries are, like so:

```
-with-apache=../apache_1.3.20 -with-ssl=../openssl-0.9.6b
```

This not only configures mod_ssl, it also goes on to apply the necessary patches to the Apache source code. With the patches in place, you can go to the Apache directory and compile it.

```
[root@ford mod_ssl-2.8.4-1.3.20]# cd ..
[root@ford src]# cd apache_1.3.20
[root@ford apache_1.3.20]# make
```

This step might take a few minutes. As with OpenSSL, you see a lot of output fly by your screen. Unless the procedure errors out (in which case you see a clearly marked error message indicating what went wrong), don't worry about the messages.

Creating the Certificate and Installing Apache

At this point, Apache is compiled and ready to be installed. But before you do the actual installation, you should create a dummy certificate with which you can test your installation. The mod_ssl folks have also made this a snap—simply type in the following:

```
[root@ford apache_1.3.20]# make certificate
```

This will begin a series of prompts regarding your locale, your business, and your identification. Because this is only a test certificate, don't worry about being specific at this point. Let's step through this one question at a time.

```
make[1]: Entering directory '/usr/local/src/apache_1.3.20/src'
SSL Certificate Generation Utility (mkcert.sh)
Copyright (c) 1998-2000 Ralf S. Engelschall, All Rights Reserved.

Generating test certificate signed by Snake Oil CA [TEST]
WARNING: Do not use this for real-life/production systems
```

The first question (Step 0) asks if you want to use RSA or DSA. For this example, use RSA.

```
STEP 0: Decide the signature algorithm used for certificate
The generated X.509 CA certificate can contain either
RSA or DSA based ingredients. Select the one you want to use.
Signature Algorithm ((R)SA or (D)SA) [R]: r
```

The next step generates a private key based on various sources of randomness in your system.

```
STEP 1: Generating RSA private key (1024 bit) [server.key]
68731 semi-random bytes loaded
Generating RSA private key, 1024 bit long modulus
.................++++++
.......++++++
e is 65537 (0x10001)
```

The system is ready to generate a certificate signing request (CSR) based on information regarding your contact information. For this, you simply fill out the form with the prompts you're given:

```
STEP 2: Generating X.509 certificate signing request [server.csr]
Using configuration from .mkcert.cfg
You are about to be asked to enter information that will be incorporated
into your certificate request.
What you are about to enter is what is called a Distinguished Name or a DN.
There are quite a few fields but you can leave some blank
For some fields there will be a default value,
If you enter '.', the field will be left blank.

-----

1. Country Name           (2 letter code) [XY]: US
2. State or Province Name  (full name)     [Snake Desert]:California
3. Locality Name           (eg, city)      [Snake Town]:San Jose
4. Organization Name       (eg, company)   [Snake Oil, Ltd]:TestCompany
5. Organizational Unit Name(eg, section)   [Webserver Team]:Systems Group
6. Common Name             (eg, FQDN)      www.snakeoil.dom]:www.xyz.com
7. Email Address           (eg, name@FQDN) www@snakeoil.dom]:abc@xyz.com
8. Certificate Validity    (days)          [365]:365
```

In Step 3, Apache automatically signs the certificate signing request using a sample certificate it shipped with. Note, this certificate isn't issued by any certificate of authority; thus, client browsers will be warned they cannot authenticate your identity if you use this certificate. However, if all you're looking for is security and you aren't concerned with identity (often the case when performing tests), this certificate will do just fine.

```
STEP 3: Generating X.509 certificate signed by Snake Oil CA [server.crt]
Certificate Version (1 or 3) [3]:3
Signature ok
subject=/C=US/ST=California/L=San Jose/O=TestCompany/OU=Systems
roup/CN=www.xyz.com/Email=abc@xyz.com
Getting CA Private Key
Verify: matching certificate & key modulus
read RSA key
Verify: matching certificate signature
../conf/ssl.crt/server.crt: OK
```

The final step asks if you want to encrypt your private key with a pass phrase. In an ideal world, everyone would want to do this. However, doing so requires a human to enter the passphrase every time the Apache web server is started. In the automated world of Web servers working in colocated data centers, this often isn't possible. So, for this example, don't encrypt the private key. Note, though, this leaves you somewhat vulnerable. If someone could break into your sever, they could steal your private key and your server's identity with it.

```
STEP 4: Enrypting RSA private key with a pass phrase for security
in the file [server.key]
The contents of the server.key file (the generated private key) has to be
kept secret. So we strongly recommend you to encrypt the server.key file
with a Triple-DES cipher and a Pass Phrase.
Encrypt the private key now? [Y/n]: n
Warning, you're using an unencrypted RSA private key.
Please notice this fact and do this on your own risk.
```

Now that you have a certificate, you can install Apache with the command:

```
[root@ford apache_1.3.20]# make install
```

This places the installed web server with SSL support in the /usr/local/apache directory. You can also find your certificates and keys in the /usr/local/apache/conf directory. The certificates are organized as follows:

/usr/local/apache/conf/ssl.key/server.key	This is the PEM-encoded RSA private key that was created in Step 1 of make certificate.

/usr/local/apache/conf/ssl.crt/server.crt	This is the PEM-encoded certificate file sent during the certificate message of an SSL transaction. It includes your public key and the information you provided during Step 2.
/usr/local/apache/conf/ssl.csr/server.csr	This is the certificate signing request (CSR) with the information you filled out during Step 2. If you decide you want a real certificate signed by a CA, you can send in this file.

Using Apache with SSL Support

To start Apache with SSL support, you simply need to run

```
[root@ford apache_1.3.20]# /usr/local/apache/bin/apachectl startssl
```

And, shazaam! You have a running SSL-enabled web server! You might want to place the startup information in your appropriate startup script, so it can automatically start at boot time.

To stop the server, simply type

```
[root@ford apache_1.3.20]# /usr/local/apache/bin/apachectl stop
```

You can place content in the /usr/local/apache/htdocs directory to make it accessible via Apache.

For additional detail regarding the configuration of the Apache web server, visit its Web site at http://www.apache.org. Apache has a complete manual online that you can browse through. Many great books are also available on Apache, such as the *Apache Web Server Administration and e-Commerce Handbook,* by Scott Hawkins (Prentice Hall, 2000). As with any book that deals with practical issues, I recommend a visit to your local bookstore, where you can page through the selections yourself and pick the book that best speaks to you.

Generating New CSRs

If you're like me, you probably blew through the make certificate section, filling in bogus information, just so you could get to the point where you could verify that the installation worked. So, now you're stuck: you have a web site with a bogus server key that was used to sign a bogus certificate-signing request and, thus, you ended up with a bogus certificate. Oops.

What you probably want to do is create a CSR that can be sent to a CA, like Verisign, so real clients on the Internet can validate your identity. Well, have no fear, for that section is here! Let's start by moving into the Apache directory:

```
[root@ford apache_1.3.20]# cd /usr/local/apache
```

Knowing Who You Are   You must begin by knowing your Fully Qualified Domain Name (FQDN) to be used for accessing your Web site. This is crucial for the CSR to work correctly. Assume for this example you want to use www.site.com.

Generating the Key   Select five large and relatively random files on your hard disk. These will be used to seed the random number generator. Let's refer to them as file1:file2:...:file5, in the following command.

Generate the key with the following command:

```
-rand file1:file2:file3:file4:file5 \
-out conf/ssl.key/www.site.com.key
```

Remember, the private key is the heart of your site's security. Protect it!

Generating the CSR   You can now generate the CSR with the following command:

```
req -new -key conf/ssl.key/www.site.com.key \
-out conf/ssl.csr/www.site.com.csr
```

You will be prompted for the attributes of your certificate.

The Follow-Up   You'll find a CSR in the /usr/local/apache/conf/ssl.csr/www.site.com.csr file that you can submit to Verisign. Visit Verisign's site for further details on processing the CSR, payment, and so forth.

Once you receive a signed certificate from Verisign, place it in /usr/local/apache/conf/ssl.crt/www.site.com.crt. You can then edit the /usr/local/apache/conf/httpd.conf file, so Apache knows to use these certificates by changing the line that starts with SSLCertificateFile to read

```
SSLCertificateFile /usr/local/apache/conf/ssl.crt/www.site.com.crt
```

You also need to change the key file so Apache uses the correct private/public key pair. Edit the same httpd.conf file, so the SSLCertificateKeyFile line reads as follows:

```
SSLCertificateKeyFile /usr/local/apache/conf/ssl.key/www.site.com.key
```

Restart Apache by running:

```
[root@ford apache]# /usr/local/apache/bin/apachectl restart
```

And, now you have your new and shiny Verisign-blessed certificate on your Web server.

SSL: THE PROTOCOL

What is arguably the key aspect to SSL's success is that it isn't tied in with any other protocol. SSL, by design, was meant to be a layer in itself, so any TCP-based protocol could use it. In essence, this is what is shown in Figure 5-3.

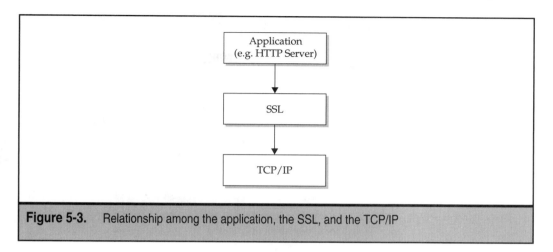

Figure 5-3.   Relationship among the application, the SSL, and the TCP/IP

The most popular application used with SSL is HTT; however, nothing is stopping anyone from using other applications. Indeed, many protocols have taken to using the additional security offered by SSL without the difficulty traditionally tied to adding an encryption to the application protocol itself. Users of Outlook might be pleasantly surprised to see they can even do Post Office Protocol (POP) over SSL, Internet Message Access Protocol (IMAP) over SSL, and Simple Mail Transfer Protocol (SMTP) over SSL.

Another key feature of SSL is its cryptographic independence. The protocol itself is merely a framework for allowing arbitrary hybrid public key/private key and symmetric key cryptosystems to work with one another. Thus, as cryptosystems evolve and improve, SSLs can continue providing the framework necessary, so they can be easily and widely used.

For the full discussion on the SSL protocol, look at RFC 2246, which can be found at http://www.rfc-editor.org/rfc/rfc2246.txt.

The remainder of this section uses the output of the ssldump and OpenSSL programs to help visualize the steps taken by an SSL client and server. If you're interested in using these tools, visit http://www.rtfm.com/ssldump and http://www.openssl.org, respectively, to fetch these tools. Note, ssldump and OpenSSL are available in source code form only. Expect to compile ssldump yourself. Precompiled versions of OpenSSL are generally findable for most Unix operating systems: most Linux distributions ship with it precompiled, FreeBSD offers it in the /usr/ports collection, and Solaris versions are available from the http://www.sunfreeware.com site. The ssldump program also requires the libpcap library to do packet sniffing. The libpcap library comes with most open-source Unix operating systems as part of the base package. For other operating systems, visit http://www.tcpdump.org.

SSL Messages

SSL uses a series of messages to communicate state changes, certificates, encrypted keys, and, of course, data. Each message contains a little information regarding the type of message, and then the content of the message itself. This section begins by examining the messages and the information contained within them. Once you understand the message types, you'll see how they come together to form a complete SSL transaction.

Client Hello

The *client hello* message is the first message to be sent after a TCP connection establishment. The message is an indicator to the server that it is to begin its negotiation phase. Within the message, you find the following:

Field	Description
Version	What is the highest version of SSL the client can support?
Random Number	A 256-bit random number the server uses for seeding its random-number generator.
Session Identifier	A 128-bit value representing this session. Subsequent connections can use the same Session-ID, so the key exchange doesn't need to take place.
Cipher Suite	A list of what symmetric ciphers can be supported.
Compression Method	A list of what compression formats (if any) the client can support. If enabled, the SSL layer automatically performs inline compression of the application data.

The version, cipher suite, and compression methods are, in a sense, asking the server "which of these do you support?" The server hello message sent from the server contains the answers.

Server Hello

The *server hello* message is the first message sent from the server to the client. This is an answer to the client hello message that also includes within it:

Field	Definition
Version	What version of SSL the server agrees to use for communication. This value is less than or equal to the version number specified in the client hello message.
Random Number	A 256-bit random number sent to the client to seed its random-number generator.
Session Identifier	If the client-specified session identifier is known to the server, the server responds with the same session identifier. This confirms both the client and server have communicated before and performed a key exchange. Because the key exchange is already done, it needn't be repeated.

Field	Definition
Cipher Suite	The client hello message contains a list of possible cipher suites. From that list, the server picks one and returns it. The selected suite is used for the asymmetric key exchange, the cipher, and the hash function type.
Compression Method	If the client specified in the client hello that it could do compression, the server picks one method and returns it. Note, returning a *null* method (meaning no compression) is valid as well.

Server Key Exchange

The *server key exchange* is the message used for the server to send its public key to the client. The format of this message is dictated by the cipher suite selected during the client hello and server hello messages. Server key exchange doesn't authenticate the server, meaning the client can only be certain the communication with the server is secure, but it cannot validate its identity.

Generating Random Numbers

Randomness is a tricky thing for computers to do. After all, computers are, by definition, deterministic in their behavior—if we always know the next thing the computer is going to do, how do we generate a random number?

The answer is we make a best effort by way of *pseudo-random* numbers, that is, numbers that simply appear random. In truth, the numbers are numerical series that eventually begin repeating themselves. To ensure the series never repeats itself, it takes a *seed*, a value that can define the behavior of the random-number generator. The trick is to get a good seed, a value that is truly random itself. If the seed is random, then the number generator also shows randomness.

Carefully picking the seed is a much easier task than trying to make a true random-number generator. Seeds can be derived from all sorts of analog events that show randomness. What's important, however, is that the seed isn't predictable. As a result, developers go through great pains to pick good seeds.

The designers of SSL, recognizing this problem, came up with a good idea: have the peer generate a seed for you. This way, the little random details in a system (such as the speed at which the disk spins, the duration the system has been running, the next available process ID, and so forth) can be spread around to others. This keeps the servers and the clients from picking predictable seeds.

Server Hello Done

The *server hello done* message is a simple information message that tells the client the server is done sending the certificate. Aside from the message type information, the message contains no additional information.

Client Key Exchange

After the server sends its public key to the client, the client uses it to encrypt a 128-bit random number destined to be used as the symmetric key. The client sends this key in the *client key exchange* message. No additional information is included in the message.

Change Cipher Spec

The *change cipher spec* message is a statement sent by both the client and the server. The message is an indicator to the recipient that all subsequent messages will be encrypted using the symmetric key. Aside from the message header (indicating it is a ChangeCipherSpec), the message has no additional data.

Finished

Once the Change Cipher Spec is sent, the sender (whether it be the server or the client) sends a *finished* message. The purpose of this message is to verify that the agreed on cipher and keys are correct. The message has three parts: the first is 12 bytes of *opaque data*, that is, data sent in clear text. The second part is the same data, except it's encrypted. The last part is the hash for the encrypted data. The receiver of the message can then decrypt the data and compare it to the opaque data sent. If the two data sets match, the client and server are in agreement over the cipher and keys.

Both the client and the server must send this message, so both sides can validate the handshake has, in fact, been executed correctly.

Certificate

The *certificate* message contains only one thing: the certificate of the server. If the certificate is in a chain, the entire chain of certificates is sent to the client. This message is sent after the server hello message by the server to enable the client to authenticate the identity of the server.

Hello Request

After the client and server have negotiated a session, the server may send a *hello request* message to ask the client to restart the key negotiation process. The client has the option to refuse doing the negotiation by returning an *alert* message. Note, the server might not send a hello request message if it's in the middle of a key negotiation.

A server might want to use a hello request message if it suspects the symmetric key has been compromised or a session has lasted too long using the same key.

Like the ChangeCipherSpec message, hello request doesn't have any data in addition to the message header.

Certificate Request

Sent by the server, the *certificate request* message is used to request the client-side certificate. This allows the server to validate the identity of the client. The message contains the certificate types the server is requesting, the distinguished name of the server (in cleartext), and a list of acceptable certificate authorities.

Certificate Verify

The *certificate verify* message is used by the client to respond to the certificate request message. Within the verification message, the client includes a hash of the client's keys, which the server can use to validate whether the client is who he says he is.

Alert

The *alert* message is an informational message sent by either the client or the server at any time to indicate a warning or fatal error. Within the message is a single byte indicating the type of alert (warning or fatal error) and the alert code that matches a predefined set of descriptions.

Application Data

The *application data* message simply indicates that the data within it is destined to the application itself and isn't to be interpreted by the SSL level. The application data is always encrypted using the agreed on cipher and symmetric key.

An SSL Transaction

Figure 5-4 visualizes the exchange of messages between an SSL client and an SSL server. Drilling deeper down into the transaction requires the use of the ssldump command. Similar to the tcpdump command, the ssldump command can understand the SSL messages that are sent back and forth, and it can display them on your screen. In this section, you examine an SSL transaction from a web browser to a secure web server.

Let's begin by running the ssldump command, like so:

```
[root@ford /root]# ssldump -An port 443 and host 10.2.2.1
```

The –A parameter tells ssldump to display all the packets, no matter how unimportant they may be, and the –n parameter tells ssldump not to do DNS resolution. Because ssldump uses the libpcap library like tcpdump, it can take similar expressions for selecting which packets to watch. In this case, we ask it only to monitor those packets on port 443 and where the source or destination IP address is 10.2.2.1. (For more details on the expressions you can use, visit the tcpdump Web site at http://www.tcpdump.org.)

For readability purposes, I made some minor changes to ssldump's output.

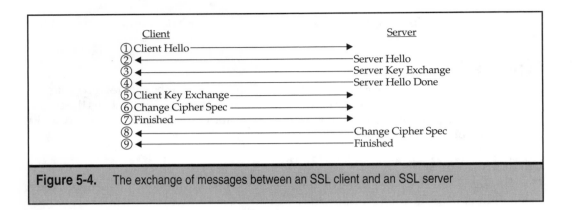

Figure 5-4. The exchange of messages between an SSL client and an SSL server

Connecting to the server, you see the first packet:

```
C>S SSLv2 compatible client hello
Version 3.0
cipher suites
SSL_RSA_EXPORT1024_WITH_RC4_56_SHA
SSL_RSA_EXPORT1024_WITH_DES_CBC_SHA
SSL_RSA_EXPORT_WITH_RC4_40_MD5
SSL_RSA_EXPORT_WITH_RC2_CBC_40_MD5
SSL2_CK_RC4_EXPORT40
SSL2_CK_RC2_EXPORT40
SSL_DHE_DSS_EXPORT1024_WITH_DES_CBC_SHA
```

The first line tells you this is a message from the client to the server (C>S) and that the message type is a client hello. The version field of the client hello states that the client can handle up to SSLv3. Finally, you see the list of cipher suites the client can support. Note, the client doesn't specify a Session-ID. This is because it doesn't have one and it wants to negotiate a new key. Also, note, the client doesn't specify a compression method. This is because it doesn't support any compression methods.

The second packet comes from the server:

```
S>CV3.0(74)  ServerHello
       Version 3.0
       random[32]=
          3b 89 7d 4d 36 6a c0 d9 ce e9 43 1c b1 b3 f9 f8
          b6 b4 77 9f 87 31 80 34 5d 01 cf b2 75 ff b7 05
       session_id[32]=
          5f e5 52 7a ad 22 17 dc f8 f9 d4 a1 f8 6b 00 90
          f2 ea 2b 44 f7 b5 15 8f ea 9a ae 4c 8b 38 c1 ff
       cipherSuite            SSL_RSA_EXPORT1024_WITH_RC4_56_SHA
       compressionMethod                     NULL
```

This packet is the server hello message that must always come after a client hello message. The server hello message begins by stating that it, too, can speak SSLv3, meaning subsequent messages will follow that protocol. If the server could only speak SSLv2, it would have answered with 2.0 instead. The next piece of information is the 32 bytes (256 bits) of randomness sent to the client. This number is returned to the server later in the session (during the finish message) in encrypted form, so the server can verify the client has the correct symmetric key. The next number is the Session-ID assigned to this session. Subsequent sessions with this server from the same client can use this Session-ID to skip the key exchange component of this handshake. The server hello ends with the server selecting the cipher suite it wants (SSL_RSA_EXPORT1024_WITH_RC4_56_SHA) and explicitly saying it won't use any compression (NULL).

The next step comes from the server. Because this is a web transaction that requires the server to identify itself, it must send a certificate message and not just a server key exchange message. The certificate message looks like this:

```
S>CV3.0(868) Certificate
      certificate[858]=
        30 82 03 56 30 82 02 bf a0 03 02 01 02 02 01 02
        <842 more bytes snipped for brevity>
```

As you can see, the only thing in the message is the certificate. Coming in at 858 bytes, the certificate message is among the larger of the messages that must be sent. The server finishes up the certificate exchange with a server hello message done like so:

```
S>CV3.0(4)   ServerHelloDone
```

With the certificate in hand, the client can verify the server is who it claims to be and pull out the server's public key (located in the certificate). Using the public key, the client sends a client key exchange message containing a random number encrypted using the server's public key to be used for the RC4 cipher agreed on in the server hello message. The client key exchange method looks like this:

```
C>SV3.0(132) ClientKeyExchange
      EncryptedPreMasterSecret[128]=
        1b 4c 73 28 6e 33 ce cd 37 b6 81 12 bc 4f 61 0b
        <112 bytes snipped for brevity>
```

As you can see, the only piece of information contained within the client key exchange message is the encrypted key.

The client now sends its last unencrypted message: change cipher spec. The message contains no information within it and looks like this:

```
C>SV3.0(1)   ChangeCipherSpec
```

To verify the encryption is working correctly, the client sends the last packet of the negotiation encrypted: the finished message. Because this message is encrypted, ssldump cannot look inside it to see what's there, so it prints "Handshake" instead. In other words, the encryption is doing what it's supposed to do: keeping packet sniffers from being able to see the contents of messages.

The last handshake message from the client looks like this:

```
C>SV3.0(60)   Handshake
```

Within these finished messages are encrypted values of the random number sent by the server during the server hello phase. Because both sides should have the correct symmetric key at this time, they should both be able to decrypt the information and validate that they do, in fact, have the correct key.

The sever now does exactly the same thing: it sends a change cipher spec message to the client to tell it that it's ready to start sending data encrypted using the agreed on key. The change cipher spec message looks like:

```
S>CV3.0(1)    ChangeCipherSpec
```

The server then tests this with its own finished message, which it sends encrypted with the agreed on key; thus, ssldump only sees a handshake message, like so:

```
S>CV3.0(60)   Handshake
```

From here on, the client and server send encrypted data destined to the application layer.

Ending SSL Communications

No required process exists for ending an SSL transaction other than simply closing the TCP connection. The client and server can explicitly send a message indicating it's done before closing the TCP connection via an alert message. This method is used to protect *truncation attacks,* in which an attacker forces a connection to close prematurely. One can visualize the significance of this by imagining what the ramifications would be if a sender couldn't send the second phrase: "Please sell my stock if, and only if, it's trading above $70." The sender of the message would be one grumpy fellow if the stock were trading at $5 and the second part of the message didn't make it through.

In HTTP, this is rarely a concern because HTTP explicitly states the size of the message being sent before sending it in the case of static content, and uses chunking in the case of dynamic content. Thus, in the example session documented in the previous section, you only see the server send an alert message like so:

```
C>S   TCP FIN
S>CV3.0(22)   Alert
S>C   TCP FIN
```

The Second SSL Session

As mentioned earlier, SSL doesn't need to go through a key exchange if the server and client already have the shared secret (the symmetric key) in their local caches. Let's step through a connection where this is the case.

The SSL session begins with the client hello message, like so:

```
C>SV3.0(85)  ClientHello
         Version 3.0
         random[32]=
             6f d1 e9 dc a7 06 db f9 ed c0 cc 70 b3 bd e0 df
             37 19 cd 22 00 57 da e5 3a 3a ee f7 7c 32 a7 96
         Session-ID [32]=
             5f e5 52 7a ad 22 17 dc f8 f9 d4 a1 f8 6b 00 90
             f2 ea 2b 44 f7 b5 15 8f ea 9a ae 4c 8b 38 c1 ff
         cipher suites
         SSL_RSA_EXPORT1024_WITH_RC4_56_SHA
         SSL_RSA_EXPORT1024_WITH_DES_CBC_SHA
         SSL_RSA_EXPORT_WITH_RC4_40_MD5
         SSL_RSA_EXPORT_WITH_RC2_CBC_40_MD5
         SSL_DHE_DSS_EXPORT1024_WITH_DES_CBC_SHA
         compression methods
                   NULL
```

Notice, this time you see some information that wasn't seen the first time the client spoke with the server. First, you see the client wants to share some randomness with the server. This randomness is similar to the server-side randomness sent during the first session—it's encrypted and sent back during the finish message, so the client can verify that the server does, in fact, have the correct symmetric key in its cache and isn't an imposter. The next tidbit you see is the Session-ID. This is the number the server sent back during the server hello during the first transaction to indicate it was caching the symmetric key. By sending this Session-ID back, the client is asking the server to recall this piece of information, so they don't have to do a certificate or client key exchange again.

Similar to the first client hello, the cipher suites available to the server to pick from are listed, as are the available compression methods.

The next packet is the server hello, as you see here:

```
S>CV3.0(74) ServerHello
         Version 3.0
         random[32]=
             3b 89 7d 4f a1 5d ec ee be b9 ec 05 e1 0d e2 45
             66 4a d4 61 c7 b9 5c f2 68 ec d0 fd 2e a0 5b f9
         session_id[32]=
             5f e5 52 7a ad 22 17 dc f8 f9 d4 a1 f8 6b 00 90
             f2 ea 2b 44 f7 b5 15 8f ea 9a ae 4c 8b 38 c1 ff
         cipherSuite              SSL_RSA_EXPORT1024_WITH_RC4_56_SHA
         compressionMethod                NULL
```

The server hello includes with it a random number to be used for verification of the client's cached symmetric key, the same Session-ID the client sent, thus telling the client it does have the symmetric key cached, the cipher suite it wants to use (as selected from the list provided by the client), and the compression method for that session (no compression).

So far, the client has told the server it has a cached symmetric key, and the server has responded with the statement of "yes, so do I." This means the server *doesn't* need to send a certificate again and the client *doesn't* need to send a random number encrypted with the server's public key. Because all these message can be skipped, the next message you see during the second SSL connection is the change cipher spec message from the server, also followed by a finished message from the server.

```
S>CV3.0(1)   ChangeCipherSpec
S>CV3.0(60)  Handshake
```

The change cipher spec message tells the client that, from now on, all the packets from the server will be encrypted. To validate that the encryption is working as expected, the random number in the client hello is hashed, encrypted using the symmetric key, and sent back to the client in the finished message (shown only as a handshake because ssldump cannot decrypt it).

The client, having validated that the server does have the correct symmetric cipher, does the same thing back:

```
C>SV3.0(1)   ChangeCipherSpec
C>SV3.0(60)  Handshake
```

Both the client and the server are now agreed on two things: they are done with the SSL handshake, and they both have the correct symmetric key. With this agreement in hand, application data can begin to flow between them, and it can be correctly encrypted/decrypted.

Once the session is done, they can close their sessions using the same method as described in the "Ending SSL Communications" section earlier in this chapter.

ACCELERATING SSL

As noted several times in this chapter, cryptographic calculations are slow. The reasons are somewhat obvious: the mathematics is complex and the raw size of the numbers to be computed are large. To solve this problem, specialized hardware capable of performing cryptographic functions (such as 1,024-bit RSA) much faster than traditional CPUs have become increasingly present.

This section examines how they work and where they fit into the scheme of your Web servers.

How SSL Acceleration Works

When engineers noticed that 32-bit (and even 64-bit) CPUs were woefully slow at processing the math required to perform cryptographic functions, they solved the problem by creating specialized processors that did nothing but cryptographic functions. Capable of both asymmetric and symmetric cryptographic functions, these chips could offload a significant amount of work placed on the main CPU. The result is a server that can keep up with the secure load demanded of it, while it can still effectively run the applications necessary to make it useful.

Turning these chips into usable features for Web servers required they be presented in a more friendly form factor. This has led to the development of PCI cards, which can be placed directly into Web servers and into proxies that take care of the encryption and decryption of packets before they even arrive at the server.

PCI Cryptographic Cards

PCI cryptographic cards, such as those that come from iVea (aka Rainbow Technologies, http://www.ivea.com), nCipher (http://www.ncipher.com), and Broadcom (http://www.broadcom.com) are designed to plug directly into web servers. They require the server software be able to communicate directly with them, so they can offload the cryptographic work to them.

From a systems administrator point of view, this implies needing to shut down your server, perform the install, and reconfigure the server. Although the engineers at these companies have made an effort to simplify the process as much as possible, it still requires work.

On the plus side, most of the common web servers have support for these cards. IIS under Windows is supported by all of the previously mentioned cards, as is Apache under Unix. If you're using a different web server, check with the manufacturer before committing to the purchase. Figure 5-5 shows what your network topology would look like with PCI-based SSL accelerators in place.

Watching an HTTPS request in progress enables us to see how the web server can use the card effectively. Immediately following the client key exchange, the Web server must decrypt the symmetric key using the private key. In a traditional server, the decryption is done in software. With a PCI card, however, the web server sends a message to the card with the symmetric key to be deciphered and the private key to decipher it with. The PCI card performs the computation and sends an interrupt back to the system indicating its completion. While the PCI card churns through the math, the web server is free to handle other outstanding tasks, including processing other connections. The result of this will be the web server being able to accept an SSL connection substantially faster than without the PCI card.

But wait, there's more! Along with being able to do the asymmetric cryptographic functions, these cards can also perform symmetric key cryptography. Thus, as the web server receives encrypted packets from the client, it's possible for the PCI card to be handed the encrypted packet for decryption. Most web servers handle the bulk encryption and decryption themselves, however, because it's often faster for them to do the work than it is to wait for the packet to be transferred to the PCI card and then brought back.

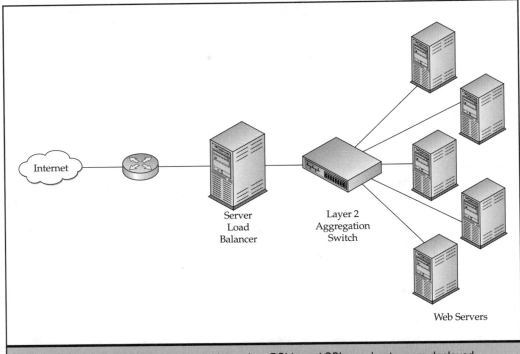

Figure 5-5.   A Web site's network topology when PCI-based SSL accelerators are deployed

Here are some PCI cards to look for:

▼ Compaq Computer, AXL300 Accelerator PCI Card
    http://www.compaq.com

■ iVea Technologies, CryptoSwift 600
    http://www.ivea.com

▲ nCipher, nForce 300 Secure e-Commerce Accelerator
    http://www.ncipher.com

Proxy-Based SSL Accelerators

Proxy-based SSL accelerators work as a point network device that resides in front of your Web server. Typically used in conjunction with server load balancers, the accelerators are configured so they only receive port 443 (SSL) traffic, while port 80 (non-SSL) traffic is passed directly to the Web servers.

The SSL accelerators accept connections from the client and use the special crypto-graphic accelerating hardware within them to speed up the process. With the session accepted, incoming HTTP requests are decrypted, and then passed on in cleartext to the Web server. The Web server seeing the request originate from the SSL accelerator, and not the actual client, sends its HTTP response back to the accelerator, which then performs encryption before passing the packet back to the client. Figure 5-6 shows the resulting network topology when using proxy-based SSL accelerators.

A significant benefit to proxy-based SSL accelerators is they are a much more plug-and-play solution for your network than are PCI-based solutions. Web servers need minimal, if any, reconfiguration, and the SSL accelerator can be dropped inline the packet path with minimal to no interruption in service.

Another significant win with the proxy architecture is that HTTP requests can be decrypted and funneled back into the load balancer, so layer 7 load balancing (such as URL- and cookie-based) can be done. This is in sharp contrast to only layer 4 load balancing that must be used for sites wanting the servers to perform SSL on the server itself. Some server load balancers have even taken to integrating SSL accelerators, thus offering tight integration. Figure 5-7 shows what a network topology would look like with such a device. SSL acceleration and offloading is discussed in more depth in Chapter 13.

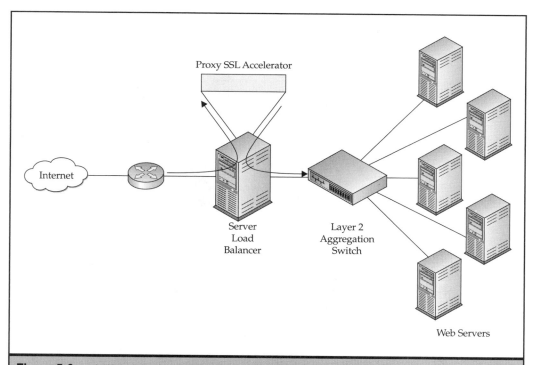

Figure 5-6.   A Web site's network topology when using a proxy-based SSL accelerator

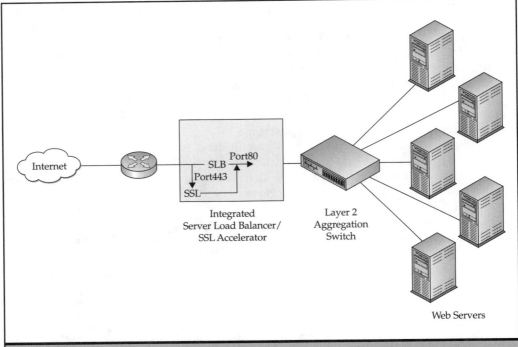

Figure 5-7. A Web site's network topology when using an integrated server load balancer and SSL accelerator

Here are some proxy-based SSL accelerators to look for:

▼ ClickArray Networks, Array 1000. Integrated N+1 clustering, Web security, server load balancing, global-server load balancing, reverse proxy cache, SSL acceleration, CDN content rewriter
http://www.clickarray.com

■ Nortel Networks (formally Alteon Web Systems), iSD-SSL 2.0. SSL acceleration
http://www.alteonwebsystems.com

■ CacheFlow, Server Accelerator 7000. Integrated 1+1 clustering, reverse proxy cache, SSL accelerator, Akamaizer
http://www.cacheflow.com

■ Intel, NetStructure 7115 e-Commerece Accelerator. SSL accelerator
http://www.intel.com

▲ SonicWall, SSL Accelerator, SSL accelerator
http://www.sonicwall.com

SUMMARY

In this chapter you learned the concepts behind cryptography, the Secure Sockets Layer (SSL) framework, and how SSL applies into real networks. Specifically, you learned:

▼ Symmetric key cryptography has limitations; however, it is very fast for bulk data encryption.

■ Public key cryptography is secure, but it requires a great deal of CPU power.

■ Hybrid solutions that use public key cryptography to exchange the key used in symmetric key cryptography appear the most effective way of providing high security.

■ Certificates are public keys plus identification information that have a hash encrypted with the Certificate Authority's (CA) private key. Clients can validate a server by decrypting the hash using the CA's public key, and then comparing the hash against a hash computed on the server's public key and identification information.

■ SSL itself is only a framework for other cryptographic functions.

■ Setting up an SSL session requires a complex handshake where public keys are exchanged and encrypted symmetric keys are exchanged.

■ Resuming an SSL session requires much less computational work because the server can use Session ID caching.

■ SSL acceleration works by offloading the intense mathematics onto a special chip dedicated to performing these equations quickly.

▲ SSL accelerators come in two form factors: PCI cards and proxy-based SSL accelerators.

As mentioned at the beginning of the chapter, reading this won't make you a cryptography expert. If you're interested in becoming one, check out the following:

▼ *SSL and TLS Essentials: Securing the Web,* by Stephen A. Thomas (John Wiley & Sons, 2000).

■ *The TLS Protocol Version 1.0 [RFC 2246],* by T. Dierks and C. Allen (The Internet Engineering Task Force, January 1999, http://www.ietf.org).

▲ *Applied Cryptography: Protocols, Algorithms, and Source Code in C, 2nd Edition,* by Bruce Schneier (John Wiley & Sons, 1995).

For the truly curious, you can examine the source code of a complete implementation of the SSL protocol at the OpenSSL project at http://www.openssl.org.

REVIEW QUESTIONS

1. **What are the differences between asymmetric key cryptography and symmetric key cryptography?**

   Asymmetric key cryptography does not require a shared secret between those communicating, whereas symmetric does. Asymmetric is also much more difficult to break than symmetric; however, this comes at the expense of being much more complex and thus slower. In SSL, asymmetric key cryptography is used for the sole purpose of sending a symmetric key in a secure manner.

2. **How does key size affect the quality of encryption? Give an example.**

   As key size grows, it becomes much more difficult to break a message. For example, in the case where numbers are used as keys, the addition of an additional bit (in the binary representation of the number) doubles the number of possible keys that exist.

3. **Explain the relationship among a Web site, a certificate of authority, a browser vendor, and a browser user. Why does this relationship work?**

   A Web site delivers the content. In SSL, it sends the site certificate to the client. The certificate of authority is the person who has signed the Web site's certificate using his or her private key. The certificate of authority then gives that public key to the browser vendor (such as Microsoft or Netscape) for inclusion in his own Web browser (such as Internet Explorer or Mozilla). When the browser user receives the certificate from the Web site, he can decrypt the certificate using the public key issued by the certificate of authority. If the resulting key certificate is valid, the decryption will work and the user will be able to use asymmetric key cryptography to send a shared secret for symmetric key cryptography. This relationship works because the user trusts the browser vendor and the browser vendor trusts the certificate of authority. The certificate of authority validates a Web site's authenticity and thus extends the trust to the Web site. A user is then able to validate whether the Web site is trusted by the certificate of authority, and if it is, the user can then trust the Web site.

4. **What is the purpose of the random number in the client hello and server hello messages? If SSL didn't use these random numbers, explain how a client could be tricked into communicating with an imposter.**

   The random number is used to validate that both sides have the correct symmetric cipher. When each side sends a random number, they know what the encrypted form should look like. Later in the SSL handshake, the number is sent back in encrypted form. Each side is able to then validate that the number was encrypted with the key they believe is shared. If SSL does not use these random numbers, it may fall prey to a man-in-the-middle attack, where someone is pretending to be a server. This happens when the client hello message has a session-id value indicating that it believes it has a cached copy of the shared symmetric key. If an imposter (posing as the server) were in place who does not really have the symmetric key but is looking to steal information, it would return the same session-id that the client sent to it. Because the client requires that the server then return the random number sent in encrypted form, the client can immediately validate whether the imposter has the shared secret or doesn't. Thus, an imposter wouldn't make it past the SSL handshake, let alone get to the point where the client may send valuable data!

5. **Explain the differences in the server key exchange message and the certificate message. Where would each be used and why?**

   The server key message is used for SSL communication where the client is looking for secure communication but does not need to validate the person it is talking to. A certificate message passes along a complete certificate proving identity as well, a feature that is necessary in e-commerce so that the client can validate whether the server is who it claims to be.

CHAPTER 6

DNS and Content Networking

OBJECTIVES

▼ Discuss the history and function of DNS

■ Become familiar with the operation of DNS

■ Identify specific Content Networking uses for DNS

■ Understand Name management and how DNS uses it

▲ Identify problems with DNS network design

In terms of the importance of current technologies, the Domain Name System (DNS) is one of the most important and useful subjects to know with respect to Content Networking. DNS can either be your friend, to be used to allow flexible and scaleable content deployment growth, or your enemy, causing nearly untraceable performance slowdowns and outages. As such, knowing at least the basics of DNS and being able to trace the critical components to evaluate any performance problems is important.

DNS, in its most common use, is used to resolve a name to some IP address. Given a name, say, www.brandsberg.net, DNS is used to resolve that to, say, 216.169.108.50. In more general terms, DNS is a distributed database that stores records of various types. The type of record that would allow the correlation from www.brandsberg.net to 216.169.108.50 would be an *A* or *address* record. Other types of records used are nameserver (NS) records, mail exchange (MX) records, and canonical name (CNAME) records. An SOA record indicates, among other things, this server is authoritative for a domain (more on this later). Also, other types of *resource* records exist (in general, known as RRs) although, in general practice, these other record types are only used in situations that don't generally impact a web site or Content Networking.

HISTORY

To understand why DNS works the way it currently does, you need to understand the history of how and why it was deployed. The original ARPAnet was conceived as a distributed network that made use of numeric addresses to label nodes. Initially, few enough nodes were in the network that a simple text-based host configuration file was useable to match each number with some memorable name. While this worked well with a smaller network, as nodes were added, maintaining it became an administrative nightmare. In addition, at the time, no standard way existed to handle mailboxes or other network configuration information, so a standard system was needed for querying various pieces of information. On top of this, each piece of information needed to be managed by different individuals. The goal wasn't to manage a single central store of information but, instead, to distribute the storage and management of the data into various domains. Thus, DNS was born.

The initial formal description of how DNS works was prepared as RFC 882 and, while out of date technically, is an interesting reference to read to understand how and why

DNS works as it does, and to understand the legacy aspects of supporting DNS. The current standard for the operation of DNS is STD 13, "Domain Names - Concepts And Facilities," prepared in 1987. While this standard has been updated by many Request for Comments (RFC), Best Current Practices (BCP), and other documents, STD 13 is still considered the "standard" for DNS operation and lays the groundwork for DNS as we know it. Table 6-1 lists all the current RFCs that update STD 13 and their titles. In most cases, these updates provide for additional resources records, clarifications needed for interoperability, or minor

RFC Number	RFC Title	Description
RFC1101	DNS encoding of network names and other types	Describes address to name encoding for reverse DNS queries
RFC1183	New DNS RR Definitions	Experimental resource record (RR) definitions
RFC1348	DNS NSAP RRs	Experimental resource record definitions
RFC1876	A Means for Expressing Location Information in the Domain Name System	Experimental RR definitions
RFC1982	Serial Number Arithmetic	Defining how to compare DNS SOA serial numbers for versioning
RFC1995	Incremental Zone Transfer in DNS	Describes IXFRs implemented in modern DNS servers
RFC1996	A Mechanism for Prompt Notification of Zone Changes (DNS NOTIFY)	Describes the Notify command, in general use
RFC2136	Dynamic Updates in the Domain Name System (DNS UPDATE)	Describes dynamic updating of DNS information from external sources, such as a server assigned its IP address via DHCP
RFC2181	Clarifications to the DNS Specification	Updates STD 13 and others with important clarifications for compatibility and security considerations

Table 6-1.   Revisions, Updates, and Extensions to STD 13

RFC Number	RFC Title	Description
RFC2308	Negative Caching of DNS Queries (DNS NCACHE)	Modifies STD 13 to require negative caching, clarifies how such caching is to be performed, and under what situations
RFC2535	Domain Name System Security Extensions	Security for DNS, supported in most DNS implementations, but not generally used at this time
RFC2845	Secret Key Transaction Authentication for DNS (TSIG)	Update on secure DNS, although not currently in wide use
RFC3007	Secure Domain Name System (DNS) Dynamic Update	Updates to Dynamic updates to provide enhanced security
RFC3008	Domain Name System Security (DNSSEC) Signing Authority	

Table 6-1.   Revisions, Updates, and Extensions to STD 13 *(continued)*

modifications needed for security purposes. Also included in the table is a brief note describing what is contained in the RFC and any important details. RFCs that impact the functions of DNS that are in widespread use or implementation are boldfaced.

HOW DNS WORKS

For the purposes of this discussion, only the basics of DNS are covered to the extent they are needed for general content networking tasks. For an administrator who needs to manage a large number of domains, more extensive training and DNS-oriented texts should be considered. This tutorial on DNS is by no means exhaustive, but does cover some subtle points whose importance can't be underestimated for Content Networking.

General Operational Overview

Consider a person typing **http://www.brandsberg.net** in a web browser. (Note, terms in italics are defined in the section following the overview.) The first thing that occurs is the web browser realizes it needs to know the IP address of the host attempting to be accessed to know who to send the request to, so it generates a request to the system's *resolver library.* The resolver library then takes the request, generates a DNS request, and forwards it to its configured *resolving nameserver.* This nameserver is responsible for then performing all further DNS requests to honor the client's request. In the case of brandsberg.net, assuming it has never resolved the address before, it uses its configuration files to determine what *root nameserver* to forward the request to first. This nameserver won't know the address of www.brandsberg.net, but it does know a list of servers that are authoritative for the domain net. These servers are known as the *Top Level Domain* (TLD) *nameservers.* The list of TLDs is returned to the resolving nameserver, which then uses the list for the next query. The request is then sent to one of the TLD nameservers, which again won't know the IP address of www.brandsberg.net, but does know of a server that knows the answer. This final server is appropriately known as an *authoritative nameserver.* The resolving nameserver receives this information back from the TLD nameserver and generates a third request to the authoritative nameserver for the "final" answer. The authoritative nameserver responds with this final answer, which is then forwarded to the resolver library on the client's computer, which, in turn, forwards the requested information to the original web browser. Once the web browser has the IP address for www.brandsberg.net, it is then able to establish a TCP connection with that address and retrieve the appropriate content.

Detailed Operational Overview

First in line from the application is the resolver library. On every client that uses DNS is a piece of code that could tentatively be called part of the operating system (OS), called the resolver library, which links applications to the global Internet nameserver network. An application calls on the library to resolve a name for the application and the library then makes use of whatever resources are available to it to perform that task. In some OSes, the resolver library makes use of resources outside DNS, such as host files or, optionally, NIS. Usually, however, DNS is the sole resource the resolver uses. In environments that make use of other resources, these other mechanisms are generally configured in a file called /etc/nsswitch.conf. In UNIX, the resolver library uses a configuration file of /etc/resolv.conf to determine how to perform DNS lookups. Here's a simple resolv.conf file:

```
search brandsberg.net
nameserver  216.169.97.10
nameserver 216.169.96.10
```

What this says is first, if necessary, append the name brandsberg.net behind any name that needs resolution if the name given didn't resolve exactly as is. Second, make use of the DNS server at 216.169.97.10 for any resolution requests and, if that server fails to respond, use 216.169.96.10. Usually, any given network or ISP has one or more nameservers that act as a resolving nameserver for any number of clients. Any number of nameserver lines in the resolution file can be used to provide redundancy for resolution requests. If the first one fails, however, it tends to slow down all the requests as they're tried in order on every request.

Next in line is the resolving nameserver. In any given resolution request, the resolving nameserver manages the request and has the most real work to do, while the resolver library simply waits for an answer (until it times out) before trying to do anything else. In an ideal situation, the resolving nameserver is connected as closely as possible to the client requesting the information to minimize the response time, as well as to allow DNS-based geographic load balancing to operate (to be described in Chapter 11). In reality, the resolving nameserver could be (and many times is) across the country from the client.

The resolving nameserver performs what's known as a *recursive* request, meaning it requests information from other servers (the root servers in general) and if that targeted server doesn't have the exact answer, it uses what information can be gained to continue the process until the request from the client can be resolved. In a typical scenario, this accounts for about two requests: one to a TLD nameserver and one to an authoritative nameserver. In complex configurations, though, the resolving nameserver could be forced to perform four or more resolution requests, although this tends to be rare and configurations that require this are discouraged.

Typically, next in line from the resolving nameserver are *root* nameservers. These servers act as the root of the DNS database tree and are all considered equal in their capability to perform a task. The list of root nameservers is hard-coded in the configuration of each resolving nameserver performing recursive requests and tends to get updated only rarely on individual servers. While this could cause a problem over time, it doesn't, because this list is used strictly to download a new list of root nameservers, so only one needs to be accurate for the system to function. Furthermore, the code used in resolving nameservers tends to avoid bad root nameservers if they have a bad list and uses only good nameservers once up and running.

A *root nameserver* acts as the server in charge of delegating requests to the TLD nameservers. As an example, if you type in the command **nslookup -type=ns**. on a UNIX machine (or any computer with nslookup installed), you'll probably get back an answer that looks like this:

```
Non-authoritative answer:
(root)   nameserver = C.ROOT-SERVERS.NET
(root)   nameserver = H.ROOT-SERVERS.NET
(root)   nameserver = A.ROOT-SERVERS.NET
(root)   nameserver = D.ROOT-SERVERS.NET
(root)   nameserver = E.ROOT-SERVERS.NET
(root)   nameserver = I.ROOT-SERVERS.NET
(root)   nameserver = M.ROOT-SERVERS.NET
(root)   nameserver = L.ROOT-SERVERS.NET
(root)   nameserver = K.ROOT-SERVERS.NET
(root)   nameserver = J.ROOT-SERVERS.NET
(root)   nameserver = B.ROOT-SERVERS.NET
(root)   nameserver = F.ROOT-SERVERS.NET
(root)   nameserver = G.ROOT-SERVERS.NET
```

```
Authoritative answers can be found from:
C.ROOT-SERVERS.NET        internet address = 192.33.4.12
H.ROOT-SERVERS.NET        internet address = 128.63.2.53
A.ROOT-SERVERS.NET        internet address = 198.41.0.4
D.ROOT-SERVERS.NET        internet address = 128.8.10.90
E.ROOT-SERVERS.NET        internet address = 192.203.230.10
I.ROOT-SERVERS.NET        internet address = 192.36.148.17
M.ROOT-SERVERS.NET        internet address = 202.12.27.33
L.ROOT-SERVERS.NET        internet address = 198.32.64.12
K.ROOT-SERVERS.NET        internet address = 193.0.14.129
J.ROOT-SERVERS.NET        internet address = 198.41.0.10
B.ROOT-SERVERS.NET        internet address = 128.9.0.107
F.ROOT-SERVERS.NET        internet address = 192.5.5.241
G.ROOT-SERVERS.NET        internet address = 192.112.36.4
```

Each of these servers can answer requests for any domain; however, the resulting answer will simply be an answer that directs you to a different server, based on how it's configured. As an example, directing a request to the previous E.ROOT-SERVERS.NET address for www.brandsberg.net results in the following:

```
$ nslookup www.brandsberg.net. e.root-servers.net
Server:   E.ROOT-SERVERS.NET
Address:  192.203.230.10

Name:     www.brandsberg.net
Served by:
- A.GTLD-SERVERS.NET
        192.5.6.30
        com
- G.GTLD-SERVERS.NET
        198.41.3.101
        com
- C.GTLD-SERVERS.NET
        192.26.92.30
        com
- I.GTLD-SERVERS.NET
        192.36.144.133
        com
- B.GTLD-SERVERS.NET
        203.181.106.5
        com
- D.GTLD-SERVERS.NET
        192.31.80.30
        com
```

```
- L.GTLD-SERVERS.NET
          192.41.162.30
          com
- F.GTLD-SERVERS.NET
          192.35.51.30
          com
- J.GTLD-SERVERS.NET
          210.132.100.101
          com
- K.GTLD-SERVERS.NET
          213.177.194.5
          com
```

This is a list of pointers to the TLD servers that are authoritative for the domain net. Any further information needs to be obtained from them for any net domain. Normally, the resolving nameserver already has this information, so this set of steps only happens occasionally when the data times out.

Next, the resolving nameserver queries one of the TLD nameservers provided by the root nameservers. For the purposes of this example, let's assume A.GTLD-SERVERS.NET is used. A query to that server returns the following:

```
> nslookup www.brandsberg.net a.gtld-servers.net
Server:   A.GTLD-SERVERS.net
Address:  192.5.6.30

Name:     www.brandsberg.net
Served by:
- UDNS1.ULTRADNS.NET
          204.69.234.1
          BRANDSBERG.NET
- UDNS2.ULTRADNS.NET
          204.74.101.1
          BRANDSBERG.NET
```

This means the two servers are authoritative for the domain brandsberg.net and, as such, the resolving nameserver now needs to ask them for information about any names within the domain, such as www. Such a query results in the following:

```
> nslookup www.brandsberg.net. Udns1.ultradns.net
Server:   udns1.ultradns.net
Address:  204.69.234.1

Name:     www.brandsberg.net
Address:  216.169.108.50
```

The address listed (216.169.108.50) is returned by the resolving nameserver to the client computer and the resolver library returns the address to the application, which then initiates a system call to make a TCP connection to that address. To determine the impact of a DNS setup on performance, consider how fast a packet can traverse the Internet. As a general rule of thumb, consider that Internet traffic can make it from the East Coast to the West Coast and back in about 90–110 ms, from the East Coast to the United Kingdom in about 80–90ms, and from the East Coast to Japan in about 185–220 ms. As a comparison, it isn't unusual for a 56K modem to introduce about 110–150ms round-trip times, and satellite Internet access to introduce about 700–1500ms round-trip times. As a good rule of thumb, if most of the users are coming in from the United States, you can use about 40–50ms round-trip times to the DNS server as a good start. Now, with this, let's analyze the time it should take to resolve www.brandsberg.net, assuming nameservers were at only one location to resolve the name:

1. The request has to travel from the client to the resolving nameserver. Assuming they're on a modem dial-up, add 55ms for the modem and 25ms to get to the resolving nameserver (half the round-trip time of each).

2. The root nameservers are configured on the resolving nameserver so, effectively, the lookup of the root nameservers is free.

3. The TLD nameservers are used frequently enough that, in general, the information is cached in each resolving nameserver so, again, this request is effectively free on any given request.

4. The nameservers to resolve individual domains in general aren't cached except for some popular domains, so the round-trip time between any given resolving nameserver and the domain's authoritative nameserver must be considered. Let's add 50ms for this request (full round trip).

5. The answer has to be sent back to the client, for another 55ms+25ms.

The total of this is about 210ms or 1/5th of a second, which isn't bad, although means exist by which this number can be reduced with proper planning and network organization. To demonstrate the impact of DNS further, consider how long it takes for the typical initial HTML page load to occur, assuming 14K of data with fully acknowledged TCP packets. The initial TCP handshake would take about 240ms, and then 10 data packets at 160ms each, and a FIN/RST (not counted). For this transaction, the total would be about 1840ms. The DNS lookup would add a little over 10 percent to this, which is dead time before anything showed up on the page. This might not seem like a significant amount, but it's also the best case. Consider what happens if a single packet gets dropped in this transaction: disaster, from a performance point of view. If the packet from the authoritative DNS server is dropped going to the resolving DNS server, a time-out generally occurs, and any additional nameservers are queried, extending the resolution time significantly at best or resulting in an error on the user's browser at worst.

Later in this chapter, optimization techniques are presented that demonstrate some of the aspects of the common DNS resolvers that aren't documented in RFCs, but can be exploited to design a good content network more efficiently.

BASIC DNS CONFIGURATION

Before getting into some of the advanced tricks you can play with DNS, an overview of how to configure a DNS server to handle a basic domain is probably a good idea. In this first example, consider that the domain somedomain.com needs to be set up. Within the domain, they'll have the following: a mail server (mail.somedomain.com) that should receive all the mail destined for anything in somedomain.com, two servers that act as nameservers (running BIND 8.2.3, a DNS server software package), a web server, and three machines, named pc1, pc2, and pc3.

The first configuration file is the named.conf, which provides the basic configuration for *named* (pronounced: *name-d*, where the *d* stands for *daemon*, which is UNIX for "server software") or the Berkley Internet Name Daemon (BIND), which is the software used for all configuration examples. Here's a basic named.conf for the domain somedomain.com:

```
options {
        directory "/var/named";
        listen-on { 192.168.0.10; 127.0.0.1; };
        query-source address 192.168.0.10 port 53;
        pid-file "/var/run/named.pid";
};

zone "." {
        type hint;
        file "named.ca";
};

zone "somedomain.com" {
        type master;
        file "somedomain.com";
};
```

The options section allows settings that operate daemon-wide to be set, such as the default directory it will use to search for additional configuration files (the directory directive), what IP addresses to listen on (the listen-on directive), and what IP address to use as its primary source IP (the query-source directive). Many other options are available, most of which aren't discussed, although several are detailed later in this chapter as appropriate to document how the code works.

For each domain (and additional subdomains) for which a nameserver is authoritative, a zone statement is configured, as shown previously. The zone "." is special, and is listed as a type *hint,* meaning it's used only to anchor the nameserver into the root nameserver mesh. The type *master* specifies the nameserver is truly authoritative for that domain and the configuration file specified contains all the records for that particular domain.

The second configuration file for this example would be named.ca, which can be retrieved from ftp://rs.intnernic.net/domain/named.ca. This file contains a list of the current root nameservers. If a bad or outdated entry is within this list, then it's effectively ignored because all it takes is one good root nameserver to ensure proper operation of a nameserver. The list will be searched and, once one good root nameserver is found, BIND uses that nameserver to retrieve a list of current root nameservers to update its internal information, as shown in the following tcpdump trace of a DNS server startup:

```
# tcpdump -n -vv port 53 &
# named
20:18:12.188444 216.169.108.50.53 > 202.12.27.33.53: 50843 NS? .
(17) (DF) (ttl 64, id 0)
20:18:12.388444 202.12.27.33.53 > 216.169.108.50.53: 50843*- q: .
13/0/13 . (436) (ttl 52, id 38624)
```

This output shows how the local server is querying one of the root nameservers for the NS records that should be used for the "." or root domain, thus overriding what's in the named.ca file.

Finally, the third configuration file, somedomain.com, is used to define the information for the actual somedomain.com domain. This file includes all the information needed to resolve any request to that domain, including those for addresses (the most common) or for mail exchangers (MX records). Here's a simple example of such a file for this domain:

```
@       SOA     ns1    hostmaster (
                       2001020600 ; serial
                       3600 ; refresh (1H)
                       900 ; retry (15M)
                       1209600 ; expire (2W)
                       43200 ; default_ttl (12H)
                       )
@       MX             5       mail
@       NS             ns1
@       NS             ns2
@       A              192.168.0.10
www     CNAME          @
ns1     A              192.168.0.11
ns2     A              192.168.0.12
mail    A              192.168.0.13
pc1     A              192.168.0.21
pc2     A              192.168.0.22
pc3     A              192.168.0.23
```

This configuration file is made purposely generic to allow adoption to any domain. The @ symbol represents the domain name itself (based on the named.conf file). Translated to fully qualified domain names, the file would look like this:

```
somedomain.com.    SOA   ns1.somedomain.com. hostmaster.somedomain.com. (
                         2001020600 ; serial
                         3600 ; refresh (1H)
                         900 ; retry (15M)
                         1209600 ; expire (2W)
                         43200 ; default_ttl (12H)
                         )
somedomain.com.       MX       5     mail.somedomain.com.
somedomain.com.       NS            ns1.somedomain.com.
somedomain.com.       NS            ns2.somedomain.com.
Somedomain.com.       A             192.168.0.10
www.somedomain.com.   CNAME         somedomain.com.
ns1.somedomain.com.   A             192.168.0.11
ns2.somedomain.com.   A             192.168.0.12
mail.somedomain.com.  A             192.168.0.13
pc1.somedomain.com.   A             192.168.0.21
pc2.somedomain.com.   A             192.168.0.22
pc3.somedomain.com.   A             192.168.0.23
```

Obviously, the first file is simpler and easier to adapt between different domains because there's less to edit. Many times when you're working with several domains, a general template can be used that's the same for all the domains, and then you simply copy the file and modify what's being used. In Content Networking, if you're virtually hosting several domains, many times you can even get away with using the exact same file for all the domains, if the template is designed to be generic enough. The first configuration example was pulled from such a file that has been used for several domains for about two years.

The format of a BIND zone configuration file line is

```
<domain> <opt_ttl> <opt_class> <type> <resource_record_data>
```

The *domain* is just that, the domain being referenced. It can be either fully qualified (with a "." at the end) or relative to the current domain (no period at the end). The *opt_ttl* is an optional value that, in general, isn't used (but its applications are described later). An optional directive $TTL can be used at the top of a zone file that allows the default to be set; otherwise, the SOA minimum (described in Table 6-2) is used. The *opt_class* value, if used, 99.95 percent of the time is the value IN, which is now the default. In older versions of BIND, this field wasn't optional and, as such, will be included in most documentation examples found elsewhere. For historical and legacy reasons, this field is still available, but it can be safely ignored. The *type* represents the type of record information following and, as such, the format of that information. Table 6-2 shows the generally used types and their format.

A	A host address (dotted-quad IP address, e.g., 192.168.0.1).
NS	An authoritative name server. Use a name as specified in an A record, not in a CNAME record.
MX	A mail exchanger (domain), formatted as "priority [0-32767] domain". Use a name as specified in an A record, not in a CNAME record.
CNAME	The canonical name for an alias (domain), used often when a name changes, or used to provide a unique name on a service by service basis (that is, WWW vs. FTP).
SOA	Marks the start of a zone of authority (domain of originating host, domain address of maintainer, a serial number, and the following parameters in seconds: refresh, retry, expire, and minimum TTL.
PTR	A domain name pointer for reverse DNS configuration.

Table 6-2.   DNS Record Types

The most common and fundamental record is the *A record*, which provides a strict mapping of a domain name to an address. When a web browser (or most any program) requests a record from DNS, it's most likely requesting an A record. *NS records* are used in the DNS resolution process and are rarely used by end-user programs themselves. They provide the maps that point from one nameserver to another, allowing delegation of maintenance responsibilities between different servers and, thus, the server maintainers. Please note: NS records should make use of names provided in A records, not CNAME records. Failure to do this results in configuration files not loading properly and strange errors in some instances, depending on the nameserver code version used.

MX records operate differently than most others and include two fields following the MX record type. The first field is a priority, indicating which MX record should be used in preference for others. When mail is being sent to the domain that has an MX record, the sending mail server will attempt to transmit the mail to the server listed in the lowest-numbered MX record. If it times out or cannot otherwise connect to that mail server, it will go to the next lowest address, and so forth. Usually, the way receiving mail servers are configured is that a single mailserver will maintain mailboxes for users, and the others act as backup relay for a given domain. An example of this is detailed later in this chapter. Important to note is the domain referenced should resolve to A records, not to CNAME records, just like NS records.

CNAME records act as aliases for another name and are generally used for the sake of convenience. They allow one name to be translated to another, either within the same domain or to a totally different domain. This is usually done completely transparently to the querying application. If several names are being so mapped to the same IP address, for management purposes, it's usually best to make use of CNAME entries for all but one record and simply point to that one entry for all other names. This allows one record to be changed for DNS updates, easing management during IP address transitions.

PTR records are used when setting up reverse DNS or the mapping of IP addresses to domain names (remember, DNS maps names to IP addresses). In general, these will be configured in the DNS servers of the IP provider, not in local DNS servers, so they won't be discussed further in any detail here. You should remember them, though, because situations exist (particularly with secure communications) that require proper configuration of these records.

Start of Authority (SOA) records provide information about the zone and settings used for updates and control. As a general rule, these records are extended across several lines for readability, although they follow the same format as other records. The first field past the *type* field is the originating host of the SOA record. This value should be the name of the most authoritative server or the one considered the final authority on a given domain. The next field is the maintainer of the domain, usually hostmaster, which should be aliased to a real mailbox within the mail system. Note, if any "." symbols are in this address, the first one should be construed to mean @ for the purposes of e-mail. This is a result of the special meaning of the @ symbol in DNS configuration files. This requirement rules out some legal e-mail names for this field, such as firstname.lastname@somedomain.com. After the e-mail contact is a set of numeric parameters, surrounded by a set of ()s.

The first of the numerical parameters is the serial number. This *serial number* is generally presented in the format YYYYMMDDXX, where YYYY is the current year, MM, is the current month, DD, is the day, and XX is the daily revision if more than one revision is created in a day. Strictly speaking, the only requirement for the serial number is that if you update the zone, you increase the serial number. Following the format given here guarantees this, though, and it's also considered the best practice for manageability. The second parameter is the *refresh interval* parameter, which is used when secondary nameservers are configured. This value is the amount of time in seconds (unless a qualifier of (d)ay, (h)our, or (m)inute is specified) between zone transfer attempts from secondary servers. Depending on how DNS is managed, this parameter may or may not matter. The third parameter, the *retry* parameter, is the amount of time a secondary nameserver waits before retrying to perform a zone transfer after it fails on its first attempt. The refresh parameter should be at least twice as long as the retry parameter, or BIND will generate warning messages on loading the zone. The fourth parameter is the *expiration* parameter, which again impacts secondary nameservers. This specifies the amount of time the secondary will continue to use nonupdated information before it considers the information to be completely out-of-date.

Last is the *minimum* parameter, or the minimum TTL for any resource records within the zone. The minimum parameter is used as the TTL if no other default TTL is specified (using a parameter of *$TTL* before the SOA record) and is used as a sanity check on any TTLs entered individually within the zone. If any TTL is lower than the minimum, it's changed to equal the minimum. Current BIND code allows for a TTL of 0; however, older code might not. In addition, many services might override such low values because they increase network traffic. In these cases, a service-dependent minimum might be imposed that overrides what is configured in DNS.

   With these examples, it should be simple enough to set up a basic domain and to track down errors. One of the most common errors is not placing a '.' on the end of a domain where it's needed. If a domain doesn't have a '.' on the end of it, such as in a CNAME, NS, or MX record, then the zone domain is implicitly and silently added. Because of such errors, it's extremely important to understand how to use two tools that come with BIND to ensure a configuration is correct: NSLOOKUP and DIG.

BASIC DNS AUDITING

Domain Information Groper (DIG) is a simple tool that can be used to retrieve records from a nameserver. As an example, the following could be executed:

```
# dig brandsberg.net any

; <<>> DiG 8.3 <<>> brandsberg.net any
;; res options: init recurs defnam dnsrch
;; got answer:
;; ->>HEADER<<- opcode: QUERY, status: NOERROR, id: 4
;; flags: qr aa rd ra; QUERY: 1, ANSWER: 5, AUTHORITY: 2, ADDITIONAL: 3
;; QUERY SECTION:
;;        brandsberg.net, type = ANY, class = IN

;; ANSWER SECTION:
brandsberg.net.            12H IN A        216.169.108.50
brandsberg.net.            12H IN NS       udns1.ultradns.net.
brandsberg.net.            12H IN NS       udns2.ultradns.net.
brandsberg.net.            12H IN MX       5 mail.brandsberg.net.
brandsberg.net.            12H IN SOA      udns1.ultradns.net.
hostmaster.brandsberg.net. (
                        2001040102      ; serial
                        1H              ; refresh
                        15M             ; retry
                        2W              ; expiry
                        12H )           ; minimum

;; AUTHORITY SECTION:
brandsberg.net.            12H IN NS       udns1.ultradns.net.
brandsberg.net.            12H IN NS       udns2.ultradns.net.

;; ADDITIONAL SECTION:
udns1.ultradns.net.    1d14h17m34s IN A  204.69.234.1
udns2.ultradns.net.    1d12h19m35s IN A  204.74.101.1
mail.brandsberg.net.   12H IN A        216.169.108.50

;; Total query time: 14 msec
```

```
;; FROM: ebrandsberg.skyport.net to SERVER: default -- 127.0.0.1
;; WHEN: Tue Apr  3 02:06:12 2001
;; MSG SIZE  sent: 32  rcvd: 241
```

The first line displays the options that were sent, most importantly, the option *recurs*, which tells the remote nameserver to do "whatever it needs to" to get a complete answer. After that, the response is displayed, parsed out into readable form. While listing the full details of every parameter is beyond the scope of this book, important to note is that all uncommented lines (without a ; symbol in front) are syntactically legal to place into a zone file and display everything including defaults. This is important to see, as hidden defaults can end up causing problems if they're hidden all the time. In addition, the option *only* prints out records that match to exactly the same domain as the name given, nothing more. As such, if you request a domain that has subdomains underneath it, you'll see no information about those subdomains, only the strict domain provided.

The command line syntax for DIG is

```
dig [@server] [domain] [q-type] [q-class] {q-opt} {d-opt} [%comment]
```

Options past the q-type generally aren't used. The first optional argument enables the user to specify the IP address of a particular nameserver to send the query to. This is an important option and should be used to verify that *all* authoritative nameservers are reporting the same information when given a particular query. Nothing causes strange problems more than when authoritative nameservers are delivering different results for the same query.

The second argument to DIG is the domain being queried; the third argument is the type being queried against. This matches the record-types described previously, but also includes the option of querying for 'any', for any type of record. This is the most useful option when debugging because it might show something that wasn't expected, allowing quicker problem resolution. The default type to query for is *A*, so you can miss information unless you explicitly request the *any* type.

The second tool, NSLOOKUP, is more commonly used, although it's not quite as friendly to decipher and use for problem resolution as DIG. NSLOOKUP can be run in two modes: one interactive and one on the command line. The command line mode has one major flaw that causes a significant amount of headaches, however, in that it attempts to perform a reverse DNS lookup on the resolving DNS server it's using and fails if it receives no response. This causes many people to believe the query they wanted failed, when in fact it had nothing to do with what they were trying to diagnose. Here's an example of this, where the DNS configured in the /etc/resolv.conf doesn't properly reply to a reverse for its own IP address:

```
# nslookup www.cnn.com
*** Can't find server name for address 192.168.0.254: No response from
server
*** Default servers are not available
```

Compare this with a nameserver that has a proper reverse resolution configured:

```
# nslookup www.cnn.com
Server:  solar.skyport.net
Address:  216.169.97.10

Non-authoritative answer:
Name:    cnn.com
Addresses:  207.25.71.30, 207.25.71.29, 207.25.71.28, 207.25.71.27
         207.25.71.26, 207.25.71.25, 207.25.71.24, 207.25.71.23,
207.25.71.22
         207.25.71.20, 207.25.71.6, 207.25.71.5
Aliases:  www.cnn.com
```

Obviously, this can cause some confusion. The key point is, in the first example, the error was for address 192.168.0.254 vs. for address www.cnn.com. The dig command with the bad nameserver address would have returned with:

```
# dig www.cnn.com

; <<>> DiG 8.2 <<>> www.cnn.com
;; res options: init recurs defnam dnsrch
;; got answer:
;; ->>HEADER<<- opcode: QUERY, status: NOERROR, id: 4
;; flags: qr rd ra; QUERY: 1, ANSWER: 13, AUTHORITY: 4, ADDITIONAL: 4
;; QUERY SECTION:
;;       www.cnn.com, type = A, class = IN

;; ANSWER SECTION:
www.cnn.com.             2h53m1s IN CNAME  cnn.com.
cnn.com.                 15M IN A      207.25.71.5
cnn.com.                 15M IN A      207.25.71.6
cnn.com.                 15M IN A      207.25.71.20
cnn.com.                 15M IN A      207.25.71.22
cnn.com.                 15M IN A      207.25.71.23
cnn.com.                 15M IN A      207.25.71.24
cnn.com.                 15M IN A      207.25.71.25
cnn.com.                 15M IN A      207.25.71.26
cnn.com.                 15M IN A      207.25.71.27
cnn.com.                 15M IN A      207.25.71.28
cnn.com.                 15M IN A      207.25.71.29
cnn.com.                 15M IN A      207.25.71.30

;; AUTHORITY SECTION:
```

```
cnn.com.                    1d23h59m38s IN NS   NS-01A.ANS.NET.
cnn.com.                    1d23h59m38s IN NS   NS-01B.ANS.NET.
cnn.com.                    1d23h59m38s IN NS   NS-02A.ANS.NET.
cnn.com.                    1d23h59m38s IN NS   NS-02B.ANS.NET.

;; ADDITIONAL SECTION:
NS-01A.ANS.NET.             1d23h59m39s IN A   199.221.47.7
NS-01B.ANS.NET.             1d23h59m39s IN A   199.221.47.8
NS-02A.ANS.NET.             1d23h59m39s IN A   207.24.245.179
NS-02B.ANS.NET.             1d23h59m39s IN A   207.24.245.178

;; Total query time: 3187 msec
;; FROM: host.domain.com to SERVER: default -- 127.0.0.1
;; WHEN: Wed Mar 21 17:16:40 2001
;; MSG SIZE   sent: 29   rcvd: 401
```

DIG returned with what it could (and answered the desired question), while NSLOOKUP returned an error when it should have continued processing. For NSLOOKUP to function properly, the nameserver it uses *must* have properly configured PTR records for its IP address, which many nameservers don't have.

NSLOOKUP does have its place, however, which is when interactive processing is needed, even if reverse resolutions aren't configured properly. If you type in the command **nslookup** with no parameters, it goes into interactive mode, enabling you to change the server you're querying interactively and setting what type of queries you want to send on its own command line. In this mode, the reverse error previously shown isn't an issue, as long as you start the session with one that does respond correctly. This capture shows how this can work:

```
# nslookup
Default Server:  solar.skyport.net
Address:  216.169.97.10

> server 127.0.0.1
Default Server:  [127.0.0.1]
Address:  127.0.0.1

> www.cnn.com
Server:  [127.0.0.1]
Address:  127.0.0.1

Non-authoritative answer:
Name:    cnn.com
Addresses:  207.25.71.30, 207.25.71.5, 207.25.71.6, 207.25.71.20
            207.25.71.22, 207.25.71.23, 207.25.71.24, 207.25.71.25,
```

```
07.25.71.26
          207.25.71.27, 207.25.71.28, 207.25.71.29
Aliases:  www.cnn.com

> set type=any
> www.cnn.com
Server:  [127.0.0.1]
Address:  127.0.0.1

Non-authoritative answer:
www.cnn.com      canonical name = cnn.com

Authoritative answers can be found from:
cnn.com nameserver = NS-01A.ANS.NET
cnn.com nameserver = NS-01B.ANS.NET
cnn.com nameserver = NS-02A.ANS.NET
cnn.com nameserver = NS-02B.ANS.NET
NS-01A.ANS.NET   internet address = 199.221.47.7
NS-01B.ANS.NET   internet address = 199.221.47.8
NS-02A.ANS.NET   internet address = 207.24.245.179
NS-02B.ANS.NET   internet address = 207.24.245.178
```

One other advantage of NSLOOKUP is it's offered on more platforms by default than DIG. As such, NSLOOKUP is the only tool that comes standard for many people to diagnose and audit their configurations. As such, anybody doing any advanced configuration of DNS should learn NSLOOKUP, no matter what's available to them.

ADVANCED DNS CONFIGURATION

Many times, Content Networking makes use of advanced DNS functions to perform various redirection and content management tasks. These functions can be for reasons as diverse as cost reduction and management simplification. By using DNS to its fullest, a better infrastructure can be implemented that allows business targets to be met more easily and with the lowest cost. In this section, several techniques for using DNS are discussed that can be used to meet such targets.

RTT Measurements

One feature of BIND that many people don't know about is that it keeps track of RTT (Round Trip Timer) measurements when there are several NS records that BIND could use for DNS resolution requests. In Bind 4.x–8.x, though, BIND rounds to the nearest value of a constant defined in the code called *noise*. In Bind 4.x, this value is defined as 128ms, while in Bind 8.x, it's defined as a value of 64ms. When a new set of NS records is retrieved, internally BIND defines the RTT measurement for each entry to be the value 0. It then uses one (effectively at random) of the entries to query against, resulting in a measurement being recorded when the response is received. It then rounds to the nearest value of 64, using the following equation (for both 4.*x* and 8.*x* code):

```
#define RTTROUND(rtt) (((rtt) + (NOISE >> 1)) & ~(NOISE - 1))
```

What this means is if a *noise* value of 64 is present (which it is almost universally), then any RTT measurements from 0–31 are rounded to 0, from 32–95, rounded to 64, 96–159 to 128, and so forth. With a value of 128 as it is in 4.*x*, the granularity is even worse, with 0–63 rounded to 0, 64–191 to 128, and so forth. Obviously, this doesn't help choose the closest nameserver effectively. The intention of this code is to allow rough selection of the best performing nameserver (and, we hope, the closest). The choice of the values allows site selection to work roughly on a continental basis (that is, between Europe and North America, and so forth).

The way the code is written opens quite a few exploitable opportunities for optimization. The first, which generally would benefit people operating resolving nameservers for clients, is to change the *noise* constant from 64 or 128 to some lower value, which would allow more efficient selection of the fastest nameserver. This also ties in with making global load balancing more efficient, as described in Chapter 11. As the value of *noise* must be a power of 2 to work properly, a value of 8 or 16 would provide a much more granular level of control. To find the appropriate place to change this value, within the source code for Bind, use the command:

```
find ./ -exec grep -l NOISE {} \;
```

If you don't have a copy of the BIND code that came with your system, the newest BIND code can be downloaded from ftp://ftp.isc.org/isc/bind/. Unless you're familiar with upgrading from one revision of BIND to another, find the most current release within the same major revision you're currently using, as configuration files have changed between major revisions.

Another method that can be used to take advantage of how BIND works is to make sure that whenever DNS servers are needed, they're distributed in an optimal fashion to ensure requests are handled in a reasonable amount of time. Many domains are hosted from two nameservers located in the same location on the same network. While this ensures that if one server goes down the site stays online, it doesn't in any way help to improve the performance of the site. Because both have roughly the same round-trip time, the traffic is distributed at random between the two boxes. If, however, the two nameservers are on the East Coast and the West Coast of the United States, then, as a general rule, the resolving nameservers on the East Coast will use the East Coast server, and the nameservers on the West Coast will use the authoritative nameservers on the West Coast. As a result, the average response time of the DNS servers for clients will roughly be improved by about 30–60 percent, depending on where the servers are located. By adding in more nameservers in Europe and Asia, the overall global response time improves significantly, without using any expensive software additions. It's all about intelligently using the features already present in Bind.

Following this is the rather counterintuitive point that using more nameservers may cause overall DNS performance to decrease. More nameservers isn't always better for performance. To demonstrate this, consider a site that has two nameservers on the East Coast vs. the West Coast. Because the RTT between the east and west is more than 32, a good division will exist between the two servers based on geography and, after at least two requests, the better of the two will be used until the data expires out. Add in a server in Nebraska or Texas and the division becomes a bit sketchier. Now, three requests would have to be made to determine the best location, and two might show up as "best" based on the logic presented earlier. In the cases where two nameservers are considered equal, some users will experience a slowdown compared with if only one nameserver was used and some would be improved. If the population distribution was even across the country, everything would probably average out, but it isn't. Because the coasts have a higher population density, placing a nameserver in the middle of the country benefits fewer people than would be benefited if it wasn't there.

One approach to provide the highest level of redundancy is to plot out the expected round-trip time windows equal to 32ms of any given nameserver based on geography and place the nameservers accordingly. Based on empirical data at press time, across long-haul data circuits, for a packet to travel about 65 miles takes about 1ms. This depends on the efficiency of the network, although the packet may travel about 90 miles in the same amount of time. As such, ensuring that each DNS server is distinctly serving a large population cluster with a radius of about 1,000–1,500 miles tends to ensure that optimal performance will be delivered. As the furthest distance in the United States between major Internet Centers is roughly 3,000 miles, this tends to support the idea of two locations in the United States for DNS servers, both roughly in the middle of each coast.

Interestingly enough, this analysis supports a different way to look at how DNS servers should be placed, in that the Internet centers of the United States are just outside Washington, D.C. and in the San Francisco Bay Area. Most, if not all, large network providers have direct connections between these two locations, and they tend to make use of these locations as the general hubs of network operations. This points to another conclusion: the network connectivity in these locations will tend to be faster and more reliable. These are key attributes in placing DNS servers for large groups of Internet users. This information should make it apparent that the optimal locations in the United States for DNS servers are in the area of Washington, D.C. and the San Francisco Bay Area, and are connected to major backbone networks. In Europe, the ideal location would be in central Europe, such as in Germany. Because of network connectivity, Frankfurt would tend to be a logical location for a European server. In the Pacific region, there are two potential logical places to place DNS servers: Australia and Japan. Because of the distances between the two, placing a DNS server in each of the regions could make sense, assuming enough demand exists to warrant the expense for each. In Japan, Tokyo is a logical choice. In Australia, Sydney is both a major Internet hub and has one of the largest population centers in the region.

In South America and Africa, the decision is a little trickier because these areas are significantly less developed than the rest of the world. As such, the distances become less of a factor compared with the locations that are wired well and can act as hubs for the rest of the area. In South America, much of the connectivity to the rest of the world goes through Sao Paulo or Rio de Janeiro, and both are close together geographically. Either would be suitable for a DNS server. In Africa, little connectivity exists outside South Africa so, as such, Johannesburg would be the logical choice if a DNS server were placed anywhere in Africa. The next most developed country in Africa, Egypt, can easily be serviced from Europe.

Obviously, the locations listed previously assume one thing: it's worth putting a DNS server in the locations given in the first place. The vast majority of content is produced and consumed in North America, Europe, and Asia, so most efforts would be to make these locations perform the best. The other locations—South America, Africa, and Australia—warrant the effort only if enough reward exists in doing so. This is more of a business case than a technical decision so, as such, it must be handled this way. One additional note in making the decision to add DNS servers: unless more advanced techniques are used for DNS server selection, every DNS server you add potentially will force users to query every one of the worldwide DNS servers to determine which is the best for future queries. Adding a server in South Africa might seem to make sense, but not when put into the context that it will slow down North American users to some degree. Ways around this problem do exist, though, and getting around this problem solves the 64ms window problems inherent in BIND, although they aren't terribly simple to implement.

To get around the issues with BIND's base implementation of RTT measurement, a technique that takes advantage of the inherent routing policies that govern how the Internet works has been developed and used by several companies. This technique involves using the same IP address block in several global locations on distinct servers, and then advertising this IP block via BGP into the Internet from these several locations. The net result is that one IP address (or more) is advertised out as NS records, and the packets traverse the shortest path to reach a server. This technique relies on the capability to make use of BGP4 peering with several providers and can be considered an advanced method to improve DNS performance.

As an alternative to making use of BGP peering to achieve the faster performance, it's possible to make use of one of several services to achieve the same goal. Companies such as Akamai (www.akamai.com) and UltraDNS (www.ultradns.com) are using techniques such as these (among others) to deliver faster responses for DNS than can be reasonably achieved with network deployments engineered for a single content provider. Because these companies are engineering solutions to work with many customers, they can afford to configure and manage server resources that otherwise would be impractical for other companies.

UltraDNS's primary service is to provide DNS resolution services for domains. As part of this service, it has installed authoritative DNS servers in several different data centers and used the BGP peering mechanism previously described to direct the requests to the nearest nameserver. As a result, there's a significantly lower latency, on average, using their resolution service than compared with the standard mechanism of simply listing several nameservers in the NS records in the TLD servers. Another advantage of using services such as theirs is the reduced maintenance headache of maintaining BIND code. Companies that specialize in this type of service generally provide users with friendly web-based tools for managing domains, making the learning curve much shorter for managing domains. They also automatically scan for common errors in configuring domains, resulting in less downtime as a result of human error. In short, unless you have specific needs, it's generally worthwhile to use services such as these for domains.

Akamai makes use of some advanced techniques to reduce the DNS resolution time, and it also provides other optimization services for customers. Akamai uses various methods of network monitoring and peering to map the overall structure of the Internet, and it makes use of this information within the DNS query level to speed the content delivery. While problems exist with the accuracy of the methods used, overall the performance gain can be considerable, although the gain focuses on the nature of the customer. This topic is explained further in the Chapter 11.

Wildcard DNS

When managing several different types of content, sometimes you need to provide several names for various reasons but, for all of these names, you want to provide the same information. To do this, the mechanism of *wildcard DNS* is used. In this mechanism, you make use of a * to represent any name not specifically defined in the configuration files and to define a record to be returned for it. This is useful to handle the situation where people type in ww instead of www or, if as part of the service being provided, a different hostname exists for each user of the service. For the configuration previously detailed (the generic one), one additional line could be added, such as the following:

```
*            IN      CNAME    @
```

This can also be used if, for instance, you're making use of virtual hosting on the web server side to provide a unique domain name for different users, such as joe .somedomain.com. This allows a single configuration to handle any number of names and the web server configuration performs the rest of the work. Each name would resolve to the same IP address, but the host header in the HTTP request would result in different content being served. On the web server, it's possible, depending on the server software, to parse the domain programmatically and to make use of a different set of content for each domain automatically without any web server configuration. Through this configuration, using both wildcard DNS and proper web server configuration, you can create domains simply by adding a directory on a server or set of servers, removing much of the complexity of DNS and web server administration.

One other use of wildcard DNS entries is to isolate what resolving DNS servers' different clients are coming from. This is demonstrated using the following logging configuration for the named.conf file, in conjunction with two simple CGI scripts, as follows. Please note, these haven't been tested for security and are used only to illustrate the technique.

```
named.conf logging configuration:
logging {
        channel queries {
                file "/var/log/named.queries";
                };
        category queries { queries; };
};
```

```
test.cgi:
#!/bin/bash
hname=`echo $REMOTE_ADDR|tr '.' 'x'`
echo "Content-type: text/html"
echo "Location: http://$hname.domain.com/cgi-bin/test2.cgi"
echo
```

```
test2.cgi:
#!/bin/bash
hname=`echo $REMOTE_ADDR|tr '.' 'x'`
echo Content-type: text/html
echo
server=`grep "$hname" /var/log/named.queries|cut -f2 \ -d'/'|cut -f2
-d' '|tail -1`
echo "<html>"
echo "Your DNS server is $server<br>"
echo "</html>"
```

This type of information can be useful in any situation where DNS doesn't seem to be working properly. Because DNS can be redirected and manipulated in several ways, this allows analytical determination of the actual path the DNS query is traversing. This is especially true when a possibility exists that a DNS forwarder might be in use. A *DNS forwarder* is a resolving DNS server that forwards all requests to yet another resolving DNS server.

RR Sets

Another way to make use of DNS for content networking is to make use of RR sets, which is when more than one answer exists for a given request. The most common case of this is the use of several NS records to be authoritative for a given domain. It's generally assumed for any given domain that at least two DNS servers can answer any given request. In a less common situation, you can answer with two (or more) A records. Most RR types can be used in RR sets, with CNAMES being (of sort) an exception. Older BIND code allowed CNAME RR sets to be created, although it's technically against the DNS RFCs to do this. In newer BIND code, there's an option to allow multiple CNAME records, aptly called *multiple-cnames*. If given in the options section of named.conf, then BIND keeps track of the CNAMES and delivers one (and only one) at a time, but delivers the different records to different individual requests. No such limitations exist for A, NS, and MX records, though.

To use RR sets, simply provide several records with the same domain, either by forcing the field to the default (of the last line's domain field) or by specifying the same name again. As an example, consider the following two examples. This

```
www     A       192.168.0.10
        A       192.168.0.100
        A       192.168.0.101
```

is the same as

```
www     A       192.168.0.10
www     A       192.168.0.100
www     A       192.168.0.101
```

While the first form is used, though, it can distract from the meaning, as well as possibly confuse some DNS management tools as to the meaning (the same could be said of leaving out any optional field, however, such as the class and TTL).

What would happen for either of these two previous examples is all three IP addresses would be returned to any requesting DNS server, who would pass that on to any application. Depending on how the application was written, it might simply use the first one in the list or it might keep track of the fact that three different IP addresses are available and use more advanced metrics to choose which one to use. In this scenario, the benefits can be enormous when the different IPs reside in different locations on the Internet, possibly in different countries. In general, though, the only applications that are intelligent enough to perform intelligent analysis of several records would be dedicated proxy servers, such as Squid.

To control the result of using several A records, various controls within are named that allow the behavior to be modified. In the named.conf file, the command **rrset-order** is used to determine the order of the returned responses in an RR set. Three options are available: fixed, random, and cyclic. The *fixed* option returns the answers in exactly the order they occur in the configuration file. In general, this would cause the first IP to be used most often because many clients will strictly use the first one in the list. The *random* option returns the responses in random order, allowing an even distribution of requests, even when the client uses only the first in the list. The *cyclic* option performs a strict round-robin order on the IPs.

One caveat to using RR sets is to make sure the reply packets aren't too large. To prevent the need to use TCP for DNS, as opposed to UDP, make sure no query response is longer than 512 bytes. To check this, a command such as the following can be used

```
dig @servername domain.com any
```

Check the last line with the reported size for the response. A value higher than 512 means, in some cases, the reply has to be fragmented, and DNS doesn't like fragmented UDP packets. As such, a TCP connection would be needed to send all the content. This won't work in many cases because of firewall rules. In an extreme case, it might be possible to reply with up to 30 A records within the response, although this can change based on the additional information provided in the reply, the length of the domain and hostnames, and so forth.

Subdomain Delegation

When a domain grows to a large size or otherwise needs to be managed in a distributed manner, subdomain delegation becomes an easy way to handle things. To do this, a line could be entered such as the following:

```
ca    NS    ns-ca.foo.com.
va    NS    ns-va.foo.com.
```

This would create a domain by the name of www that would reside on the nameservers NS-CA.FOO.COM and NS-VA.FOO.COM. On each of these servers, they would manage the IPs for the computers in each location (CA and VA, respectively), allowing the administrator of the overall domain to free himself from the responsibilities of tracking the local machines. Or, you could register domains in the various country domains, such as .jp and .uk, and have all of them point to the same resource file. As an example, the named.conf could contain

```
zone "domain.uk" {
      type master;
      file "generic";
};

zone "domain.jp" {
      type master;
      file "generic";
};
```

By doing this, the various machines and IP addresses are all managed in one file, yet virtual hosting can take advantage of the different locals in the names to default to different languages and such. This is a much more generic and easily manageable technique than trying to use configured languages on individual browsers, and it can still be used in conjunction with such configurations when available. Another reason to do this is if several domains were registered, to account for people misspelling a domain name. All the misspelled domains can be directed to one file that contains a wildcard CNAME entry to direct users to the real domain or to force an HTTP redirect to the proper domain.

Using delegation also makes sense when different companies are working as partners to provide a service to a customer. Consider the situation where a content provider wants to offload some content that's become popular enough that its local Internet connections can't handle it. Instead of using a URL for a third-party hosting company, the content provider can delegate a name such as www2.domain.com instead of www.someotherdomain.com to ensure brand recognition stays with the originating company. The domain www2 can be delegated to the nameservers of the third-party company, so it can maintain control of what final IPs are delivered to the customer, but the original company keeps control over the name.

Remember this one key point: any single name can be considered a domain and it can be delegated as such. In the previous example of using www as a subdomain, there's no requirement that any other hostnames be within that subdomain. Further tricks you can play with subdomains are discussed in Chapter 11.

DNS Thrashing

One of the problems in using delegated domains and multiple domain names in a web page is *DNS Thrashing,* or the overuse and dependence on DNS to deliver content to a user. On a recent visit to the CNN homepage, a prime example of this was found. Following is a tcpdump trace of DNS requests from a client requesting the CNN homepage, resulting in no less than five DNS requests. If the user had been on a satellite connection (as this one was), this would force a minimum of about four seconds extra time to download this web page and many times, depending on the service, much longer than that.

Here's an example using WWW.CNN.COM:

```
17:59:21.521211 148.71.62.138.34580 > 216.169.96.10.53: 20201+ A?
www.cnn.com. (29) (DF) (ttl 64, id 0)
17:59:25.697666 148.71.62.138.34580 > 216.169.96.10.53: 8962+ A?
i.cnn.net. (27) (DF) (ttl 64, id 0)
17:59:37.513220 148.71.62.138.34580 > 216.169.96.10.53: 27815+ A?
toolbar.netscape.com. (38) (DF) (ttl 64, id 0)
17:59:53.965228 148.71.62.138.34580 > 216.169.96.10.53: 14125+ A?
a388.g.akamai.net. (35) (DF) (ttl 64, id 0)
18:00:06.105980 148.71.62.138.34581 > 216.169.96.10.53: 8855+ A?
a18.g.akamai.net. (34) (DF) (ttl 64, id 0)
```

A similar trace to Yahoo!'s homepage led to:

```
18:29:47.165370 148.71.62.138.35114 > 216.169.96.10.53: 52080+ A?
www.yahoo.com. (31) (DF) (ttl 64, id 0)
18:29:50.847895 148.71.62.138.35114 > 216.169.96.10.53: 25461+ A?
us.a1.yimg.com. (32) (DF) (ttl 64, id 0)
```

In Yahoo!'s example, us.a1.yimg.com is served by Akamai and is needed to serve distinct content from Akamai's server network. The initial URL forces www.yahoo.com to be requested, and all images use the same name for absolute references, resulting in a fast download. The only way to get better performance would be to use a single name and relative references, although many times in today's environment this lofty goal is only achievable with simple web sites. In the case of CNN, one way to reduce the resolution time is to make sure Akamai is referenced with only one name, and all the content that isn't local to the origin server should be delivered through Akamai, as it is with Yahoo!. Another example of thrashing comes from NBCI, also for seven DNS resolutions:

```
19:09:08.260180 148.71.62.138.35133 > 216.169.96.10.53: 11063+ A?
www.nbci.com.(30) (DF) (ttl 64, id 0)

19:09:13.445652 148.71.62.138.35133 > 216.169.96.10.53: 30729+ A?
a1356.g.ak.nbci.com. (37) (DF) (ttl 64, id 0)

19:09:13.780354 148.71.62.138.35136 > 216.169.96.10.53: 7039+ A?
ad.doubleclick.net. (36) (DF) (ttl 64, id 0)

19:09:16.836399 148.71.62.138.34592 > 216.169.96.10.53: 830+ A?
www.ibuyjunk.com. (34) (DF) (ttl 64, id 0)

19:09:16.899116 148.71.62.138.34592 > 216.169.96.10.53: 831+ A?
www.geocities.com. (35) (DF) (ttl 64, id 0)

19:09:18.165631 148.71.62.138.35136 > 216.169.96.10.53: 48327+ A?
m.doubleclick.net. (35) (DF) (ttl 64, id 0)

19:09:19.793025 148.71.62.138.35136 > 216.169.96.10.53: 51714+ A?
a1356.g.ak.snap.com. (37) (DF) (ttl 64, id 0)
```

Many of the DNS Thrashing sites are ones that have a wide variety of business arrangements with different partners and direct traffic to different ad servers at different times, which might end up redirecting traffic to yet another server elsewhere. While solving the problems these arrangements cause is difficult, performance and the possibility of failure in any one of these resolutions should be considered, and solutions that include caching might be warranted. With caches, much of the redundant resolution requests can be removed, while placing logs of all the transactions that have occurred in the content owners' hands, even if the logs end up being retrieved from other locations for business reasons.

REGISTERING DOMAIN NAMES

To make use of a name for your company, the name must be purchased through any one of several companies called *registrars*. These companies work together through a group called the Internet Corporation for Assigned Names and Numbers (ICANN), which is responsible for managing the TLDs, as well as coordinating the management of the root nameservers (although other organizations run the root nameservers themselves). In the initial Internet boom, you had to go through one company to register domain names in the .com, .net, and .org TLDs and that company was Network Solutions. Any company that advertised it could register domains for you was simply acting as a middleman for the process and, while that company might make it simpler for you to register domains, all it did was pass the information on to Network Solutions for registration.

Now, however, the list of "Registrars" has gotten significantly longer, and Network Solutions no longer has a monopoly on the actual registration process. For a complete list of all the TLD domains available, as well as a list of companies registering names within each TLD, please check the web site http://www.icann.org/, the home page for ICANN. As the exact process differs now for each registrar, the overall process of registering will be discussed and, although the registrars now hide many of the pieces, the process on the back end is still the same.

General Process

One of the largest benefits of having several registrars in place has been the simplification of DNS registration and the enhanced ease of management once a domain is registered. The process of registering a domain is roughly to

1. Find an available domain to register,
2. Provide contact information for the domain, and
3. Provide payment information.

By default, most registrars provide a DNS server and, many times, a base web page with most packages. When you go through the initial registration process, the registrars default the authoritative nameserver to their own nameservers, making it easier to get going. If the registrar requests a DNS server to point to, you should have the DNS server already configured and ready to serve the domain. One trick to this: the name the registrar asks for is *not* explicitly the NS record for the domain in your zone file, although it should match what's in the zone file. Instead, this is a name registered specifically for resolution at the TLD nameservers. Through your registrar, there should be a means to manage nameservers or to register a nameserver. What happens is a record is created that can be queried directly from the TLD nameservers. Remember how in the configuration of an NS record, a name needs to be pointed to? At the TLD level, they need a name to point to also, such as ns1.somedomain.com. If the information weren't available at the TLD level, no way would exist to obtain the information from the authoritative nameserver level because the IP addresses of the nameservers at that level aren't available. The issue of registering such records simply won't exist if you're making use of a third-party nameservice system, such as UltraDNS, because their records are already registered. As an example of a zone file that would make use of their nameservers, the following could be used

```
@              SOA      udns1.ultradns.net.     hostmaster (
                        2001040102 ; serial
                        3600 ; refresh
                        900 ; retry
```

```
                          1209600 ; expire
                          43200 ; default_ttl
                          )
@          MX     5          mail
@          NS     udns1.ultradns.net.
           NS     udns2.ultradns.net.
@          A      192.168.0.1
www        A      192.168.0.1
mail       A      192.168.0.1
*          CNAME  www
```

One final note on this, you can't have more than one NS record at the TLD nameservers registered for a given IP. If you're hosting several domains and want to have the names NS.DOMAIN1.COM and NS.DOMAIN2.COM point to the same IP, you can't do it. You can, however, place two IPs on one server and register a different IP for each of the nameserver entries.

Contacts

For any given DNS registration, up to five contacts are registered or associated with the registration. These contacts are titled the organization contact, administrative contact, technical contact, billing contact, and zone contact. One or more of these contacts might be missing, and many registrars now default one or more of these on initial registration. In general, at least the administrative and technical contacts are filled in.

The *administrative contact* is the contact information for the person responsible for significant decisions about the domain. If all the other contacts are the same person, then generally the administrative contact is the only one filled in. The *technical contact* is usually the contact info for the person or group managing the network resources (that is, the DNS and web servers). The *billing contact* is for the group responsible to make sure the domain bills are paid. If this contact is missing, you can assume the administrative contact carries out this responsibility. The *organizational* and *zone contacts* generally aren't used, but they can be used to list the formal corporate name of the owner of the domain and the manager of the zone file, if this is different than the technical contact. Not all registrars even offer the zone contact to be modified.

Properly configuring these contacts is *very* important, not only for any communication between your registrar and yourself, but also because bills are sent via e-mail to the contacts. These contacts also provide the means by which spam warnings and security notifications from third-party organizations can be sent to you, in case someone is making use of resources they shouldn't use. Unfortunately, the contact information is public information to anyone who queries for it, so make certain the e-mail address is a "role" address, usually to be forwarded to a person or group that takes care of the answering and reading the e-mail. *Never* use a person's personal e-mail address for this because it can cause a significant problem if that person leaves the company or otherwise is unavailable.

WHOIS Databases

The information provided for each contact, as well as the information associated with the domain itself, is stored in publicly accessible databases called *WHOIS databases*. To access this information, either the whois command can be used from UNIX or you can use any one of several windows or web-based WHOIS tools. Because these all access the same information, the UNIX (Linux-specific) WHOIS tool will be described for the purpose of examples.

In its simplest use, the command **whois** [domain] will provide some sort of information about a particular domain. For example, the command **whois cnn.com** returns the following:

```
[whois.networksolutions.com]


Registrant:
Turner Broadcasting (CNN-DOM)
   1 CNN Center
   Atlanta, GA 30303


   Domain Name: CNN.COM


   Administrative Contact:
    TBS Legal Department   (TL92-ORG)    TMGROUP@TURNER.COM
    Turner Broadcasting System, Inc.
    One CNN Center
    Atlanta, GA 30348
    US
    404-827-3470
    Fax- - - - 404-827-1995
    Fax- - 404-827-1995


   Technical Contact:
    TBS Server Operations  (TS309-ORG)   hostmaster@TBSNAMES.TURNER.COM
    Turner Broadcasting System, Inc.
    One CNN Center
    Atlanta, GA 30348
    US
    404-827-5000
    Fax- 404-827-1593
   Billing Contact:
    idNames, Accounting   (IA90-ORG)   accounting@IDNAMES.COM
    idNames from Network Solutions, Inc
    440 Benmar
    Suite #3325
    Houston, TX 77060
```

```
     US
     703-742-4777
     Fax 281-447-1160
```

```
Record last updated on 03-Nov-2000.
Record expires on 23-Sep-2009.
Record created on 22-Sep-1993.
Database last updated on 27-Mar-2001 01:56:00 EST.
```

```
Domain servers in listed order:
```

```
NS-01A.ANS.NET            199.221.47.7
NS-01B.ANS.NET            199.221.47.8
NS-02A.ANS.NET            207.24.245.179
NS-02B.ANS.NET            207.24.245.178
```

As an alternative example, the command **whois register.com** returns

```
[whois.networksolutions.com]
```

```
  Organization:
        Register.Com
        Domain Registrar
        575 8th Avenue - 11th Floor
        New York, NY 10018
        US
        Phone: 212-798-9200
        Fax..: 212-629-9305
        Email: domain-registrar@register.com
```

```
  Registrar Name....: Register.com
  Registrar Whois...: whois.register.com
  Registrar Homepage: http://www.register.com
```

```
  Domain Name: REGISTER.COM
```

```
        Created on.............: Wed, Aug 04, 1999
        Expires on.............: Tue, Aug 04, 2009
        Record last updated on..: Thu, Jun 01, 2000
```

```
  Administrative Contact, Technical Contact, Zone Contact:
        Register.Com
        Domain Registrar
        575 8th Avenue - 11th Floor
```

```
New York, NY 10018
US
Phone: 212-798-9200
Fax..: 212-629-9305
Email: domain-registrar@register.com
```

Domain servers in listed order:

```
DNS1.REGISTER.COM                              209.67.50.220
DNS2.REGISTER.COM                              209.67.50.241
DNS3.REGISTER.COM                              209.67.50.253
DNS4.REGISTER.COM                              209.67.50.254
```

Register your domain name at http://www.register.com

```
The previous information has been obtained either directly from the
registrant or a registrar of the domain name other than Network
Solutions. Network Solutions, therefore, does not guarantee its
accuracy or completeness.
```

In the first case, the WHOIS server that WHOIS contacts by default is run by Network Solutions. In the second case, REGISTER.COM—a registrar in its own right—runs its own WHOIS server and references what that server is. In any case, the TLD's configurations are generated from the same information displayed in the WHOIS queries, so if that information isn't correct, problems will exist. Take particular care in modifying this information because it can take 24–48 hours to effect changes and make corrections.

PROBLEMS WITH DNS

Although DNS, as implemented in BIND (usually), has taken the Internet a long way since it was conceived, issues revolve around it that any responsible administrator needs to know. The first issue is the need to keep on top of updates to DNS software, particularly BIND. Numerous holes have been found in BIND that make it vulnerable to serious attacks. Some of these holes are simple denial of service attacks, causing BIND to crash and resulting in the inability to resolve the names for which the server is responsible. Other attacks cause corruption of the internal databases, allowing someone to take over your web site by substituting his IP addresses for your names. When this happens, a distinct possibility exists that a user will be able to capture credit card numbers, and so forth. As such, any administrator managing his own DNS servers should subscribe to any one of several security mailing lists, such as CERT's (http://www.cert.org) mailing list or bugtrack (http://www.securityfocus.com). Failure to stay current on such matters can inevitably lead to the nameserver being compromised or taken offline. This isn't a matter of if, but of when.

Another problem with DNS is the tendency of ISPs to make use of centralized DNS servers for their clients. This prevents optimizations, such as using DNS for global load balancing, from working as effectively as it could, as well as significantly slowing the overall resolution time for users. On average, each DNS resolution on such a central DNS configuration can lose about 40–50ms because of the cross-country trip to its resolving DNS server. On top of this, if enough users are using the same resolving DNS server, the response times can go down, degrading performance further. If any packet loss occurs, though, this can cause the most significant performance drop, resulting in pages that might never come up.

THE FUTURE

While DNS has gotten the Internet as far as it has, the problems with its design have started to weigh it down. Many site failures are DNS-related issues, preventing people from accessing the content efficiently and effectively. While other major Internet protocols are changing and morphing into forms that are more efficient, DNS as a protocol has remained relatively unchanged for years. Some major areas of development are being performed, though, some to improve DNS and others to replace it.

One of the more fundamental changes to the DNS protocol implemented in the newest versions of BIND is the support of IPv6, which is slowly gaining use in research environments and wireless networks. Most of the resolver libraries now in use support receiving IPv6 addresses, as do many of the nameservers. Currently, code exists for Windows, Linux, Solaris, as well as the various flavors of BSD. Many router vendors support IPv6, although most routers in use need to be upgraded to support these features. As IPv6 isn't in widespread use, most content networks needn't worry for a few years about content availability on the IPv6-enabled Internet; mechanisms are in place to bridge between IPv6 and IPv4 as needed.

Another important change to DNS is the rapidly developing area of DNSSEC, or Secure DNS. While Secure DNS is an evolving technology, keeping track of it is important because this enhancement solves many of the security issues involved with DNS, primarily with session hijacking. If a site is handling sensitive content, DNSSEC should certainly be investigated, if only to give users the option of using the more secure mechanisms. Further references to DNSSEC and documentation on its installation can be found within the BIND 9.x code releases. Note, if you plan on installing and working with DNSSEC, the implementations are still rapidly changing and might not work together between different versions (for example, between versions 9.1.1 and 9.1.2 of BIND).

Another change to the Internet that impacts the functionality of DNS is a technology called Internet Keywords. *Internet Keywords* enable a user to interact with the web browser using natural language words, as opposed to strict DNS syntax. While the goal of using Internet Keywords is good, the technologies are driven more by marketing than anything else. While both Netscape and Internet Explorer provide a default service to manage Internet keywords, competing solutions operate as plug-ins that users can install. The main players in this area are RealNames (www.realnames.com), Netword (www.netword.com), and Netscape (keyword.netscape.com). By far, RealNames has the lead in this technology because of the built-in functions in MSIE to support RealNames, as well as many partner sites that make use of the technology when performing general searches. While wide support exists for this type of technology, whether the public will take to it over using general search engines is still uncertain, so relying on this technology to develop for content networking is a fairly limited prospect.

SUMMARY

While DNS is an important technology for content networking, it isn't a utopia. Many of the performance improvements that can be gained with DNS over normal configurations are statistical improvements, whereas misconfigurations can be devastating in their impact. More than one company has seen its sites totally removed from the Internet for days simply because of misconfigurations or failure to pay bills for domain names. Understanding the subtle interactions that impact DNS performance is critical to ensure a well-performing site, as is how delegation can occur and how subdomains can be used to group and manage content. DNS configurations should also allow flexibility where needed, and they should be instituted to allow different types of content to be distributed in more efficient manners. By remembering the future, as well as other content networking technology, redundancies and inefficiencies can be reduced, creating a fast, efficient, and profitable site configuration.

REVIEW QUESTIONS

1. **Under what conditions would it make sense to use an image's name distinct from a www name for content distribution?**

   The conditions under which using an image's name distinct from a www name for content distribution would make sense are when the image's name can be handled more efficiently using a different set of servers, through a content distribution network for improved client access, or if a possibility exists of using such techniques later with site growth.

2. **Why would the following be considered invalid in a zone configuration file?**

   ```
   @    CNAME    www
   ```

   Aliasing a domain to a subdomain within the same domain can cause recursive errors and lead to other names and information that might reside in the primary domain becoming inaccessible. If cached, such an entry can cause the wrong servers to be queried for any future domain records from the main domain.

3. **If you had a satellite link to the Internet, would you want your clients to make use of a local resolving nameserver or a nameserver on the other side of the satellite link, and why? For a local nameserver, assume no DNS forwarding is active.**

    You would want to make use of a remote nameserver if possible. This is as a result of resolving nameservers having to make several DNS requests for many locations, as opposed to a resolving library making a single request for a given domain to its resolving nameservers. The number of satellite traversals should be kept to a minimum to improve performance. If a DNS forwarder were used, then a local nameserver would be preferred because it would cache answers for local clients and only issue one request for unknown names to its resolving nameserver.

4. **Why would adding more authoritative DNS servers in remote areas slow down a majority of clients?**

    Adding more authoritative DNS servers into remote locations forces many resolving DNS servers outside the 64ms RTT window to resolve at least once against every DNS server listed as being authoritative before choosing the best one. If many remote DNS servers exist, this slows the average DNS resolution time and results in slower performance for clients.

5. **What techniques can be used to avoid excessive DNS queries when partnering with other sites?**

    Using caches and content distribution networks can allow the content delivered by several companies to be accessible via one name, allowing for faster resolutions and improving overall content delivery time. This also enables better logging of activity, allowing for better statistics and control of content.

6. **On a frequently used site, how could delegating a holder subdomain be used to improve performance to groups of customers? Does this mean using an extra domain, such as www.a.domain.com instead of www.domain.com?**

    When several names are within a domain, using a holder domain allows for interesting tricks to be played. When the subdomain a.domain.com is resolved, a small set of DNS servers can be used in distinct geographical locations, which the clients' resolving nameserver can choose the best of, without many iterations. Based on the choice, the second level of delegated domains can deliver a different set of NS records based on the local chosen. As an example, consider the following set of configurations excerpts.

For domain.com:

```
a      NS     new_york.americas
a      NS     munich.europe_africa
a      NS     tokyo.pacific_rim
```

In europe.domain.com:

```
www    NS     munich.europe_africa
www    NS     johannesburg.europ_africa
```

In americas.domain.com:

```
www    NS     new_york.americas
www    NS     san_jose.americas
www    NS     rio.americas
```

In pacific_rim.domain.com:

```
www    NS     sydney.pacific_rim
www    NS     tokyo.pacific_rim
```

With this configuration, the overall choice of what main nameserver for a.domain.com will be done in three resolution attempts and, at the second level, it also will take no more than three attempts. In addition, by using the same nameserver name at both the a.domain.com level and the region.a.domain.com level, a round-trip time will also already be entered for the name in the second request. This further reduces the number of resolutions that need to be done to narrow the choice of the best nameserver.

CHAPTER 7

Internet Structure
and Function

OBJECTIVES

▼ Discuss the general Internet hierarchy

■ Describe the role of the POP

■ Differentiate between various types of service providers

■ Discuss the importance of NAPs and Peering

▲ Provide an overview of BGP

The Internet is the global arena in which Content Delivery Networking (CDN) occurs, by and large. Discussing CDNs by ignoring their context seems a bit backward, so it's worth taking a few moments to discuss it. This chapter is intended to provide a basic introduction to high-level Internet organization, such as it is. To optimize a thing, understanding a bit about what it is can help. The Internet is a complex place, and that complexity seems to be accelerating at a nonlinear pace. Unfortunately, that complexity isn't readily amenable to interpretation, characterization, or anything approaching a complete description. Much like that monolith in 2001, it simply is. This wasn't always so. Back in the day, the Internet was a simple interconnection of networks—it wasn't until somebody realized money was to be made that its organization got completely out of hand.

For many, the Internet is AOL, Yahoo!, or until recently, Excite@Home—confusing content providers and web portals with the structure of the Internet. This is an important, if somewhat obvious, point: the Internet is a physical thing. Cyberspace is an abstraction, the Internet isn't. Unfortunately, the Internet is also commonly abstracted. While the physicality of the Internet is a sea of cables and landlines, linking users in a specific manner at regional point of presence (POP), it could be (and frequently is) diagrammed as a cloud into and out of which frame-relay connections, serial links, and virtual private networks (VPNs) disappear and reappear. The Internet as a black box is not terribly helpful when trying to understand its organization, however.

In its simplest form, the Internet is a network of networks. It's a mesh of many thousands of interconnected public and private computer networks that interoperate without any central governing authority. The physical infrastructure is composed of copper wire, wireless RF, and fiber-optic cables connected to computers, routers, and switches, all of which operate a variety of OSI Layer-2 data-link protocols, including PPP, ISDN, X.25, SONET ATM, frame-relay, and point-to-point serial links. Data movement within a network is made possible by layer-3 protocols, such as any number of Interior Gateway Protocols (IGP). More relevant to our Internet-structure discussion is the protocol responsible for moving data from one network to another: Border Gateway Protocol (BGP). These media and protocols are all embedded into the basic building blocks of the Internet: the POPs, Network Access Points (NAP), and backbones.

This information is provided with the intent of equipping a CDN designer with some of the tools and lingo required to understand some of the issues surrounding the Internet as a whole.

GLOBAL STRUCTURE

"There is no architecture, but only a tradition, which was not written down for the first 25 years." (RFC, 1958).

In this section, we're going to look at two things. First and foremost is a description of how the parts of the Internet are put together. There are problems with such a proposal, however. The Internet was, about 20 years ago, relatively simple and easy to document. That was 20 years ago, and things have changed somewhat. Now, the actual structure of the Internet, that is, the physical layout of cables and fiber, changes on a daily basis. Any description of such a seething mass of metal and glass is bound to be fundamentally inadequate.

An approach more useful and applicable might be to look at the Internet in a functional manner, instead of a physical one. The problems with functional descriptions are they're only approximations and tend to be oversimplified for any particular case. However, while not literally accurate, functional descriptions can be quite instructive. At a rough gloss, the structure of the Internet yields itself to three functional levels of analysis, which are discussed in turn.

Functional descriptions of network topologies need to include the ingress and egress points. All network connections not directly pointing at a user base are described as peering, which is the next topic. *Peering* is how service providers connect to each other, how traffic gets exchanged between carriers. These relationships are often complex and political, but critical for Internet function. Peering occurs at specific points, NAPs, and these can be public or private, free or fee-based. A basic requirement for routing across NAPs is BGP, and this is discussed in the section "Internet Routing with BGP."

Hierarchical Organization

The difference between a hierarchy and a heterarchy is deciding who's the boss. In a *hierarchy*, that's easy, the one on top is the boss. In a heterarchy, this is a bit more problematic. *Heterarchies* are unusual, and authority tends to depend on circumstance, function, and domain. Depending on the glasses you're wearing, the Internet could be described either way.

In a heterarchical sense, the cellular unit of life in the Internet is a single network segment. The Internet is simply composed of lots and lots of such cells. When looked at too closely, this is all there is to see. No structure, no semantic patterns, just fractals from here on up.

Switching glasses, some artificial intervening stages lend themselves to an alternative view. If the networks are grouped into organizations and companies, all is no longer created equal on the Internet. Some networks are obviously larger than others. Some are more critical to the functioning of the whole. Some carry more traffic; some lease bandwidth on their networks to others. At this point, useful distinctions within such networks can be made. We turn to this first.

POP

The first layer is the one most ISP users are familiar with, the point of presence. ISPs create POPs in the markets they're attempting to serve, providing a local access ramp onto their network. A POP (see Figure 7-1) can be quite complex, involving an entire Internet Data Center, or relatively simple, such as a rack in a colocation facility with a modem bank set up behind a hunt group.

The vast majority of POPs will be small-scale for reasons of economy. To become a world-class Internet service provider (ISP), local POPs are the keys to success. A POP in every city will provide a marketing edge over the competition, as well as provide access

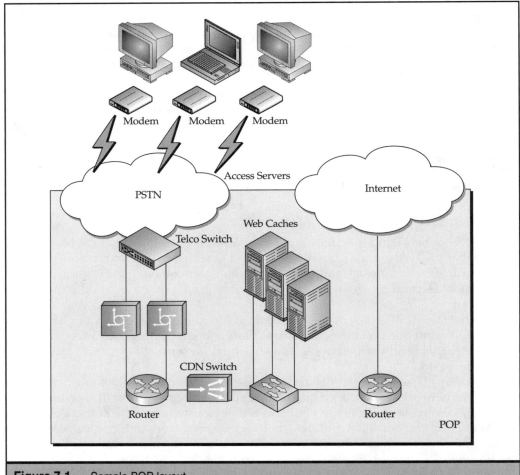

Figure 7-1. Sample POP layout

to a larger potential client base. ISPs that provide hosting, colocation or application services—application service provider (ASP)—will require something more robust than a rented rack in someone else's facility. In addition to power, air, and security concerns, these services require space and the infrastructure to support these designs. Such data centers are expensive, so their numbers tend to be few and strategically placed geographically to provide services to the largest number of clients possible.

Three primary technologies are used to ramp into a POP: Point-to-Point Protocol (PPP) over a modem dial-up, DSL, and cable. Of the other two (un)common technologies, ISDN tends to be out of favor because of cost and relatively slow access speeds, and most satellite implementation still requires a modem uplink. Most ISPs will provide some combination of service, for example, DSL and dial-up. Whichever technologies are chosen will dictate the hardware required in the POP, for example, a DSLAM for DSL, an access server for dial-up, and so forth.

Subscriber-edge CDNs could focus at this level to provide service. Some managed services, such as those provided by Akamai Technologies (http://www.akamai.com/), will install content distribution servers at the major ISP POPs worldwide, in an attempt to put content delivery mechanisms as close to the potential client as possible.

The types of CND appliances that might be fitted here depend on who's building the CDN. If it's the ISP itself, then there's no better place to install web caches than here in the POP. The more traffic off the WAN links the better, and caching can eliminate a lot of HTTP traffic overhead. Chapter 13 deals with this issue at some length.

Another service commonly deployed here is some kind of bandwidth management (BWM). Usually bundled into the access device, what this service does is ensure Service Level Agreements (SLA) are met satisfactorily. BWM is dealt with in Chapter 14.

ISP

A company that provides Internet access to end users is called an Internet service provider (ISP). This definition, like most, is somewhat oversimplified. ISPs generally come in one of two flavors: those that provide access to end users and those that provide access to those that provide access to end users. Both are helpfully called ISPs (though the latter are sometimes called network service providers, or NSPs). InterNAP, AboveNet, and Savvis are all examples of NSPs: Earthlink (http://www.earthlink.com), AOL (http://www.aol.com), and MSN (http://www.msn.com) are all examples of "traditional" ISPs. For the sake of ease, we'll recognize the distinction here and ignore it because it isn't relevant to our discussion.

A distinction that *is* useful to our discussion has to do with reach of service, that is, between regional and national/international service providers. The distinction has a lot to do with infrastructure; regional carriers needn't have it, national carriers ought to. National carriers, in large part, have their own backbone or, more likely, lease a lambda off a DWDM circuit operated by a backbone provider, like Qwest, AT&T, or Sprint. Three of the major national carriers have already been mentioned: AOL, Earthlink, and MSN. Thousands of regional carriers exist. Here are a few: Excel (http://www.excel.net), which serves Southeastern Wisconsin; Drizzle (http://www.drizzle.net), which serves the Puget Sound; and Catskill On Line (http://www.catskill.net), which serves (strangely enough) the Catskill

Mountains area. The boundary between regional and national is pretty thin, and quite a few national carriers began as regional success stories, such as Annapolis' own Toad (http://www.toad.net).

ISPs, at the very least, own or maintain a POP to provide access to their end users. The more POPs, the more users the ISP can support and give simultaneous access to, and the more revenue the ISP can generate.

Another lucrative trend among ISPs, both regional and not, is to offer *hosting* or *colocation* to their business customers. These services allow a company that needs or wants a web presence to have someone else manage the general operating facility and, optionally, the hardware, software, access, bandwidth, and security of that web site.

Backbone Providers

Compared to ISPs, few backbone providers exist. These companies have a tendency to be telco companies as well, for example, AT&T, SBC, and Sprint (see Figures 7-2 through 7-4). Their backbones were installed for handling long-haul voice traffic and, as data network became more and more popular, were upgraded to keep pace. One of these companies' primary revenue streams derives from leasing space on their networks to other, national ISPs.

What differentiates backbone providers from national ISPs is that one provides service to the other. National ISPs lease lines from Sprint and WorldCom, not the other way around. But, to make matters more confusing, almost all of the backbone providers have

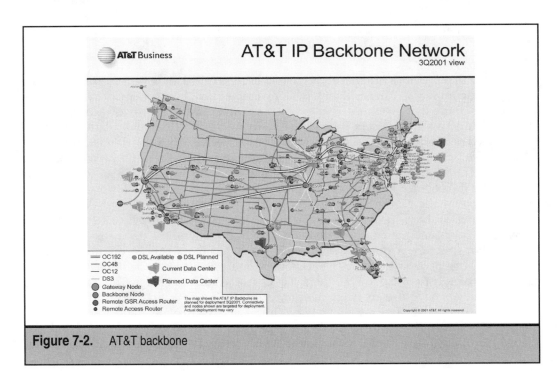

Figure 7-2.   AT&T backbone

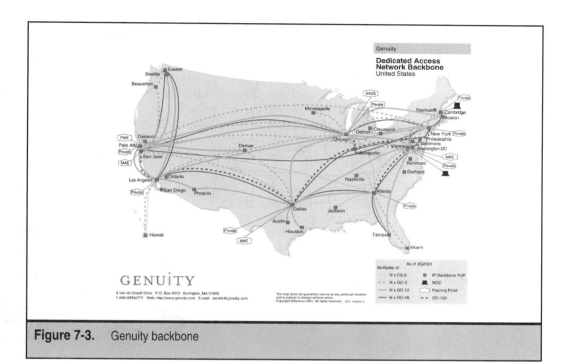

Figure 7-3.   Genuity backbone

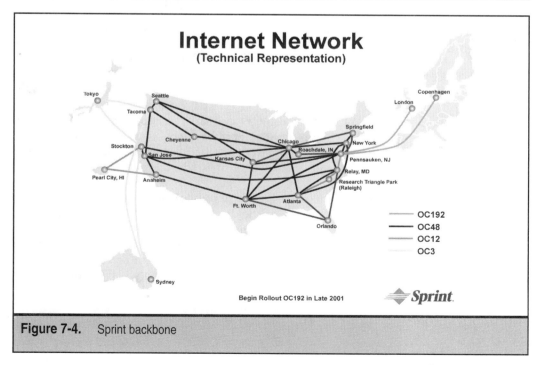

Figure 7-4.   Sprint backbone

entered the national ISP market, providing access to end users and establishing hosting and colocation facilities throughout their networks. AT&T, Qwest, Metromedia Fiber, and Cable & Wireless all offer ISP services, at least down to the level of small businesses, if not individual subscribers.

The benefits of using backbone providers as your ISP are obvious—better reach, better network, better range of services. The caveat is that most backbone providers tend to run their ISP businesses as separate and distinct from their backbone business units, so the benefits might not be all that great.

Backbone providers, to be considered such, will have a significantly large bandwidth connection across most of the regions they serve. These days, that means somewhere between OC-3 (155 Mbps) and OC-192 (10 Gbps). Often, these high-capacity pipes criss-cross the country, and maps of these networks tend to be colorful affairs.

The thing to notice in most of the backbone topology maps is that most providers serve the same cities, that is, their circuits all seem to terminate in the same cities across the countries they serve. There are several potential reasons for this. One, they're using each other's lines, that is, one is leasing from the other, perhaps different lambdas off the same DWDM circuit. Or, the fiber between those two cities was laid more or less around the same time and runs through the same conduits with the other carrier's fiber strands. Or, most probably, these metro areas have large potential customer bases that need to be served, and the provider needs to terminate there to dump off local traffic. How this is done is covered in the next two sections.

NAP

A subscriber attempting to access a provider's web site has no way of knowing where his requests are going to or coming from. At its heart, CDNs are an attempt to ensure the subscriber never has to sit there, drumming his fingers, thinking about it.

In the ideal circumstance, the distance from subscriber to provider is short. More realistically, this would mean the provider is located in the subscriber's network or, at the very most, somewhere in the same ISP. Most large ISPs have numerous content providers as customers, so this isn't as unusual as it might appear. The problem is that if the targeted site were off the ISP's network, getting to it might not be as straightforward as you would hope. If an ISP is a city-state of the Internet and backbone providers are the roads, then NAPs are the places those roads cross. Without NAPs, there is no way to get from one ISP to another.

This is a two-edged sword. With only a couple of public NAPs, this could lead to odd traffic patterns. As we just discussed, if the provider and the subscriber are on the same ISP, there are few architectural reasons why content couldn't be retrieved. When the networks are different, the NAP will be the bridge between them, even if the NAP happens to be significantly far away from the two endpoints. A subscriber in Toledo, connected to ISP #1 attempting to get to a web site located in a co-lo facility also in Toledo, but connected to ISP #2, might have get there by way of Chicago. Not ideal, but without the NAP, the connection might not have been possible at all.

Originally, there were four public NAPs, or exchange points (EP). MCI WorldCom operates the NAP in Washington, D.C. (http://www.mae.net), Sprint the NAP in New Jersey, and SBC the NAPs in San Francisco (http://www.pacbell.com/Products_Services/Business/ProdInfo_1/1,1973,146-1-,00.html) and Chicago (http://nap.aads.net/ main.html). WorldCom added another in San Jose (MAE-West) and many more have sprung up worldwide. Backbone providers and National ISPs would connect to these facilities and arrange to connect to each other in some sort of peering agreement (discussed in the next section). Places where these sorts of arrangements are made available to one and all are called *public peering points*. Alternatively, ISPs have of late begun to adopt a more restricted approach, *private peering*, so the ISPs can restrict who it connects to and attempt to gain further control over its internetwork routes.

The physical layout of NAPs can vary from NAP to NAP. It can be as interesting as a *provider hotel*, where several dozen backbone providers are present in a single facility with a variety of high-speed and very-high-speed connections pumping into a single or small set of high port density switches or routers, such as a big Juniper M160. On the other hand, NAPs can be simple, existing within one of a backbone provider's POPs, and consist of a Fast Ethernet run into a common layer-2 switch. The types of allowable connections also vary from NAP to NAP, but public NAPs tend to require fast, high-capacity links. The connection technologies are a mix of LAN and WAN standards, including FDDI, Fast Ethernet, Packet-Over-SONET (POS), Frame Relay and ATM. While ATM and POS over OC-48 (and OC-192) have a higher bandwidth, Gigabit Ethernet (GigE) interfaces are much cheaper, so GigE is slowly phasing out these other technologies.

The problem with NAPs is a function of the success of the Internet itself. Given only a relative handful of NAPs, and thousands of backbone and access providers, the specter of a problem arises. All these ISPs require interconnection to serve their customer bases; this requires a NAP. The possibility of overcrowding the NAP becomes a real problem, and the sheer volume of traffic forced through these exchange points becomes truly staggering. Traffic delays become inevitable as the NAPs become the biggest bottleneck on the Internet.

The proliferation of private NAPs (PNAP) has been in response to some of these problems (see Figure 7-5). Instead of dragging a long-haul circuit to a public NAP and routing all off-net traffic through it, it might make more sense to find local places to offload local traffic. This would allow more direct routing and more efficient network traffic handling, instead of dumping more and more traffic on the increasingly congested NAP. Carriers arrange for EPs whenever a direct financial and engineering benefit exists (cheaper than long-hauling to a public NAP; fewer hops to a local destination). PNAPs, typically being by-invite-only, can be implemented anywhere there's equipment for the crossover, so quite a few of these peer-to-peer EPs occur within the already-built POPs of one of the carriers. Conversely, locating a POP wherever there's a PNAP makes good sense. Subscribers of ISP #1 can get shunted off to their destinations in ISP #2 almost immediately if they connect through a POP at a PNAP for ISP #1 and ISP #2.

Note, some confusion exists as to the difference between a public exchange and a private one. For marketing reasons, then, many public exchanges are called private, and

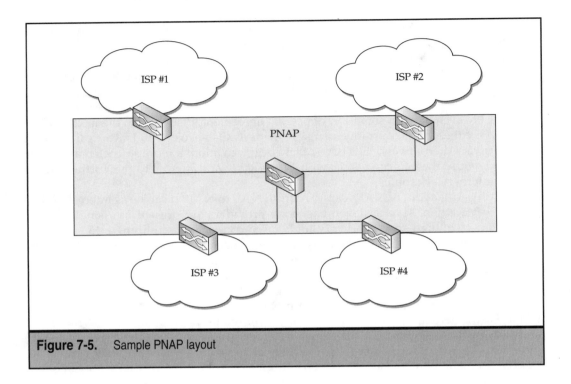

Figure 7-5. Sample PNAP layout

some private exchanges, public. The primary distinction is there are only a few NAPs—everything else is a PNAP. *PNAPs* are, numerically, exchanges between local carriers for the purpose of optimizing local traffic flows. *NAPs* are, by tradition and design, the only other place where traffic is exchanged between providers.

However, several other interesting approaches to PNAPs have been implemented, both for fee and for free, completely blurring the lines between public and private. All are public in the sense that if you can afford to, you are welcome to connect. All are private in the sense that they aren't a traditional NAP. Some require openness in business dealings, discouraging or even forbidding nondisclosures with respect to the peering arrangements made there. Some are more hands-off, having no stance whatsoever to the dealings among the actual providers connecting there.

Cooperative PNAPs, such as BNAP (http://www.Baltimore-nap.net), and SIX (http://www.altopia.com/six) are fee-free, though costs might be associated with racking a router in the former, and running cable in the latter, and possibly a nominal "donation" for upkeep. These PNAPs were created with the express purpose of enabling intelligent routing in the Internet and avoiding the remote-NAP problem. Handoffs are accomplished via 10/100 Ethernet through relatively simple, low-end Cisco layer-2 switches. These cooperatives are basically NAPs, but suited to metropolitan areas instead of regional ones. A partial list of the public exchange points is maintained at the Exchange Point web site (http://www.ep.net).

Commercial PNAPs are a bit more robust, as they must be, and survive by throwing quite a few value-added features on top of the basic promise of potential connectivity. These for-profit EPs claim their architectures provide access to many top-level backbones and ISPs; by connecting at their PNAP, the customer can gain one-hop routing to nearly any network one could want to get to. In addition, rack space, emergency tech support, physical security, and ease of use are touted as invaluable add-ons that should be part of any NAP—but, because they aren't, wouldn't you like to interconnect at a facility where they are?

InterNAP (http://www.internap.com) is a commercial PNAP provider that specializes in colocation and hosting. The idea is, connect to/host with InterNAP because InterNAP is connected to everybody else, a sort of one-to-many relationship. Hence, no matter what network you want to get to, you are only one hop away. InterNAP has a significant client list, so now has the clout necessary to get special treatment from the other backbone providers and can pass that on to its customers. InterNAP advertises that each of its connection points is fully redundant (including hot-spares) and practically guarantees connectivity, regardless of the problems any single backbone provider might experience. Its offering rounds out with dedicated, on-site tech support 24×7. InterNAP has service points all across the United States, Europe, and Japan.

ICS Network Systems (http://www.bigeast.net) is another PNAP provider, located on Long Island, New York. ICS's claim to fame is its proximity to one of the largest backbone providers in the United States, AT&T. ICS advertises that its PNAP is zero hops away from AT&T's backbone—that is, its EP is within that backbone. Diverse connectivity options are available from Sprint and Digex. Colocation services are available, as are various network security options. More interestingly, ICS offers caching and server load balancing as options for its colocation service.

Metromedia Fiber Network (http://www.mfn.com/) is the parent company of both AboveNet and PAIX. *AboveNet*, before the acquisition, offered services similar to InterNAP, including colocation/hosting and one-to-many network connectivity. As part of MFN, its services now include the capability to lease space on or transit the MFN backbone, which has OC-48 connections within and throughout the United States and OC-192 connections overseas. MFN is also one of the largest metro fiber providers, with fiber rings in many major metropolitan areas. *PAIX*, which touts itself as "The Original Neutral Internet Exchange," is more along the lines of a cooperative PNAP in that PAIX isn't placing itself in a position to bias or leverage the peering connections one way or another—it is, in fact, "neutral" to such arrangements and simply provides the facility and 24×7 support for doing so.

In terms of congestion, there's significant value to PNAPs over the traditional public NAPs. Somewhere north of 80 percent of the traffic on the Internet travels through one or more of the WorldCom Metropolitan Area Ethernet (MAE) facilities. PNAPs help to alleviate some of that stress.

The EP, being the natural crossroads in the Internet, is a natural point for injecting CDN technologies. Even without a POP, an EP might offer the basic CDN services such as SLB (Chapter 9) and GSLB (Chapter 11), web caching (Chapter 8), application redirection (Chapter 13) and Bandwidth Management (Chapter 14). Again, remember, the idea is to get content and content services as close to the subscriber as possible; penetration into the EP is only one logical step removed from the POP. For the service provider, an EP is a traffic ingress point. Deploying web caching services at the EP adds yet another tool for eliminating traffic from the backbone.

Another driving factor behind adopting CDN technologies at the EP has to do with the way Internet routing works. Shortest-exit routing, as is used with BGP, requires that traffic egress the network to the target network at the earliest possible point. Even if staying on the network will provide significantly better performance. For example, both a backbone provider and a national ISP have a connection to a single POP off an EP. The backbone provider will most likely have a significantly higher bandwidth connection to that EP, for example, an OC-12, whereas the national carrier only has a T-3. If the two networks cross at an EP nearer to the source, the traffic will leave the backbone in favor of the national carrier's network because that network is the destination network, and shortest-exit routing will force the switchover (see Figure 7-6).

In such cases, deploying CDN technology in the EPs will be even more critical to decrease transit distances and optimize traffic flows.

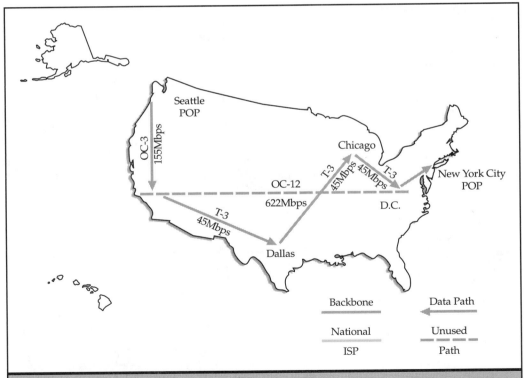

Figure 7-6. Shortest-exit routing

Peering

Peering is the term used to describe the relationship that providers negotiate to determine how traffic will be exchanged at an EP, but there isn't any formal, codified definition of what is and isn't peering. However, what seems to be common across usage is that this relationship is formal, and may or may not involve fees. There are three primary models for peering. The first is a *bilateral settlement*, where each provider bills the other based on use, and actual payments are determined based on the imbalance of traffic. A variation of this is a *multilateral agreement*, where each ISP executes a single agreement with a PNAP, and gains access to the other networks via the PNAP operator. The second model involves transit, where one provider pays another to carry its traffic, usually across a backbone. The third is called Sender Keep All (SKA), where no billing occurs for the exchange of traffic. This last is more properly called peering in the more general sense of the term peer and, for the sake of clarity, we'll use the term in that sense here. The actual benefits of peering are technical and are discussed in some detail in the previous section. From a technical standpoint, peering is accomplished via some physical connection and setting up BGP. The requirements for peering typically include some hardware connection specification, BGP-4, and an ARIN-assigned ASN.

The parties that generally engage in any of these arrangements are of three not terribly distinct types: Tier-1 ISPs, or backbone providers; Tier-2 ISPs, or national providers; and Tier-3, which are the regional ISPs. The requirements for peering generally depend on which of the three, in combination, are involved. Tier-1 providers generally peer freely with each other, as do Tier-2 providers. The relationship between Tier-2 and Tier-3 is almost invariably one of transit, where the regional carrier pays the national. The relationship between Tier-1 and Tier-2 is more complex.

Peering has become something of a snobby Internet club. Large-scale backbone providers such as WorldCom, Cable & Wireless, and Genuity have all become less and less willing to peer freely with smaller service providers. Their reasoning is more business oriented than engineering driven, namely, their infrastructure costs are considerable and required for sustained growth. Providing free access across that infrastructure, then, is unsound business practice. However, there are exceptions. When a Tier-2 or Tier-3 provider has infrastructure in a region desirable to the Tier-1 provider, peering might be implemented to off-load off-net traffic in an expeditious manner. Or, when the provider finds it exchanges significant (that is, roughly equivalent) amounts of traffic with another particular ISP, it will make sense for those two networks to peer.

"Roughly equivalent" traffic exchange is another tricky concept to pin down, but roughly what is meant is the following. Each network, if it has users, generates traffic. These user requests are then sent out to some destination. The destination then, in turn, sends back whatever is requested. The requests themselves are more or less inconsequential, as, typically, they are only a few, small packets. The return traffic is the problem. One little request can start a flood for a response. The flood adds up in terms of sourcing traffic. If two Tier-1 or Tier-2, or a Tier-1 and Tier-2 provider discover there's an equal amount of responses going to each other's networks, then peering will most likely be implemented. Local ISPs tend to accept more traffic than they generate. Co-lo providers tend to generate more than they accept. ISPs that are both, which is the current trend, can both send and receive prodigious amounts of traffic.

Backbone providers have come up with a variety of minimum infrastructure requirements for a given provider to be eligible for a SKA-style peering relationship (see Table 7-1). The most interesting requirement is the number of public NAPs at which the candidate has already established a peering connection. With this one requirement, the backbone provider is attempting to ensure that the regional carrier isn't simply getting a free (or at least, dramatically cheaper) ride across its expensive backbone.

The problem with peering and, more specifically, the withholding or conversion of a peering relationship into one with more of a client feel, is the criteria for the decision. Notably, there don't seem to be any hard-and-fast rules. Prima facie, this isn't a big deal, until you consider who the players are. When in the context of a relationship between a Tier-1 and a Tier-2 provider, this becomes a big deal. Tier-2 providers have nationwide networks and, in some cases, a backbone of their own. However, if cut off from their Tier-1 provider, the Tier-2 provider then becomes an island outside of the Internet as a whole. More subtly, if the relationship becomes bilateral or transit-oriented, the client then could pay enormous sums just to provide access. If that same Tier-1 provider then chooses to peer with a competitor, the advantage goes to that competitor for not having to pay the interconnection fees. The power, then, is in the hands of the Tier-1 provider and, with no standards to require a Tier-1 network to peer with a Tier-2 network, the possibility arises for anticompetitive and possible monopolistic practices. This is a worry, especially because all those that peer with Tier-1 providers are required to sign a nondisclosure agreement. Even worse, the ISPs that peer with Tier-1 providers aren't disclosed and neither are the terms for any peering arrangement made with a Tier-1 provider. In the last five years, there has been a tremendous amount of ISP consolidation; the number of Tier-1 providers has shrunk dramatically. These factors, and others, have led many to start discussing intervention by federal regulators.

Into the Looking Glass

While not terribly relevant, a looking glass is relatively interesting. Essentially, what a *looking glass* enables you to do is access a web-based interface to the user EXEC mode on a router running Cisco IOS. What makes it interesting is these are core Internet routers, running in various backbones and EPs worldwide.

The common commands allowable are

access-list	bgp	bgp summary	environmental
flap-statistics	mroute summary	ping	trace

This enables a network administrator to run trace routes and pings to a particular network or network device (for example, the one they're administering) from just about anywhere in the world. Further, the looking glass can be used to see if the network they want advertised actually is advertised. This is an amazing troubleshooting tool.

The web site is called Traceroute (http://www.traceroute.org). One of the sites listed therein (http://nitrous.digex.net) is a looking glass into the MAE-East and MAE-West

Backbone Provider	Web Address	ASN	Reqs Min Vol	Max. Traffic Ratio	Peer BW	Backbone	Min NAPs
Genuity	http://www.genuity.com	1	1 Mbps	~1:1	?	155 Mbps	3
UUNet/WorldCom	http://www.uu.net	701	150 Mbps	1.5:1	OC-12	OC-12	4
Cable & Wireless	http://www.cw.com	3561	45 Mbps	2:1	OC-3	OC-48	4

Table 7-1.   Backbone Peering Requirements

facilities itself. While the looking glass won't let you do a full **show bgp** (it gives the following error: "A full BGP table dump would cause too much stress on the router and this machine"), a summary is also quite interesting and tells you how many routes the router knows (over 100,000 networks), how many AS paths it knows (over half a million), how much memory it takes to hold it all (over 30MB), and how many peers it has (almost 300!). It's pretty neato.

Internet Routing with BGP

The BGP defined in RFC 1771, allows for the creation of loop-free interdomain routing between autonomous systems, where an AS is simply some group of routers that happen to fall under a single technical administration. ASNs are 16-bit numbers, with the resulting range from 0–65535. The range 32768–64511 is reserved by the IANA, and 64512–65534 are designated for private use, much as RFC 1918 sets out private IP address ranges. The basic topology is shown in Figure 7-7.

Routers within an AS can and do use one or more interior gateway protocols (RIP, OSPF, EIGRP) to exchange routing information inside the AS and an exterior gateway

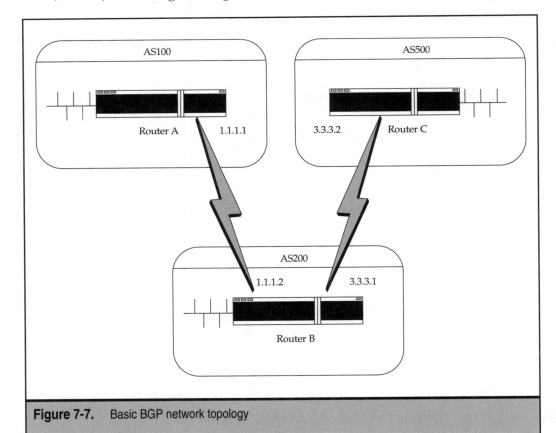

Figure 7-7.   Basic BGP network topology

protocol, such as BGP, to route packets outside the AS. Like some other routing protocols, BGP uses TCP as its transport protocol, with its own connection to TCP port 179. Two BGP routers form a TCP connection between one another and exchange messages to open and confirm the parameters governing the connection. Any two routers that have formed a TCP connection to exchange BGP routing information are considered peers or neighbors. Within an AS, routers running BGP processes are required to peer with each other (this is called internal BGP, or IBGP), but peering with external BGP routers is strictly optional (keeping the distinction, this is called EBGP). BGP peers initially exchange their full BGP routing tables. After this exchange, incremental updates are sent only as the routing table changes.

How BGP Works

When a router configured for BGP comes online in a network, either for the first time or after it has been power cycled, it tries to establish connections with any other BGP routers that might be adjacent to it. Once a connection has been established with neighboring routers, the initial router begins to download the entire routing table of each neighboring router. After this initial update, BGP routers needn't exchange the entire routing table unless a new BGP router joins and requests a full routing update. Subsequent updates will be much shorter and will be triggered by changes in the topology and periodic updates.

Updates in BGP are typically messages that indicate a change in the preferred path to reach a given IP segment. Once a router receives this update from a neighbor on a preferred path, it has a choice to update its own routing tables if it sees this new path is more efficient. If a BGP router makes any changes to its routing tables, it must subsequently propagate this information to all other neighboring routers to which it's connected. In turn, these neighboring routers must follow the same rule and decide on taking the update and, if they do, must propagate the changes, and so on and so forth.

As part of an exchange between BGP routers, a unique digital signature is attached to every packet exchanged between the routers. This signature is used for security purposes and makes it extremely difficult for intruders to masquerade as another BGP router and propagate false routing information. The BGP packet header is shown in Figure 7-8.

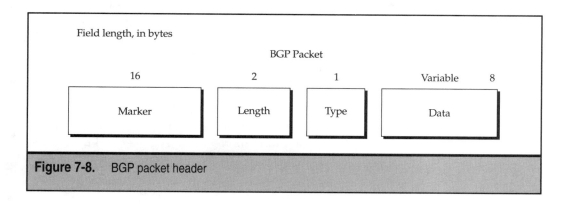

Figure 7-8. BGP packet header

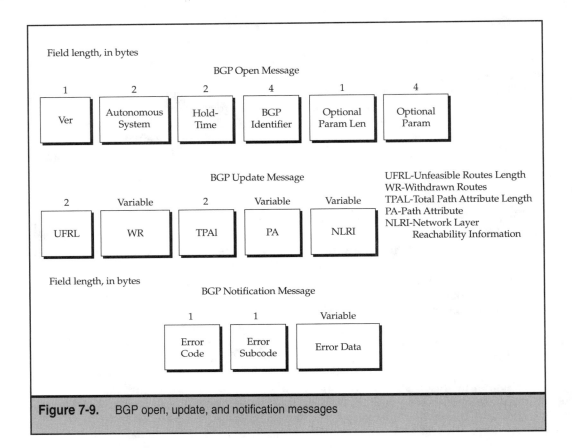

Figure 7-9.   BGP open, update, and notification messages

BGP routers exchange information using four types of messages (see Figure 7-9 above). These are as follows:

▼ **Open**   Used to establish the initial connection with a participating BGP neighboring router.

■ **Update**   Contains updates and changes to existing preferred paths. Update messages are sent out to neighboring BGP routers only and are sent when a change in topology occurs. The two types of updates are as follows:

   ■ **Withdrawn Routes**   This message is sent out when a route no longer exists and needs to be deleted from the routing table.

   ■ **Paths**   This message is sent out to indicate a new preferred route. This path consists of two pieces of information—the IP segment and the address of the next router in the path that's used to route messages destined for that address.

- ■ **Notification**   Used to indicate BGP errors, such as an incorrect or unreadable message received. Immediately following a notification message, the connection between the sender and receiver is closed.

- ▲ **Keepalive**   Sent out to each neighboring router every 30 seconds by every BGP router to let them know it's still active. The 19-byte Keepalive messages sent can be configured to exchange at different intervals, however, as long as both routers are configured with the same interval. If a router doesn't receive a Keepalive message from an adjacent router within a set amount of time, it closes the BGP connection with that router and removes it from its Routing Information Base, repairing what it perceives as damage to the network.

BGP routing messages carry the highest precedence of any traffic over the Internet, and each router that receives a BGP routing message gives it first priority over all other traffic. This is done to ensure that routing can take place under any circumstances. Without BGP fully operational, it would be difficult to get all nonlocal traffic off-Net, and could well result in isolating the AS from the rest of the Internet.

As part of every BGP router, a detailed database of information used is maintained to derive the routing table. This router database is called a Routing Information Base (RIB), and it contains three types of information:

- ▼ **Adj-RIBs-In**   This is the raw routing information received from neighboring BGP routers.

- ■ **Loc-RIB**   This is a processed version of the routing information derived from the Adj-RIB-In and is the routing table used by the router.

- ▲ **Adj-RIBs-Out**   This information is information the router chooses to send to neighboring routers in the form of updates.

The BGP algorithm, run after the router receives an update message from a neighboring router, consists of the following three steps for each IP address sent from the neighbor:

- ▼ **Update**   If the path information for an IP address in the update message is different from the information previously received from that router, then the Adj-RIBs-In database is updated with the newest information.

- ■ **Decision**   If it was new information, then a decision process is run that determines which router, of all those presently recorded in the Adj-RIBs-In database, has the best routing path for the IP address given in the update message. The algorithm for the decision process isn't mandated, and administrators can set local policy criteria, such as how long it takes to communicate with each neighboring router and how long each neighboring router takes to communicate with the next router in the path. If the best path chosen as a result of this decision process is different from the one currently recorded in the Loc-RIB database, then the database is updated.

- ▲ **Propagation**   If the decision process found a better path, then the Adj-RIBs-Out database is updated as well, and the router sends out update messages to all its neighboring routers to tell them about the better path. Each neighboring router then runs its own BGP algorithm and decides whether to update its routing databases, and then propagates any new and improved paths to its neighboring routers in turn.

One of the other important functions performed by the BGP process is to eliminate loops from its routing information. A *routing loop* occurs when a packet sent out by a router returns to the same router without ever reaching its destination. BGP addresses this problem in a simple way. Each routing entry in BGP contains a list of ASes that must be traversed to reach the specific destination. This list of ASes acts as an audit string of the path that must be taken to arrive at the destination. If a list ever contains an AS number twice, the BGP process knows immediately that a loop exists in the path and that entry is subsequently discarded.

The BGP protocol has been periodically revised and is now at version 4. Each version can support all earlier versions. Different routers can run different versions of BGP, so the protocol includes an interesting method for ensuring that different versions can communicate. When one BGP router tries to communicate for the first time with a second BGP router, the first router sends the second router an Open message, including the highest version of BGP it supports. If the second router can't support that version, it sends back a Notification message with the highest version it *can* support. The first router then opens a connection using that version, so the two routers can then communicate at the highest version of BGP they both support.

Some BGP Manipulation

To move packets efficiently across the Internet, a routing protocol must take into consideration the AS paths that must be traversed. As some ASes are larger than others and, therefore, require more time to traverse, charting an optimal path can be somewhat of a challenge. Although it can be impractical to implement, the path of packets as they transit peering points can sometimes be adjusted. Once manual intervention is placed into the routing decisions, however, optimization is often forsaken.

You can manipulate several attributes within BGP, aside from simply creating route-maps and filters to shunt traffic. Depending on the network topology configuration, the following attributes can be particularly useful AS_PATH, MULTI_EXIT_DISC, and LOCAL_PREF.

By itself, AS_PATH isn't terribly interesting (see Figure 7-10). A mandatory attribute in BGP routing updates, it includes the string of ASNs that represent a route to a particular destination. As routes are exchanged between BGP routers, the routers prepend their ASNs to the AS_PATH, to indicate they're a transit area to reach the destination. AS_PATH attributes can be manipulated manually, especially by the router injecting the route in the first place. By prepending its own ASN to the AS_PATH *before* advertising it, the router effectively *discourages* that path, provided another path exists to that AS with a shorter AS_PATH. Remember, with BGP, it's all about the shortest AS_PATH; the shorter the path, the more preferred the route. In the case of a large corporation with multiple egress points onto the Internet (or at least, onto an upstream ISP), prepending one of the two paths will bias the incoming traffic toward the path not prepended. To make this

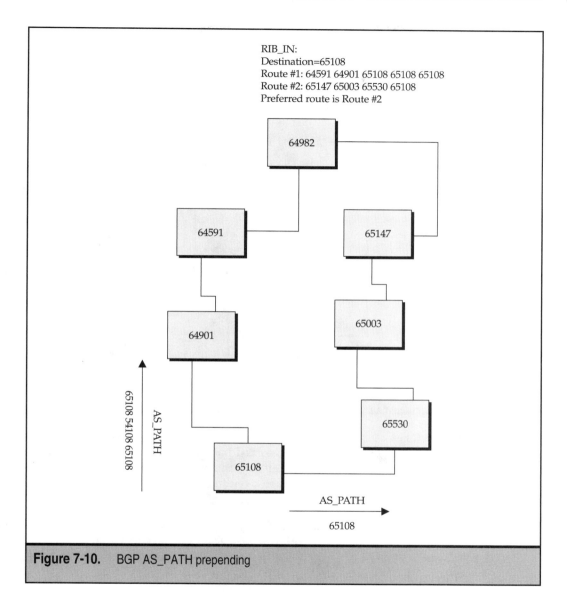

RIB_IN:
Destination=65108
Route #1: 64591 64901 65108 65108 65108
Route #2: 65147 65003 65530 65108
Preferred route is Route #2

65108 54108 65108

AS_PATH

AS_PATH

65108

Figure 7-10.   BGP AS_PATH prepending

even more explicit, network administrators will bias against one path by prepending the ASN multiple times. These prepended ASNs will be embedded into the AS_PATH attribute and sent out into the Internet, available for any and all to use.

MULTI_EXIT_DISC (MED) is an optional attribute that happens to be nontransitive, that is, if set, the attribute won't be passed along beyond the neighbor it's advertised to (see Figure 7-11). Essentially, MED works the same as AS prepending in that it tells the

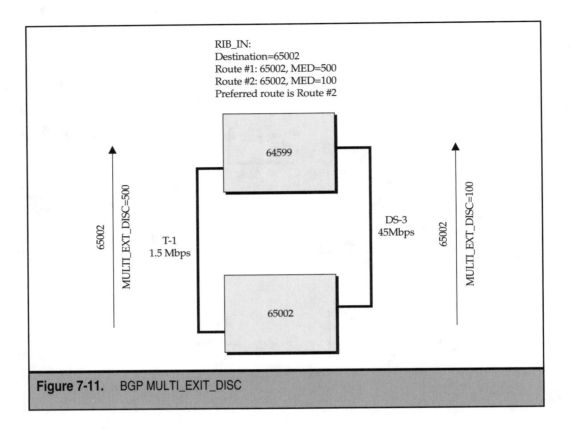

Figure 7-11. BGP MULTI_EXIT_DISC

neighbor which of two or more paths is preferred back into the AS that advertised it. Lower values are more preferred, where 0 (zero) means no-value or null, and not always. MED values are compared within an AS when deciding which route to take into an AS, when more than one choice occurs. MED, then, can be used to keep traffic from a hot-standby link or a link being used for specific application traffic, or to point traffic to a particularly fast/higher bandwidth link. MED values for routes to the same destination via different ASes aren't compared, by default, as they're meant only to be a hint from one single AS to another single AS as to how to get to it. If reasons exist to violate this rule, for example, the directly connected path is, in fact, a backup-only path, and then, in a Cisco router, the **bgp always-compare-med** command will enable this functionality. MED is important because by using MED, you can avoid shortest-exit routing (see the previous) but, note, not all providers support MED, or derive or interpret the MED values in a systematic way. Your provider can help you with this.

LOCAL_PREF, like MED, is another optional attribute included in BGP updates for a particular route (see Figure 7-12). Unlike MED, LOCAL_PREF doesn't get communicated beyond the AS. As its name implies, LOCAL_PREF is relevant only to routing decisions within the AS itself. LOCAL_PREF is intended to help discriminate between multiple paths to the same destination and bias in favor of the one with the highest LOCAL_PREF value. In other

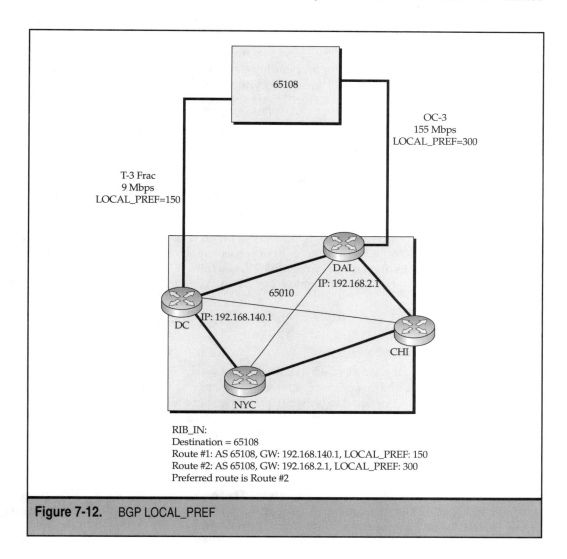

65108

OC-3
155 Mbps
LOCAL_PREF=300

T-3 Frac
9 Mbps
LOCAL_PREF=150

DAL
IP: 192.168.2.1

65010

IP: 192.168.140.1

DC

CHI

NYC

RIB_IN:
Destination = 65108
Route #1: AS 65108, GW: 192.168.140.1, LOCAL_PREF: 150
Route #2: AS 65108, GW: 192.168.2.1, LOCAL_PREF: 300
Preferred route is Route #2

Figure 7-12. BGP LOCAL_PREF

words, LOCAL_PREF defines the egress from the AS to some destination, when multiple egresses can be chosen. Again, this can help defeat shortest-exit routing behaviors.

Simple BGP Load Balancing

BGP will install only the best route to a destination into its routing table, even though it maintains up to six alternatives in its database. These EBGP alternatives won't be communicated to IBGP peers, however. In these cases, the router replaces the list of alternatives with itself as the next hop, and then advertises that route instead. Exceptions do exist. If a router learns of the same route via two different routers, for example, the routers in AS

65108 in learning about network 192.168.0.0/16, then the router will maintain two routes to that network, one via each viable path. These two routes are automatically load balanced, all else being equal (that is, no MED or prepending was set). This is done by round robin on a per host basis, so 192.168.1.1 will go across link 1, 192.168.1.2 will go across link 2, 192.168.1.3 will go across link 1, and so forth. This automatic load balancing is a feature of Cisco routers.

Cisco offers another option to attempt load balancing across BGP. If multiple routes are learned from the *same neighboring AS,* then the router can be configured to load balance across them. By default in such circumstances, the router will select the path with the lowest router-ID (usually, the configured loopback address) and install that as the preferred route. With *maximum-paths* configured, however, the router can maintain up to six alternative paths to a single destination.

Neither of these options is terribly sophisticated, and the use of both is somewhat restricted (namely, to Cisco routers). Chapter 9 deals with Load Balancing in more detail and Chapter 10 covers some High Availability protocols. For a deeper look into BGP, its use and configuration, you can't do better than Sam Halabi's *Internet Routing Architectures,* now in its second edition. Available from Cisco Press, this book is still the be-all, end-all BGP reference.

SUMMARY

This chapter has been an attempt to do the nearly impossible—put structure where none exists. The Internet is a hodge-podge of networks, some big, some small, some providing access, some transit, all connected together at innocuous but all-important transit points.

POPs are the quintessential on-ramp to the Information Superhighway. Most providers will have them all over the place, with the idea that more is, indeed, merrier. The more POPs, the more reach, the more reach, the more revenue. POPs are used by both regional and (inter)national ISPs, and, currently, no farther away than a local call to nearly every area code in the United States. Regional ISPs connect to their larger brethren, and the larger carriers connect to the backbone providers. These backbone providers are the ones with all the glass under the concrete of the major metro areas, across the long empty spaces in the nation's interior, and lying at the bottom of the oceans. These long-haul providers are largely the same ones that provide long-distance telephone service, which makes sense, because in many cases, voice traffic is going across the same strands! Regardless of the kind of service provider, all exchange their data with the others in some way or another. The primary method for doing so is via a NAP. These NAPs are increasingly and incredibly oversubscribed, which has led to private peering as the new model for connectivity, for good or for ill.

Even with this simple set of characters, the reality of the physical infrastructure that is the Internet is awesome to behold. The sheer number of cables and fibers interconnecting the world is easily beyond counting. All the backbone and metro topology maps combine with the LAN and WAN maps, to create something almost meaningless to the eye. Some interesting attempts have been made to try to make sense of it all, however. Caida (http://www.caida.org) has some of the most startlingly beautiful maps of the Internet ever created—and some are even available for sale! Another site with quite a few mind-bending maps is the Geography of Cyberspaces site (http://www.cybergeography.org).

Moving data across the Internet is no simple task. Moving data across the Internet *well* is even trickier. BGP is the de facto standard for interconnecting networks, and you've seen briefly what it is and does, and some of the things that might be done with it. While not intended to be definitive by any means, this chapter has put some of the basic concepts at your disposal.

REVIEW QUESTIONS

1. **What is the difference between an ISP and a backbone provider?**

   The difference between an ISP and a backbone provider is what they sell. ISPs sell access, backbone providers sell transit. Of course, backbone providers, in most cases, do both!

2. **Why are NAPs important?**

   NAPs are important because, without them, networks will be unable to exchange traffic, and all networks would become isolated from each other.

3. **What are the three types of arrangements network providers make to exchange data at NAPs?**

   The three types of arrangements network providers make to exchange data at NAPs are bilateral/multilateral, transit, and peering.

4. **What are two mechanisms administrators can configure in BGP to avoid shortest-exit routing?**

   In BGP, administrators can configure AS_PATH prepending, MED, LOCAL_PREF, route maps, and filters to avoid shortest-exit routing.

CHAPTER 8

Web Servers, Cookies, and Web Caches

OBJECTIVES

▼ Understand the relationship between HTTP requests and responses, and how web caches fit into that model

◼ Learn about the HTTP headers that control the cache's behavior

◼ Discover how the various components of caching fit into web infrastructure

◼ Understand cache-related protocols

▲ Learn how HTTP cookies work

In a land long, long ago, in a server farm far, far away, the world was introduced to web servers. The intent: make the sharing and referencing of physics papers a lot easier. But, then, two seemingly insignificant things happened. The fine people at the National Science Foundation decided it was time to open up the doors to commercial use of the Internet and this guy named Marc, who was working on a graphical web browser, decided to help start a company called Netscape.

The world flocked to the Web, as it was called by those who used it, because a few creative types realized that along with sharing physics papers, you could share all sorts of other (usually useless) information. As this happened, two interesting events occurred. The first was the desire for content providers to customize information on a per-user basis. And the second was legacy applications that called for centralized management could use the web browser, which has a cross-platform, highly available application interface.

The desire to use applications on web servers left us with some interesting problems:

▼ What is the interaction between web servers and their applications?

◼ How do applications retain the user's state using a protocol (HTTP) that is, by design, stateless?

▲ How does a web site effectively deliver content when the servers are pulled between the task of running applications and serving static content?

In this chapter, we examine all three problems and their corresponding solutions.

THE PROCESS OF FETCHING CONTENT

The Hypertext Transfer Protocol (HTTP) is a simple request/response system meant to solve two key problems inherent in other file transfer protocols, such as FTP. First, HTTP uses a simple text-based request format. This makes writing clients and proxies much easier, and it makes the protocol easy to expand on. Second, HTTP removes unnecessary state information between the server and client. The web server has no concept of a user session from click to click, thereby making HTTP easier to write. In fact, a simple web server could take only a few dozen lines of C code.

From a caching point of view, content comes in two flavors: dynamic and static. The important difference between the two is that *static content* can usually be cached, whereas *dynamic content* cannot be cached. The following section explores the difference between the two types.

Requesting Static Content

Let's examine a simple HTTP request from a web browser to a web server. Figure 8-1 visualizes the process for you. Stepping through the process, you see

1. The client begins by opening a TCP connection to the server. The server accepts the connection and waits for a request.

2. The client sends the following HTTP request:

```
GET /sample.html HTTP/1.1
Accept: */*
Accept-Language: en-us
Accept-Encoding: gzip, deflate
User-Agent: Mozilla/4.0 (compatible; MSIE 5.01; Windows NT 5.0)
Host: www.planetoid.org
Connection: Keep-Alive
```

The request ends with the sending of a blank line.

3. The server then processes the request and gets the /sample.html file off the disk.

4. The server sends an HTTP response header that looks like this:

```
HTTP/1.1 200 OK
Date: Mon, 03 Sep 2001 22:08:05 GMT
Server: Apache/1.3.14 (Unix) PHP/4.0.4
Last-Modified: Mon, 03 Sep 2001 22:05:22 GMT
ETag: "8b84c-1c-3b93fea2"
Accept-Ranges: bytes
Content-Length: 28
Keep-Alive: timeout=15, max=100
Connection: Close
Content-Type: text/html
```

A blank line then ends the response header.

5. The content itself is sent from the server.

6. The server closes the TCP connection, thereby ending the transaction.

And that's it. Not terribly complex, is it?

For additional detail on what the headers mean, see Chapter 4 or RFC 2616 (http://www.rfc-editor.org/rfc/rfc2616.txt).

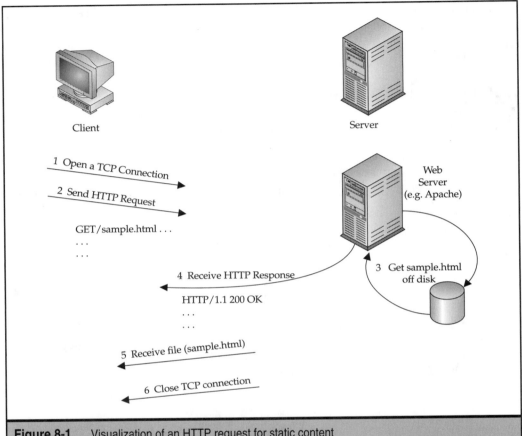

Figure 8-1. Visualization of an HTTP request for static content

Web pages are a series of independent objects that are requested separately. The first page that comes down is the HTML code itself, which tells the browser what text will be on the page and how it will be laid out. Part of this page description includes references to images and their location on the page. Each image referenced in the HTML code is requested from the web server using separate HTTP requests. Thus, a single web page might incur many HTTP requests.

Requesting Dynamic Content

Dynamic content is simply those web pages generated on-the-fly for a specific user, for a specific instance. An excellent example of this is the My Yahoo! service at http://my.yahoo.com. Every page generated requires that the server check its database, determine the format in which users want to see their content (for example do users want to see headline news before seeing their stock ticker?), and then generate the HTML necessary to render that page.

Because every page requires that the server execute a program, check a database, or otherwise do more work than simply reading a file from disk, dynamic content requires much more horsepower from your servers than static content does.

While the server handles dynamic content differently than a client does, a client doesn't see any difference between static and dynamic content. The HTTP requests generated are the same and the handling of the responses are the same.

Let's step through a dynamic request and see what the server is doing to process it. Looking at Figure 8-2, you can see the inside of a web server handling dynamic requests.

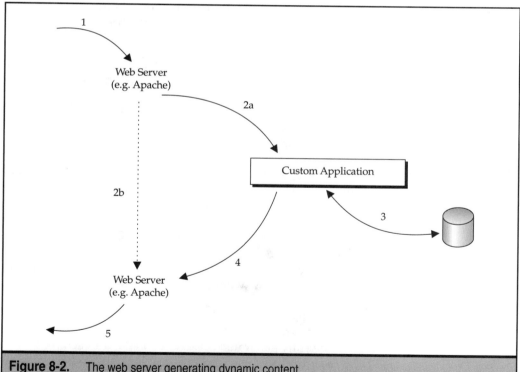

Figure 8-2.   The web server generating dynamic content

1.   The server receives an HTTP request from a client.

2a. The server calls on the custom application.

2b. The web server waits for the custom application to finish.

3.   The application (optionally) requests information from a database.

4.   The application generates HTML code and returns it to the web server.

5.   The web server forwards the resulting HTML to the client.

Pretty straightforward, isn't it?

CACHING

Another key design improvement HTTP made over protocols like FTP is it was designed to allow for the easy use of proxy servers and for proxy servers to be able to cache content. This has led to a proliferation of caching servers that fit in many places and can improve system performance in various ways.

In this section, two types of caching are discussed: client-side caching and edge caching. Fundamentally, both types of caching do the same work; however, they accomplish different things and, thus, have differing features that make them special from one vendor to another.

The Basics

For content to be cached, it must go through a proxy server. A caching proxy has the task of receiving a new HTTP request, checking to see if it's available in the cache, and, if it isn't, contacting the origin server and getting the content.

With respect to the transaction, proxy servers act a lot more like web servers than they do web clients. In that respect, the client-side behavior when using a cache doesn't change, but server-side responses and actions based on responses do change.

Let's begin by examining how proxies determine whether an object can be kept in cache.

Can an Object Be Cached?

HTTP headers have the option of including in them a special line that specifies whether the object being sent can be cached and, if so, what parameters should affect the cache's treatment of that object.

In their simplest form, there exists the Pragma: no-cache header. This header is compatible with the HTTP 1.0 spec and simply tells the proxy the content isn't to be cached. This is typically applied to dynamically generated content. To make the caching options more flexible, the HTTP 1.1 spec introduced the Cache-Control header. This header can be used by both requests and responses to dictate the behavior of caches.

HTTP requests can use the following values for Cache-Control:

Cache-Control Directive	Meaning
no-cache	Cache must refetch object from origin server.
no-store	Cache cannot save a copy of the response.
max-age=*delta seconds*	Client will only accept cached object if it's less than *delta seconds* old.
max-stale=*delta seconds*	Client will accept a cached object even if it has expired, but only if it's not more than *delta seconds* older than the expiration date.
min-fresh=*delta seconds*	Client will only accept cached object if the object has at least *delta seconds* remaining before it expires.
no-transform	Cache cannot alter the object in any way. This is most significant to proxies that perform some type of service, e.g., lowering the resolution of images for slow link downloads. Few proxies do this type of transform anymore.
only-if-cached	Cache should return the object if it's cached; however, it shouldn't contact the origin server if the object doesn't exist in the cache. If a cache receives this message and doesn't have the object, it should return with a 504 message (Gateway Timeout).

HTTP responses can use the following responses for the Cache-Control header:

Cache-Control Directive	Meaning
Public	Object can be cached.
Private	Object cannot be cached by any shared cache (browser caching is okay).
no-cache	Object cannot be cached by anyone.
no-store	Object cannot be put on to any permanent store by the cache.
no-transform	Object cannot be altered in any way by a proxy, e.g., the reduction of image quality for low bandwidth users is an example of a transform.
must-revalidate	Object cannot be sent after the expiration date, even if the client specifies a max-stale control. Object must be refetched from the origin server.
proxy-revalidate	Same thing as must-revalidate, except this applies only to proxy-based caches, not to browser-based caches.
s-maxage=*delta seconds*	Maximum object life as defined in *delta seconds*. This value can override the Expires header.

Expiring Content

Caches must have a mechanism for knowing when content has become stale. This is accomplished by using four tags: Cache-Control, ETag, Last-Modified, and Expires.

In the previous section, we explored the use of the Cache-Control header to force expiration or revalidation. For instance, a client could force the reload of a file by including within its request the header Cache-Control: no-cache. The server can control how (or even if) an object is cached by means of the same header, but with different values. For details, see the previous section that discussed all the values and their meanings.

When an object sent by a server can be cached, it sends along with the object an *ETag* header. The format of the header is

```
ETag: "hash-value"
```

where *"hash-value"* is the computed hash of the object being sent. This hash is like a checksum: if the object changes in any way, the hash value also changes.

The first time a client requests a static object from a server using the GET method, it receives an ETag for the object. The client can then keep this object and associated ETag in its local cache. If the user calls on a page that has the same object, the client can then send a HEAD method to request only the header of the object. The server's response will contain the most recent ETag value for the object, which the client can compare to its cached value. If the two values are the same, then the client knows the object hasn't changed, and it can safely use the cached object instead of having to fetch it from the server again.

Proxy caches can also use the ETag to determine if an object in its cache is current and whether it needs to fetch a specific object from the server again.

Another header used for content expiration is the *Last-Modified* header. The format of this header is as follows:

```
Last-Modified: Date
```

where *Date* is the full POSIX-compliant date and time the object was last modified. Similar to the ETag, the first request from a client to fetch a static object will include the Last-Modified header. The client can then use the HEAD method to get an object's Last-Modified date, so it can decide whether an object has changed. If the object has changed, the client can use the GET method to fetch the revised object from the server again.

Finally, the *Expires* header explicitly defines the time and date at which a cached object should be considered stale. The format of this header is as follows:

```
Expires: Date
```

where *Date* is the full POSIX-compliant date and time the object should be considered stale. If an object in a cache isn't stale, the cache needn't contact the origin server to validate whether the object has changed yet. Thus, if your web server has static objects that don't change often (such as company logos, and so forth), be sure to configure your web server to generate Expires headers for these objects. This is so both browser caches and any proxy caches along the path can cache the object and avoid the bandwidth incurred with validation processes.

Invalidating Content

Some HTTP methods exist for which caching simply doesn't make sense. Specifically, these methods are PUT, DELETE, and POST. In each of these methods, the cache must pass the request to the origin server because it will cause the origin server to perform some content-changing action.

Should a proxy cache have the URI that's being acted on by these content-changing methods, the cache should immediately invalidate the content if it has a local copy. For example, if a server-side CGI script generates content that can be cached, a proxy cache can keep a local copy of its output. If a client sends a POST method to that CGI script, the result of the script might change and, thus, the cache must invalidate its copy as it forwards the POST to the origin server.

Transparent vs. Nontransparent Caching

Proxy caches require the TCP connection to be *terminated* at the cache. This means the cache will accept the TCP connection on behalf of the server, and then, if necessary, generate a new TCP connection to the server. The server will see the connection as having originated from the cache's IP address.

In *nontransparent caching,* the client explicitly addresses the proxy cache as the destination IP. If the cache doesn't have the content, the cache must know the IP address of the origin server from which it can get the content. Depending on whether the cache is a forward or reverse proxy cache, the configuration for this is different. (See the following section titled "Forward vs. Reverse Proxy Caching"). Figure 8-3 shows this relationship.

In *transparent caching,* the client addresses the destination server. The proxy cache is configured to accept connections for any destination IP, thus the client thinks it's talking to the server. If the proxy cache doesn't have the necessary content, it fetches that content from the origin server automatically to fulfill the client request. Figure 8-4 shows this relationship.

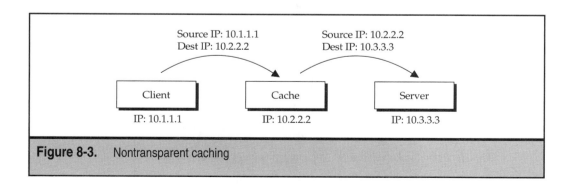

Figure 8-3.   Nontransparent caching

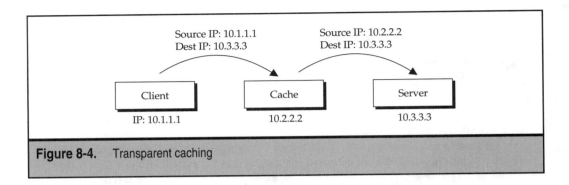

Figure 8-4. Transparent caching

Forward vs. Reverse Proxy Caching

Caches currently come in two flavors: forward caches and reverse proxy caches. Each of these uses the same fundamental technology; however, each cache differs in the details in its deployment and the types of requests for which it optimizes itself. This section covers what each of these technologies is and how each differs from the other.

Forward Proxy Caching

The original intent with proxy cache was to make client-side content delivery faster. The assumption was that latency on the Internet was significant enough to justify the use of caches, and the bandwidth savings for ISPs could be enormous. This method of caching is called *forward proxy caching*, or simply *forward caching*.

Figure 8-5 shows forward caching in action.

Let's go through the steps:

1. The client makes the first request for the object. The cache receives the request.

2. The cache finds it doesn't have the content requested and forwards a request to the origin server.

3. The origin server returns the content back to the cache. If possible, the cache stores the object.

4. The cache returns the object to the client.

5. At some future time, the client requests the same object again. The cache receives this request.

6. Seeing it has the object, the cache immediately returns the object to the client.

Forward proxy caches are typically configured to be transparent. This allows sites such as ISPs not to have to make any changes on the customer PC. Nontransparent forward caches require the client browser to be configured to use a proxy cache. In doing this, the browser always contacts the proxy server directly; however, it changes the

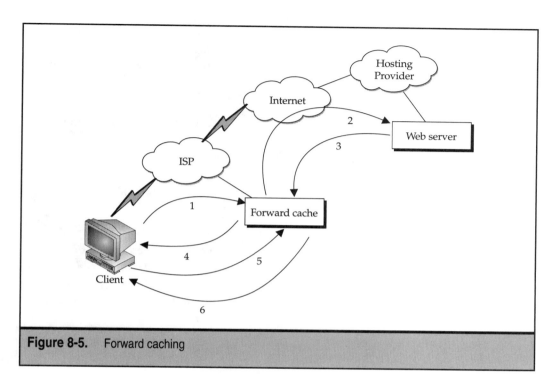

Figure 8-5.   Forward caching

method, so instead of referring to a URI, it refers to the URL. This lets the proxy server know what origin server it should contact. The following is an example of this.

```
GET http://www.clickarray.com/ HTTP/1.0
Accept: */*
Accept-Language: en-us
Accept-Encoding: gzip, deflate
User-Agent: Mozilla/4.0 (compatible; MSIE 5.01; Windows NT 5.0)
Host: www.clickarray.com
Proxy-Connection: Keep-Alive
```

Reverse Proxy Caching

As servers moved to dishing out more dynamic content, administrators found a lot more servers were needed to handle the same amount of traffic. Intermixed into that dynamic traffic, however, is still a good deal of static traffic. Logos, icons, navigation maps, and so forth still needed to be sent to clients.

To help deal with this, reverse proxy caching came into play. With reverse proxy caches, HTTP requests from clients are sent to the server-side cache. The cache attempts to service static requests out of its cache, thereby alleviating load from origin servers. Those requests that call for dynamic content are automatically passed on to origin servers.

In Figure 8-6, you can see the path of an HTTP request from client to server with a nontransparent cache in the middle.

Let's go through the steps of an HTTP request:

1. The client makes a request to the web site. The reverse proxy cache receives the request on behalf of the web server.

2. Seeing it doesn't have the requested content, the reverse proxy cache forwards the request to the server.

3. The server responds with the content. If the content can be cached, the reverse proxy cache keeps a local copy.

4. The reverse proxy cache returns a copy of the content to the client.

5. Another client makes a request for the same object for which the first client made a request.

6. Seeing it already has a copy of the object, the reverse proxy cache doesn't bother the origin server and automatically returns a copy of the content to the client.

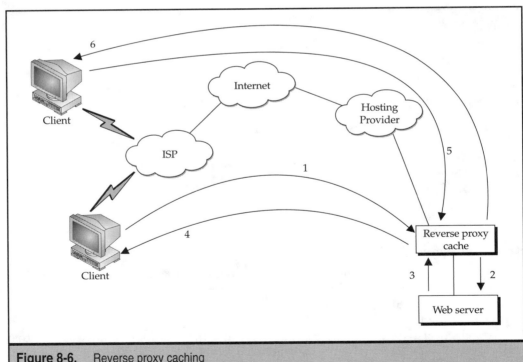

Figure 8-6.   Reverse proxy caching

Depending on how a site is configured, reverse proxy caches can appear in both transparent and nontransparent configurations. In transparent configurations, server load balancers (SLBs) are used to do *cache server redirection,* that is, the SLB redirects the HTTP request from the virtual IP to the cache that's configured to work in transparent mode. If the cache doesn't have the content, it requests the content from the origin server via the SLB, thereby allowing the request from the cache to be load balanced across the real server pool. (For additional information on SLBs, see Chapter 9.) The SLB can also be configured with content rules, so certain types of requests are never forwarded to the cache (for example, anything with /cgi-bin in the URL should go always go directly to a real server group).

In nontransparent configurations, the cache should be configured with a virtual IP of its own and set up to terminate all incoming HTTP requests. The cache can then check to see if it has the content and return it if possible. Otherwise, the cache should forward the request to an SLB, so the real server pool can be properly load balanced.

Some reverse proxy caches, such as those from ClickArray Networks (http://www.clickarray.com) and CacheFlow (http://www.cacheflow.com), now come with SLBs as part of their standard offering and, thus, eliminate the need for a separate load balancer in the network.

Edge Caching and Content Delivery Networks

As the Internet has grown, increased point-to-point latency has become an issue for sites wanting to provide a higher quality of service to their users. To deal with this problem, companies such as Akamai (http://www.akamai.com) and Speedera (http://www.speedera.com) have started services that consist of thousands of forward proxy caches that are topologically spread out across the Internet.

Subscribers to CDN services rewrite their content so references to static objects, such as images, point to a CDN cache. When a client wants to fetch the image, a DNS query is made to find the IP address of the CDN cache. The CDN's DNS servers differ from standard DNS servers because, instead of blindly returning an IP, they examine the client's IP address and, using proprietary technologies, determine which CDN cache cluster is topologically closest to it. The DNS server then returns the IP address of the appropriate CDN cache cluster, and the client makes a request for the content from there.

Because the cache clusters are topologically closer, their respective latencies are much lower. This results in the client having a better web experience, which can result in more repeat visitors to a web site. A web operator's dream. . . .

In addition to providing a better response time to a client, the distribution of web traffic across thousands of forward proxy caches translates to reduced load on origin servers. Depending on your site architecture, the reduced load and improved performance can make the steep per-megabit price offered by CDNs worth the money.

The CDN DNS query doesn't reply blindly with an IP address but, in fact, checks the originating IP address and tries to locate the closest CDN Servers. The questions are what method will it use and how does it work?

The answers to the previous questions can help the intended audience understand the benefit of using CDN over any other cache technology.

"Akamaizing Content"

In the way the term *xeroxing* became a synonym for photocopying, the term *akamaizing* has become a synonym for automatically rewriting content so it's CDN-aware. Typically, web sites go through a manual akamaization process where they convert all their existing content, so it becomes CDN-aware. These web sites must also update their web applications, so the applications generate CDN-aware HTML code, and the production of new HTML must undergo an additional step of being made CDN-aware. When all is said and done, the process of making content CDN-aware can be a time-consuming one, despite the automation tools offered by companies like Akamai and Speedera.

To assist with this problem, some reverse proxy caches now offer the capability to rewrite content dynamically, so it becomes CDN-aware without any additional work. The ClickArray Networks (http://www.clickarray.com) Array series sports a feature that allows content to be rewritten for any CDN. The content can then be stored in its internal cache for future delivery. Similar to the ClickArray solution, the CacheFlow Server Accelerator series allows content to be dynamically rewritten; however, this only works for the Akamai network. Both solutions are then able to deliver the rewritten content from their cache, thereby reducing even more load on origin servers.

Let's look at a quick example for www.example.com. Assuming no CDN, a web page might look something like this:

```
<html>
<center><h2>My Vacation<hr></h2></center>
<img src="pic1.jpg">
<img src="pic2.jpg">
</html>
```

Now, assume the content is rewritten for the Akamai network. The resulting content would look like this:

```
<html>
<center><h2>My Vacation<hr></h2></center>
<img src="http://a9.g.akamai.net/6/9/21/000/www.example.com/pic1.jpg">
<img src="http://a9.g.akamai.net/6/9/21/000/www.example.com/pic2.jpg">
</html>
```

Speedera, on the other hand, uses a slightly different method of rewriting content. A Speedera-ized site would look like this:

```
<html>
<center><h2>My Vacation<hr></h2></center>
<img src="http://cdn.example.com/pic1.jpg">
<img src="http://cdn.example.com/pic2.jpg">
</html>
```

Notice, in both cases, the resulting rewrite was essentially inserting a static string before the pic1.jpg and pic2.jpg filenames. The specific prefix changed from CDN to CDN (thus, making them incompatible) but the underlying principle remains: have the web client do a DNS lookup against the CDN DNS server, so the CDN can redirect the client to the closest cache cluster.

Cache Interception

Depending on your site architecture, web traffic can be a subset (albeit, a large one) of the total traffic that's going over your links. Thus, putting web caches off to the site is often necessary, so non-web traffic can be forwarded correctly. To accommodate this, you can use *cache interception*, which is a method of network design that allows a TCP-aware router or switch to redirect traffic to a cache without disrupting normal traffic flow.

Cache interception can currently be done by two methods. The first is by port redirection on layer 4-aware switches or Unix-based routers. The second is via the Web Cache Coordination Protocol. Both methods are examined in this section.

Port Redirection / L4 Switch Redirection

The concept behind port redirection is a simple one. Requests passed through a Unix router or server load balancer can be redirected to a cache. If the cache cannot service the request, the cache passes the connection back, so the request can be properly forwarded to the origin server.

The key difference for requests forwarded through the cache is the source IP address changes from the client to the cache's, thus allowing the cache to see the content as it's returned from the server. The cache then keeps a copy of the content (if the HTTP headers allow it to do so) and forwards the content back to the client.

Figure 8-7 visualizes this process.

1.   The client sends the packet destined to the web server.

2a. The packet is *not* HTTP, the packet is directly forwarded.

2b. The packet *is* HTTP, the destination is changed to the cache.

3.   On a cache-miss, a new HTTP request is made to vip1. Because the request originates from the cache, the redirection doesn't happen.

4.   The request is load balanced and forwarded to a real server.

Using a Unix-based router (such as a PC running Linux) is often a good solution for a small- to medium-sized business that wants to offer Network Address Translation (NAT), firewalling, and transparent caching to its users. Placed in conjunction with a Squid cache, you have a great solution for providing a forward cache solution for your users. (Squid, placed on a beefy PC costing no more than $1,500, should give you enough throughput to keep up with 3-4 T1 links.) For configuration details, visit the Squid homepage at http://www.squid-cache.org. For specifics on cache redirection for multiple operating systems (including Linux), read section 17 of Squid's FAQ.

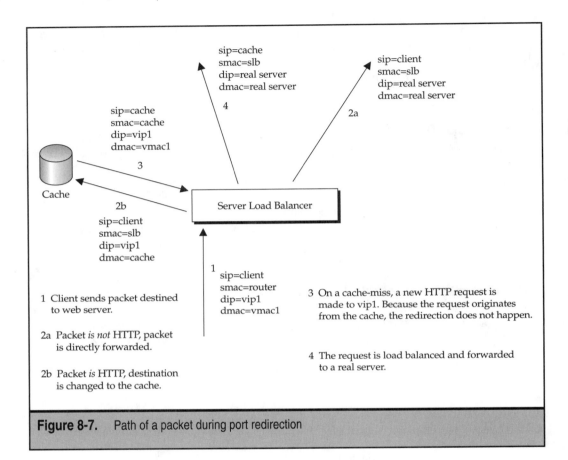

sip=cache
smac=slb
dip=real server
dmac=real server

sip=client
smac=slb
dip=real server
dmac=real server

4

2a

sip=cache
smac=cache
dip=vip1
dmac=vmac1

3

Cache

2b

Server Load Balancer

sip=client
smac=slb
dip=vip1
dmac=cache

1

sip=client
smac=router
dip=vip1
dmac=vmac1

1 Client sends packet destined
   to web server.

2a Packet *is not* HTTP, packet
   is directly forwarded.

2b Packet *is* HTTP, destination
   is changed to the cache.

3 On a cache-miss, a new HTTP request is
   made to vip1. Because the request originates
   from the cache, the redirection does not happen.

4 The request is load balanced and forwarded
   to a real server.

Figure 8-7.   Path of a packet during port redirection

Using an SLB to provide port redirection is a better choice in higher throughput environments or in server environments where multiple web servers need to be load balanced. Almost all SLBs provide this feature with the exception of those balancers that integrate a reverse proxy caching solution (for example, ClickArray Networks). If you're in a forward caching environment (for example, an ISP), consider load balancers from Nortel (previously Alteon) or Cisco (previously Arrowpoint). Both vendors provide web cache redirection as part of their standard layer 4 server load-balancing solution.

Web Cache Coordination Protocol (WCCP)

The Web Cache Coordination Protocol (WCCP) came to life as a Cisco proprietary solution. Its intent was to allow its routers (normally layer 3 devices) the capability to redirect web traffic to caches it also made. Unfortunately, some limitations existed to this proto-col, namely:

▼   Redirection of TCP port 80 traffic only

■   Support for up to 32 caches, but only one home router

▲   Support for only a single services group

In the second incarnation of the protocol, Cisco went the standards route, thus allow-ing other caching and router vendors to interoperate with what became WCCPv2.

WCCPv2 expands on the idea behind port redirection in many ways. The first is the option to encapsulate packets and ship them to web caches via GRE tunnels. This allows web caches to exist outside the routers' broadcast domain (read: another subnet) and still properly handle redirected packets. All the web cache has to do is remove the encapsula-tion and inject the packet into its TCP stack. The TCP stack, configured as a transparent proxy, would properly terminate the connection and continue functioning like any trans-parent proxy.

The second major difference is WCCPv2 allows web caches to work with more than one router. Thus, in a network where many routers are connecting many networks, a cluster of caches could work, in theory, with all possible ways into and out of the network.

The third major difference is WCCPv2 allows for the web caches to turn down a request if it doesn't want to (or is too busy to) handle it. The router can then simply con-tinue forwarding the packet to the destination where the request can be serviced, albeit with a greater latency. This is in sharp contrast to port redirection, which forces the web cache to handle whatever load is thrown at it because the switch has no state information regarding any one connection.

The last major difference is the capability for routers to specify web caches based on some information in the packet. This method of web cache selection (also referred to as the *hash*) can be used so the same cache is referenced when working with the same web server. Doing this guarantees that if content gets cached once, subsequent requests from different clients will get a cache hit because they'll be directed to the same cache. The only threat to this feature is similar to the megaproxy problem, where a given web site could be large enough and busy enough that the traffic could overwhelm the web cache.

WCCPv2 Messages   *WCCPv2* is comprised of a series of messages serving specific requirements that are sent via UDP on port 2048. Four messages exist.

▼   Here I AM

■   I See You

■   Redirect Assign

▲   Removal Query

Let's step through what each of these messages means and what information it passes between the router and the web cache.

Here I AM

The *Here I AM* message is transmitted by a web cache to each router it wishes to work with. The transmission of this message allows the web cache to join the *service group*, that is, the group of web caches the routers can pass HTTP requests to. Each web cache must send this message once every ten seconds.

Within the message is a series of submessages that specify the following:

▼ Are the remaining packets in this transaction password protected? If so, the MD5 hash of the password is included.

■ Is the service being redirected well known? At press time, the only well-known service is HTTP. If the service isn't well known, a list of which TCP and UDP ports to redirect must be provided.

■ Which parts of the headers (IP address and TCP/UDP ports) are to be hashed, so packets either originating from or destined to the same place will always hit the same cache.

■ The identity of the web cache.

▲ A listing of what other routers and web caches are thought to be in the service group.

I See You

The *I See You* message is the response sent by the router to a web cache on receipt of a Here I AM message. If the Here I AM message was unicast, the corresponding I See You is unicast as well. Ditto with multicast.

The purpose of the I See You message is to allow the router to pass some information back to the web cache. The information within this packet is as follows:

▼ Are the remaining packets in this transaction password protected? If so, the MD5 hash of the password is included

■ A confirmation of services the router is passing to the web cache

■ The router's identity

■ The router's view of what web caches are in the service group

▲ The router's view of how HTTP requests are spread to all the web caches in the group

Redirect Assign

Once a web cache joins a service group, the group must elect a group leader. Although no well-defined protocol exists for this, the recommended method is by the members getting together and picking the web cache with the lowest IP address.

Once a web cache is elected, it must periodically send Redirect Assign messages to confirm the distribution of redirected packets from routers to web caches. If a router doesn't hear this message from a web cache for 50 seconds, the routers assume the network topology has changed and that their table telling them what web caches to redirect traffic to is invalid. This leads to the tables being flushed and forcing the web caches to rejoin the service group for that particular router.

The contents of the Redirect Assign packet are a subset of the I See You packet. These contents include

▼   The MD5 hash of the password (if one is being used)

■   A confirmation of services the router is passing to web caches

▲   Assignment information regarding which caches are getting what traffic

Removal Query

Each web cache is required to send the Here I AM message to the router every ten seconds. If a router doesn't hear from a member cache within 25 seconds, the router sends the offending web cache an explicit Removal Query packet, which, essentially, asks the web cache whether it wants to continue being in the service group. If the web cache does want to remain in the group, it must send back three Here I AM messages, each within one second of each other. If the router doesn't hear from the web cache within five seconds, the router will remove the web cache and announce this change during the next set of I See You packets it sends to the other web caches.

The contents of the Removal Query packet are as follows:

▼   The MD5 hash of the password (if one is being used)

■   A confirmation of the services the router is passing to web caches

■   The last IP address that sent a Here I AM message

▲   The IP address of the specific web cache being queried

WCCPv2 Forwarding Models   During the I See You message, the router tells the web cache what forwarding model it wants to use. A *forwarding model* is simply the method by which the packets will be redirected from the router to the web cache. Two models are available.

The first model comes from WCCPv1, which uses a GRE tunnel between the router and the web cache. When a packet in the router is tagged for redirection, it's encapsulated in a GRE tunnel and passed to the web cache. The web cache then must remove the encapsulation and inject the packet into its TCP stack. The nice aspect of using this method of forwarding is the web cache needn't be directly accessible to the router in the same way as the L4 redirection. The bad side to this model is overhead is incurred when encapsulating packets for transmission, which both the router and the web cache must deal with. On an already congested router, this can easily lead to dropped packets.

The second method is to use L4 redirection. This is clearly a faster method of redirecting packets, but comes at the expense of limiting what the network topology can look like. With GRE tunnels, web caches could, in theory, exist anywhere on a network, thus enabling service providers to unify their caching structure. The reality is, however, that most web caches end up adjacent to the router, thus eliminating the benefit from having the GRE tunnel.

Which is better? This depends on your needs in the network. If performance is the number one criterion for you, L4 redirection is a better choice. If flexibility is more important, use the GRE tunnels.

A Sample WCCP Configuration   Configuring WCCPv2 under IOS can be straightforward. Begin by logging into the router and entering enable mode. Once you are in enable mode, the following commands configure the router to redirect web-related packets without a destination of 192.168.196.51 to a cache:

```
Router# configure terminal
Router(config)# access-list 100 deny ip any host 192.168.196.51
Router(config)# access-list 100 permit ip any any
Router(config)# ip wccp redirect-list 100
Router(config)# interface Ethernet0
Router(config-if)# ip web-cache redirect-list
Router(config-if)# end
Router#
%SYS-5-CONFIG_I: Configured from console by console
```

Caching Products

Many caching products exist in the market today. Unfortunately, because of the rapid rate at which their feature sets evolve and performance numbers change, this chapter isn't the ideal place to cover their specifics or discuss marketing buzzwords. The following short list, however, should give you a starting point from which you can look into caches. Note, this list is a far cry from an exhaustive list of available caches, and the author highly recommends you do your homework before making any commitments. All of the cited numbers are based on marketing literature found on their respective web sites.

ClickArray Networks

The *Array 1000* from ClickArray Networks (http://www.clickarray.com) stands out among the caches because it's only meant as a reverse proxy-caching solution. Using only RAM for storage, the cache trades capacity for performance, which as a server-side cache only is something quite workable for most sites. Of course, this means it makes for a poor choice as a forward proxy or edge cache solution but, then again, that's not what its engineers had in mind when it was developed. What's unique about this cache is it's integrated with a sever load balancer, global SLB, SSL accelerator, content rewriter (Akamaizer), and firewall.

Peak Throughput	500 Mbps
Peak Requests/Sec	20,0000
Supports HTTP 1.1	Yes
Supports Streaming Media	"Early 2002"
Appliance	Yes

Cacheflow

Cacheflow (http://www.cacheflow.com) is a name well recognized in the world of caching, mostly for its work in forward proxy caches and edge caches. With the release of the SA-7000, Cacheflow has designed a product that's optimized for server-side reverse proxy caching. The SA-7000 uses a disk for holding content and sports an optional SSL accelerator and content rewriter (Akamaizer).

Peak Throughput	300 Mbps
Peak Requests/Sec	"Thousands"
Supports HTTP 1.1	Yes
Supports Streaming Media	Yes
Appliance	Yes

Network Appliance

Network Appliance (http://www.netapp.com) is well known for its network attached storage (NAS) devices, especially in the realm of corporate NFS servers. Network Appliance has applied its underlying disk technologies to make the Netcache C6100, a web cache that can be used as either a forward proxy cache or a reverse proxy cache.

Peak Throughput	155 Mbps
Peak Requests/Sec	"Thousands"
Supports HTTP 1.1	Yes
Supports Streaming Media	Yes
Appliance	Yes

Cisco Systems

Cisco Systems (http://www.cisco.com) rolled out a complete CDN suite that included the Cache Engine 590. The *Cache Engine* series from Cisco is designed to work in tight conjunction with the Cisco router family (in the case of the 590, requiring a Cisco 7000 class router). The cache uses a disk for storing content and has the unique feature of being part of a complete "roll your own CDN" suite of products.

Peak Throughput	25–40 Mbps
Peak Requests/Sec	Not stated
Supports HTTP 1.1	No
Supports Streaming Media	No
Appliance	Yes

Inktomi

Inktomi (http://www.inktomi.com) has been in the caching business for a long time and is now entering the CDN marketing with its own suite of tools for allowing customers to build their own CDNs. The Traffic Core cache can be used by its system as either a reverse or forward proxy cache. The cache is a software solution available for Solaris, Linux, Windows 2000, HPUX, and Irix. Because the cache is a software package, the system performance is dependant on the hardware platform on which the user deploys it.

Peak Throughput	Hardware-dependent
Peak Requests/Sec	Hardware dependent
Supports HTTP 1.1	Yes
Supports Streaming Media	Yes
Appliance	No

Volera

Volera (http://www.volera.com) is the Novell spin-off dedicated toward Internet infrastructure, specifically regarding caching. Like other caching vendors, Volera's Excelerator product is part of a larger CDN product offering. The cache can be configured as either a forward or reverse proxy cache, and it uses disk to hold content.

Peak Throughput	Not stated
Peak Requests/Sec	12,300
Supports HTTP 1.1	Yes
Supports Streaming Media	Yes
Appliance	Yes

ADDING STATE: HTTP COOKIES

During the design of HTTP, other file transfer protocols, such as FTP, were examined and compared. The decision was that one of the flaws of protocols like FTP is they require the server to maintain state. That is, the server must track what each user was doing from request to request. This requires a lot of server-side resources and brings the overall system performance down measurably.

Seeing that maintaining server-side state wasn't a good thing, HTTP was designed so each request/response pair was independent of one another. This made the server side much more streamlined, easier to implement, and able to handle greater loads than a single FTP server.

But there was trouble in paradise. As people turned to adding applications to the server side, the need for maintaining state became increasingly important. From the simplest need for maintaining whether a client had authenticated themselves to more complex features, such as shopping carts where the server had to remember what products were in the customer's cart, something was needed to maintain state.

Understanding "State"

Every application has a number of variables it must keep track of for what a user is doing in the program at any given time. Those variables, collectively, form the application's *state* information. In the context of HTTP transactions, the intent of clearly defining an application's state is so the application can give the client a tidbit of information when sending it back an HTML page. The client would then send this tidbit back to the server during the next click, so the server application could plug that information back into its variables and remember where it left off when dealing with the user.

The classic example of needing state information is with shopping cart applications. When a user wants to purchase something, the application sees a request has been made to put an item in the shopping basket. The system cannot uniquely identify the user at this time, however, so the application sends a tidbit of information back to the client to store. This tidbit of information is simply a list of those objects that have been added to the shopping basket.

When the user is ready to check out and pay for those items in his shopping basket, the system must be able to see what's in the basket, and then associate those items with the billing information provided by a user in a form. By having the client send the tidbit of information back, listing what objects are in the basket, along with the form containing the billing information, the shopping cart application can properly compute the total and bill the credit card. If the client didn't send the list of items in the cart back, the billing application would have nothing to bill!

Cookies

In the previous section, we discussed "tidbits" of information that get placed on the client's browser for maintaining state information. In the world of HTTP, these tidbits are called cookies. A *cookie* is simply some arbitrary information sent to the web browser from the web server stored as a name/value pair. Along with the name and corresponding value, a cookie includes information about which web sites can view the cookie and how long the cookie is valid.

Cookies are sent by web servers to browsers in HTTP response headers. When a client generates an HTTP request, the cookie information is placed in the HTTP request header and sent back to the site.

The Set-Cookie: Header

The format of the cookie is as follows:

```
Set-Cookie: NAME=VALUE; expires=DATE; path=PATH; domain=DOMAIN
```

where *NAME* is the name of the cookie, *VALUE* is the value being stored in the cookie (up to 4,000 bytes long). *DATE* is the date on which the cookie becomes invalid, stored in the format Tue 19-Sep-2001 12:03:00 GMT. Note, GMT is the only valid time zone that can be used in a cookie.

A cookie can be selectively sent to a web site. If the developer only wants to have a cookie sent to the /cgi-bin directory, she can set *PATH* as /cgi-bin. Thus, visits to other directories in the site won't result in the cookie being sent. In most cases, the root is specified, thereby causing the cookie to be sent on every click in a web site. For modem users on a web site, selectively sending cookies can make a great difference in the "user experience" arena.

To control which web sites can see a specific cookie, the developer setting the cookie can specify which Internet domain can receive a copy of the cookie. This is done via the *DOMAIN* setting. Browsers match *DOMAIN* to the tail end of the web site being browsed. If a match occurs, the cookie is sent. For example, if *DOMAIN* is set to acme.com, a user browsing www.acme.com, shopping.acme.com, and roadrunners.acme.com will transmit the cookie. If no *DOMAIN* is specified, the cookie is transmitted to every web site the user visits.

Optionally, the end of a Set-Cookie: header can include the phrase "; secure" to tell the browser the cookie should only be sent if the page it is contacting has been connected to via SSL.

The Cookie: Header

Once the cookie is sent by the server, the client keeps a local copy of it on disk. When the user clicks the site again, the browser automatically sends the cookie back to the server as part of the HTTP request. The cookie, as it's sent to the server, is formatted as follows:

```
Cookie: NAME=VALUE; NAME=VALUE
```

where the *NAME* and *VALUE* pairs are the same set in the Set-Cookie: header. Many cookies that need to be sent back to the site are done so in a single line, however, with each pair separated by a semicolon.

SUMMARY

In this chapter, you learned about the key issues in web cache deployment, web Cache Control, and HTTP cookies. Specifically, you learned

- ▼ The path of an HTTP request differs only in server path when it comes to dynamic versus static content. To a web cache, it's all just another HTTP object.

- ■ HTTP is a simple text-based stateless protocol.

- ■ The behavior of HTTP objects in a web cache is controlled by the request and response headers.

- ■ Web caches can exist either in path proxy solutions or out of path redirection solutions (L4 redirection, WCCPv2).

- ▲ HTTP cookies allow web applications to introduce state into what is otherwise a stateless protocol.

If you're interested in more details regarding the treatment of caching by the HTTP protocol, visit http://www.rfc-editor.org and read up on the HTTP 1.1 specification in RFC 2616. For more information regarding the WCCP protocol, read the WCCPv2 specification at http://www.ietf.org.

REVIEW QUESTIONS

1. **How does the Cache-Control header alter the behavior of a web cache?**

    The Cache-Control header is used by web servers to inform web caches on whether they should cache an object. The default behavior of a web cache (in the absence of a Cache-Control header) is to cache the object.

2. **When redirecting web cache requests, must the switch and/or router be aware of Layer 4 (TCP) headers? If so, why?**

    The switch and/or router must be aware of layer 4 (TCP) headers so that the TCP port field can be examined. Only if the TCP port field matches a preconfigured value will the switch redirect the request to a web cache.

3. **Under what condition will a WCCPv2-enabled router remove a web cache from its list of web caches?**

    If the web cache does not respond to Here I AM messages for 25 seconds and does not respond to Removal Query messages for an additional 5 seconds, the web cache is removed from the list.

4. **How does WCCPv2 redirect HTTP requests to web caches in other broadcast domains?**

   The router and web cache must use GRE tunnels.

5. **Should a Set-Cookie: header be cached by a web cache?**

   Yes. If the object was deemed cachable, the Set-Cookie: header should remain; otherwise, the object would not have the same effect on future receivers of the content. If the web site administrator wants unique cookies to be sent to each user, he should make sure that the object uses the Cache-Control header and mark the response as uncachable.

CHAPTER 9

Server Load Balancing

OBJECTIVES

▼ Define the scope and role of server load balancing (SLB)

■ Differentiate the technology applications for SLB

■ Identify the two primary solutions from Cisco and Nortel Networks

■ Examine what applications can be load balanced in Layer 3 - 7 of the OSI model

■ Explore the concept of virtual server group and virtual IP

■ Discuss the technical and business benefits of server load balancing

■ Describe the enterprise and e-commerce environments that benefit from server load balancing technology

▲ Explore some server load balancing scenarios and provide the step-by-step configuration required

In the past few years, the World Wide Web has grown from a speculative medium to a robust infrastructure that handles mission-critical business traffic. Industry pundits indicate that the number of e-commerce users over the Web increased to 142 million in 1998 and is forecasted to surpass 500 million by 2003. This increase in use is expected to drive commerce on the Internet to more that $1 trillion by 2003. To support this growth, Web sites must be able to set up and maintain millions of connections every second. This requires bandwidth, more powerful and scalable servers, high-speed access, high availability of servers, and fault-tolerant links.

SCALING THE INTERNET

Quick response time and continuous availability have become mandatory requirements as sites compete to offer users the best online experience. The utmost requirement in all mission-critical web-computing infrastructures is a solution that can scale server capacity dynamically to match aggregate client demand, while ensuring continuous service availability.

Single Server Approach

These requirements brought several challenges. Let's examine some of the challenges from the context of a single server web site.

▼ A single server no longer is able to provide services efficiently to meet the growing demands of users, either in terms of load or availability. Quick response time is a key factor for an online user to promote loyalty.

■ A single server doesn't offer any kind of redundancy or high availability. When the server goes down, whether scheduled or unscheduled, the whole site is down. The effect on business for an e-commerce site is severe, resulting in lost loyalty of users.

▲ Scalability is a critical factor for a web site to ensure growing demands are met. In the case of a single server, however, any software or hardware upgrades require the server and, in turn, the web site must be brought down indefinitely.

Server Farm Approach

From the limitations imposed by a single server web site emerged the concept of *server farm*, where multiple servers catered to high volumes of user requests. This satisfies the mandatory requirements of fast response time, high availability, and scalability.

Although the server farm provided solutions for many of the challenges presented for a single-server web site, it imposed many new issues of its own, as follows.

▼ How is traffic directed to the appropriate server in a server farm?

■ How is traffic distributed equitably among all the servers?

■ How is traffic distributed so no servers are overloaded?

▲ If a server is overloaded, how do you resolve it?

WHAT IS SERVER LOAD BALANCING?

So, the question is, how do we resolve the previous challenges? One increasingly popular answer is to deploy server load balancers that provide the infrastructure to scale application-processing power, maximize server efficiency, and ensure high-application availability.

First-generation server load balancers are PC-based software products, and tend to have limited performance and connectivity. New generations of server load balancers are special-purpose devices, based on a switching platform that consolidates multiple web infrastructure functions with server load balancing and multilayer switching. Examples of these functions include redirecting traffic to caches, load balancing traffic across multiple firewalls, packet filtering, and bandwidth management.

Load balancers are sophisticated, and use protocol information in OSI Layers 3, 4, and 7 to identify and manage application-layer sessions. For example, an advanced device could use embedded URLs strings, TCP or UDP port numbers, the SYN/FIN bits that mark the start and end of TCP application sessions, as well as the IP source and destination addresses to make their decisions. What is selected for parsing generally depends on what application the load balancer is actually load balancing. Some examples include the following:

▼ URLs for HTTP traffic

■ UDP ports for DNS load balancing

■ TCP ports for load balancing SMTP

▲ IP Destination Addresses for default gateway load balancing.

Alteon Web Systems, the load balancer pioneer, coined the term *Web switch* to represent this new, more flexible class of device that front-ends server farms and provides Internet traffic management. The terms "Web switch" and "load balancer" are used interchangeably in this chapter.

Virtual Server Group and Virtual IP

The key to load balancing is dynamically distributing the traffic load across a group of servers running a common application (or set of applications), while making the group appear as if it were a single device to the client.

For example, a number of Web servers with access to the same content can be logically combined into an HTTP cluster or virtual server group (VSG). The VSG provides a "virtual" HTTP service to clients in that the clients aren't aware a number of "real" servers are participating in providing this service. The clients access the service using a virtual IP (VIP) address, which is configured in a Web switch that front-ends the real servers. As connection requests arrive for the virtual service, the Web switch passes these requests on to one of the real servers in the VSG based on knowledge of the servers' availability, load-handling capability, and present load. Once the Web switch assigns a session to a real server, it must recognize all successive packets associated with that session. These packets are processed and forwarded appropriately to make sure the client continues to be associated with the same physical server for the duration of the session. See Figure 9-1 to illustrate server load balancing using the VIP and VSG server group.

Web switches also monitor the completion of sessions, at which time the binding of the session to the physical server can be removed. This ensures that the next time the client connects, he'll be connected to the most available server at that time, providing the best possible service to each client. The administrator can invoke special mechanisms if the application requires persistent connections, such as with FTP control and data connections from the same client, SSL, and some online shopping cart applications.

Technical Benefits

The benefits to an SLB configuration are fairly straightforward: reliability, scalability, independence, optimality, and simplicity. We'll review each in turn.

▼ **Reliability** Web switches can be deployed to increase the availability of a given application. This is done by removing the *single point of failure*, which is a dependency on the availability of a single device in the web data center infrastructure, whether that be a server or router, or some other device. The switch is configured to monitor the availability of physical devices through a process called *health checking* (described in the following) and, at the failure of any one device, it automatically routes new incoming sessions to the other remaining healthy devices. Also, by spreading the active sessions across multiple devices, the number of sessions actually disrupted during a failure of a single device decreases.

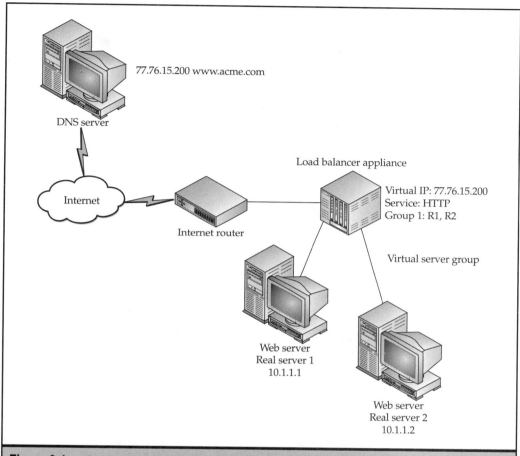

77.76.15.200 www.acme.com

DNS server

Internet

Internet router

Load balancer appliance

Virtual IP: 77.76.15.200
Service: HTTP
Group 1: R1, R2

Virtual server group

Web server
Real server 1
10.1.1.1

Web server
Real server 2
10.1.1.2

Figure 9-1. Simple server load-balancing configuration

More advanced load balancers allow for backup servers to be configured. These backups come online if a single server, or even an entire VSG, fails. Some of the more advanced load balancers can support multisite load balancing to protect against failure of the entire site. See Chapter 11, "Global Server Load Balancing," for more details.

▼ **Performance Scalability** The implementation of Web switches can provide the infrastructure to match resources with demand. During periods of peak load, a Web switch can dynamically and gracefully increase the capacity of the VSG by enlisting overflow servers into the load balancing process.

- ■ **Platform Independence**   Interestingly, a Web switch introduces server agnosticism into the server farm, generating a kind of application server platform independence. In a group or cluster, different types of servers—Unix, Windows, Linux, Netware—can be combined to host the same application, providing relatively painless build-outs of an undersized web farm with maximum flexibility.

- ■ **Optimal Resource Use**   Web switches can dramatically improve server resource use simply by distributing that traffic across multiple servers. Clients can be dynamically directed to the least used server, servers best configured to handle particular types of requests, and so forth. This decreases server costs and improves site performance.

- ▲ **Operational Simplicity**   When a VSG is configured, the load balancer detects offline resources and reroutes accordingly. This allows devices to be removed for maintenance purposes, without disruption of user services. This decreases administration cost and total cost of ownership (TCO).

Business Benefits

From a business perspective, the benefits of using SLB technology are also fairly straight-forward: satisfaction and utilization go up, TCO goes down.

- ▼ **Increased Customer Satisfaction**   With Web switches, customers get faster, more consistent response time, with the Web switch directing traffic to the least loaded and most responsive web server. Web sites can consistently deliver superior performance by managing the load on web servers and preventing web servers from getting overloaded.

- ■ **Improved Resource Utilization Based on Business Policies**   Preferred customers and mission-critical application traffic can be given higher priority by the Web switch. Server and network resources can be allocated for high-priority users and applications with the bandwidth management feature. Mission-critical applications and users accessing these applications get consistently good performance.

  Most Web switches offer features that can differentiate users and guarantee a superior level of service for preferred users. ISPs and corporate IT managers can use these features to control their infrastructure resources to deliver negotiated Service Level Agreements (SLA). Also, this gives them an opportunity to increase profit margins by offering tiered service levels.

- ▲ **Decreased TCO**   The Web switch helps in simplifying infrastructure architecture and optimizing resource use. This decreases administration and server cost.

Applications

Environments that benefit from server load balancing include Web hosting services, e-commerce services, online service providers and corporate data centers with high-availability requirements. Server load balancing supports many TCP-based or UDP-based applications where common content is available across a group of servers. Internet/intranet applications, such as Web servers, FTP servers, DNS servers, and RADIUS servers have been the first to take advantage of server load balancing to support the high growth and unpredictable volume of web-oriented traffic.

Web-Hosting and Online Services

Web hosters and *online service providers* typically deploy multiple HTTP, FTP, and other application servers today, with the load distributed across them via round-robin DNS. This approach isn't the most desirable because it isn't fault-tolerant, requires a high degree of administration, and is generally limited in the number of configurations available. Server load balancing enables transparent use of multiple servers with built-in high-availability support.

E-Commerce Web Sites

E-commerce sites are becoming mission critical for most businesses. For many new businesses, the Web is the only channel for generating revenue. These sites must have superior performance and high availability.

Online Retail Sites

Online retail sites experience sudden surges in user traffic because of a promotion campaign, demand for a new product, and so forth. Web switches help manage the load on the site, prevent servers from getting overloaded, and guarantee high-application availability. They also help in easily scaling the site to meet demand with minimal effort.

Online Trading Sites

Online trading sites have more dynamic content and experience sudden traffic surges. For example, a change in political scenario or availability of new economic data could result in large fluctuations in the financial market. This results in a sudden, multifold increase in online trading activity. Also, when servers are overloaded, the performance degrades and session completion rate rapidly degrades. Planning and overprovisioning to meet these sudden traffic surges is expensive. Web switches help to optimize resource use and dynamically control the load on servers to provide good performance.

Business to Business E-Commerce Sites

Enterprises are setting up extranets to automate sales, marketing, and procurement processes. These extranets must be highly available and provide consistent performance. Web switches enable enterprises to build reliable and scalable infrastructures that support mission critical solutions.

Application Hosting Services

Application service providers (ASPs) are using the Web to deliver applications on demand. This enables enterprises to rent applications and decrease their IT expenses. To meet the requirements of large enterprises, hosted solutions must be scalable and highly available, and must deliver superior performance. A Web switch enables ASPs to build an infrastructure that supports these business-critical solutions.

SERVER LOAD BALANCING OPERATIONS

Any TCP-, UDP-, or IP-based application can be load balanced as long as common content is made available across the VSG supporting the application.

Grouping Options

Servers can be grouped into VSGs based on administrative requirements. Common ways to administer server content are duplicated content and centralized content back-end data servers.

Duplicated Content

Servers with duplicated content on local disks can be grouped into a VSG. This approach is low cost and ideal for applications with mostly static content requiring little replication.

Centralized Content on Back-End Data Server

Alternatively, data can be stored directly in a back-end database server. Application servers retrieve data from the back-end server in real time through file- or database-sharing techniques, such as a Network File System (NFS). Each application server runs any or all of the load-sharing applications, as long as it has access to the associated content on the back-end server. Shared access to a single copy of data also enables server load balancing for read/write applications.

To allow the data server to keep up with aggregate requests from multiple application servers, a general recommendation is to connect back-end data servers with a higher-speed switch port than the application servers. The same Web switch platform enables clients to access the application servers via layer 4 switching and allows the application servers to access the database server via layer 2 or layer 3 switching.

SOLUTIONS

Several solutions are presently available from various vendors for server load balancing application. Certain solutions are designed around purpose-built appliances whose sole application is server load balancing. Other solutions are integrated appliances providing multipurpose applications, including server load balancing.

The latest trend appears to be modularizing the server load balancer and inserting it as a blade into a high-end L2/L3 switch, as is the case with both Cisco and Nortel.

Let's examine several of these solutions presently available in the market.

The Cisco Solutions—Local Director

In discussing the Cisco solutions, we examine two distinct server load balancing platforms. The Local Director was the premier load balancing solution from Cisco prior to the ArrowPoint acquisition in June of 2000. Soon after, this became the foremost Cisco server load balancing solution especially in the ISP, ASP, and dot-com companies. The Local Director continues to be a popular load balancing solution for Cisco customers, however, both in the enterprise and ISP market space.

The *Cisco Local Director* is a network appliance with an embedded operating system that intelligently load balances the requests of users across multiple cluster of low-cost servers. It lets you build a highly redundant, fault-tolerant, and scaleable server farm system, where servers are automatically and transparently placed in and out of service.

All physical servers appear as one virtual server in the view of the user, with only one IP address and one URL address required for the server farm.

Hot-Standby Stateful Fail-Over Mechanism

To increase fault tolerance further, the Local Director architecture enables you to equip an optional hot-standby stateful fail-over mechanism eliminating the Local Director as the single point of failure in a Web infrastructure.

Stateful fail-over maintains the state of the user connections to servers, so that when a Local Director fails, a second Local Director takes over the user's sessions. Additionally, the configuration of the active Local Director is automatically replicated to the standby Local Director, reducing potential configuration errors.

See Figure 9-2 for a Hot-standby network configuration for Local Director.

Cisco Local Director

The Cisco Local Director 430 appliance is a high-end load balancing solution that supports the highest-traffic Internet sites, with up to 400 Mbps throughput and 30,000 connections per second. This model also supports 10/100, FDDI, and Gigabit Ethernet connectivity. It boasts a 384MB memory, 2MB of Flash memory, and supports 64,000 virtual and real IP addresses.

The Cisco Local Director 416 appliance is a value-priced solution for TCP applications, such as database access or intranets. It delivers up to 80 Mbps throughput and 7,000 connections per second. This model also supports 10/100 Ethernet connectivity. It boasts a 32MB memory, 2MB of Flash memory, and supports 8,000 virtual and real IP addresses.

Health-Checking Applications and Servers

The Local Director has the capability to place Web servers in and out of service automatically and transparently, based on their dynamic availability. It applies a three-point system

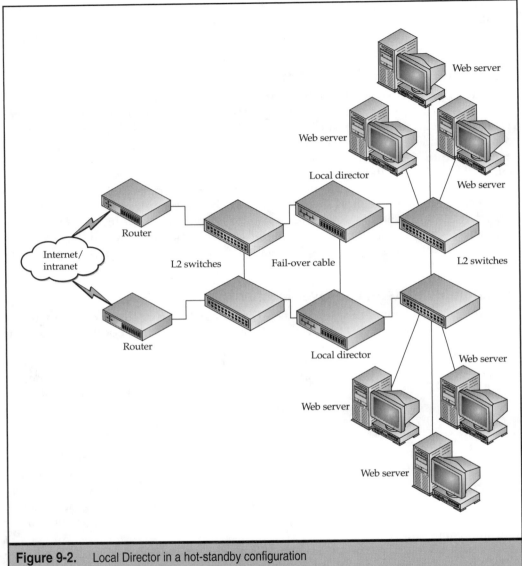

Figure 9-2.   Local Director in a hot-standby configuration

for detecting the health of applications resident in the Web servers and routing to new servers when necessary. This includes the following:

▼   Monitoring the TCP handshake between client and server

- Verifying active content
- ▲ Providing a Dynamic Feedback Protocol (DFP) for servers to communicate directly to the Local Director.

Monitoring the TCP Handshake

To determine application availability, the Local Director snoops the TCP handshake between the user and the server to the port level. If an application or server isn't responding to the TCP handshake or is responding with TCP RSTs (resets), then the Local Director fails the server immediately. This process is transparent; therefore, clients are rarely sent to a dead application. In the case where the server issues TCP RSTs, this could be caused by the server being too busy to accept more connections or the daemon servicing that type of traffic has failed, that is, the HTTP daemon on port 80.

The administrator can also configure the RSTs threshold and, thus, can calibrate how quickly the Local Director will pull a server out of service.

Local Director transparently can bring a failed server back in service if it responds with data on an existing connection. The server is then put into testing or transmission mode and, if it responds to a new live connection, then it's put back in service.

Content Verification

The Content Verification System (CVS) enables the Local Director to use user-definable and customizable HTTP requests to probe Web servers proactively to determine application availability. These probes can be run for each real server associated with a virtual server. The CVS probe monitors the health of Web servers, applications, and content.

A CVS probe, which can consist of numerous steps, makes a specific HTTP request to the server, evaluates the response based on user-defined criteria, and, thus, determines the health of the real server. You can also specify whether a probe failure will result in the real server being taken out of service immediately or in a warning message being generated. These probes can run automatically on a user-specified schedule on all the real servers or they can run manually by the administrator on a particular Web server.

Some of the criteria used by the CVS probe to determine the health of the server and application are the following:

- ▼ Response time of a real server when a request for a particular URL is made
- Response of a real server when cookies are present in the request
- Response of a real server to a particular browser agent
- Type of content returned by the real server
- Status code returned by the real server
- ▲ Presence and content of any cookies returned by the real server

As e-commerce sites become mission-critical assets of a business, the deployment of CVS has also become more complex and multiple tiers have been a common implementation scenario, especially a three-tiered e-commerce site that includes Web servers, application servers, and data base servers. Proactive probing of these servers is, therefore, an important requirement for any successful e-commerce site. Active content verification is a powerful tool that can identify not only whether a Web server is up, but also whether the application is up and the data base server is healthy. Likewise, active content verification can determine if the content is corrupt at any tier.

Dynamic Feedback Protocol (DFP)

The DFP protocol provides a mechanism for real servers to send feedback information intelligently to the Local Director, ensuring the Local Director doesn't route traffic to downed applications and that it's sent instead to the correct real server.

Agents resident in the real server use DFP to communicate the real server's health, availability, and load condition to the Local Director. Cisco envisions DFP to be a widely embraced standard for server feedback, and some current DFP providers that have interoperated with Cisco on DFP are Hewlett-Packard, Platform Computing, Sterling Software, and WebSpective Software.

DFP is the first protocol that allows servers to provide feedback and input into a load balancing decision. It provides the following benefits to the customer:

▼ A server agent can inform a Cisco network of a server congestion

■ A server agent can inform a Cisco network when a server is underused

■ A server agent can inform a Cisco network when a server shouldn't be used for a certain period of time

■ A server agent can prioritize a certain application (such as HTTP) over other generic applications

▲ A server agent can perform content verification services

Cisco and its DFP partners are creating an environment of truly integrated networks and server resources. The business benefits are lower costs and fully used investments in a distributed computing infrastructure, good traits appealing to CIOs where ROI is always an appealing story.

Distributed Director and DFP

With DFP, the Local Director can also now communicate load and availability information to *Distributed Director,* the multisite, load-balancing solution of Cisco. This is possible because Distributed Director also supports DFP, and the Local Director acts as a DFP server, communicating load and availability information of its web servers to Distributed Director using the DFP protocol.

Distributed Director transparently redirects end users to the closest responsive server, determined by such factors as client-server proximity and client-server link latency. Assume an organization has two sites: one in Paris and another one in San Jose. HTTP requests of users based in the United States are redirected to the San Jose site, while European users are redirected to the Paris site.

With the DFP protocol, each site communicates its server's health and availability to Distributed Director, ensuring that users are sent to a site not only in close proximity to it, but also with healthy and available servers.

The Cisco ArrowPoint Load Balancers

ArrowPoint Communications, based in Acton, Massachusetts, was founded in 1997 and, with its 300-plus employees, was acquired by Cisco in June 2000. Its feature-rich and popular server load-balancing appliances soon became an integral part, together with the Load Director of the Cisco content networking suite of products.

Several products are now part of the CSS family of Cisco load-balancing Web switches. The high-end platform is the modular chassis-based CSS 11800, designed for extremely large Internet sites. The CSS 11100 is a stand-alone appliance designed for smaller sites.

Most recently, Cisco introduced two members of the CSS family: the CSS 11050 and the CSS 11150. These superseded the original CSS 11100, which claimed to offer a three-fold increased in performance over its predecessor.

In terms of market positioning—with the CSS 11800 being the top-line product for extremely large Internet sites and data centers—the CSS 11050 is now considered the entry-level load balancing solution, while the CSS 11150 is the medium solution designed for moderate traffic Web sites and POPs.

A key point to remember is this: the full feature set of the high-end CSS 11800 is available to the other two products, except for their limited scalability.

Now let's explore the CSS 11800 Web switch architecture and feature sets.

Cisco CSS 11800 Load Balancer

The CSS 11800 is a 15-slot chassis-based system, with a wide range of module combination options of 10/100 Ethernet, Gigabit Ethernet, and Management line cards. The switching fabric module has a 20 Gbps back plane, and, for redundancy, the management module can take up four slots. Eight slots are available for pure I/O modules.

The content policy engine resides in four MIPS RISC processors running a real-time operating system with over 512MB of memory. These resources provide the flow setup required by the users, capability to read full URLs, ability to dynamically locate cookies anywhere in the HTTP header, and application of multiple policies to route the user to the best site and server in real time.

After that, 16 distributed ASICs are then assigned to deliver the user content requests at wire speed across the switch.

The CSS 11800 supports all TCP and UDP-based web protocols, wire-speed NAT, and integrated IP routing. This is designed for optimized content requests and delivery of HTTP, passive FTP, and streaming media protocols. The CSS 11800 has an integrated firewall, called its FlowWall Security feature, providing wire speed per-flow filtering of content requests. Its security policies can be based on a combination of source and destination IP addressees, protocol, type, or content URL. The CSS 11800 protects against Denial of Service (DoS) attacks, such as SYN flooding, ping flooding, and smurfs.

The CSS11800 is also designed to redirect to and load balance cache engines, as well as server farms. Cisco claims a performance of up to 400 percent in web cache efficiency for transparent, proxy, and reverse proxy configurations.

The CSS 11800 can also be used to load balance external firewalls.

In the load-balancing functionality is the capability of the switch to provide high-speed HTTP flow setup, dynamic and intelligent real-server selection criteria based on load and content availability, and URL and cookie-based policy and traffic prioritization. It can dedicate real servers based on a particular content type. For example, Real Player type video feeds can be redirected to a server or server farm that has suitable bandwidth of CPU power. It can also configure redundant fail-over, backup, and over-spill real servers.

Cisco Content Switching Module

Discussions on the Cisco load-balancing solutions isn't complete without mentioning the Content Switching Module (CSM), which is a load-balancer blade designed for integration into the Catalyst 6500 switch. The CSM can establish up to 200,000 layer 4 connections per second and provide high-speed content switching, while maintaining 1,000,000 concurrent connections. It supports the most common load-balancing algorithms, such as round robin, least connection, and Client IP has. The CSM also supports URL and cookie-based load balancing. It supports the use of DFP probes to monitor the health and availability of web servers and interoperates with Distributed Director for use in global content networks.

The Nortel Web Switch

Alteon Web Systems, acquired by Nortel Networks in October 2000, pioneered server load-balancing integrated appliances. Founded in May 1996 and based in the heart of Silicon Valley in San Jose, California, it quickly became the market leader with 50 percent market share worldwide in the 1998 and 1999 time period. Here are the operational details on the Alteon Web switch.

The Web switch, with server load balancing, acts as a virtual front-end processor to clusters of real servers connected via direct attachment to switch ports or indirectly through hubs and switches. A VIP address is configured for each VSG, presenting a single address for the server group to the rest of the network. Domain Name Services (DNS) must advertise this VIP address.

For example, if www.alteon.com were available on three servers and load-balanced by the Web switch with a VIP of 215.176.12.3, DNS would advertise 215.176.12.3 as the address of www.alteon.com, not the individual IP addresses of the real servers. Clients who want to access the load-balanced application would be directed by DNS to send their requests to the VSG hosting the application. The Web switch receives these packets and uses the destination TCP port number to identify the application to be load balanced.

Packets addressed to anything other than the configured VIPs on the Web switch are forwarded at layer 2 or layer 3, as appropriate. This allows real servers to be accessed through the Web switch simultaneously via their real IP addresses. This also enables nonload-balanced applications, such as system management and administration, to access the servers directly through the switch.

TCP/IP Server Load-Balancing Operation

The Web switch recognizes when a client is requesting a new TCP session by identifying the TCP SYN packet. The request is forwarded to the best available server, based on the configured load-balancing policy. Once the switch determines the best server, it binds the session to that server's real IP address. The Web switch maintains a binding table that associates each active session with the real server to which it's assigned. After the Web switch binds a connection request to a real server, it performs address substitution, so the real server will transparently receive packets for that session. The switch replaces the VIP in the IP destination address with the server's real IP address and replaces the switch's MAC address in the MAC destination address field with the server's MAC address. See Figure 9-3 to illustrate how IP addressing substitution takes place as traffic flows inbound from the client to the real server.

After performing the necessary address substitution, the Web switch forwards the connection request to the chosen server. All subsequent packets belonging to that session undergo the same address substitution process and are forwarded to the same real server until the switch sees a session termination packet (that is, a TCP FIN packet). Likewise, the Web switch intercepts packets traveling from the real server to the client and performs the reverse address substitution. It replaces the real server's actual IP address in the Network Layer source address field with the VIP and forwards each modified frame to the client (see Figure 9-4).

On receipt of a TCP FIN packet, the Web switch performs the necessary address substitution and forwards the FIN packet to the appropriate real server, causing the server to tear down the connection. Then it removes the session-server binding from its binding table.

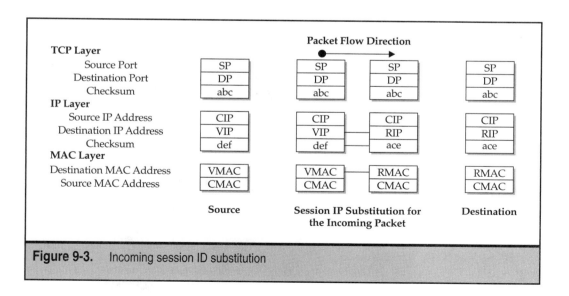

Figure 9-3.   Incoming session ID substitution

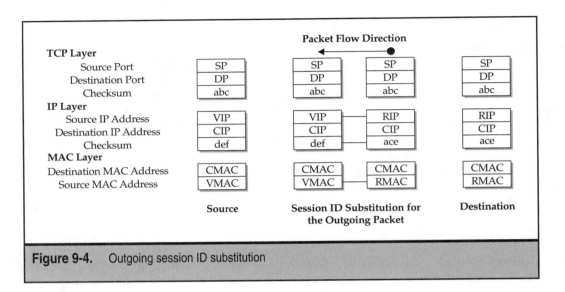

Figure 9-4.   Outgoing session ID substitution

UDP/IP Server Load-Balancing Operation

Because UDP is a connectionless protocol, it technically doesn't support the concept of session. Nevertheless, Alteon Web switches support server load balancing for UDP-based applications. If UDP load balancing is activated on the Web switch, the switch identifies UDP packets arriving from clients addressed to a VIP. If an incoming packet destined for a VIP has a source IP address not presently found in the Web switch's binding table, the Web switch uses the configured load-balancing algorithm to determine to which real server the "new session" should be bound.

While this binding is in effect, all UDP packets from this source IP address are sent to that same real server. When no UDP traffic from the source IP address is seen in a user-specified period of time, the session is removed from the switch's binding table. In this context, *session* means the flow of packets during the time a specific Source IP address is bound to a particular real server.

Performing Health Checks on Servers

The most important consideration when making load-balancing decisions is whether the servers and their load-balanced applications are working properly. The Web switch uses special mechanisms to monitor servers and ensure that connection requests are directed to healthy servers. The different mechanisms available for health checking are

▼ Monitoring physical connections

■ ICMP (PING) monitoring

- TCP connection monitoring
- Active content verification
- ▲ Dynamic application verification

Monitoring Physical Connections

The Web switch monitors the physical link status of switch ports connected to real servers. If the physical link to a real server goes down, the Web switch immediately places that server in the Server Failed state and doesn't forward new connection requests to that server. In addition, the switch doesn't forward any more traffic associated with existing sessions to that real server and immediately removes all existing sessions bound to that real server from its binding table. This ensures existing connections are closed quickly with minimal impact to the user.

Monitoring Through ICMP Pings

At the most basic level, the Web switch can monitor server health by sending ICMP ping requests to servers. Based on the servers, the switch can verify the health of the server's networking stack. This is recommended when all IP traffic, or a UDP-based application other than DNS, is being load balanced.

The rate at which ICMP pings are sent is a user-configurable parameter. If a user-configurable number of consecutive ping requests fail, the target server is placed in the Server Failed state. While in this state, no new connection requests are sent to the real server.

TCP Connection Monitoring

A more sophisticated health-checking mechanism is for the Web switch to send TCP connection requests (that is, TCP SYN requests) to the real servers and determine that the server responds. This is recommended when a TCP-based application for which the switch doesn't support content-based health checks is being load balanced.

A more sophisticated health-checking mechanism is for the Web switch to send TCP connection requests (that is, TCP SYN requests) for each load-balanced application to each real server and determine that the server responds. These connection requests identify both failed servers and failed services on a healthy server. The rate at which these connection requests are sent is a user-configurable parameter. If a user-configurable number of consecutive connection requests to an application fail, the application on the target server is placed in the Service Failed state. While it is in this state, no new connection requests are sent to the application on that real server. Connection requests continue to be sent to the other, however, with healthy applications running on the same server.

When an application on a real server is in the Service Failed state, the Web switch continues to perform health checks. When the Web switch has been successful in connecting to a load-balanced service, the real server is slowly brought back into service, using mechanisms that don't overwhelm the newly available server.

Active Content Verification (ACV)

To verify the availability of a Web service and associated content, users can configure a reference URL to instruct the Web switch to access the data represented by the URL during its periodic server health checks.

To check HTTP service availability, the Web switch makes a request for the specific content via an HTTP GET, and then verifies the received content and return code. This test not only checks the TCP connection, but also checks the Web server and content server. In the example in Figure 9-2, the HTTP request is sent through Web Server A and File Server A. If the verification request is successful, it proves a path exists from the switch to the data. If the verification request fails, the switch redirects the request through another path.

The ACV feature supports not only HTTP but also other services, including NNTP, FTP, SMTP, POP3, IMAP, DNS, and RADIUS.

Dynamic Application Verification (DAV)

Dynamic application verification (DAV) expands on active content verification. With DAV, the Web switch can verify the availability of dynamic applications like .asp applications, GGI scripts, forms, and so forth on Web servers. This feature enables users to write their own tests that emulate user actions and supply the switch with a URL of the test script.

The DAV feature can also be used to monitor the health of other Internet services, like mail service.

Backup Servers

A server or link failure, as well as administrative action, can cause a Web switch to remove a server from the load-balancing VSG. Users may configure the Web switch to introduce a backup server into a VSG when any or all of the servers within the VSG fail.

A backup server introduced into the VSG after the removal of a single server processes connections until the Web switch determines the removed server is once again operational. At that point, the backup server is removed from the mix.

In the case where the switch introduces the backup server into the mix after the removal of all servers in a VSG, the backup server is taken out of the VSG when the Web switch determines all servers in the group are once again operational. Note, a backup server being taken out of the mix means no new connections are made to it. Existing connections remain operational until they're terminated by normal mechanisms.

Load Balancing Policies

The Web switch makes decisions regarding which server within a VSG to assign a new connection based on user configured load-balancing policies. The different policy options available in the Alteon Web switch are

▼ Least used or most available server selection

■   Persistence-based server selection

▲   URL-based load balancing

Most Available Server Policies

Various policies can be used to drive the load-balancing decision. On the Web switch, the load-balancing policy for each VSG is a user-configurable parameter. Most Available policies include the following:

▼   Simple Least Connections

■   Weighted Least Connections

■   Simple Round-Robin

▲   Weighted Round-Robin

In addition, a maximum-connections threshold can be configured for any or all real servers in conjunction with any of the previous policies.

Simple Least Connections   In the method of *simple least connections,* the number of active connections being processed by each real server is tracked.

When a request for a new connection is received, it's forwarded to the real server in the VSG with the fewest active connections. This is often viewed as the fairest policy because servers that close connections faster get more connection requests forwarded to them over time. Implicitly, this algorithm takes into account feedback from the real servers in that faster or less-loaded servers close connections more quickly, indicating they're available for more workload.

Weighted Least Connections   In the solution of *weighted least connections,* a weighting function is added to the simple least-connections policy. The number of connections to each server is normalized based on each server's static weighting, and each connection request is directed to the server with the fewest active normalized (as opposed to actual) connections. The idea is this: servers with greater inherent capacity should support a larger number of active connections.

Simple Round Robin   With the *simple round-robin load balancing* algorithm, new connection requests are forwarded to the real servers in a round-robin fashion so that, over time, each server in the application server group gets the same number of connections. This doesn't mean each server will have the same number of active connections because some will close connections faster than others. Round robin is commonly used when the servers in a VSG are roughly equal in capacity.

Weighted Round Robin   *Weighted round-robin balancing* is similar to round-robin load balancing, but each server in the application VSG is assigned a static weight based on some view of the capacity of each server. Servers are presented connection requests in proportion to their weighting.

Configuring Basic Server Load Balancing on an Alteon Web Switch

Look at what's involved in configuring an Alteon Web switch to perform server load balancing on a pair of web servers. Refer to Figure 9-5 for the network diagram showing a web site with a server farm composed of two servers. The users from the Internet access a virtual IP address by resolution from a DNS server. In this example, the web site Alteon.com has a DNS entry of 170.20.1.100, which will be the VIP configured in the Web switch. The Web switch will select either Real Server 1 or 2 to process that particular user based on the configured metric. And *Leastconns* will be used as the metric, which over time has proven to do the best job of load balancing among the servers in a server farm. Leastconns is also the Web switch's default metric. We configure health checking of the real servers using the default TCP method.

Let's examine the steps required to configure basic server load balancing on an Alteon Web switch. The following are the required configurations tasks:

1. Define the IP interfaces on the switch.

2. Enable server load balancing and define each real server. Assign an IP address to each real server.

3. Assign the real servers to a group.

4. Define a VIP (virtual IP address).

5. Configure the HTTP service for the virtual server.

6. Define the port configuration.

7. Apply and save the configuration

The following configuration exercise implements basic server load balancing based on the network diagram in Figure 9-5. We configure the Web switch so all user requests for VIP 170.20.1.100 will be load balanced between Real Servers 1 and 2.

Here is the step-by-step procedure:

1. Define the IP interfaces on the Web switch:

```
/cfg/ip/if 1
ena
addr 170.20.1.1
mask 255.255.255.0
/cfg/ip/if 2
ena
addr 10.1.1.1
mask 255.255.255.0
```

2. Enable server load balancing on the Web switch and assign real servers:

```
/cfg/slb/on
/cfg/slb/real 1/ena/rip 10.1.1.2
/cfg/slb/real 2/ena/rip 10.1.1.3
```

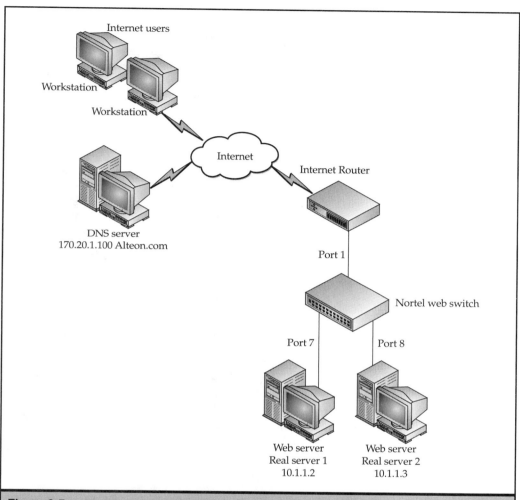

Figure 9-5. Basic server load balancing

3. Assign the real servers to a group:

   `/cfg/slb/group 1/add 1/add 2`

4. Define a VIP (virtual IP):

   `/cfg/slb/virt 1/ena/vip 170.20.1.100`

5. Configure the HTTP service for the virtual server:

   `/cfg/slb/virt 1/service http/group 1`

6. Define the port configuration:

    ```
    /cfg/slb/port 1/client ena
    /cfg/slb/port 7/server ena
    /cfg/slb/port 8/server ena
    ```

7. Apply and save the configuration:

    ```
    apply
    save
    ```

Persistence Policies

Many e-commerce sites maintain stateful information for each customer on web servers. The Web switch must forward all incoming requests from a particular user to the same server, until the completion of the transaction. Also, users returning to an e-commerce session after a temporary disconnect should be redirected to the same server to avoid having to restart their shopping activity.

The persistence policies supported on the Alteon Web switches are

▼ Hash

■ Minimum Misses

■ SSL Session ID Tracking

▲ Cookie-Based Tracking

Hash   With the *hash* policy, the server is chosen based on source IP address. The IP address is used to generate an index into a table that contains all servers in VSG. Because server selection is based on source IP, all requests from a given user are sent to the same server. This is particularly useful in e-commerce applications and firewall load balancing where session state must be maintained.

With this policy, the server selection table is recomputed every time a server leaves or enters the VSG. No existing connections are rehashed unless the server they go to has gone down.

The hash policy is better than minimum misses (see the following) for most applications because it generally offers a more even distribution of connections across servers. If server load-balancing statistics indicate that using hash causes one server to process more requests over time than others, consider using minimum misses, SSL session ID tracking, or cookie-based tracking. One of the biggest challenges with the hash algorithm (as well as minimum misses) is that all clients coming from behind a proxy may use the same source IP address and, therefore, cannot be differentiated. In this case, traffic from all clients is sent to the same server, defeating load balancing.

Minimum Misses   The *minimum misses policy* is similar to the hash policy in that the source IP address is used to generate an index into a table that contains all servers in VSG. Unlike hash, however, when a server leaves the VSG, the server selection table is recomputed only to reassign users associated with the failed server. This policy results in less perturbation of server assignments when a server fails.

SSL Session Tracking   Many e-commerce sites use secure connections for transporting private information about clients. When a client connects to a server using an encrypted SSL session, a unique SSL session ID is assigned. Using SSL session IDs to maintain server persistence is the most accurate way to bind all a client's connections during an SSL session to the same server.

SSL session tracking is most useful in scenarios where other persistence policies cannot be used because one source IP address (belonging to a proxy) is used to represent a large number of clients. For example, in large networks, proxy firewalls typically change users' IP addresses on outgoing packets for security reasons, overloading the source IP address. If persistence is determined solely by source IP address, many users are redirected to the same real server and load balancing in the VSG is ineffective. In these environments, using SSL Session ID persistence for load balancing is the best algorithm.

When SSL-session ID tracking is enabled, Alteon Web switches examine the TCP SYN handshake and subsequent packets to examine the SSL session ID and determine if it belongs to an existing SSL session or a new one. If the session is new, the Web switch assigns it to a real server, based on the configured load-balancing algorithm (least connections or round robin). If the packets are associated with an existing session, the connection is assigned to the same server involved in previous portions of the SSL session.

Cookie-Based Session Tracking   This algorithm uses HTTP cookie information to direct the client connection to the appropriate server. This load-balancing mechanism offers more granularity than IP address because the switch can now identify a specific user to send to a server.

With *cookie-based session tracking*, the Web switch sends the first incoming request to the most available server. The server modifies the cookie and inserts its IP address. Based on this information, any subsequent request from this user is forwarded to the same server.

Maximum Connections Option

The maximum connections feature, configurable in conjunction with any of the load-balancing options described earlier, enables users to set the maximum number of active connections to be assigned to a particular server.

When a server reaches its maximum connection limit, it receives no more connections until it drops back below its maximum connections limit. If an overflow server has been assigned, it is then brought into service. If all the servers in the VSG reach their maximum connections limit and no overflow servers are available, no additional connection setup requests are handled until at least one server drops below its limit.

The maximum connections option enables users to enforce service quality by preventing key servers from being overloaded.

URL-Based Load Balancing

URL-based load balancing allows the Web switch to observe each client URL request and forward the request to the appropriate server based on predefined rules. Typically, every page download consists of multiple TCP requests. URL-based load balancing looks into incoming HTTP requests and, based on the URL information, forwards the request to the appropriate VSG. Server selection within a VSG is based on user-defined polices and dynamic load on the server.

The example in Figure 9-6 shows a large e-publishing site that has graphic images (.gif and .jpg) and script files (.cgi, .bin, and .exe) on separate servers. Also, the static files are stored on a separate server farm under the /product, /company, and /information directories. The Web switch observes the incoming HTTP request and forwards it to the appropriate server based on user-defined policies. I/O intensive requests like reading image files, video files, and so forth, are sent to Web Servers 1 or 2 (call this VSG A), and computer-intensive tasks like executing applications are sent to Web Servers 3 or 4 (call this VSG B). Based on this configured policy, all requests for images (.gif) files or (.jpg) files are sent to VSG A. The requests are also load balanced among servers in VSG A, based on a user-configured Most Available server policy. All requests with .cgi, .bin, and .exe in the URL are sent to VSG B. All other requests for static pages are sent to Web Servers 5 and 6 (call this VSG C).

Configuring URL-Based Server Load Balancing

Let's examine the steps required to configure URL-based server load balancing, one of the most popular applications of the Alteon Web switch. The following are the required configurations tasks:

1. Define an IP interface on the switch.

2. Define the URL strings to be used for server load balancing.

3. Enable server load balancing and define each real server. Assign an IP address to each real server. Assign each real server to its designated string.

4. Assign the real servers to a group.

5. Define a VIP (virtual IP address).

6. Configure the HTTP service for the virtual server and enable urlslb.

7. Define the port configuration.

8. Apply and save the configuration.

That's it. Now let's perform the actual commands on the Alteon Web switch necessary to implement URL-based server load balancing.

The following configuration exercise implements URL-based server load balancing based on the network diagram in Figure 9-6. We configure the Web switch so all user requests for .gif and .jpg files go to virtual server group VSG A; all user requests for .cgi, .bin, and .exe files go to VSG B; and the rest go to VSG C.

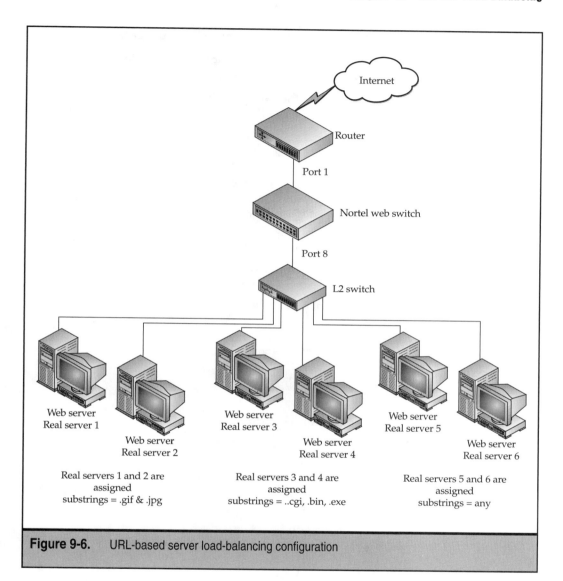

Figure 9-6.   URL-based server load-balancing configuration

Here is the step-by-step procedure:

1. Define the IP interfaces on the Web switch:

```
/cfg/ip/if 1/ena/addr 10.1.1.1/mask 255.255.255.0/broad
10.1.1.255
```

2. Configure the URL strings to use to load balance the Web servers:

```
/cfg/slb/url/lb/add "any"/add ".gif"/add ".jpg"/add ".cgi"/
/cfg/slb/url/lb/add ".bin"/add ".exe"
```

3. Enable server load balancing on the Web switch and assign real servers:

```
/cfg/slb/on
/cfg/slb/real 1/ena/rip 10.1.1.2
/cfg/slb/real 1/layer7/addlb 2/addlb 3/
/cfg/slb/real 2/ena/rip 10.1.1.3
/cfg/slb/real 2/layer7/addlb 2/addlb 3
/cfg/slb/real 3/ena/rip 10.1.1.4
/cfg/slb/real 3/layer7/addlb 4/addlb 5/addlb 6
/cfg/slb/real 4/ena/rip 10.1.1.5
/cfg/slb/real 4/layer7/addlb 4/addlb 5/addlb 6
/cfg/slb/real 5/ena/rip 10.1.1.6
/cfg/slb/real 5/layer7/addlb 1
/cfg/slb/real 6/ena/rip 10.1.1.7
/cfg/slb/real 6/layer7/addlb 1
```

4. Assign the real servers to a group:

```
/cfg/slb/group 1/add 1/add 2/add 3/add 4/add 5/add 6
```

5. Define a VIP (virtual IP):

```
/cfg/slb/virt 1/ena/vip 10.1.1.100
```

6. Configure the HTTP service for the virtual server:

```
/cfg/slb/virt 1/service http/group 1/httpslb ena urlslb
```

7. Define the port configuration:

```
/cfg/slb/port 1/client ena
/cfg/slb/port 8/server ena
```

8. Apply and save the configuration:

```
apply
save
```

Here are some of the benefits of URL-based server load balancing.

Ease of Management   Large Web sites have so much content associated with their domain name that splitting this content up across multiple file systems on multiple servers not only makes it easier to manage, it also improves site performance and availability. With URL-based load balancing, incoming requests can be easily redirected to the server group with the correct content.

Resource Optimization   Partitioning content across multiple servers enables web sites to use servers optimized for a specific task. Servers optimized for computer-intensive functions are better at serving web pages with dynamic content, while servers optimized for disk I/O functions are better at delivering large static pages. With URL-based load balancing, the switch forwards dynamic requests to powerful server groups optimized to handle computer-intensive requests and static requests to I/O optimized servers. This improves performance and optimizes resource use.

User Differentiation and Service Level Provision   Partitioning users among different virtual server groups gives web site managers the ability to use different types of servers to service different classes of users. URL parsing helps in forwarding incoming clients to different servers based on user type, type of request, and so forth. This feature can be used to give preferred customers a larger share of system resources and better response time than best effort users.

Prioritization of Transactions   URL-based load balancing can also be used to give certain types of transactions higher priority, so a payment transaction or an order transaction can be given a larger share of virtual server resources.

Parallel Execution   Large web sites have their content partitioned across multiple servers. With this feature, processing tasks for each session and page request can be split and distributed to multiple servers for parallel operations. For example, you can retrieve the image and text portion simultaneously from different servers. Parallel processing improves session performance and scalability.

Management of Traffic Surges (Flash Crowd)

A phenomenon known as *Flash Crowd* results when an unusual heavy surge of access descends on a popular web site for a temporary period of time. An example would be a music recording company's web site introduction of hit music for download and purchase. Deploying overflow servers would be one solution in this kind of scenario.

The Web switch can be configured to introduce overflow servers when any or all of the servers in a VSG hit their maximum connections threshold. The Web switch can also bring in backup servers when it detects that any or all of the servers in a VSG have suffered from a service or physical link failure.

A server that normally performs another function can be configured with the load-balanced application(s) and given access to the associated data. Under normal circumstances, the Web switch won't forward any connections for the load-balanced application to this server.

If one or all of the real servers supporting the load-balanced application hit their maximum connections limits, however, the Web switch introduces the overflow server into the load-balancing virtual service group. When the load on the real server(s) falls to an appropriate level, the Web switch stops forwarding connection requests to the overflow server, removing it from the load-balancing service group.

High Availability Configuration

The Web switch monitors the real servers and the load-balanced applications to ensure client requests are forwarded only to healthy servers. To improve fault tolerance further for the entire system, Web switches can be put into *Active-Active* load-balancing configurations to build topologies with no single point of failure.

Advantages of Active-Active Configuration

Active-Active configurations are always preferable to the alternatives, which incorporates some sort of standby device. Standby devices typically don't *do* anything unless and until something breaks. Definitely nice for peace of mind, but this can be brutal on the checkbook. With Active-Active, the configuration allows for full utilization of the resources you've implemented. As the name suggests, both (or all, depending on how many we're talking about here) devices *fully* participate in whatever activities are being performed. The additional benefits of this are outlined below.

Improved Resource Utilization   Both Web switches are actively performing load-balancing activities for the same virtual service. This doubles the virtual service's effective usable performance and capacity.

Improved Session Availability   Because both Web switches are active, if one fails, only half the user sessions to the web server farm are affected. With traditional hot-standby configurations, only one of the switches is being used and, when it fails, all the user sessions to the web server farm are lost.

Ease of Configuration   Because both switches are active all the time, it's much easier to configure the switches in this mode.

Improved Performance During Traffic Surges   Because both switches are being used, any sudden surges in traffic load are handled more easily.

Switch Processing

Load balancing thousands or tens of thousands of connections per second over dozens of real servers requires vast amounts of processing capacity and memory. Traditionally, three types of processing take place in a server load-balancer: background processing, per-session processing, and per-frame processing.

Background processing includes tasks such as server and service health checks, topology communications, and statistics reporting. These tasks tend to be single-threaded, and the load is light. A coprocessor inside a switch can do the job.

Per-session processing includes a variety of activities, such as identifying incoming session requests, determining the best server for each session, creating a binding that recognizes session terminations and unbinds each session, and handling persistence and timing out idle sessions. Session processing is CPU-intensive, particularly when traffic to be load balanced arrives simultaneously from many 100 Mbps or 1 Gbps ports. Executing per-session processing from a centralized processor limits the number of total session throughput of the load balancer. In addition, routing each session packet to and from the centralized processor puts an additional load on the back plane of any server load-balancing device.

Finally, *per-frame processing* includes session address substitution (IP, MAC, and Layer 4 port number), recomputing checksums, and, in some cases, examining actual frame data. For example, load-balancing FTP sessions requires the load balancer to examine every packet sent by an FTP server to the client over the control channel, so it can derive the dynamic port number to be used for data transmission. Per-frame processing can be extremely CPU-intensive and is best distributed to dedicated processors on each data path. Executing per-frame processing from a centralized processor on traditional server load balancers limits the total frame throughput of the device.

Many other applications have unique session establishment characteristics. This further heightens the need to equip a load balancer with enough capacity and flexibility to support future application load-balancing needs.

SUMMARY

In the past few years, the number of users accessing web sites has grown rapidly. Enterprises are also using their web sites to increase revenue, improve customer service, and optimize business processes. Server load balancing enables IT managers to build an infrastructure that can support mission-critical solutions. For web-based solutions, the switch provides high availability, performance scalability, platform independence, resource optimization, and operational simplicity. The business benefits of a Web switch–based solution are increased customer satisfaction, improved resource use, and decreased total cost of ownership.

The features of Web switches that are important for any web solution are layer 3 and 4 load balancing, URL-based load balancing, real server health monitoring, peak load or traffic surge management, and policy-based service level management.

Several solutions based on purpose-built appliances, integrated switches, and blade modules were discussed in this chapter. Clearly, the Cisco and Nortel solutions are premier implementation of server and global server-load balancing and will continue to compete for market leadership in the months and years to come.

The real winner, however, is the user, whose Internet and web experience is richer and more fulfilling as a result. The concept of $24 \times 7 \times 365$ availability is finally here and waiting for the comeback of the dot-coms.

REVIEW QUESTIONS

1. **What is the Flash Crowd phenomenon? Name one solution a web site uses to protect itself from Flash Crowd.**

   A Flash Crowd phenomenon is a temporary surge of heavy user traffic usually triggered by an event. An example would be the initial release from a hot singer being introduced for sale for the first time at a music store's web site. To protect itself from the Flash Crowd and ensure that Internet users don't experience undue delays while browsing this web site, the web administrator configures one or more overflow servers, which come online when any regular server hits its maximum connections' threshold.

2. **Why is an Active-Active server load-balancing configuration a preferred method when web administrators are concerned with getting full return on investment (ROI) of their web infrastructure?**

   In an Active-Active server load-balancing configuration, two load balancers are configured to process user traffic at the same time, both enhancing the ROI potential of the load balancers and ensuring no single point of failure is in the infrastructure.

3. **What is health checking? Name some health-checking methods the Web switch employs.**

   Health checking is a method used by the load balancer to determine the health and availability of web servers. One method used is periodic ICMP pings of the web servers. A better method is a periodic TCP handshake with Web servers, which not only shows the web server is functional, but also ensures the TCP/IP stack is likewise operational. More sophisticated health-checking checks the contents of the web server ensuring the web site is fully operational.

4. **What is "persistence" or "stickiness," and what are some persistence policies deployed?**

   Persistence ensures every request from a user is handled by the same server, until the completion of the user's transaction. Additionally, when a user suffers a temporary disconnect, persistence ensures the user is directed to the same server. This is important if, for example, the user of an e-commerce web site is engaged in a shopping activity and filling a shopping cart. Some of the persistence policies supported by a load balancer are hash, SSL session ID, and cookies.

5. **Discuss some benefits of URL-based server load balancing.**

    URL-based server load balancing allows the Web switch to redirect a user's request to a web server based on the URL string present in the initial request. Two of the benefits of URL-based server load balancing are ease of management, which allows an administrator to split up the contents of its web site among several servers for both ease of management and improved site performance; and resource optimization, which allows the administrator to use more powerful Web servers to serve CPU-intensive requests for dynamic contents and less-powerful servers to serve static contents.

6. **What function does a backup server perform?**

    When any server in a virtual server group fails or is taken out administratively for maintenance, an administrator usually configures a backup server to take the place of the functions of the downed server.

7. **What is the Dynamic Feedback Protocol (DFP)?**

    The DFP is a proprietary Cisco protocol, providing a mechanism for real servers to send feedback information intelligently to the Local Director—a Cisco load-balancing appliance—ensuring that the Local Director doesn't route traffic to downed applications and that the traffic will be sent to the correct real server.

CHAPTER 10

VRRP and HSRP

OBJECTIVES

▼   Understand the reasons and applications of protocol-based redundancy

■   Understand the elements and operations of VRRP and HSRP

▲   Demonstrate real-world examples of successful protocol deployment

In the last chapter, you learned about the technology solutions used to add redundancy into the server infrastructure. SLB techniques enable CDN designers to create bulletproof server farms and, further, to ensure that no matter what, requests for content can get served.

That is, unless the SLB devices can't get those requests. Or send them anywhere.

Designing for redundancy is like trying to remove a bottleneck. Every time you eliminate one, another crops up in what seems to be the ultimate network-design whack-a-mole.

At every level, there seems to be something that can go belly-up and, thereby, cause the complete and utter failure of the content delivery infrastructure. Starting at the bottom, the servers connect into a single switch. What if a network card goes bad? No problem: dual-home the servers. What if the server goes bad? No problem: use SLB and create a server group. What if the layer-2 switch goes bad? No problem: divide the servers into groups and add each group to its own layer-2 switch. What if the router goes bad? What if the site gets sponged off the face of the Earth? What if . . . !

The latter, we'll address in Chapter 11, the former, now. The problem this chapter attempts to address is redundancy at the gateway level. Every egress point off a network goes through a gateway. That gateway, at least for servers, is the *default gateway*. Everything in the Internet is typically reached by sending traffic to it. The default gateway gets configured one of two ways: manually or dynamically. For client hosts, it tends to be dynamically, through the Dynamic Host Configuration Protocol (DHCP). Most network design guides direct designers to implement this service wherever and whenever possible. For servers, configuration is statically configured, that is, configured by hand. Servers have a nasty habit of being located by name through a service like the Domain Name Service (DNS). DNS, a static database, will have one or more addresses for any given name. DHCP can hand out any old address to any old server, and each handout could be different—not a problem for clients, but for servers accessed by static name-IP address mappings, it could get ugly. While Dynamic DNS (a DNS service that coordinates with DHCP and possibly WINS) is on the way, it hasn't arrived. The long and short of it is content servers get manually configured addresses, including their gateway of last resort. And this isn't a problem—until the gateway fails.

You can fix this in several ways. One way is to configure a routing protocol, like RIP, on the servers in question. Each server can then snoop on local routing broadcasts and select its gateways accordingly. This tends not to be a popular solution, mainly because no one seems to want to implement RIP on their server networks. There are too many broadcasts, too many weird routing possibilities, and it takes too long to converge.

Another solution is to implement a protocol-based solution, such as VRRP or HSRP. These two protocols are functionally identical, that is, they serve the same purpose and are deployed in the same situations. Essentially, these protocols are used to provide hot-standby gateway failover protection. If the primary gateway is going belly up, these protocols ensure a backup can step in, take control, and continue service, all in seconds, and completely transparent to the end users. The way this is accomplished is through deploying dummy addresses that are assumable nearly instantaneously by any of the devices participating in the protocol.

Both protocols enjoy a wide deployment currently. HSRP is a proprietary Cisco-developed protocol, but is available for licensing to third parties for some fee. As such, HSRP hasn't enjoyed wide market acceptance. VRRP is the standards-based equivalent and is, therefore, free of licensing issues It seems to be enjoying a wider market/platform penetration because of it. High-end Cisco routers support both protocols, but for CDN devices, VRRP seems to be the de facto standard. Cisco's Arrowpoint product line, Nortel Networks' Alteon product line, Foundry Networks' product line—all support VRRP (of some variety—more in the following).

CDN designers need to be aware of these two protocols and how to deploy them. The RFCs that cover these two protocols are still the single best reference available and can be found at the IETF web site (http://www.ietf.org).

VIRTUAL ROUTER REDUNDANCY PROTOCOL

Virtual Router Redundancy Protocol (VRRP) is an Internet Engineering Task Force (IETF) protocol, specified in RFC 2338. It fulfills a role similar to Cisco's proprietary Hot Standby Router Protocol (RFC 2281), where the goal is "to eliminate the single point of failure inherent in the static default-routed environment (RFC 2338)."

VRRP is used when high availability is needed to access a gateway device where redundancy is provided through a virtual router (VR), a logical object that acts as the default gateway for a set of hosts on a given network. The VR is comprised of two routers running a common VRRP process. When a packet is sent to the VR, either of the two routers can handle the request and forward it on to the appropriate next hop. Each router can participate in one or more VRs, adopting the role as either *master* or *backup* router in each relationship. In case of failure, the backup device takes over for the master. Figures 10-1 and 10-2 show the difference between a single and redundant gateway network.

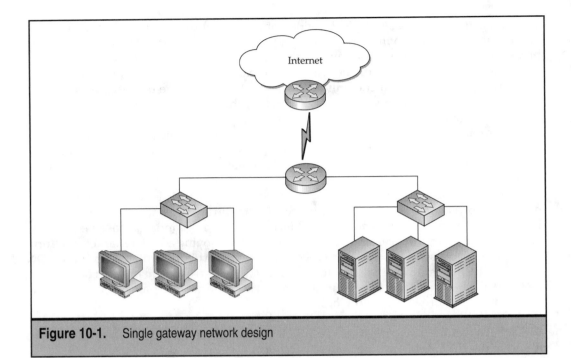

Figure 10-1. Single gateway network design

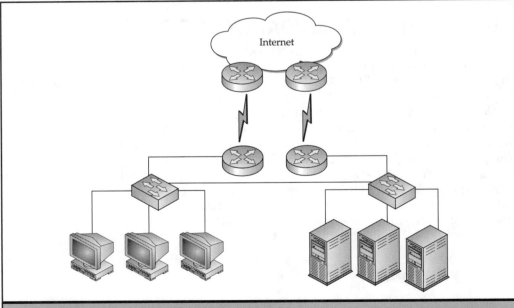

Figure 10-2. Redundant gateway network design

Operations

The way this works is as follows: the basic element in VRRP configurations is the router running the VRRP process. Of course, one router alone won't do much in the way of High Availability! But when two or more routers, on the same layer-2 segment and running VRRP processes, are then configured with the same 8-bit virtual router ID (VRID), these devices are combined to create a single VR. Each router can (and often does) participate in multiple VRs. More on this later.

In a given VR, unless a failure occurs, the master controls, or *owns,* the IP addresses assigned to the VR, called the virtual IP (VIP). What this means is the device that has the VIP as one of its own already configured interface addresses will be said to own that address. The master handles all protocol requests for that VR address and does so at both OSI layer 3 and layer 2. At layer 2, a VR also creates a virtual MAC (VMAC) address for layer-2 handoffs. The VMAC has a standard format of 00-00-5E-00-01-*xx*, where the last byte is the VRID for the VR. A downstream ARP request for the MAC of the VIP will yield the VMAC.

The VMAC is important because MAC addresses are stored by network nodes, either in the ARP cache (for end stations) or in the CAM tables (for switches). These stored entries can remain in the tables from several minutes to over an hour. Upstream failures during this period could result in errors, lost data, and broken connections. By using a fabricated, logical MAC address, either of the two VRRP routers can assume control of it and continue operations even in a failure, without the need for a possibly lengthy timeout period.

When configured and operational, the master sends out periodic advertisement messages, by default, once per second. A certain number of these advertisements must be missed to have a backup initiate the takeover procedure, usually set to three, but this is configurable. When a failure is detected, a backup initiates an election to see who becomes the master for that segment. This election protocol is vendor-specific because it isn't covered in the RFC, but it works something as follows. After three missed advertisements, the first backup on a segment (and, remember, there could be several) to reach the timeout then sends out an advertisement showing, with a special *priority,* a variable set from router to router (and *is* part of the RFC spec).

This 8-bit field is included in the VRRP header of every advertisement and is set to 100 by default. All other backups on the segment will match that priority. If a given backup can beat that value with a higher priority, it sends its advertisement out onto the network. The router with the highest priority wins, becoming the master. The priorities can range from 1–254, with higher being better. A value of 255 is reserved for the VIP owner, so the owner always becomes the master during an election. A value of zero is special and means an election must begin immediately. This is the priority value that the first backup detecting the failure will most likely send to start the election process.

NOTE: This is dependent on implementation—not every vendor will, should, or must implement elections this way.

A corollary to the election process, however it's implemented, is called *preemption*. Each router has an option under the VRRP setting either to allow or deny the preemption of the current master. When a router with this setting on sees an advertisement by a router with a lower priority, the higher priority router gratuitously issues an election challenge. This can be turned off for all cases except for the VIP owner. When the owner comes back online, it will force (and win) an election.

VRRP is usable only on a single layer-2 segment. What keeps the packets isolated on the segment they were generated on is the TTL, which is set to 255. By design, if a VRRP Router receives a packet with at TTL value of anything other than 255, the router must discard it. Because all routers decrement TTLs with every forward, the sending router sets the TTL to 255, it reaches the next hop, and can go no farther.

Figure 10-2 shows an example of this VRRP configuration in operation. Each of the physical routers is master in one virtual router and backup in the second. If Router 2 fails, then Router 1 takes over the routing functionality of Router 2. It assumes control of the MAC and IP address of Virtual Router 2, and then responds to all requests intended for those addresses. This failover to the backup router is transparent to hosts sending traffic across the network and should occur in less than five seconds.

Protocol

This section explores the VRRP header info and packet structure. The goal is to identify the various fields, and their uses, meaningfully. This information will be useful in packet traces.

VRRP is a layer-4 IP protocol, like UDP or TCP (its IANA-assigned protocol number is 112), and is encapsulated in IP for transport. VRRP uses a variable-length header (48+ bytes), depending on the number of VIPs being advertised under the process. Also, VRRP is multicast-based, so the destination address is always a Class-D address. VRRP has a reserved IP, for advertisement, of 224.0.0.18.

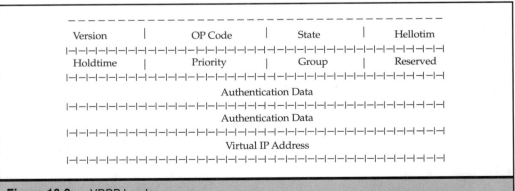

Figure 10-3. VRRP header

Version Field   The 8-bit version field specifies the VRRP protocol version of the packet. The most common, standardized version is version 2. Version 3 is for IPv6.

Type Field   The 8-bit type field specifies the VRRP type of this packet. Only one packet type is defined in this version of the protocol, the advertisement packet type, identified by a value of 1. Any packet received with a value other than 1 must be discarded by the router.

Virtual Router ID (VRID)   The 8-bit VRID field identifies which VR this packet belongs to.

Priority   The 8-bit priority field contains a value from 0–255 that signifies what role a specific device holds. See the previous for a description.

Count IP Address   The 8-bit count IP address field identifies the *number* of IP addresses contained in the VRRP advertisement.

Authorization Type   The 8-bit authorization type field identifies the authentication type used, on a per interface basis. If no authentication is set, the value is 0. For simple clear-text passwords, the value is set to 1 or, if IP header authentication is being used, the value is set to 2.

Advertisement Interval   The 8-bit advertisement interval field indicates how much time should elapse before the next advertisement is sent. This value is in seconds, with the default of one second.

Checksum   The 16-bit checksum field is used to detect errors in the VRRP message.

IP Address   Multiple 32-bit IP address fields are used, if necessary, to identify the IP addresses associated with the VR.

Authentication Data   The 64-bit authentication data field is used to pass simple text authentication information. The value of the information passed is the binary representation of an eight-character string of plain text.

VRRP Router States

A VRRP Router can hold one of three states according to the protocol state machine. The *state machine* is simply a functional description of how the VRRP router will behave and what its duties are, depending on its role.

Initialize   Before a Start command is given to the process, for example, **enable**, the process will remain in the Initialize state. It doesn't do much, except allow configuration of the process. When a start command is given, the Initialize state has a couple of duties to execute, depending on its priority.

If the priority is 1 and 254, the process will set both the Master-Down-Timer and the Master-Down-Interval. The first indicates it hasn't yet heard an advertisement; the second indicates how long it will wait for one before initiating an election. The default interval is just over three and a half seconds.

If the priority is 255, which is automatically and only set if the device is the VIP owner, then the Initializing device has some other duties. First, it sends an advertisement. Next, it sends a gratuitous ARP request response to the network segment containing the VMAC for the VIP. The device then assumes the role of master.

Master A VRRP Router in the Master state functions as a forwarding router for the IP address associated with the Virtual Router. It must respond to ARP requests, forward packets with a MAC address equal to the MAC Address of the VR, and manage and forward IP packets meant for the VR. It also sends an advertisement message at the frequency set by the Advertisement Interval, again, by default, once every second.

If the VRRP process on the master is given an administrative halt or stop command, the master responds by sending out an advertisement message with the Priority set to 0 to force an election, and then transitions to the Initialize state.

Backup A backup VR has only one job: to monitor the availability of the master router by receiving and processing advertisement messages. It cannot respond to ARP requests or forward packets. If the Master-Down-Interval expires, then the backup assumes the role of the master by some election criteria and transitions to the master state.

Case Studies

VRRP configuration on each device is different. Each device has its own command line and parameter formats. In this section, configurations for two product lines are presented.

Juniper

The following is an example of how to configure one VRRP Master Router and one VRRP Backup Router to create a Virtual Router 1. Figure 10-4 illustrates this.

VRRP Master Router

```
[edit]

interfaces {
    ge-0/0/0 {
        unit 0 {
            family inet {
                address 10.10.10.100/101 {
                    vrrp-group 1 {
```

```
                    virtual-address 10.10.10.200;
            priority 255;
                    advertise-interval 3;
                    preempt;
                    authentication-type simple;
                    authentication-key UnSeCR;
                }
            }
        }
    }
}
}
```

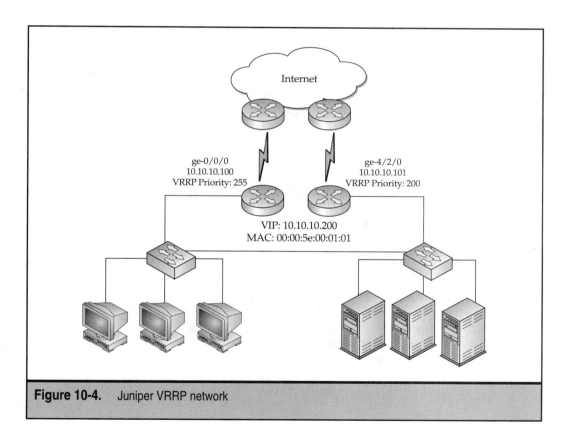

Figure 10-4. Juniper VRRP network

VRRP Backup Router

```
[edit]

interfaces {
     ge-4/2/0 {
          unit 0 {
               family inet {
                    address 10.10.10.101/101 {
                         vrrp-group 1 {
                              virtual-address 10.10.10.200;
                              priority 200;
                              authentication-type simple;
                              authentication-key UnSeCR;
                         }
                    }
               }
          }
     }
}
```

The following is an example on how to configure the MAC address on a Juniper Gigabit Ethernet interface.

```
[edit interfaces]

ge-0/0/0 {
     gigether-options {
          source-filtering;
          source-address-filter {
               00:00:5e:00:01:01;
          }
     }
     unit 0 {
          family inet {
               address 10.10.10.100/101 {
                    vrrp-group 1 {
                         virtual-address 10.10.10.200;
                         priority 255;
                         preempt;
                    }
               }
          }
     }
}
```

Cisco

Cisco has supported VRRP since version 12.0 on its high-end platforms, and is supported on their Ethernet interfaces, from 10/100 up to GE, as well as on MPLS VPNs and VLANs. The following configuration is for a 3 VR implementation of VRRP (see Figure 10-5) on a pair of Cisco routers. Each VR will have the following properties.

For Group 1, the VIP is 192.168.2.1, and NY-Localnet-DG-1 is the owner. As the owner, NY-Localnet-DG-1 will become the master for this group. The advertising interval is 2 seconds, preemption is enabled, and the password is 'password'.

For Group 12, the VIP is 192.168.2.12, and NY-Localnet-DG-2 is the owner. As owner, it will become master for this group. The advertising interval is 5 seconds, preemption is enabled, and the password is 'swordfsh'.

For the last, Group 100, the VIP is 192.168.2.100. However, there doesn't appear to be an owner (perhaps a router not yet online). With no clear priority, and assuming that both routers start their processes simultaneously, NY-Localnet-DG-2 will become master for

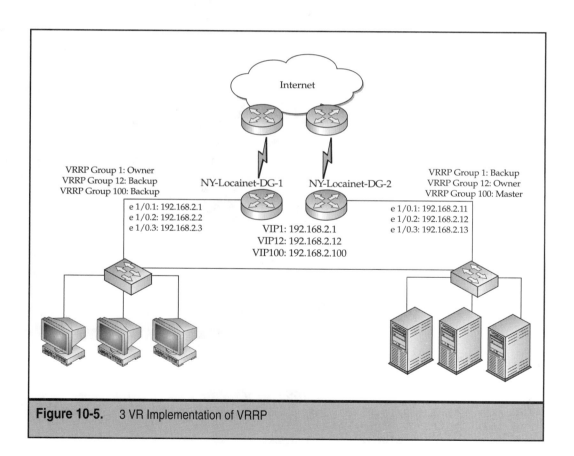

Figure 10-5. 3 VR Implementation of VRRP

this group. Cisco implements a tiebreaker for VRRP elections by choosing the winner for holding the highest manually configured IP address (192.168.2.13).

Here are the (partial) configurations:

```
hostname NY-Localnet-DG-1
!
interface ethernet 1/0.1
ip address 192.168.2.1 255.255.255.0
!
interface ethernet 1/0.2
ip address 192.168.2.2 255.255.255.0
!
interface ethernet 1/0.3
ip address 192.168.2.3 255.255.255.0
!
vrrp 1 priority 200
vrrp 1 authentication password
vrrp 1 timers advertise 2
vrrp 1 timers learn
vrrp 1 ip 192.168.2.1
vrrp 12 priority 100
vrrp 12 authentication swordfsh
vrrp 12 timers advertise 5
vrrp 12 timers learn
vrrp 12 ip 192.168.2.12
vrrp 100 timers learn
vrrp 100 preempt
vrrp 100 ip 192.168.2.100
```

And for the second router:

```
hostname NY-Localnet-DG-2
!
interface ethernet 1/0.1
ip address 192.168.2.11 255.255.255.0
!
interface ethernet 1/0.2
ip address 192.168.2.12 255.255.255.0
!
interface ethernet 1/0.3
ip address 192.168.2.13 255.255.255.0
!
vrrp 1 priority 100
vrrp 1 authentication password
vrrp 1 timers advertise 2
```

```
vrrp 1 timers learn
vrrp 1 ip 192.168.2.1
vrrp 12 priority 200
vrrp 12 authentication swordfsh
vrrp 12 timers advertise 5
vrrp 12 timers learn
vrrp 12 ip 192.168.2.12
vrrp 100 timers learn
vrrp 100 preempt
vrrp 100 ip 192.168.2.100
```

VRRPe

VRRPe (*e* for *extensions*) is a proprietary enhancement to VRRP, implemented by Foundry Networks, HP, Nortel Networks, and others. VRRPe differs from VRRP primarily in that there's no owner for VIPs. That is, it's no longer required to use an IP address already configured on one of the switches as the VIP. The VIP, in this case, can be completely independent of the IP interfaces configured in the layer-3 switches and, therefore, no restriction exists on which router can be the default master router. This is in contrast with VRRP, where the owner must be the default master.

VRRPe can differ architecturally from VRRP in minor ways. For example, the Foundry implementation of VRRPe sends messages to destination MAC address 01-00-5E-00-00-02 and destination multicast address of 224.0.0.2—the multicast address for "all routers". By way of contrast, the Nortel Networks/Alteon implementation uses the standard VRRP addresses. In what seems to be a standard characteristic, the VRRPe master and backups are selected based on their priority, not ownership. You can configure any device as master simply by giving it the highest priority.

Foundry, HP ProCurve, and the Alteon product line all support functionally identical versions of VRRPe. However, it's worth noting this isn't a standard and, as such, it isn't surprising that intervendor VRRPe interoperation isn't terribly reliable. Yet.

HSRP

The Hot Standby Router Protocol (HSRP) is specified in RFC 2281. According to the RFC, "HSRP provides a mechanism which is designed to support non-disruptive failover of IP traffic in certain circumstances. In particular, the protocol protects against the failure of the first hop router when the source host cannot learn the IP address of the first hop router dynamically." Note how similar this is to the stated goal of VRRP!

In HSRP, VRs are implemented by a set of routers, called an *HSRP Group* or a *standby group*. The *active* router in the HSRP Group assumes responsibility for forwarding the packets sent to the VIP. The routers that are part of the standby group and not currently active are considered *standby* and have the responsibility of taking over for the active router if it fails.

Like VRRP, the routers can be members of multiple standby groups simultaneously. Similarly, a single group can implement multiple VRs. If the hosts that use the VR are divided into separate groups—for example, along subnets, VLANs, or DHCP scopes—the standby group can achieve some rudimentary load balancing. Remember, within a standby group, the active router is the only one doing anything. By making one router in an pair active for one VR and the second active for the other, then both routers will be doing work at the same time.

Each device will have an IP and MAC address. When the device becomes part of the HSRP Group, another IP and MAC address are assigned to the VR. In contrast to VRRP (and more strongly than VRRPe), the VIP must be unique on the network.

Protocol

As you'll see, HSRP and VRRP are functionally equivalent, but differences occur in the way the two implement failover.

HSRP Header

HSRP is encapsulated in IP and uses UDP as its transport, using UDP port 1985. Packets are sent to a multicast address of 224.0.0.2 with a TTL of 1. Recall that VRRP uses a TTL of 255, but adds this catch: if that TTL isn't 255, it must be discarded. With HSRP implementing a TTL of 1, the same is accomplished without having to add the additional injunction.

Figure 10-6 illustrates the HSRP Packet format for IPv4.

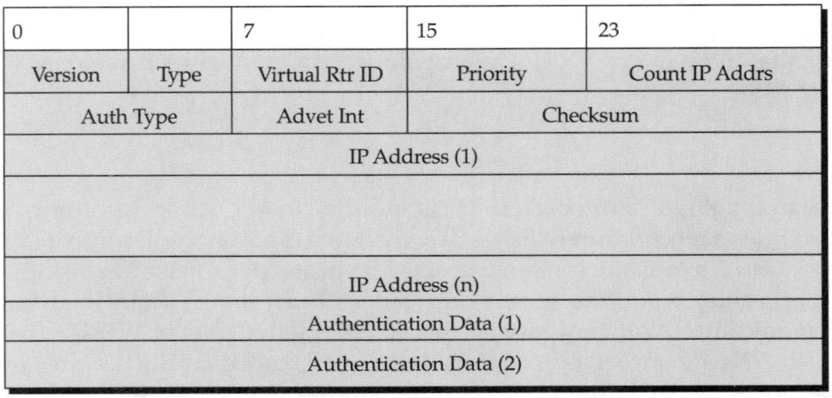

0		7	15	23
Version	Type	Virtual Rtr ID	Priority	Count IP Addrs
Auth Type		Advet Int	Checksum	
IP Address (1)				
IP Address (n)				
Authentication Data (1)				
Authentication Data (2)				

Figure 10-6.   HSRP Packet header

Version   The 8-bit version field specifies the HSRP protocol version of the packet. The current specified version is version 0. (Beta software? You be the judge!)

Op Code   This field specifies the HSRP packet type operation. Three values are possible. If the value is set to 0, then the message is a "Hello", which is the standard keepalive, and indicates the router is capable of being active or standby. If the value is set to 1, then the message is a "Coup". This is exactly what it means—revolution! Or, more precisely, the Coup is an indication the sender wants to go active. When the value is set to 2, the sender is indicating it wants to "Resign" from being active (and probably should have been called "abdicate").

State   This 8-bit state field indicates the current state of the router sending the message. The details are discussed in a later section, but six states are possible. The following table shows them, with their codes.

Value	State	Value	State	Value	State
0	Initial	2	Listen	8	Standby
1	Learn	4	Speak	16	Active

Hellotime   This 8-bit field is used with Hello messages to indicate the number of seconds between messages. The default is three seconds.

Holdtime   This 8-bit field describes the amount of time, in seconds, before the current active is considered AWOL, and is only included in Hello messages. The default is ten seconds, or three times the hellotime, plus a bit for jitter.

Priority   Identical to VRRP, this 8-bit field is used to determine the outcome of elections. The router with the highest value wins and, in the case of a tie, the router with the highest active IP address wins.

Group   This is an 8-bit group field that indicates which routers belong to a given standby group.

Reserved   This 8-bit reserved field is reserved for future use.

Authentication Data   This 64-bit field can contain an eight-character clear text password for authentication.

Virtual IP Address   The 32-bit virtual IP address field indicates the VIP used by this group.

Operational Parameters

Certain information must be configured for each router in a standby group. This information includes the following: group number, VMAC, router priority, any authentication password, hellotime, and holdtime. At least one router must be configured with the Virtual IP address. The other routers in the group can learn it from that router.

Note, all routers in the standby group are transmitting periodic hello messages, which is unlike VRRP, where only the master is sending out such advertisements. Elections occur, but more along the lines of selecting the vice president, not the president—in a failure, the one that will take over has already been selected and can step in immediately. The elections are then held to see who will step into the VP/standby role.

Router States

The *router* states are similar to those used in VRRP, except HSRP identifies six distinct states to VRRP's three. These states are logical categories that identify the responsibilities each of the roles must execute.

Initial   As the name suggests, the *initial* state indicates the HSRP process is either not currently running or is just starting up on that router/interface.

Learn   Before the router receives a hello message, it's considered in the *learn* state.

Listen   In the *listen* state, the HSRP process has received a hello message and might have thereby learned the VIP, the hellotime, and the holdtime, but isn't yet participating in the standby group.

Speak   In the *speak* state, the router definitely knows the VIP and is actively participating in the election of the active and/or standby router by sending hello packets with its own priority enclosed.

Standby   The *standby* state indicates the HSRP router is fully functioning in the standby group and has been recognized as being next in line to take over the responsibilities of the active router. Only one router is in the standby state at any given time.

Active   As the name implies, the *active* state indicates the router is the active router. The active router forwards packets sent to the VIP. This router, like the others, sends Hello messages periodically to indicate its status. Like the standby router, only one router is in the group in this state.

HSRP Timers

Three timers are used to trigger events: the active timer, the standby timer, and the hello timer. The *active* timer is used to monitor the hello messages of the active router, and it expires after the holdtime expires. The *standby* timer does exactly the same thing as the active timer. Finally, the *hello* timer is used to trigger hello messages. If the router is in speak, standby, or active status, it needs to send out a hello message.

Case Studies

The following are a pair of configuration examples on how to configure HSRP in a Cisco environment.

Simple HSRP

The goal is simple default gateway redundancy. Currently, network addressing is assigned via DHCP, which includes the gateway address of 192.168.2.1. This address will be the VIP handled by the standby group.

Two routers connect to a pair of layer-2 switches downstream and provide connectivity off-Net. The layer-2 switches are cross-connected to provide some downstream redundancy and to enable the passing of HSRP hellos. See Figure 10-7 for a network diagram.

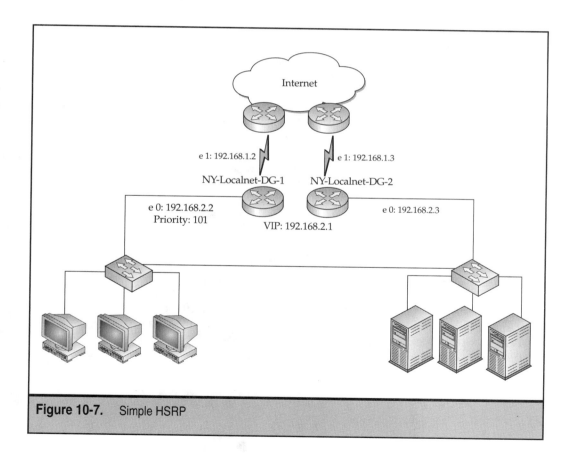

Figure 10-7.   Simple HSRP

With the following configuration, NY-Localnet-DG-1 will be the active router for the LAN (with priority 101) and NY-Localnet-DG-2 will be backup.

```
hostname NY-Localnet-DG-1
!
interface ethernet 0
ip address 192.168.2.2 255.255.255.0
standby 1 ip 192.168.2.1
standby 1 preempt
standby 1 priority 101
standby 1 authentication swordfsh
standby 1 timers 2 7
!
interface ethernet 1
ip address 192.168.1.2 255.255.255.0
!
hostname NY-Localnet-DG-2
!
interface ethernet 0
ip address 192.168.2.3 255.255.255.0
standby 1 ip 192.168.2.1
standby 1 preempt
standby 1 authentication swordfsh
standby 1 timers 2 7
!
interface ethernet 1
ip address 192.168.1.3 255.0.0.0
!
```

HSRP w/ 2 VIPs

The decision to migrate from a single HSRP group to a dual-group environment was made to fully use the network devices and egress links. Again, a pair of layer-2 switches provide host connectivity and allow for HSRP hello passage. Figure 10-8 shows the changes.

Additionally, a second DHCP server has been added to the network, so each layer-2 switch can have its own local DHCP server. Each server will hand out separate scopes, and each scope will have a separate default gateway—both of which are VIPs—handled by the standby group.

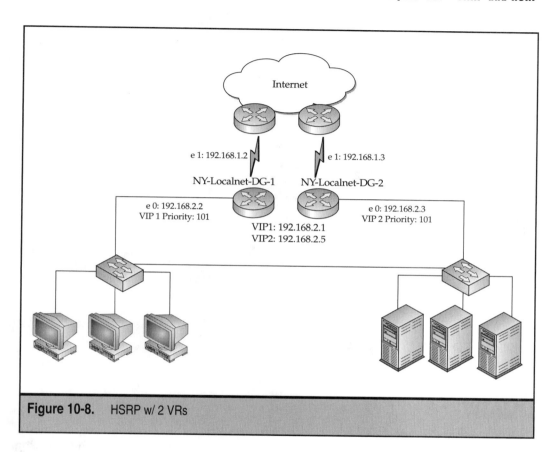

Figure 10-8. HSRP w/ 2 VRs

With the following reconfiguration, NY-Localnet-DG-1 will still be active for VIP 192.168.2.1 (priority 101), and NY-Localnet-DG-2 will be active for VIP 192.168.2.5 (also priority 101).

```
hostname NY-Localnet-DG-1
!
interface ethernet 0
ip address 192.168.2.2 255.255.255.0
standby 1 ip 192.168.2.1
```

```
standby 1 preempt
standby 1 priority 101
standby 1 authentication swordfsh
standby 1 timers 2 7
standby 2 ip 192.168.2.5
standby 2 preempt
standby 2 authentication password
standby 2 timers 2 7

hostname NY-Localnet-DG-2
!
interface ethernet 0
ip address 192.168.2.3 255.255.255.0
standby 1 ip 192.168.2.1
standby 1 preempt
standby 1 authentication swordfsh
standby 1 timers 2 7
standby 2 ip 1.0.0.4
standby 2 preempt
standby 2 priority 101
standby 2 authentication password
standby 2 timers 2 7
```

SUMMARY

The primary goal is to provide content services, "at all costs," and gateway redundancy is yet another step in that high-availability chain. CDN designers interested in providing the highest level of service to and from their data centers should look closely at protocol-based solutions, such as those outlined in this chapter.

Whether a particular implementation settles on either VRRP or HSRP depends more on the solution being implemented. More specifically, it depends on which of the two the relevant vendors support! While functionally on par, the support base varies wildly, with most CDN technology vendors providing support for the standards-based VRRP, and Cisco, while holding out HSRP for licensing, still is the primary supporter of HSRP.

Remember, gateways can occur at nearly any level in any network—whenever traffic needs to go off-Net, it will go through a gateway to do so. Any of these are possible points of failure. With protocol solutions, they needn't be *single* points of failure.

REVIEW QUESTIONS

1. **Which of the two protocols, VRRP or HSRP, fails over faster?**

   Both are user-configurable, and actual fail-over timers are set by vendor. As such, neither will necessarily operate faster than the other.

2. **Can I implement an HSRP solution on a pair of Foundry devices?**

   No. Foundry supports VRRP and VRRPe.

3. **Can I implement a VRRP solution using both a Foundry switch/router and a Cisco router?**

   Yes, VRRP is standards-based.

4. **Can I implement a VRRPe solution using a Foundry switch/router and a Nortel Networks Alteon web switch?**

   No, VRRPe is *not* a standard, and each vendor's implementation is different. In this case, the Foundry is using a different advertisement multicast address than the Alteon.

CHAPTER 11

Global Server Load Balancing

OBJECTIVES

▼ Describe purpose and use of Global Server Load Balancing (GSLB)

■ Describe major technologies employed in site selection

■ Discuss packet loss and its impact

■ Discuss major problems with DNS-based solutions

■ Compare/contrast Footraces with probing techniques

■ Explore complex routing technology solutions

▲ Demonstrate technology solutions for GSLB

Global Server Load Balancing (GSLB) is an attempt to extend the concept of SLB by an order of magnitude. Instead of providing load balancing services to a set of servers in a single server farm, GSLB provides a mechanism whereby multiple, geographically diverse server farms can be deployed to provide a significantly enhanced level of service. Most vendors will agree that the stated goal of GSLB is to improve the availability and performance of some set of web-enabled content. This chapter reviews the various technologies and techniques for achieving this and analyzes some solutions currently on the market.

Imagine that an online content provider, such as CNN, has a content server farm in New York City. This server farm is where all its streaming media comes from, and that media is comprised of local news bulletins, live broadcasts covering disasters and presidential election debates, video journalism articles on biological warfare, weather and market reports, and news from the war in the Middle East. And, of course, all their paid advertising is disseminated from here as well. CNN is reliant on its web site to be accurate, current, and, above all, useable.

Suppose the unthinkable happens. A nuclear bomb gets detonated in Los Angeles. A meteor the size of a Volkswagen Bug strikes the Kremlin, leveling all of Moscow. Aliens seize the Space Shuttle. Whatever. In such situations, three critical ways exist in which GSLB can help content providers like news organizations stay plugged in and shoveling content, regardless of the circumstance.

First, what can happen to news web sites in such events is a fairly common problem and, in fact, happens to them every time some tremendous event occurs. It's called *flash traffic,* and is, simply, a massive traffic spike. Online news organizations use server farms to serve their content and, depending on the amount of advertising dollars at risk, likely use sophisticated SLB tools to ensure prompt, efficient delivery. Even with these tools, however, the sheer volume of traffic for our hypothetical disaster might well be enough to overwhelm them completely. With GSLB, multiple remote sites could have offloaded the traffic, allowing users to be shunted to backup server farms.

No one can plan for a meteor taking out your server farm. Such site failures can be the result of something so dramatic or as simple as a cleaning crew accidentally unplugging a crucial switch. Things happen. The Internet itself was designed with this kind of extreme flexibility in mind. You can "lose" large hunks of the California coastline and still have data moving from west to east. GSLB can work with the robust Internet routing protocols and enable clients by dynamically rerouting to live content distribution sites if a large failure at the primary site occurs.

Users come from all over the world to view CNN's content. How efficient is it to have those requests go hither and yon? How enjoyable is it for the user to sit at his desk, drumming his fingers while some service provider routes his request to the Arctic Circle and back again? With GSLB, it's possible to discriminate some level of geographic relevance. That is, send your clients in China to your server farm in Beijing, not London.

Many uses exist for GSLB. This chapter examines a few of them and discusses some of the more subtle aspects to globalizing content.

SOLUTIONS

A natural question is whom this technology targets. The quick and dirty explanation would be any company deriving a significant portion of its revenue from delivering web-based content. Another less dramatic category will be any company trying to offer services that require a global distribution mechanism, whether the clients for those services are internal or external.

GSLB implementations have three primary categories. The first is a simple failover technique, whereby GSLB technology can be used to provide site redundancy. The second is a bit more robust, where GSLB acts in concert with DNS to load balance across multiple, distinct sites. The final variation carries this last category a bit farther and uses GSLB to determine client redirection to the best site, depending on the world location of the client.

Simple Failover

A particular type of client, a news organization, was discussed previously. Extrapolating a bit from here, a simple case could be made that *any* business relying on its content distribution via the Web would be a potential beneficiary of such a technology solution. Online retailers, in particular, should be and are looking closely at whether GSLB would make sense for their enterprises.

Drilling down a bit deeper, GSLB can be implemented within a particular organization as well, providing support for mission-critical applications and databases. Enterprises with nationwide or international reach have problems particular to size—resources not local to the end user tend to cause tremendous burdens on long-haul circuits.

For example, an LDAP database containing all the corporate user accounts, their rights and privileges, as well as their contact info, can be fairly central to the way a large corporation does business. Placing a local server at each of the remote offices is a great way to remove LDAP traffic from the WAN and to increase user satisfaction. In the event of a local LDAP server failure, however, the users will be forced to do without.

That is, to do without unless some form of GSLB is deployed. With GSLB, a local failure can be translated into simply making a nonoptimal connection across the backbone WAN to the next available site. Performance might not be fantastic, depending on the robustness of the WAN, but work will be able to continue.

High Availability

When designing a data center, a point in the design appears to exist where the Law of Diminishing Returns takes over. You can stuff only so many servers into a data center and install only so many routers and switches. You can deploy only so many backup power systems. After a certain point, all the server clustering solutions and SLB devices in the world aren't going to buy you any more redundancy or availability. If that site goes down, that's it. A major construction project in the area could generate a backhoe-induced failure. It isn't a stretch to imagine that even though separate circuits were purchased from different providers—circuits that used different Lambdas on physically separated fiber strands—the two strands of fiber run through the same conduit, lying next to each other, and could get cut by the same backhoe.

The approach many large portal sites use is to create several smaller data centers. The content-generating mechanisms are duplicated across the sites, as is the content itself. GSLB mechanisms are then implemented to ensure that even if a failure at one data center takes it entirely offline, another fully functional data center is already handling traffic. As mentioned earlier, news organizations and online retailers greatly benefit from this distributed approach.

The way this works is by manipulating DNS. As discussed in Chapter 6, DNS is the service by which clients retrieve IP information based on server name (and vice versa). First, the GSLB device is configured to provide authoritative DNS responses for the names of the sites being load balanced. Much like an SLB device, the GSLB device is also configured with a list of sites being served, each hidden behind some unique VIP. The VIPs are stored as A-records, and the GSLB device can use some sophisticated techniques (described in the following) to determine which of them to hand out to any particular DNS request.

Geographic Load Balancing

Taking the distributed approach a step farther, the data centers can be strategically located to minimize the impact sheer distance can have. Obviously, the latency between a user in New York City and a resource in Manhattan is going to be considerably less, all things being equal, than the latency of a user in Madagascar attempting to connect to the same resource. Now, if only that site were in Johannesburg. . . .

The design goal for geographic load balancing is closely in line with general Content Networking design principles. Specifically, put the content as close to the consumers as possible. The reach the content provider wants or needs should dictate the strategic locations where local sites should be deployed. Two primary sites, located on the East and West Coasts of the United States, preferably near large Network Access Points (NAP) such as

MAE-East and MAE-West, service most providers' needs. The next staging areas are typically in Europe, Asia, Australia, South America, and South Africa, usually in that order.

The more sites, the better the reach, but the higher the cost. At some point, the Law of Diminishing Returns kicks in again and the choice becomes more of a business decision than a technical one.

Geographic Load Balancing works exactly the same as the High Availability solution previously outlined. Through active site monitoring, the GSLB device can and will dictate which sites remain active and available for use, as well as manipulating the DNS returns to the requesting client, thereby deciding which of the sites is most relevant to that client.

HOW IT WORKS

How it all works is something of a tricky subject to set down. The problem isn't technical but, rather, is that of a moving target. GSLB is still in its infancy, technologically speaking, and new and clever approaches to solving its problems are being invented daily. The approach taken here is to outline some of the more clever approaches, describe the technology as clearly as possible, and show some of the advantages and disadvantages with the approach.

Dynamic Site Selection

At its heart, GSLB is all about site selection. Which site should a particular client be sent to and what criteria are used to make that choice? Painting with broad strokes, the two criteria most relevant will be some measure of load and some measure of proximity. Load should be able to dictate which site is most able to handle the request, proximity dictates which site is most likely to introduce the least amount of latency.

Load algorithms will be the same as those used in SLB to determine which server to route individual requests to. In GSLB, we're looking at site load, not server load, so the metrics will be more of an average instead of a specific. Metrics such as least connections (leastconns) will be able to track the number of connections into a particular site, where metrics such as *hash* will attempt to spread all connections evenly across the available sites. More sophisticated polling techniques on the part of the GSLB device would allow the tracking of numbers of servers up or down, the average response times of a site, thresholds for the maximum connections and CPU utilization, network bandwidth load, Quality of Service (QoS) metrics, and, perhaps, security concerns.

Proximity algorithms are where GSLB and SLB start to diverge. The notion of proximity incorporates an expectation of speed—it will be faster to get resources locally instead of having to go far away. Basic latency bears this out—the more intervening steps, the longer a response will take, period (all else being equal). Round-trip-timers (RTT) are important measures in this regard, as are average bandwidth along the path, the number of hops, the number of ASes that need to be traversed, and so forth.

No protocol standards specify how to implement these functions as yet, so it's a matter of individual vendors exploring and creating what they need. As a result, the protocols built for these functions are all proprietary to the solution vendor implementing them.

You can implement GSLB solutions in many ways, and some general categories immediately follow. Whichever the implementation, some sort of proximity/load protocol will be embedded in the solution proffered by the vendor.

Backup Servers

Purists say using GSLB technology for site failover or backups isn't really GSLB at all. Pooh on them. Any technology that takes the original client request and sends it to a better site, whether that site is more geographically appropriate to that client or is simply more able to handle their request, is GSLB, and the rest is simply nitpicking.

That said, using GSLB for site failover or backups isn't really GSLB, at least in the sense that it includes little or no necessary notion of proximity. Not that it can't, but it most likely won't. What we're doing with this type of solution is identifying a secondary site that can handle traffic if and when the primary site goes kablooie, and not focusing on making clever decisions on where to send traffic. The configurations are relatively simple and look alarmingly like: "if there's a failure, send all traffic here." This backup site can be a simple server or a load-balanced server farm, it doesn't matter to the primary site. What does matter to the primary site is what constitutes a failure.

There are failures and there are failures. Server seizing up? A failure. Unplugging a server from the switch? A failure. Sudden power loss to the server? Also a failure. Power loss to the entire building? Definitely a failure, but a bit more catastrophic than the others. In the failover-GSLB scenario, the tolerated failures aren't quite as robust as the other two, described in the following.

The GSLB device, here probably just a layer-4 switch, holds the configuration information on the failover site. If it's unable to respond to client requests and send them the failover information, then so much for failover. Hence, the other two solutions, while more expensive, are preferred.

Before moving on, it's worth noting that layer-4 switches typically have metrics that can specify when a backup/overflow site should be activated, in addition to outright failure. *Maxcons* set a cap on the allowed incoming connections to a particular server in an SLB group and, if all servers have exceeded their allowable number of connections, maxcons send the new incoming connections to the backup until the local servers become available.

This is typically implemented on layer-4 devices in two ways. The first is literally as a backup server option, somewhere in the menus under the server group configuration. The other likely approach is as a remote server option and is configured into the server group as any other local server. When configured in this way, such as it is on Foundry's Server Iron series, the remote server won't be used until the local servers are unusable.

DNS Based

When GSLB is discussed, as it usually is, over an expensive lunch paid for by an eager vendor, the DNS-based approach is invariably implied. The main difference between this approach and the one before it is the addition of a proper GSLB-based device. This device can, and will, in the case of the Alteon Web Switch and the Foundry Server Iron, act as a layer-4 switch, as well as a GSLB device.

The way this works is by no means simple. Essentially, the GSLB device is going to take over DNS name-resolution functions for the name that would resolve into the site being served by GSLB. In other words, when a client wants to get to a GSLB resource, like a web portal such as http://my.aol.com/ (not that AOL uses this, but you get the idea), the client's DNS server will get a request to turn this name—my.aol.com—into an IP address. There's no reason to expect the first DNS server will have this information. In this case, what the DNS server will do is initiate a complicated lookup process to find out who might have this information. What it's looking for is the authoritative name server for the name my.aol.com. Normally, that server would be one of the DNS servers serving the aol.com domain, but when using the DNS-based version of GSLB, things are a bit different. Instead of configuring those DNS servers with an A-record with the name-address pair, the name my.aol.com is converted into a subdomain, and the request is then forwarded to another DNS server that's authoritative for that domain, specifically, the GSLB device itself. Trust me, its complicated, but see Chapter 6 for a more robust discussion of DNS and its vagaries.

The recommendation is not to implement this variety of GSLB in line with a server group needing to be load balanced, however. More specifically, this works best if the GSLB device isn't also performing load balancing functions at one of the sites (even if it's the primary site) being serviced by the GSLB process. The reasons for this are straightforward. If that site fails, the GSLB device goes with it, which won't help future clients much.

The recommended implementation is to locate the GSLB device close to the DNS servers that serve the corporation using GSLB. In some cases, a decision to load balance DNS might make sense. Couple this with a GSLB implementation and you'll have a configuration nightmare, but an interesting one. Just make sure the filters inbound into the DNS server group don't block DNS traffic to the GSLB process! See Chapter 13 for a discussion on DNS load balancing.

When the GSLB device is located here—away from the server segments hosting content—a failure on one of those segments isn't also likely to take down the GSLB device. Taking paranoia to a level of safe thinking, locate the GSLB device in a separate site entirely to ensure full flexibility. Even better, using a colocation facility such as InterNAP, AboveNet, or Exodus.net would be a great idea.

Anyway, once the DNS servers are configured to send the GSLB device DNS lookups, the GSLB device can then be configured to keep track of as many sites as the individual device-vendor allows. Some of the methods for tracking site availability and suitability are described in the following section, "Globalization Techniques."

Also, in passing, we should mention a "poor man's GSLB" exists that relies entirely on DNS. By default, DNS will round-robin responses based on configured addresses in an A-Record. In other words, if you want a resource globally load-balanced, simply adding a second or third IP address into the A-record will cause resolution requests to rotate through the configured IPs. This isn't recommended, of course, because if one site is down, DNS could care less and will continue to send out bad IPs just as happily as it sends out good IPs. Caveat emptor, you get what you pay for, and so forth.

Routing Protocol Based

Again, the purists will look askance at this being included here. The problem is this type of solution focuses on the reachability decisions for content retrieval, and these aren't necessarily GSLB issues. To those who would so complain: point taken and conceded.

As the name suggests, with this approach, the routing protocol will be relied on to get traffic to the content servers, regardless of where that content is. Through trickery and sleight of hand, the clever network architect can engineer a situation where the VIP the content servers are hiding behind can be advertised throughout the network, and then local routing decisions can decide which VIP is most suitable for use by each particular request.

Good reasons exist for not relying on the DNS-based solution for providing the only avenue for GSLB. The problem is with DNS itself, and the way DNS information, once retrieved, is stored.

The process of a recursive DNS lookup is expensive. The originating DNS could have to step through many levels of the DNS hierarchy to reach an authoritative nameserver, and each of those levels requires its own lookup to take the next step. To prevent these lookups from occurring each time a client makes a request of a resource for which the DNS server is not authoritative, the DNS server will cache the responses it gets so it can serve subsequent requests that much faster. Clients do the same thing, for the same reasons. The problem arises when a failure happens after the DNS lookup has occurred. In such cases, the client already has received the DNS information and has cached it. All its requests will continue to go toward the downed site, regardless of the machinations of the GSLB device—it has already been cut out of the loop, so to speak. Clients will get nothing but timeouts. Restarting the browser, which one hopes will flush the cache, will only cause another DNS lookup, will then retrieve outdated information from the DNS server itself, and will then continue to fail to reach the downed site.

The configuration of name records in DNS servers has the option of setting a minimum TTL value in the SOA record, which specifies how long requesting servers should cache the DNS responses. By default, this is set to 3,600 seconds, or one hour. Note, this applies to all records in the zone and not to any one record specifically, so making GSLB services special in the sense that they're treated differently from other records (that is, have a short TTL) will be impossible. That is, impossible unless all that's in the zone is the GSLB service!

Microsoft DNS has a known bug affecting all versions of Windows 2000 Server/Advanced Server, Service Packs1 and 2. This bug causes the default TTL on resource records to be extended to 24 hours, regardless of the minimum TTL assigned by appropriate SOA record. 24 hours! And, most helpfully, this bug will disguise this fact from the administrator by not showing these cached responses in the management console or via the command line tool! The only way to detect this is what is happening will be through packet traces (and the noncircumventable errors this causes). This, by and large, will completely annihilate any chance of having GSLB function correctly for users resolving to GSLB resources after a failure via a Microsoft DNS server. C'est la vie, Microsoft says—network engineers will have to wait until Service Pack 3 for a fix. See Microsoft Knowledge Base article Q303964 (DNS Server Caches NS Records Longer Than the TTL) for a description of the problem.

Microsoft's Internet Explorer, until version 4.x, used to cache DNS responses in its web cache for 24 hours! All later versions, up to and including Version 6, now default to 30 minutes, and Microsoft Knowledge Base article Q263558 (How Internet Explorer Uses the Cache for DNS Host Entries) explains how and why adding a key to the registry of Windows operating systems will lengthen this default setting, further "optimizing" the user's performance. This is madness, of course, and strongly discouraged. If anything, this setting should be *shortened*, not lengthened, especially because this value will override the minimum TTL setting on any particular DNS response.

With these known problems with DNS implementations, some other mechanism for ensuring a client gets to the appropriate resource in case of failure is warranted. Routing protocols are designed with this sort of fast-failover in mind.

The most likely approach will be manipulating Border Gateway Patrol (BGP) because this is the most commonly used protocol on a scale useful enough to have impact. BGP is mostly used for exchanging reachability information with other, neighboring, large-scale networks, but it can and does interact with Interior Gateway Protocols (IGPs), such as IS-IS, RIP, and OSPF. The IGPs-EGPs (Exterior Gateway Protocols) interactions are complicated. On a router running the Cisco IOS, the learned routes are given preferences based on how they're learned. These preferences are called *administrative distances*, and they're a measure of the reliability of the source protocol. For example, routes learned via IS-IS are more trusted than RIP and are less trusted than those learned by OSPF. Further, external routes learned by BGP (E-BGP) are much more trusted than internal routes learned by BGP (I-BGP). More strongly, E-BGP is a source more trusted than any other method or nonproprietary protocol, with the exception of directly connected networks and manually configured static routes. E-BGP, then, is highly believable. Using BGP in this way—that is, injecting BGP routes into another autonomous system—is, by default, one of the best ways to be believed on the Internet.

If one can manipulate BGP in such a way that the same advertised GSLB address is made to appear to come from separate locations, well, that might be worth looking at, and it's examined in the following "Hybrid DNS/Routing System" section.

Taking a step closer, it's worth remembering that, at some point, the IGP takes over the routing decisions for any particular packet. More to the point, it doesn't make sense for every router in a network to be asked to maintain the full (or even partial) Internet routing database, as routers running BGP do. BGP is complex and most IGPs aren't. The average enterprise user will deploy BGP at the edges of the network, at autonomous system boundaries and, typically, not at local segment boundaries—not even at content server segment boundaries.

BGP will take the packets only so far, and then it's up to the IGP to take it the last mile. From the perspective of the IGP running in a single area, there might only be one way to get to the resource in question, but there might be multiple areas. Each of these areas might have the same notion: to get to x, send it to y. The trick is that physically different $x$es exist, and each IGP will only know one. The skill is in getting BGP to announce all of them to the rest of the world.

PACKET LOSS—AN ASIDE

Packet loss, usually measured as a percentage, represents the number of packets dropped during transmission because of network congestion or data corruption. A simple method of measuring packet loss is by use of *ping*, a tool that sends ICMP echo-request packets to a specified destination and then waits for a corresponding echo-response packet. Ping uses this data to determine two things: the latency of the link and the reliability of the link. When ping fails to receive an echo-response packet for an echo-request packet it sent, ping increments its packet loss counter and continues.

By dividing the total packets sent by the number of packets lost, ping can report the packet loss as a percentage. When an Internet link is monitored over the course of time, packet loss of less than 1 percent is normal. If the percentage grows higher, you'll find the quality and performance of TCP connections over this link will have degraded because of their inherent retransmission mechanisms.

Exactly how poorly TCP performs during packet loss is largely a function of the window size and Maximum Transmission Units (MTU). When a larger packet is dropped, it requires more effort and time on the sender's part to retransmit the packet. As a result, TCP performance tends to fall quickly during packet loss if large windows/MTUs are at work. The trade-off is that when packet loss doesn't occur, larger windows/MTUs usually give better throughput.

Packet loss usually occurs at one of three places on the Internet: 1) at the local ISP the client is using, 2) within the content provider's network itself, and 3) at the peering points between two different network providers because of congestion.

Unfortunately, the first cause of packet loss (the local ISP) isn't under the control of the content provider in any way and, regardless of where the content is delivered from, results in poor performance. While this might reflect poorly on the overall experience the client has with the Internet, it's usually an overall experience and not one that reflects specifically on one site, although some content might be impacted more by this than other types.

The second cause of packet loss—the local content provider's network—is obviously under the control of the local network administrator and should be closely monitored to ensure no particular degradation results in poor performance to the clients. In general, the low cost and high quality of network equipment available these days permit and encourage tremendous overdesign on the local infrastructure, and this helps to ensure local bottlenecks won't result in future problems. Trying to match the network design closely to the current demands of the content generation eventually results in wasted productivity and potentially lost revenue. A workable, if crude, rule of thumb is simply to estimate how much traffic you think you currently need to pipe over your local network, and then bump that up by a factor of ten, when it makes financial sense to do so.

So, if the estimated bandwidth is going to be 20 Mbps, then using a 100 Mbps Ethernet data path in the server farm is probably a good idea. The Internet circuit might be another matter and acquiring a 100 Mbps Fast Ethernet upstream connection (assuming the content is hosted in a data center, where such service is possible) or a 45 Mbps DS3 should be sufficient, but expect it to be costly. Remember, in most cases today, billing is done on a utilization basis, with a base charge derived from the capability of the media to burst. As an example, a 100 Mbps link might be used, with the utilization billed at the 95th percentile of actual use on that. In general, actual use will be significantly lower than 100 Mbps, even if the full capacity is used during peak times. Ensuring that adequate physical bandwidth exists for growth is prudent. Paying for a dedicated, but underused, link might not make good financial sense.

The third significant cause of packet loss is peering connections. In many cases, the peering between two companies might be significantly less reliable than it should be because of political or financial issues. Sometimes, one company will deny an upgrade to another company because of the lack of balanced traffic on the links. Many peering agreements require "roughly equal" bandwidth on both the transmit side and the receive side of the link. This forces companies that, in general, only transmit or receive traffic to or from another network to pay for additional bandwidth, in effect, creating a more customer-oriented relationship, instead of having a relationship of peers. This has been of particular significance with the rise of companies that specialize in running data centers such as Exodus and AboveNet because, in general, these companies generate traffic as opposed to passing it. Many of the traditional backbone providers believe these companies are going after the revenue generators (the content providers) and are leaving the costly job of providing the distribution network for users to them.

One last significant, but underappreciated, factor that plays a role in performance is the consistency of the bandwidth as measured by standard deviation of the RTT or other, similar, metrics. *Standard deviation* measures the variability of a set of data, in our case, the RTT. A *standard deviation of zero* means the connection between the client and the server is completely consistent and, in general, represents a lightly loaded set of connections between the two endpoints. The higher the standard deviation, the more traffic and, for the most part, the more bottlenecks are occurring on the same paths between the two.

To imagine how this works, consider a trip on a major freeway. If little traffic were on the road (say, at night), then the amount of time it would take between point A and point B would tend to be constant and based on the distance between point A and B, as well as the relevant speed limits. When more traffic is on the freeway, the chances of encountering a bottleneck and having congestion occur becomes higher, and results in more variability in the time between point A and B. Once a certain amount of traffic is reached, the variability starts to skyrocket, which if measured at different times would result in a rather high standard deviation. On the Internet, similar mechanisms of queuing exist: if too much traffic is seeking to go through a particular pipe, the most recently received packets would be queued while other packets are transmitted. The greater the traffic, the more likely any given packet will need to be queued, thereby increasing the variance in RTT calculations.

Irregular latency between two connected systems tends to reflect some intermediate condition that can also result in packet loss and, in many cases, in certain types of data flows becoming unstable, such as streaming media. For streaming media software to properly estimate the amount of data needed before starting the playback of a particular piece of content, the software must be able to estimate how fast the connection is and use that information to determine how much of the clip to buffer before starting to play it. If this estimation is off because of fluctuations on the network, the result is the conclusion of the buffered content being played to the user before the next piece of content is available for playback. This is seen as a pause in the playback and, when it occurs frequently, results in erratic and unviewable content. Consistency at its most basic level can be measured by determining the standard deviation of the RTTs between a client and server. In terms of a network, if the standard deviation of the RTTs is higher than half the average RTT, the connection can be considered to be irregular; on the other hand, if it's less than 1/10 of the average, then the link is considered extremely consistent.

CAVEATS

Before any administrator begins the selection process of how GSLB should be done and with what products, many issues must be analyzed to ensure no problems occur in the process. The first and most important issue to contend with is the issue *of data replication*. In nearly every web site, some content is updated on a regular basis, be it inventory in the case of e-commerce, or news and stock quotes for a news site. Failure to keep all the sites current can result in the sale of an item that has already been sold to someone else from another data center, misquoting of stock quotes, or other issues. As such, a detailed plan must ensure the data used for operations at one site is available at another, and problem resolution is handled in a clear and distinct manner. While the actual database synchronization issue is beyond the scope of this chapter, this issue is one that should be addressed with the database vendor or developers to ensure a solution is either in the works or in place. Otherwise, most globalization attempts are doomed to failure.

Another question that needs to be addressed is how to deploy content. We've already discussed the role of backup/failover GSLB, but in an *Active-Active* scenario, more than one site is handling the load and the sites are acting as relative peers. Normal requests and site demand are handled by the GSLB metrics. With an Active-Active solution, synchronization becomes something of a problem because transactions are occurring at both sites in real time.

The alternative, and one that helps with the synchronization issue, is to work off an Active-Standby model. In the *Active-Standby* model, only one location delivers the content to users, but another site is ready to assume the traffic load at any time, à la the backup model previously described. In general, this type of solution is easier to implement on a back-end basis, and if used correctly, it can be a successful staging area for new hardware, software, and services. When new stuff is being rolled out, the primary site is cut over to the backup and, if a failure occurs, the old primary can be used as a fallback. Cutovers of this sort can be rolled out via DNS and use zone propagation as the mechanism for gracefully cutting over.

Of course, if DNS is being used as the cutover mechanism, then the problem of caches and change propagation needs to be addressed. If the primary site fails after the address record is cached, additional clients might end up being sent to the failed primary site anyway. As such, a means of tunneling requests from the primary to the secondary site should be put into place. With HTTP, this can be as simple as an HTTP redirect, although other protocols such as HTTPS, FTP, and POP3 aren't handled so easily. Many times, these protocols should be handled via some sort of Internet Protocol (IP) tunnel, such as with Generic Routing Encapsulation (GRE)—see RFC 2784—to make the remote site appear as a local entity for backup purposes. Another solution is to change the source IP address of packets destined for a failed server farm to a local IP, and then transmit them to the remote site. When packets are returned to the failed site, the reverse process is done, allowing the failure to appear seamless to clients—if the primary site has the capability to do this. If a complete failure of the primary site occurs, in general, nothing can be done to resolve this issue.

An alternate way to handle an Active-Standby setup is to make use of BGP peering. While a bit more complex to implement, the advantage of BGP is it can avoid DNS problems entirely and allows routing to take care of the issue. This assumes both sites are set up with ISPs that accept and will handle the BGP peering properly and equally, or that both sites are connected to the same ISP, but at different locations. The disadvantage to using BGP peering is it's an all-or-nothing game: when you turn it on, all the traffic—even from preexisting connections—is directed to the new sites, which could result in a period of inaccessibility for those already using a site. While this is acceptable during a complete or near-complete failure at one location, it isn't acceptable if the failover was intended to be graceful for maintenance purposes.

The third issue with an Active-Standby configuration is how to activate the switchover. The issue, called the *split-brain problem,* is this: many failures that could possibly activate a switch are only partial failures, in that each site can't see the other, but half the Internet can access one site, while the other half can see and access the other. If automated tools are set up at the backup site that monitors the primary site and implements the failover via DNS or BGP, unintended effects might occur. Both sites might now have active databases and active e-commerce activities going on, resulting in an inconsistent and potentially fatal data corruption. This situation either needs to be addressed or a nonautomatic means of triggering the failover should be used. Because of this issue and others surrounding Active-Standby solutions, the recommendation is that Active-Active plans be implemented. Active-Active solutions tend to scale better and the planning necessary for such an installation tends to help ensure complete availability at all times.

GLOBALIZATION TECHNIQUES

Particular implementations of GSLB are many, varied, and probably proprietary. As mentioned, the state of the art is a moving, evolving target. Discussions as to specifics are, therefore, likely to be outdated quickly, but generalities are always useful. Several approaches are currently in use for implementing GSLB. The technology approaches discussed in the following involve three primary methods: passive, Footraces, and active probing. Each is discussed in turn.

Worth noting is that any solution will probably combine the best of all these technological approaches. A blend of passive and active strategies, perhaps involving Footraces of some sort, will generate the most flexible and interesting solutions.

Passive Techniques

Passive globalization techniques rely on the fundamental nature of how the Internet works to allow distribution of content to occur. Within this category are two commonly used methods: the Berkeley Internet Name Domain (BIND) DNS RTT measurement and BGP routing. Both these protocols are designed to help the Internet operate and, at a fundamental level, allow one computer to find and communicate with another. DNS operates at a textual name level to find an IP address, and BGP performs much the same task, but at the IP level instead. Some techniques make use of both in combination, to allow for the most flexible solution.

BIND DNS RTT

The simplest method to globalize content is to make use of BIND's built-in RTT measurement facility when using multiple NS records. As described in Chapter 6, BIND records the RTT of a response for a given nameserver and uses this information in determining where to send DNS queries in the future. This can be used to help optimize content distribution better than pure DNS round-robin load balancing would allow and to help overcome offline sites.

To use this feature, DNS servers need to be placed at each location serving content, and the configuration of each DNS must return the addresses that exist within that local site only. As an example, consider the domain domain.com, which has two sites: one in Virginia and one in California. The following records could be the records in the TLD name servers.

Domain.com	NS	192.168.0.10	;VA name server
	NS	192.168.1.10	;CA name server

Within the VA name server, the following records could exist:

www	A	192.168.0.11

and in the CA name server:

www	A	192.168.1.11

The net result of this configuration is this: if the VA name server is queried (which will be the tendency for clients closer to that site), it will return the A-record for that content server. If the CA name server is queried, it will return its A-record. This isn't the same as using both A-records for DNS round robin; when configured that way, the tendency is to use either A-record indiscriminately.

BGP VBI for DNS

Along the lines of the simple DNS RTT trick, a shared BGP space can be used to similar effect, although taking advantage of a different aspect of how the Internet works. With BGP, you can inject a virtual network block (VBIVirtual Block Injection), say, a /24, from several locations, and then advertise a DNS server within that shared IP block. From the perspective of the Internet, several paths would appear to exist to the same DNS server. Note, BGP enables you to source a route from only a single AS, so that places constraints on how this will work. In Figure 11-1, you can see the solution uses a pair of ISPs, one for

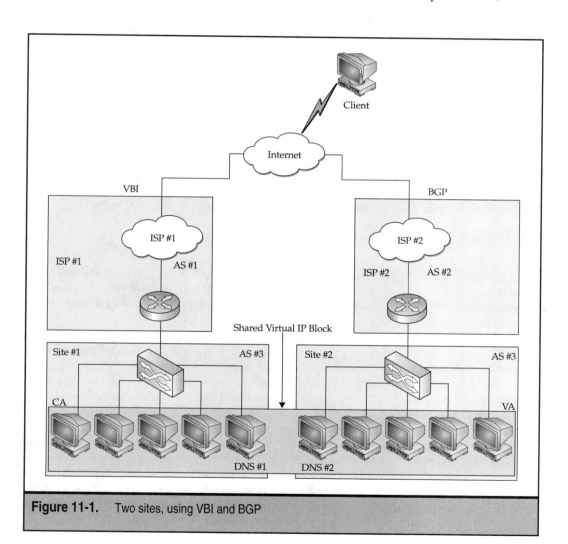

Figure 11-1. Two sites, using VBI and BGP

each region. Each ISP has its own unique AS number, and the content provider, in turn, has one. The two sites are connected by a dedicated link, at the very least for synchronization reasons.

BGP peers downstream from the DNS servers will see, and maintain, multiple paths to the destination AS, which appears to be hosting a single DNS server: one route via AS #1 and another via AS #2. As traffic traverses the Internet toward the sourcing AS, the routing protocol will send traffic along the shortest path to the AS.

In point of fact, more than one DNS server will deliver information, information that will be different depending on which path was chosen. To illustrate how this would work, again refer to Figure 11-1. Both DNS servers would appear to have the same IP address (standard VIP stuff here), so you would only have one IP address advertised at the TLD server (or two IP addresses if you had two servers at each location). As an example, you would have

```
Domain.com          NS          192.168.0.10          ; DNS server #1
```

The trick is what the A-records within each DNS server say. For example, within the California server, there could be the following:

```
www                 A           10.0.0.10
```

while in the Virginia server, there would be the following:

```
www                 A           10.0.1.10
```

Two distinct addresses! Each entry would refer to a local VIP. This would give the appropriate VIP to the client, depending on what path that client took to get to the DNS server. This is a bit crude, of course, and it relies on the fact (hope) that the client is located proximally to its local DNS.

While this shared IP approach works with DNS, it isn't necessarily recommended that any TCP-based services (such as HTTP) use a shared IP block in this same way. The problems with this approach are twofold. First, BGP allows for equal-cost multipath routing. What this means is any given router could have two or more equally good routes to a single destination. The problem is, in this case, BGP could load balance across them. This could result in, for example, SYN packets going to one site, while ACK packets go to another site entirely! Second, route fluctuations will occur over time, which could well disrupt and change the path on the fly that a particular packet takes, especially at points with equal chances to go in either direction. As a result, TCP connections could become scrambled, as sequence numbers are all jumbled, and might be delivered to the wrong sites. Persistence, sometimes useful to content providers, might be lost entirely (see Chapter 9 for a discussion). By contrast, the single UDP packet that makes up DNS queries would either go one way or another in these border cases and, as a result, would simply pick one site or the other, more like a random coin toss. In the cases where a favored path exists, in general, that path would pick a better site, resulting in better performance overall.

Hybrid DNS/Routing System

Each of the two solutions so far has its limitations. Relying on DNS-based GSLB solutions is fine, but works only insofar as DNS itself works. Solving problems inherent with DNS is tricky, but using routing protocols to do so isn't going to be fail-safe either. Routing client requests to content servers still remains a problem.

It seems the appropriate solutions must include a two-tiered approach. The first tier implements some DNS-based solution. The BGP VBI approach, just outlined, is viable if complex. However the DNS is handled, the next tier will have the goal of handling the actual client requests. With a multitiered solution, addressing some of the issues raised in the last section might be possible, with the unsuitability of BGP VBI for TCP-based services like HTTP.

As mentioned previously, one of the problems with simply using DNS to select a site is this: once the site is selected, no way exists to flush the caches located on the DNS server and the client itself to force them to a new site on failure. The solution would then be one to eliminate the need to do so.

One complex way to get around this is to share not only the virtual IP block the DNS servers reside in, but also the IP blocks the HTTP servers reside in, but with different metrics to ensure that one site is primary for each shared virtual IP block. Configured correctly, client requests could continue to be sent to out-of-date IP addresses and still get service.

The final element required would be some sort of mechanism that allows the sites to sort out which connections belong to which site. The way this is usually done is with TCP sequence numbers. If, during a given session, part of a session is mistakenly routed to the wrong site, the TCP sequence numbers won't match any given current sessions, so a TCP-reset will most likely be sent to the client at this point, resulting in a failed session. The solution would be to implement a method of handling the sequence numbers in such a way that either site could readily identify which site ought to handle the traffic. Two different sets of sequence numbers, separated and reserved, could be implemented this way. Couple this with a mechanism for redirecting these errant packets back to the appropriate site, and you're off to the races.

In Figure 11-2, you inject multiple virtual IP blocks: one for the DNS server segment (with equal cost out of both sites) and one for each of the two server segments. The DNS servers at each site are handing out VIP addresses of the server segments that are local, as in the last section. This is fine, but now failover becomes a problem, again, as outlined in the last section. If both sites are configured to respond to both VIPs, however, which site gets the requests no longer matters—all the real servers are serving identical content. You can get this to work by making the VIP blocks shared across both sites. Ideally, you'd still like to prefer the more local site to the remote, so biasing one site over the other *might* be a good idea.

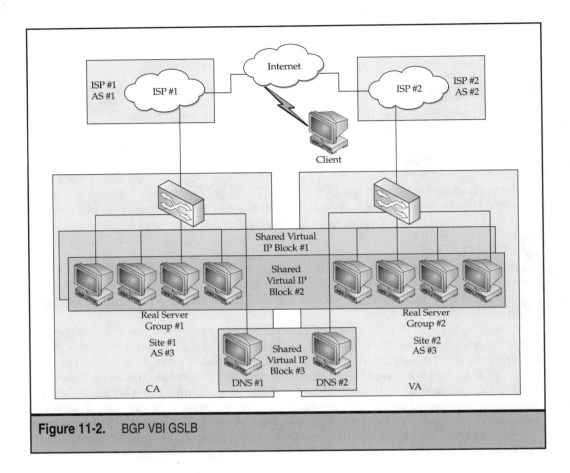

Figure 11-2. BGP VBI GSLB

To make this work, each site advertises its own virtual IP block for its server segment. In addition, each advertises the virtual IP block for the opposing server segment, but at a dramatically reduced preference. On the load balancer, each of the local server groups is configured with the same two VIPs in the range of the virtual IP blocks being advertised by BGP.

In CA, inject the DNS block, the local server block, and the opposing server block with heavy AS prepending, to significantly decrease the preference of that route. In VA, do the same, but make sure you reverse the preferences. Depending on the arrangements with the peering ASes, you could use MED instead of, or in conjunction with, massive prepending.

If the VA site falls off the map, the new traffic will be routed to CA dynamically via BGP. Existing connections to the VA site will be lost regardless, unique TCP sequence numbers notwithstanding. New connections would be then routed to the remaining site.

This eliminates the problems with bad DNS caches, but requires three separate, publicly routable IP blocks, and an inordinate amount of BGP expertise. This is a fairly expensive solution, but the current state of the art.

Footrace Techniques

A *Footrace*, as the name implies, is a general technique where several packets race each other to see who gets to the client first. More specifically, a Footrace can be performed any time a client requests a piece of content that can be modified on transmission to deliver several answers: the first answer that reaches the client is the one used, and the losers are discarded as duplicates. A Footrace tends to add additional latency because all the sites need to coordinate their information with the other sites and transmit their answers at about the same time. In addition, most Footrace techniques require the spoofing of IP addresses at various sites to mimic the data being transmitted by other sites. While different configurations might keep this from being a problem, most ISPs are now introducing filters into their networks to prevent spoofing. As a result, these techniques might not work with particular ISPs.

DNS Footraces

One technique used is a DNS Footrace. This involves the following process: a client's DNS server requests an A-record for a particular resource, say, www.domain.com. The authoritative nameserver for domain.com transmits this fact to other servers at each location and, through constantly measured built-in delays, all the sites' servers respond with different information at the same time. One of the packets will be received by the client's DNS server first and will contain an A-record for the resource, as it exists at the site of the "best performing" DNS server.

This technique is functionally measuring only the performance of the site to the client's DNS server, not the overall performance between the site and client, which is the first weakness. The second weakness is that the client's DNS server can be in a remote location from the user itself, so the time needed to synchronize the site's DNS servers to provide a response is adding latency to a statistically marginal benefit. As such, the benefit to the average user is even less, although in conditions where one site is having problems (such as during an ongoing DOS attack), the benefit can be immensely valuable.

HTTP-redirect Footraces

HTTP-redirect Footraces are another, although less-used, technique that's similar to DNS Footraces. In an *HTTP- redirect Footrace*, a single site receives an HTTP request. Instead of responding directly, the site that received the request sends coordination messages to all the other sites and waits based on the known delay it takes to transmit this message to the remote sites. After the required delay, all the sites would then, in unison, send a data packet for the HTTP response that includes an HTTP-redirect to a distinct address that resides at each site, which then becomes the URL from which the subsequent content is retrieved.

As an example of how this works, consider our sites in California and Virginia. A client requests http://www.domain.com, and the request is sent to California. After the initial TCP handshake, the GET request is sent to California. At the California site, a device that monitors the Virginia site knows it takes about 30 ms for the request to be forwarded to Virginia, so it sends a copy of the request to Virginia and waits 30 ms. In Virginia, the request is received and a response is sent to the client, containing a redirect to http://www-va.domain.com and, in California, at the same time, a response is sent that contains a redirect to http://www-ca.domain.com. The user will be directed to one or the other site, depending on which of the packets is received by the user first. The second packet—because it contains the same sequence number and length—is considered a duplicate by the TCP stack on the client and is discarded.

The benefits of this approach over DNS footraces are twofold. First, because the client is directly interacting with the sites, this allows the client's location to be accurately used for site selection. Second, information such as can be contained in cookies can, in theory, be used to direct users to specific sites. For example, the presence of a cookie specifies that the user should be directed to one site or another because of prior shopping cart data, and so forth.

Four drawbacks still exist to this approach, though. First, if the redirect is done by name instead of by IP, this will force another DNS lookup to be performed by the client, increasing its latency over a simple request. Second, the drawback of having to synchronize the responses is the same as with footraces in general. Third, the URL displayed in the browser window will be different depending on the name, which can cause issues with some clients. Fourth, the method is dependent strictly on HTTP and doesn't support other common protocols, such as HTTPS, FTP, and SMTP.

TCP Handshake Footraces

The final currently common mechanism for Footraces is to perform one at the TCP handshake level. In the *TCP handshake Footrace* system, each site would have a range of TCP sequence numbers they're allowed to use when establishing TCP connections with a client. A client will transmit a SYN packet to a particular site, which will then coordinate with the rest of the sites, much like the previous example. In this method, though, each site will send back a SYN-ACK with a different sequence number set. The client will acknowledge the SYN from the server site, and whichever ACK is received by the first site tells that site who won the Footrace. At this point, one of two things could occur. One, either the connection could operate in a tunnel mode, where the first site that received the SYN would forward any packets to the proper site, and data is generated and transmitted from that site. Two, this initial site can make use of protocol-supported redirection (in the case of HTTP) to pin down the client to the proper site.

One final advantage of this approach needs to be explored, though. This method can be used in conjunction with DNS footraces and/or BIND's DNS RTT measurement and, in conditions where the local site is the best site at the initial onset, no tunneling needs to be done. This helps to prevent the additional overhead of tunneling many connections to another site, yet allows tunneling to be done when this is logically the best solution.

Again, though, drawbacks exist to this approach. First, in tunnel mode, two sites, instead of one, are now involved in the transmission of traffic. This increases the chance of problems occurring that can slow a client or cause errors. Second, if HTTP redirects are used, the DNS lookup time and changed URL issues are the same as with HTTP Footraces. Third, in tunnel mode, more latency is added when data is received from the user over more direct methods, as well as increased traffic, which potentially adds additional cost to bandwidth.

Active Techniques

Probing is the process where each site determines how far away a particular address or subnet is by some metric, and all the sites make use of that information to direct clients to different sites. *Active Probing* can take the form of explicit probes directly against a client as the client attempts to access the content, or it can be a mechanism that maps the Internet constantly and uses whatever information is available at any given time to direct users to a particular site. The goal is to elicit a response of some kind from the client, for example, an RST, so data can be collected and an appropriate site selection calculated. Being able to calculate RTTs would be most useful in this regard. Some specific probe methods that have been used before include opening TCP port 53 against querying nameservers, sending a TCP packet originating from port 80 (or other ports as desired) to the client's IP and a random high-order TCP port (resulting in an RST packet), and direct ICMP echo requests.

Many active probes are blocked by firewalls and can often irritate firewall administrators if the unexpected and unexplained packets keep bouncing off their firewall. While not all firewalls are configured by default to simply discard these packets, as they're disguised as parts of legitimate sessions, most stateful firewalls might still eliminate them and can certainly be configured to do so. The firewall itself might issue an RST packet, however, and that would do fine for calculating an RTT. If the firewall does block the packet, and then discards it and fails to send any notice back to the probing device, a traceroute back to the client can be initiated, and the last responding hop could be used on which to base site selection.

Note, probing and Footraces are rather similar in operation. The primary difference between them is when they're performed. Footraces are initiated on a client query and introduce a lag into the initial service offering. Probing can be initiated as a Footrace, and then continue in a periodic fashion for some interval of time. Dynamic tables can be built and updated by the probing device, to be used as necessary and appropriate. The obvious benefit of continuous polling is information can be disseminated immediately, and changes can be detected and acted on quickly, instead of having to run a Footrace for each client request. Probing can help determine the stability of a particular path, allowing consistency to be measured, specifically by looking at statistical data on RTT and packet loss information as well as standard deviation of the RTT.

DNS Probes Measurement

DNS probes work by configuring the device performing the GSLB to answer DNS queries for the web site. When a query arrives, the GSLB device solicits all the sites to send a DNS query back to the originating DNS server. In this way, the closest site can be determined based on the latency of the response, that is, whichever response was received first.

Probing will continue at configurable intervals for some configurable period of time, so subsequent requests from that DNS server will be met with the most optimal information.

Tracking this information might seem unwieldy at first because potentially thousands upon thousands of DNS servers are installed on the Internet. Keeping tabs on every single one seems unnecessary, cumbersome, and resource prohibitive. Statistically, this isn't the case. True, thousands of DNS servers exist but, statistically averaging recursive DNS lookups over time, it becomes readily apparent that certain DNS servers will request information much more frequently. Tracking those more thoroughly makes sense and will decrease the number of DNS servers that must be tracked at least by an order of magnitude. Most likely, DNS servers will be those serving large client bases, such as AOL, MSN, Earthlink, and other large-scale ISPs. The odd corporate DNS server that accesses the GSLB site for authoritative information will also be tracked, of course, but the bulk of Internet traffic doesn't originate from these sites.

HTTP Probes

HTTP probes work in a manner similar to the DNS probes just outlined. When making the GSLB decision for a particular client, the GSLB device will initiate a Footrace by forwarding the HTTP GET messages to each of the sites in the GSLB site table. The requests are then processed by the individual sites, and then returned to the original sender. The first response reaching the client is the one that's accepted, and then used throughout the duration of the session. All late arriving responses are discarded as duplicated packets.

At this point, site selection is complete and active probing can begin. The individual sites in the GSLB table will attempt to elicit a response from the client and use this information to maintain a site preference table for that client. By itself, this isn't all that useful; the sheer number of potential clients far outstrips the number of potential DNS servers by several orders of magnitude. By extrapolating from a single client, however, the GSLB device can start populating the site preference table based on the network mask to which the client might belong.

This information is completely unknowable to the GSLB device, of course, but guesstimates will serve just as well. The goal is to assign sites based on network address, the assumption being that, at some point, it's reasonable to assume clients coming in from the same network will be somewhat proximal to each other.

One way this could work might be as follows: the first client arriving might have a network mask assigned to it, starting at, say, a /8 CIDR block. The next client that requests resources will either fit into that block or not and, if so, would get the same site selection without having to run a Footrace, which results in a faster response for that client. Now, a /8 isn't even a remotely accurate mask but, at this point, that isn't relevant.

Probing works on statistical averages over time, and its results are applied to groups, whereas Footraces are individual efforts.

The second client that hits from that network block will be assigned its own probe, and another Footrace could be run so more accurate measurements are taken. If the same site selection results are obtained, the two clients can be analyzed to see if a /16 netmask would, perhaps, better fit them. If so, all subsequent clients would receive the same site selection they did. If not, then the GSLB device can sort them into two different blocks, assigning them the same sites or not, as dictated by the GSLB site selection metrics. The more users that come in from a particular network, the finer grained the probes can be made, say, down to a /20 or /24. The broader the netmask is, the larger the groupings of potential clients will be, generating fewer entries in the table. On the other hand, the broader the netmask, the more likely it will be that the network subdivisions won't all be proximal. A /20 is about as large a mask as would be desired and will probably be about as large a network as can be expected in a single geographic area. CIDR blocks this large are usually cut up into smaller parts and used throughout an enterprise, where some addresses are for the local offices, others for the remotes, and still others are for the WAN links between them. The larger the block, the more likely are remote offices and the more likely that "remote" will mean "overseas." Smaller blocks are more likely to be grouped together, but this means more networks exist to probe and track, which might require significantly more resources on the part of the tracking device.

The extreme end of this will be the mega-POP ISPs, such as AOL, MSN, Yahoo! and others, which hide large sections of their user base behind proxies. A /24 would normally be expected to cover only 200 or so clients, but with proxy-based ISPs, these 200 or so proxies could hide millions of users, spread out worldwide. This is fine because the way the proxies work is as a two-way funnel—all user traffic flows into and out of these proxies, and the proxies serve specific geographic areas. Hence, all that's needed is to map site selection to the proxy! Proxies should be relatively easy to spot in the site selection tables because the amount of content requests coming from them will be statistically anomalous.

HTTP Redirection

HTTP redirection begins with a simpler method of DNS-based load balancing. In the first step, the server load balancer is configured to answer DNS queries for the web site. All the sites are configured to answer such requests.

During its normal operation, each web site sends information according to a variety of metrics, which allows every site to know how busy the other sites are. When a DNS query is received, the client is given the IP address of the site with the least load, regardless of geographic locality. While this might seem simplistic, the method works well enough for most people and is often the easiest deploy, especially compared to the complexity involved with Footraces.

This isn't to say this method can't, shouldn't, and isn't coupled with Footrace techniques to create more complex and flexible approaches. It's simply that the primary implementation has more to do with load than with proximity.

Where HTTP redirection becomes useful is with DNS-based GSLB decisions. Remember, the problem with these methods is that DNS responses tend to get cached. As discussed earlier, this was at least 30 minutes with Internet Explorer and up to 24 hours if using a Microsoft DNS server. During the period when the client is still making HTTP requests, but isn't making DNS requests, it's reasonable to expect a specific site could become overloaded. This is where HTTP redirection comes into play: the busy site can turn users away from it and toward another less-loaded site by sending it an HTTP-redirect response to any given query. Thus, web sites can continue offering load balanced sites without needing to wait for the client to make another DNS query.

CASE STUDIES

In the following section, we try to bring it all together and discuss the technologies in specific contexts. The examples are all fictional, but should give you a flavor of how they might be implemented.

Directory Services for J. Magellan and Sons

J. Magellan is one of the last great privately owned financial investment companies. With over 100 branch offices across 48 continental U.S. states processing over $100 trillion dollars in transactions in the last calendar year, J. Magellan is poised to go public in the next nine months. To show serious value-add to its clientele and to Wall Street, the company has decided to centralize its corporate resources and enable next generation technology to do so.

GSLB has been selected as a technology to globalize these corporate resources. Implementation will be staged, with the proof-of-concept being an initial rollout of the service for an LDAP-based phone and user directory for use within the corporation. Successful implementation will lead to a rollout of other services within the same infrastructure designs.

Infrastructure and Goals

Los Angeles and New York City: GSLB services will be implemented in the data centers in both LA and NYC. The goal is to provide proximity-based site selection and provide HA for the three distributions centers. The solution proposed includes three GSLB-enabled load balancers, one per site. Each site will have the full complement of databases, web servers, and application servers. A dedicated fractional T-3 is in place between NYC and LA. Using bandwidth management techniques (see Chapter 14), 1 Mbps will be allocated for the database software to synchronize content between the two sites.

Stage One

The first stage of the implementation is to ensure site redundancy. On the site in NYC, the load balancers are configured with the local real server group for standard load balancing, at addresses 10.5.100.0/26, and have a VIP of 192.168.10.100. The subdomain www.yournewscorp.com is registered in DNS, and the local GSLB device is registered as the authoritative nameserver for this domain, at 192.168.50.1. In LA, the local server group is on 10.120.100.32/27 with the VIP set to 192.168.20.100. The GSLB device is registered as the DNS secondary to the www.yournewscorp.com domain, at 192.168.50.2. (See Figure 11-3.)

To the NYC local server group, 192.168.20.100 will be added as a remote/backup server. To the LA local server group, 192.168.10.100 will be added as a remote/backup server. At this point, the first stage is almost complete. Testing will be scheduled to ensure that failover occurs, and NYC's local server group will be taken offline to test failover; the same should be done in LA.

Stage Two

The second stage will be to implement GSLB. A DNS Footrace will be implemented to ensure some measure of proximity to the most appropriate site. The GSLB devices at each site are already configured to respond to DNS requests. Now, when responding, whichever receives the request will forward it to the other site and synchronize its responses so both are sent to the requesting DNS at the same time.

While this isn't perfect, the solution is simple, relatively easy to implement, and meets the design objectives.

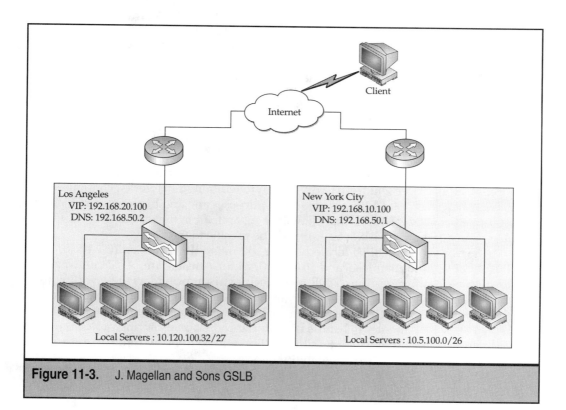

Figure 11-3.   J. Magellan and Sons GSLB

Your News Corp.

Your News Corp. (YNC) is a media organization that makes use of the Web to distribute world-class, front-line news reporting by ordinary people. It's a 24/7 news site, competing directly with CNN, and the Web is its only distribution outlet. As a multimillion dollar advertising revenue media engine, YNC is interested in ensuring that its distribution channel remains hiccup-free.

Infrastructure and Goals

YNC has chosen to upgrade its current network services portfolio to include GSLB. Currently, its primary distribution site is in an Exodus colocation facility in New Jersey, just across the river from Manhattan. YNC has secured rack space in an AboveNet facility in San Jose, California, and a third in the InterNAP facility in Amsterdam. Colocation facilities were chosen for the quality and number of immediate upstream peers; Exodus has excellent NAP connections to the major backbone providers. Multiple providers were chosen for reasons of redundancy. Dedicated T-1 connections were provisioned to each of the three sites, using the NYC site as the hub site. These connections are implemented for back-end data synchronization.

The content provided by YNC is of two flavors: a large amount of static text supplemented with Real Audio audio/video streams. The goal is to provide a high-end HA solution as impervious as possible to the localized Internet failures and to provide as high a quality of service as possible to clients, so all users are directed to the most local site and/or to the site most able to handle their requests.

A routing protocol-based solution has been chosen for implementation. BGP VBI will be used to provide both site selection via DNS and dynamic routing to the content server farms. The GSLB device will provide additional error-correction services in the event of a misroute. (See Figure 11-4.)

Stage One

Stage One of the implementation will be to configure SLB in each of the three locations. Each local load balancer will have five VIPs (on five different networks) configured: one unique nonshared VIP for GSLB-based failover purposes and another four shared VIPs for advertisement via DNS. The backup VIP will be separate from the virtual IP blocks—not a member of any of the virtual blocks—and will be specific to the site.

Local server groups will be located on the following IP networks: 10.1.100.0/24 for NYC, 10.15.22.0/24 for San Jose, and 10.193.9.0/24 for Amsterdam. A /24 network was chosen because of the minimum CIDR block the upstream providers were willing to re-advertise. Each server group will be configured so its members include the local servers and the backup VIPs of each of the remote server groups. A maxconns setting will be implemented at each of the sites to handle flash traffic and load measuring protocols implemented to track site readiness. Note, site selection will be done by routing protocol, but failover will be guided by load/availability metrics.

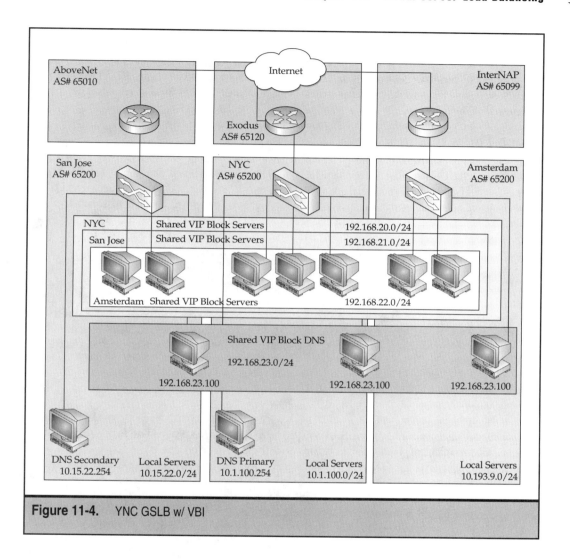

Figure 11-4. YNC GSLB w/ VBI

All three sites will be configured with BGP, advertising a single AS (65200) into all three co-location providers, each with its own AS numbers.

The primary YNC DNS server, located in NYC, will be located at 10.1.100.254, with the secondary DNS located in San Jose at 10.15.22.254. These DNS servers will be configured with the new subdomain, www.yournewscorp.com, and the authoritative nameservers will be the GSLB devices, hiding behind the single VIP 192.168.23.100, but located separately in NYC, San Jose, and Amsterdam. Each GSLB device will respond to client requests with the VIP from its preferred segment (refer to Stage Three for these).

Stage Two

Stage Two will implement the BGP VBI for the shared GSLB DNS server segment. One of the virtual IP blocks, 192.168.23.0, has been reserved for the virtual GSLB DNS servers. All three sites will advertise this route via BGP, all with equal cost (that is, no AS prepending).

Stage Three

Stage Three will implement the BGP VBI for the three server segments. NYC will advertise 192.168.20.0/24 as its preferred VIP block, San Jose will advertise 192.168.21.0/24 as its preferred block, and Amsterdam will advertise 192.168.22.0/24 as its preferred block. Each site will advertise the other two blocks, but will prepend the AS number multiple times to bias toward the routes to the local site. MED won't be used, as all three co-location vendors don't support it and a standardized configuration is required for company IT troubleshooting and support policies.

Stage Four

Last, but not least, errant packets must be dealt with in Stage Four. On each of the GSLB devices, TCP sequence number ranges will be reserved, so each site can immediately recognize sessions belonging to remote sites. Packets received by the GSLB devices will be scanned for these sequence numbers, and all errant packets will be forwarded via the private links to the appropriate sites.

PRODUCTS

Many choices are available for GSLB solutions in the marketplace. The following is a brief discussion of some of the major vendors and their solutions.

ClickArray Networks (http://www.clickarray.com) produces the Array 500 and Array 1000. Both devices include features such as a firewall, reverse proxy caching, server load balancing, content rewriting, and SSL acceleration, in addition to Global Server Load Balancing. Their GSLB features tie into their clustering solution to provide both site-to-site load balancing and site-to-cluster load balancing, where multiple clusters might exist within a single site. Available port interfaces include two 10/100/1000 TX/SX Ethernet, and the GSLB features include proximity and overflow capabilities.

Radware (http://www.radware.com) Web Server Director (WSD) offers layer 4–7 server load balancing and GSLB. Two offerings exist, only one of which (WSD-NP) offers proximity-based GSLB. The WSD-NP-enabling, GSLB-based solutions include HTTP redirection, Radware's proprietary Triangulation™ technology (a Footrace mechanism), and DNS redirection, all of which can be used in combination. Available ports are eight 10/100 TX, and two 1000 SX Ethernet.

Nortel Networks' (http://www.alteonwebsystems.com) AceDirector and 180 Series offer layer 4–7 server load balancing and GSLB. Unlike most others, the implementation is ASIC-based, instead of software-based, resulting in significant performance gains. The AceDirector's GSLB feature uses an easy to configure DNS-based load balancing option to allow web sites to be selected based on their availability. The Alteon Content Director is a dedicated GSLB platform, offering more sophisticated technologies, including site selection based on client-to-server Footraces, RTT, path reliability/packet loss, and latency. Available ports include nine 10/100 TX, dual-PHY 10/100 TX/1000 SX ports on the 180 series.

F5 Networks' (http://www.f5.com) 3DNS is part of the F5 Networks family of load balancers. The 3DNS is offered as a separate product or as an integrated feature on its Big-IP server load balancer and includes a fully compliant BIND 8.*x* DNS server. The 3DNS uses either DNS or network proximity to make global server load balancing decisions. Proximity technologies are derived from ARIN lookups against assigned IP addresses to determine the client country-of-origin and matched against a most-local server configuration. 3DNS also supports site persistency and QoS metrics. Available ports include a single 10/100 TX Ethernet, with Gigabit Ethernet as an upgradeable option. (See Figure 11-5.)

Foundry Networks' (http://www.foundrynet.com) Server Iron product is a layer 4–7 load balancer with built-in GSLB functionality. The Server Iron can employ DNS-based Footraces to determine site selection, in addition to monitoring RTT and load metrics. Manual configuration of site preferences for known IP blocks is possible and, with site monitoring, failover options are viable. Available ports on the Server Iron include between 8 and 24 ports of 10/100 TX or 1000 SX Ethernet. (See Figure 11-6.)

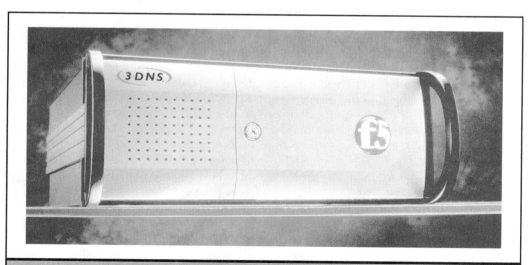

Figure 11-5.   F5: 3DNS Controller

Figure 11-6.   Foundry Networks: Server Iron

SUMMARY

In this chapter, you learned about many of the technologies hidden under the umbrella of GSLB. As you discovered, quite a range of technologies comprise GSLB, from simple site redundancy to full geographic site preferences. The ways to implement these technologies range from extensions of SLB to capitalizing on the way BGP works.

Important to remember is who and what GSLB is for. Essentially, the goal is to provide optimized HA solutions. "Optimized" so clients are getting to the most proximal distribution sites and/or sites that will respond best to the client requests. "HA" so if something goes wrong, clients can still access content in a straightforward, transparent fashion.

The solutions available so far are all first-generation and, as such, have significant shortcomings. DNS-based solutions are problematical at best because of caching problems, and Footraces aren't necessarily effective if the Footrace isn't back to the original client. Footraces to every client aren't necessarily an effective use of resources, either—probing is better in that it aggregates requests into a statistically meaningful set, but probing may or may not be possible because of security concerns. Relying on routing protocols is a second-generation approach, but such techniques are incredibly complex and difficult to troubleshoot.

The old adage "something is better than nothing" isn't always true. In most cases, GSLB won't be a cost-effective route. Solutions that provide next-generation-like results might require the purchase of a dedicated GSLB platform, a cost that can be significant, and not dual-purposed. Further, unless the content requires a global reach, the performance gains might only be minimal outside of normal Internet operating parameters and, where the gains could be dramatic, performance on the Internet might well obscure them entirely.

This isn't to say GSLB isn't ready for prime time. It is. It just isn't for everybody. But, for those clients that are heavily invested in online content distribution, GSLB might not be an option—it might be a requirement. The seven-second rule still applies: a significant chance exists that, given viable alternatives, a client won't wait longer than seven seconds for accessing a given resource. In that type of competitive arena, any advantage, no matter how slight, is going to mean dollars going to the bottom line—yours, or your competition's.

REVIEW QUESTIONS

1. **What are the three places packet loss can occur?**

   Packet loss can occur in the ISP (client side), the content provider network (the server side), and peering connections (links between service providers).

2. **Why are DNS Footraces a poor strategy to pick the site best suited for serving content to a particular user request?**

   DNS Footraces are a poor strategy to pick the site best suited for serving content to a particular user request because measuring the latency between the web sites and the DNS server might be a poor representative of the actual user's experience. This is because the DNS server is likely to be on another network and, thus, to have differing latencies. This is also because the DNS server might be located far away from the user. Take, for example, the AOL network: many of its services are housed in the state of Virginia, but its users are spread all over the globe.

3. **Why would a site send an HTTP redirect to a user after telling the user to come there in the first place?**

   On high-traffic sites, the moment-to-moment traffic patterns can vary considerably. Thus, a site could believe it's the ideal location to send a client, and then experience a burst of traffic. During that burst, the site might find it prudent to redirect some of the users to another mirror site in a transparent manner, so no user receives an error page.

CHAPTER 12

Content Networking and Security

OBJECTIVES

▼ Describe the threat to content providers

■ Define filtering and describe what filtering contributes to content security

■ Define what a firewall is and what it contributes to content security

■ Review some basic High-Availability solutions for content security

▲ Define and describe Firewall Load Balancing

More and more organizations are placing an ever-increasing amount of systems and resources on the Internet. This simple fact has, of course, created the field of Content Networking! But availability, obviously, isn't without risk. Without a means of protection between the systems and the Internet, these resources are potentially vulnerable to malicious attacks. These attacks can cripple a site, as is the case in a Denial of Service (DoS) attack, change the content of a web site, or even gain access to the systems and their data.

SECURITY

There's an old saw about security, told to me by a friend who spent a summer working for a towing company: "If a good thief really wants it, it's gone." Of course, this was in the context of car theft, but the spirit applies to all security domains. There is only so much you can do and, no matter what you do, someone really clever (and with way too much time on their hands) can and will find a way around it. Now, this isn't meant to make you feel warm and fuzzy—remember, most software security patches are issued as a result of someone reporting a hole. That is, someone actually diddled around enough to exploit someone, somewhere, and out of the goodness of their heart, bothered to tell the manufacturer (or told someone else, who then told the manufacturer) about it. To make matters much, much worse, the extremely accomplished "data terrorists" never let their pet hacks out, so what the manufacturers patch may well be a small subset of what is vulnerable.

Of course, this doesn't mean your IT security officer will or should simply bury his head in the sand and keep it there until his next job. The whole point of security is to seriously discourage the attempt. "The Club" is a perfect example. The Club is a bar of metal that "locks" a car's steering wheel in place and, thus, deters theft. The Club is worthless. To steal a car with The Club, you saw through the steering wheel, and The Club slips off. The whole point is this takes effort. The thief who really wants a "Clubbed" car simply takes it, Club or no. But the thief who isn't so committed to *your* car may well look elsewhere in search of easier prey. This is the heart of a successful security plan. Deterrence. I mean, why make it easy? In fact, studies show that even minimal security deflects the vast majority of external attacks. The reasoning goes: the more security, the fewer attacks, simply because it simply isn't worth the bother. Not that the would-be attacker can't get through, good security requires an investment of time and energy that only the most perverse are willing to generate.

Be aware also that most external hacks are pretty generic, and they're generated by someone "just testing" a freeware application they downloaded from the Internet. By the time such applications become readily available, manufacturers have already implemented their patches. The upshot of this is twofold. First, most hackers are at least several steps out-of-date and, therefore, are mostly harmless. Second, if you don't stay current on your patches, you can safely upgrade the aforementioned class of hackers to potentially lethal. Also, as for the class of hackers that's *already* potentially lethal, regardless of the negligence on the part of the maintainer of the system being exploited, very, very few exist. So many web sites are currently in place on the Internet that, statistically speaking, these folks are most likely focusing on someone else, so why worry? Yeah, right.

NOTE: I keep drawing the distinction between external and an implied internal attack. As most readers are aware, common wisdom has it that over 80 percent of successful damaging attacks originate from within the network, the disgruntled (soon-to-be-former) employee being the prime candidate.

In addition to the disgruntled employee, Kevin Mitnik made social hacking well known. Many studies have shown that social hacking is one of the easiest and more practiced ways to obtain information, enabling a would-be hacker to penetrate and possibly cause damage to network resources.

But moving on, what's with all the worry, anyway?

Mitigating Denial of Service

The primary threat to data center and web site security is DoS. A DoS attack is the prevention of normal service and an attempt to disrupt Web operations by overwhelming or interrupting servers. Such attacks have gained notoriety in recent months as visible Internet sites have fallen victim. These attacks are launched by new, more sophisticated software that can solicit the assistance of innocent third parties whose computers are infected.

DoS attacks can have a crippling effect on business. They prevent legitimate users from accessing the site and can degrade site performance substantially. In today's point-and-click economy, this means potential customers could end up looking elsewhere. Detecting and correcting these attacks is also costly, involving close interaction between service providers and IT personnel, and perhaps disrupting normal business activities within the company. Bad press resulting from successful attacks can have a negative effect on capital markets and vice versa: buy.com sustained attacks in its first day of trading as a public company. Finally, these attacks can render servers temporarily unavailable, causing crashes that might destroy data and require downtime for corrective action.

How Can We Be So Vulnerable?

Why are attacks so hard to resist? In the rapid innovation of the Internet, why haven't wily engineers devised protection from these assaults? The answer comes down to four key factors: software bugs, anonymity, necessary weaknesses, and the involvement of innocent third parties.

Software Bugs   Today's operating systems are complex and broadly available, often with millions of lines of code. As Microsoft has repeatedly proven, such complex systems cannot be perfectly tested for every possible condition and still get to market in a timely fashion. This means hackers can find *boundary conditions*—unlikely or unanticipated circumstances in which an operating system stops working or grants a hacker access—and then apply these hacks to public systems. While vendors are constantly issuing patches and fixes to software, many organizations lack the knowledge or personnel to maintain the latest code on all their systems.

Standardization   At the root of many vulnerabilities is standardization. Hackers thrive in highly standardized environments. On the Web, a few protocols link a few varieties of operating systems running a few types of web server software. Back-end infrastructures, such as databases and application servers, are undergoing a similar standardization. What this means, of course, is once a weakness is discovered in a particular system, it can be exploited across a wide range of targets.

Anonymity   The Internet lets hackers cover their tracks. Often, attacks come from *staging areas*—servers to which hackers have gained access—so when the machine performing the attack is finally tracked down, the hacker is not only long gone, but was never administratively connected with the machine in the first place. The Internet's protocols also let attackers hide. Every packet of data sent across the network carries a source and a destination address that uniquely defines a sender and receiver. But certain attacks enable the hacker simply to make up source addresses, a process known as *spoofing,* and render the attack nearly untraceable.

Underlying Weaknesses   This lack of traceability is a function of some necessary weaknesses in the underlying protocols of the Internet. The Internet is a connectionless medium in which packets are sent back and forth across many paths. This is in sharp contrast to a connection-oriented system, such as the telephone network, where a link is established to send data.

Because the Internet is connectionless, certain protocols, such as TCP, need to simulate a reliable, point-to-point link across it. Setting up this link happens in several stages, known as the *TCP synchronization process,* during which the sender and the receiver agree to talk. This process is called *three-ways handshaking.*

Because the Internet is an unreliable, best-effort medium, delays can occur in synchronization. The receiver responds to a synchronization request from a sender, and then waits patiently for the receiver to acknowledge the response. During this time, the TCP session is embryonic: it hasn't yet been established, but the receiver is keeping track of it.

By default, servers track embryonic TCP sessions for several minutes. This enables clients and servers to establish sessions despite long network delays, and is necessary for a ubiquitous, global Internet. But the patience of the receiver can be exploited. The default value for max timeout is four minutes for most TCP stacks.

Attacking a server by establishing many embryonic TCP sessions is one example of taking advantage of a necessary weakness in networking protocols. Many others exist.

Innocent Third Parties   The final reason attacks are hard to defend against is they often involve innocent third parties. Today's leading sites have huge amounts of capacity at their disposal. To hurt such sites, hackers need to enlist the help of other networks and devices. Some attacks trick other devices into responding to what appears a legitimate request from the victim, and these responses overwhelm the victim. Others infect systems with *Trojans*, attacking software that can later be used to target a victim. With the broad deployment of DSL and "always online" local loop connections from cable providers, hackers have an even broader base of unwitting third parties to exploit.

Types of Attack

Three basic forms of attack can bring down a site.

Poison Attacks   A *poison* attack sends toxic information to a target. This can take the form of a malformed packet the receiver doesn't understand or an oversized packet that exceeds the buffers of the target system. In some cases, a properly constructed poison packet can include code the receiver inadvertently executes when buffers are exceeded.

State Resource Attacks   A *state* attack consumes resources on a destination server by forcing the server to expend much more effort than the receiver in processing and tracking state information. The TCP SYN attack is the best example of such an attack, although other attacks include flooding a server with SSL session requests that force it to perform heavy cryptographic computation.

Capacity Resource Attacks   Even if a site is relatively well defended against poison and state attacks, attackers can still overwhelm bandwidth into the site. In recent Internet attacks, even when the target sites were aware of the problem, it was way too late: upstream providers' peering points were already handling more capacity than most countries generate all year. A *capacity* attack simply uses up more capacity than the victim owns.

General Prevention

Preventing attacks requires work at both ends of the network. Internet service providers (ISPs) and system administrators can take steps to ensure that the devices under their control don't participate in an attack. This begins with a good security policy, but can also include steps to cripple would-be attacks from infected machines.

Preventing Zombification   Machines can't participate in an attack if they aren't infected in the first place. Good security practices and clean servers are an essential preventative measure but, in today's complex server environments, malicious code can masquerade as legitimate software and hide unnoticed in myriad subdirectories. Scanning tools can detect and remove some malicious code, but scanner vendors are in a constant race with hackers.

Blocking Marching Orders   Even if a system is infected, it still needs to get instructions so it knows which systems to attack. These "marching orders" are stealthy, often encoded in seemingly innocuous traffic, such as ICMP response messages. Some firewalls can block a portion of this traffic, but attack systems are surprisingly robust and hard to detect.

Ingress Filters   Many of the most dangerous attacks involve spoofing the true source address of the attacker and replacing it with either random addresses (to hide identity) or the address of the victim (to trick devices into responding to the victim instead of the attacker.) By filtering downstream traffic, an ISP can prevent attacking machines from masquerading as another system. With the advent of "zombie" attacks, however, spoofing is less and less an issue. Furthermore, inspecting traffic is costly in terms of processing and can discourage some service providers from implementing such mechanisms.

Zombie attacks might be stopped through infection prevention, ingress filtering, or blocking the "attack" signals hackers send to infected systems.

Don't Bring a Knife to a Gunfight   These preventative measures are all wise, responsible steps to take. But they rely on altruism and assume that systems administrators have the time and knowledge to implement them. To make matters worse, several of them will simply be bypassed in later revisions of hacker code, with morphing Trojans or new attack messages, for example. In other words, we can't rely on preventative measures to solve the problem.

The rest of this chapter deals with two of the most common approaches to dealing with DoS attacks: filtering and firewalling. The chapter rounds out with a discussion on how to make these solutions robust, by means of High-availability solutions.

FILTERS AND FIREWALLS

In security, nothing beats a lock and key. This method is tried and true, unless, of course, someone happens to have a key or, perhaps, a lock pick. A padlock effectively blocks the unprepared but, overall, the security is only as good as that surrounding the keys. Even worse, it doesn't do anything to stop the thief from getting to the lock in the first place. In network security, the parallel to this approach is the password. Despite its inherent limitations, this is still the primary method of providing network security. And, like the padlock, passwords do nothing to prevent someone from whacking away with a password cracker.

In physical security, installing card readers is probably a good next step. In networking, I generally equate this back to setting Access Control Lists (ACLs) on strategically placed network devices, such as a router or a switch. By preventing access to all but a select few, you at least can restrict who gets to bang away at the lock. Installing card readers throughout a secured area might not be as effective a deterrent as a pair of aspiring WWF wrestlers, but the intention is the same. I tend to think of a good firewall as something akin to a door guard because, hopefully, it has somewhat more intelligence than a padlock or card reader. Using both ACLs and firewalls is bound to be much better than a simple lock and, when combined with one, are quite effective at reducing and eliminating most external threats.

With DoS firmly in mind, lots of things can be implemented to deter all but the most foolhardy. Ask your average network engineer what can be done to protect a network from an external attack. The first thing they're liable to mention is the implementation of a good firewall. Going back to my analogy, this is a bit out of order, but what it tells you is firewalls are extremely high profile and are widely considered as the minimum requirement for security. Essentially, a *firewall* is a network appliance (or PC with specialized software) that sits on the data path, inspecting packets as they pass. The rules that firewalls use to pass (or deny) packets are generally called *filters*. Filters that are applied by anything other than a firewall we'll call ACLs, so I expect I'll use the two terms loosely and interchangeably.

The benefit of firewalls is they can massively restrict access, and then maintain logs of what data is accessed when and by whom. For example, a firewall can be configured to allow access only to or from certain IP addresses and for specific ports. Firewalls can also be used to log where packets originate, if they were allowed to enter the network or if they were denied. These logs can then be used to show what systems might have been improperly accessed, as well as provide a basis for possible litigation.

Advanced firewalls are also used to maintain session state information. What this means is advanced firewalls examine the traffic flow for all sessions between systems (across the firewall). If a given packet matches the rules database in the firewall or is part of an exiting already-authenticated session, they can be passed through. This is a nice way of neutralizing certain types of IP address spoofing and inserting specialized packets into an existing traffic stream.

Function

Firewalls and ACLs function in much the same way and, of the two, ACLs are usually acknowledged as inferior to firewalls. Generally configured and installed on network devices, such as a router or switch, ACLs don't do much more than deny traffic based on certain packet parameters—source and/or destination IP, source and/or destination port, source and/or destination MAC address, and so forth. Basically, they're restricted to whatever is found in the header of a particular packet and also are restricted to making decisions on a packet-by-packet basis. As mentioned, think of these as the simple passcard readers installed at doorways into secured areas—not a whole lot of intelligence and as long as your card is cleared, you're good to go.

Firewalls, on the other hand, tend to be a bit smarter than that. Using state information, firewalls can track the progress of an actual conversation between two end stations and allow or deny that traffic based on parameters a bit beyond what the individual packet header may or may not contain. For example, most filters can be configured to allow a normally denied packet, as long as the ACK-bit is set in the header field, implying this packet is a valid response to a request. However, IP addresses can be spoofed and header attributes changed—what guarantee could a filter provide that the packet just passed isn't, in fact, such a one? With *stateful inspection* (a term coined by Checkpoint Software Technologies), a firewall can maintain a record of the context of a particular session. In effect, the firewall keeps a record of who sent what requests and, within a timeout period, will match up "returning" packets with this original request. If a match is found, all is well; if not, the packet can be dropped. This is significantly stronger than simply allowing traffic by a static set of rules, such as what is accomplished typically by filtering. Again, think of a firewall as an actual guard, controlling access into or out of a network.

Performance

Guard or card reader, firewall or ACL? You should probably use both, on the "better safe than sorry" principle. But where do you use them? ACLs can be placed nearly anywhere a router or switch exists. Firewalls can be placed similarly, but generally aren't for two good reasons. First, firewalls are expensive. A good licensed firewall package and associated hardware can run into the tens of thousands of dollars. A filter, on the other hand, goes on the device you've already bought and so adds nothing new in the way of expense. Second, firewalls are slow. Despite the plethora of marketing propaganda by firewall vendors, firewalls aren't faster than routers, and they're nowhere near as fast as switches. A good rule of thumb is hardware is faster than software. No matter how optimized a device, a firewall is almost invariably a software package installed on a PC. Checkpoint and the Cisco PIX are, perhaps, despite their labeling, devices of this sort. Routers and switches are hardware, and are designed to do nothing but move packets and, invariably, they'll be faster at doing so than any PC. Exceptions to both examples exist, of course. NetScreen Technologies manufactures a lightning quick firewall—its trick is in using ASICs instead of a centralized CPU for processing, in effect moving filtering decisions to the port instead of the queuing up to the CPU. At press time, NetScreen firewalls are generally considered the fastest firewalls on the market. Similarly, Nortel Networks builds network hardware using an ASIC over the centralized CPU design favored by Cisco Systems in its networking hardware. As a result, its gear tends to be significantly more adept at moving packets. Something that should also be noted is this: no matter how fast a firewall or network device, adding filters or rules to a firewall database can tremendously impact performance and invariably does so in a negative fashion. The larger the rule set, the more pronounced this effect would be.

Logging

Occasionally, having a record of what was done, by whom, when, and for how long proves useful. Such occasions might be immediately after all the web servers spontaneously began to display banners that say, "Kilroy was here," even though the site hosted had nothing to do with WWII. Or, perhaps, your online banking clients are reporting that their balances were unexpectedly zeroed out—all of them. Or, maybe during a scheduled update, you realize the reason your web server is so slow is simply because it's busy. *Very* busy. Any of these things might give rise to the desire to have reasonably accurate information on the activities in question. When did it start? How long has it been going on? Who is responsible? What in heaven's name is going on?

Logging is a good way to sort out some of these issues. Most network devices, including routers and firewalls, include some sort of logging mechanism. So, if you've configured a log event to track the number of ICMP Echoes that hit your firewall, each PING will generate its own log message, which will either show up on the console, as on a Cisco router, or be written to disk, as with a Checkpoint firewall. Firewalls, being essentially special-purpose PCs, tend to be much better suited to tracking events as they occur and logging them against future need, especially as they have some sort of storage ready to hand. Depending on the firewall, these logs can be incredibly detailed, and, if needed, can be configured to track and log every single decision made by the firewall. Note, this is an excellent way to drive performance solidly into the ground, but it can be done if needed. Remember that any CPU time devoted to logging isn't devoted to moving and analyzing packets, and performance will suffer.

Routers and switches, being designed along lines different from PCs, generally don't have a hard drive to use for storing log messages. Hence, their memory buffers tend to be rather limited, and they tend to get overwhelmed quickly, so an off-loading mechanism would be a better solution. A syslog server to which the router or switch can forward such messages, as they occur, would be ideal. The same caveat about system performance applies here as well: the more you log, the less time you spend processing packets.

To log or not to log, is it even a question? The tradeoffs are generally worth it, so long as you're smart about what you log. Again, just don't go nuts. Log what you need or what you're concerned about. If you set up rules on a firewall to discourage DoS attacks, then logging occurrences of such events will probably be in your best interest. If you're interested in getting an idea of the total traffic flowing into your data center, well, logging all incoming traffic probably isn't a bright idea. In this case, statistical summaries might be more useful. Most devices will track statistics automatically and, depending on the sophistication of the device, these statistics could be broken down in any which way. Check with the manufacturer for specifics.

Generally, a good idea is for the network administrator to spend some regularly scheduled time reviewing the logs. Logs can get quite unwieldy in size if left unread too long, and what's the purpose of logging if no one ever reads the logs? Most logs will wrap, in that, over time, the log will begin to overwrite itself, instead of simply filling the disk partition and crashing the server. How long you keep a log, and how often you check it, will be part of any company's security policy.

Basic Network Design

The placement of security devices throughout the network is something of an art. The goal is to place them strategically enough so no resource is left unprotected, but also to place them in such a way that irrelevant traffic is unimpeded. The idea is to avoid choke points wherever possible or to minimize any choke point that isn't avoidable. Network devices are bottlenecks, congestion areas, and aggregation points. At this point in the network path, a packet is likely to experience a delay of some sort. Filtering and firewalling make this worse, not better. Indiscriminately numerous filtering agents can easily exacerbate an already bad situation, and improperly restrictive rules can reduce the functionality of a network below required levels.

The trick is to place the right security at the right location. What this translates to is a fairly simple rule of thumb: place the most restrictive policies closest to the resource it protects. Be thoughtful and choosy.

Figure 12-1 illustrates a simple network with a firewall and several routers. The trick is to place and configure the firewall to protect the network as a whole, but to allow necessary traffic to pass to the network behind it. The question to ask is "What needs to go

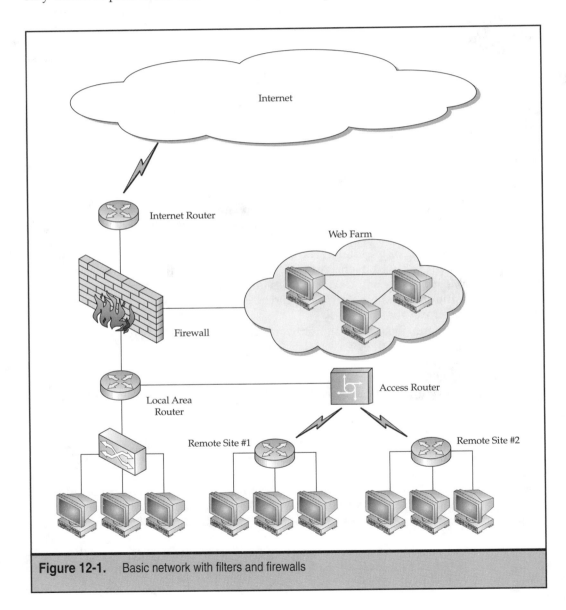

Figure 12-1. Basic network with filters and firewalls

through?" for each of the devices being configured, be it firewall or ACL on a router or switch. In most cases, erring on the side of caution is a better approach than a laissez-faire approach—having to endure the bother of opening yet another port on the firewall (or router) is better than cleaning up after realizing too late that a port should have been closed in the first place.

Figure 12-1 shows several devices where security could be applied. First and fore-most is a firewall that sits astride the data path out to the Internet. This firewall has three interfaces: one each for the routers to which it's directly connected and one for the web farm. Rules on the firewall will not only restrict data flow into the corporate network to traffic types relevant for business, but will deny anything except FTP and WWW traffic to the web farm. The Local Area Router might have ACLs that prevent traffic from the re-mote offices from traveling to the workgroup switch below it. The other routers could have similar rules.

Filters and Filtering

A *filter* is a rule with two parts. First, there's an *identification* criterion: when will this rule apply and to whom? The identification criterion can be so general as to specify anyone at all or so specific as to pick out only certain packets generated by a certain application on a specific workstation. Identifying the traffic is only the first step, of course. Now, some-thing needs to get done—what's supposed to happen and how should the packet be treated? The range of specific *actions* depend on the capabilities of the device itself.

Important to note is not all devices perform filtering actions in the same manner. Ad-ministrators tasked with designing any filter set are urged to become familiar with all the ins and outs of that particular product's filtering engine before getting started. Poorly planned filtering can cause serious disruptions in network service. The following is a list of typical filtering actions:

▼ **Allow** An *allow* action tells the filter engine to allow the packet to pass through the device on its way to a destination.

■ **Deny** A *deny* action tells the filter engine to drop the packet, thus prohibiting it from moving on to its final destination. A typical deny action sends no notification back to the sender to indicate the packet has been dropped.

■ **Reject** Similar to a deny action, a *reject* action causes a data packet to be dropped. Where it differs from a deny action is that a reject action initiates a notification to the source informing it the packet has been rejected.

■ **Redirect** On some devices, filters can be used to redirect packet traffic from its intended destination to some other device or group of devices. Redirection filtering is covered in greater detail in the next chapter.

■ **Network Address Translation** Some devices use filters to determine where to perform network address translation (NAT). NAT is used to "hide" a set of private network addresses behind a valid one. A company can use a large private network from a reserved IP address range, such as 192.168.0.0, and do so free of cost. To communicate with the rest of the Internet, however, that network must be translated into a valid range, usually of a much smaller size (and, hence, lower cost). NAT filters are typically found on routers or firewalls, and are processor- and memory-intensive.

▲ **Other** Depending on the manufacturer, filters can be used for identification, rather than initiating some action. Quality of Service (QoS) filters are used to queue certain traffic more expeditiously than others. Dial-on-demand routing (DDR) filters are used to identify "interesting" traffic. Then, if the filter fires because the router sees specified traffic, it can generate a dial-up connection into another network and, thus, minimize expensive connect-time charges. Route filtering can be done with ACLs as well, so certain routes can be removed or altered (summarized) in a routing update going from one network to another. Other applications depend on the vendor.

Filter Use

Filters can be applied in various ways, so the next step is to determine *when* you want the switch to apply the filter. While many devices give the administrator the capability to choose when inspection occurs, such as IOS-driven Cisco devices, some don't. Typically, packets are inspected on ingress, egress, or both.

▼ **Ingress** The filter engine inspects traffic as it enters some port on the device. The appropriate action is immediately applied *before* any route/switch decisions are made. By applying filters on *ingress*, packets the filter engine has been configured to drop or reject don't get processed by other functions of the device. For example, a filter designed to deny all private IP traffic would drop that traffic before any route/switch calculations were performed, saving time and resources on the device.

■ **Egress** The device's filter inspection engine fires *after* route/switch actions are determined, as the packet is about to exit some port on the device. Filtering actions might be more desirable on egress for two reasons. First, the administrator might have other rules or route/switch actions that must be performed before filter engine inspection. And, second, this might only apply to a particular egress port (among several). Note, however, that by not filtering on egress, the device itself could be more susceptible to attack.

▲ **Both** The device's filter engine fires as the packet enters the device, and then reinspects packets on egress, applying additional actions as necessary. Separating ingress from egress rules might be a bit tricky, but this is usually accomplished by source address ranges. Many firewall applications provide inspection on both ingress and egress for increased security. This option allows any packets generated at the firewall device to be filtered and provides ingress filtering for traffic originating outside the device. While this provides the highest level of security, it does have a negative impact on traffic flow.

Filter Numbering

Filter numbering and how a device treats the order in which the rules are applied dictates the actual behavior experienced by a filtering device. By way of a pair of examples, filters on an Alteon Web switch are single-action rules and have a numbering scheme that ranges from 1 to 224. Low-number rules are processed and applied before high-number rules, and many rules can be applied a single interface. Cisco Systems, on the other hand, has a slightly different filter procedure. A single ACL configured for a Cisco IOS device can have multiple actions, but each interface can only have a single ACL (per direction). Each rule within an ACL is still processed in terms of order: highest in the list is processed first. Cisco's ACL numbering has nothing to do with precedence of processing but, rather, dictates the settings and options available through the command line for that particular ACL. For example, an IPX access list would need a different set of options than an IP access list and, therefore, would get a number out of a different range to indicate to the IOS the specifics relevant to that type of ACL.

ACLs are processed from the top down. Processing continues on a packet-by-packet basis until a match is found. In most cases, as soon as a filter match occurs, the relevant action is performed and no further filter processing is done on that packet. This simple fact requires caution in filter creation—general rules that come before specific rules are applied first, and this might mean the specific rule won't get applied at all.

The following are some good rules to remember when designing filters:

▼ When using multiple rules, always place the most specific rules first. Because most devices apply only one filter per packet, be sure to order very specific filters *before* you order filters that are more global in scope. For example, is a very specific filter

```
Filter 10
Source 10.1.1.50
destination 10.10.10.50
sport any/dport 69/action allow
```

allowing a particular IP host to TFTP to a specific IP host? This would obviously need to come before the next filter:

```
Filter 200
source any/destination 10.10.10.50
sport any/dport 69/action deny
```

■ This one denies all TFTP traffic to the same IP host. If the order of the two rules were reversed, no one, including host 10.1.1.50, could send TFTP traffic to the 10.10.10.50 server, even though the next line would permit it—the second line would be irrelevant in this case because it would never fire.

▲ Process high hit rate filters as close to the top of the list as possible. Remember, filtering slows down the operation of the filtering device. The more filters that need to be processed, the slower the performance will be. Therefore, filters designed to catch the majority of packet traffic should be placed as high up on the chain as possible. This ensures that the appropriate actions are performed quickly, minimizing any potential delay.

Default Filters

Many devices that perform filtering have default or implicit rules applied and, on many devices, this is implemented as something called the implicit *deny all* rule. This rule states that all traffic, regardless of source or destination, should be dropped. This rule is designed as a catchall and is included for security purposes. The argument for the inclusion of the rule is that if a packet enters the device and the administrator of the device hasn't specifically created a filter to handle that packet, then that packet is undesirable and should be dropped. This is something of a mixed blessing: for security purposes, this is great and fills in when an administrator gets a bit lazy. This is also bad because it can cause serious network disruption if manually configured filters aren't created to allow all types of desirable traffic to pass unhindered through the device. Unfamiliarity with this rule often leads to several trouble tickets, generated from users wondering why their applications no longer function. As such, it's critical for the administrator to be aware of all the various default filters that exist on a filtering device. Typically, Cisco IOS implements a default deny all rule and appends this to the bottom of all ACLs. This *requires* that the ACL include specific lines for allowable traffic. Ideally, this is something other than the rule to *allow any*. However, in the case where general security isn't an issue and the entire goal is to block a single address range, or traffic type, with a small set of deny rules, including an allow any at the end of the ACL then allows all other traffic to pass unmolested.

Filter Placement

Figure 12-2 shows the network down to the relevant interfaces on each of the networks. The goal for successful filter placement is to identify locations where filters could be placed to increase the security of the network.

Router A is the first line of defense for traffic ingressing from the Internet. Also, this is the sole connection to the Internet, so any security you implement here should be minimal. This router should be left to route. Even so, an antispoofing filter on S0 would be simple to implement—all nonlocal traffic (inbound from the Internet) cannot have a local source address. If it does, dump it. This prevents these spoofed packets from penetrating the network at all. Outbound, S0 can have a filter blocking or summarizing routing updates heading to the Internet.

Likewise, Firewall A is going to be minimally configured to keep it functioning at a high level. A rule that specifies that only traffic on ports 80 and 443 should be allowed to pass when sourced from the Internet and destined for the DMZ would do. Firewall B will be more complex and needs to have rules allowing all update traffic from the corporate networks into the DMZ, but blocking any other traffic destined for the corporate networks that originate in the DMZ or the Internet. Also, any disallowed traffic destined for the Internet from the corporate network (that is, streaming media, online gaming, adult web site URLs, or Internet file sharing programs) needs to be blocked here. These rules

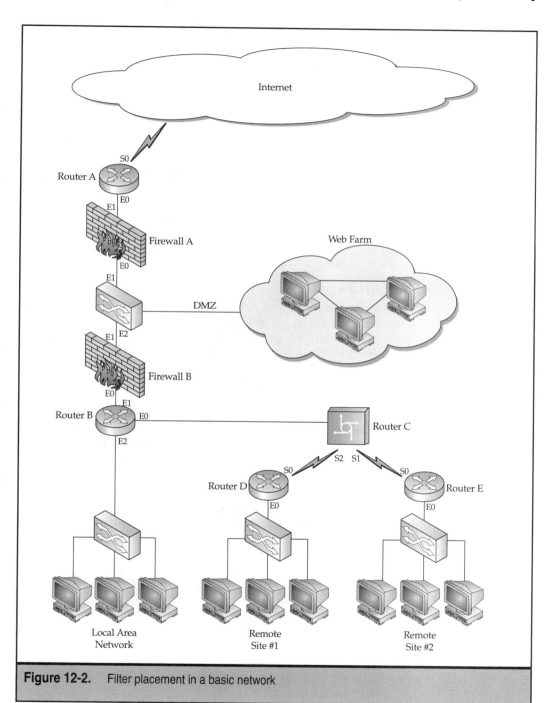

Figure 12-2.   Filter placement in a basic network

will all be interpreted as they ingress the firewall, regardless of the interface. The rule it-self will dictate how it should be interpreted.

Router B functions both as a default gateway to the local corporate network and an aggregation point for the remote sites. Primary responsibilities at this junction will be moving packets, but some security is also due. An inbound filter on E2 can prevent traffic from traveling to the remote sites and another inbound on E0 can prevent traffic from traveling from the remote sites to the corporate network or limit it to a specific set of ad-dresses, say, the corporate servers. Router C is another aggregation point for both of the remote sites and, as such, might be performing NAT on both S1 and S2. Routers D and E will have antispoofing filters as well as filters on their E0 interfaces preventing traffic to the opposing remote site.

In short, there's a cost for implementing firewalls and ACLs that doesn't involve money: that cost is latency and performance. Again, vendors such as NetScreen thrive on making this limitation as transparent as possible by relying more and more on hardware- and not software-based solutions.

Firewalls and Fire Walling

We've already described a firewall as akin to using a guard in the lobby of a building. Most Content Networking implementations include at least this level of security and do so in place of, or in conjunction with, ACLs. By no means is a good firewall the entire scope of good security, however. Strong password policies, virtual private networks (VPN), intrusion detection systems (IDS), and an ever-vigilant network administrator ap-plying all the latest security patches—these elements will probably also be included in any high-profile network. Remember, the more traffic your site is expected to attract and carry, the higher the risk posed—high profile = high risk. However, whatever security is implemented, a good firewall will likely be the cornerstone of the security effort.

Many firewall vendors exist in the world. Checkpoint Software Technologies manu-factures the, arguably, most popular firewall today. Cisco Systems' PIX Firewall product line can accommodate data pipelines into the gigabit range, and it also produces an IOS-based firewall that works with the majority of its router hardware. NetScreen fire-walls have fewer features, but are comparatively cheap and are implemented as an ASIC-based solution, and, hence, are blisteringly fast. Checkpoint's rules are all applied on ingress (or all on egress, or all on both directions). Both NetScreen and Cisco allow for the specification of the direction for each rule.

Overall, firewalls vary wildly in performance, features, support, and cost. Factors that weigh in on any purchasing decision also vary, and seem to have more to do with name recognition and brand loyalty than anything the vendors build into their gear. To be honest, which firewall you choose to implement is less important than the decision to implement one at all.

SYN-ing and SYN-ers

The SYN-Attack, or SYN-Flood, is probably the most difficult DoS attack to deflect. IDS, such as RealSecure from Checkpoint or Net Ranger from Cisco Systems, can be used to see this one coming but, by then, it's probably too late. Defenses against this attack are best implemented on a firewall or on another network appliance that sits between the servers and the outside world. Because the firewall is a network appliance that's likely to be installed anyway, using it to watchdog a connection to ensure it's legitimate makes sense. Web switches (such as Nortel Networks' Alteon Web Switches) typically have the brains and brawn required to do the job, and are likewise situated atop the data path.

The attack unfolds by exploiting a weakness in TCP. A typical TCP session will always kick off with the TCP three-ways handshake. First, the client requesting the session will indicate this desire with a packet with the SYN-bit set. The response from the server will be a SYN-ACK, straightforwardly, an acknowledgement of the received SYN request. Normally, a SYN-ACK-ACK, follows this and this is simply the client acknowledging that the server acknowledged the initial request.

The problem arises when the server doesn't receive this last packet. Until this last packet is received, the session is considered *half open* or *embryonic*. The TCP standards indicate that a server should wait several minutes before declaring this session dead and timing it out. The problem is that the backlog queue on a given TCP/IP stack isn't large. Because all TCP sessions still in the embryonic state need to be tracked, memory resources must be allocated to them. Piling enough half-open sessions on to a single server that would overwhelm this backlog queue is relatively trivial. When that happens, the machine can no longer accept new, legitimate sessions. For all intents and purposes, this means the site is down. To make matters worse, this attack has a nasty tendency to induce instability in the protocol stack and could cause the server to crash. Finally, the attack is almost always spoofed—so who knows where it actually came from! There are no known ways to neutralize the SYN Attack completely. Candidate solutions have been implemented by Cisco, Checkpoint, and others.

TCP-Intercept   Cisco implemented TCP-Intercept in the Enterprise IOS version 11.2. Two implementations—*intercept* and *watch* modes—of this feature exist. In *intercept* mode, the IOS device (usually a router) acts as a type of TCP proxy for a web server. As incoming TCP connection requests are transiting the router, it holds the incoming request in memory and opens a TCP connection to the server. When the final ACK is received in the TCP handshake, the router then merges the two sessions together, and all subsequent traffic for this session is switched through. In *watch* mode, the router allows all TCP requests to go through to the server. If the session request isn't completed in a timely fashion, however, the router sends a reset to the server, killing the embryonic session.

The simplest TCP-Intercept configuration has two steps. The first step is the creation of the ACL that identifies the target servers that need protection. The second step is activating the TCP-Intercept function. The two commands are as follows:

```
Router(config)# ip tcp intercept list 111
Router(config)# access-list 111 permit tcp any 192.168.100.0 0.0.0.255
```

This tells the router to use TCP-Intercept when transiting packets are destined for the 192.168.100.0/24 network. As the default implementation of TCP-Intercept is intercept mode, the command to alter this would be

```
Router(config)# ip tcp intercept mode watch
```

As activity increases, so does the level of protection provided by TCP-Intercept. Two thresholds are defined (and user configurable): total incomplete connections and requests that have occurred in a one-minute interval. The default values for these are 1100. If these values are exceeded, the router assumes an attack is underway and begins a more aggressive approach to TCP filtering. After the threshold has been reached, any new requests are permitted only at the expense of an existing connection—that is, a new connection is allowed as an older embryonic connection is deleted via a reset. Effectively, this limits the number of half-open TCP sessions a server will have to deal with to some nonfatal number. The commands for setting these thresholds follow: *high* indicates the threshold at which this "aggressive" behavior begins, and *low* indicates the value at which behavior returns to normal.

```
Router(config)# ip tcp intercept max-incomplete [high|low] [value]
Router(config)# ip tcp intercept one-minute [high|low] [value]
```

Monitoring the activity of the TCP-Intercept function is done by way of a pair of show commands:

```
Router# show tcp intercept connections
Router# show tcp intercept statistics
```

SYNDefender   Checkpoint Technologies incorporates the same functionality in its Firewall-1 product. Capable of operating in either the gateway or passive modes, the SYNDefender functionality allows for a method of deflecting the SYN Flood before it reaches the vulnerable web servers. In *gateway* mode, the firewall will proxy TCP sessions for the web server, allowing the connection to go through to the server only when the three-way handshake has been completed. In *passive* mode, the firewall simply tracks the inbound TCP SYN packets and keeps tabs on the session, waiting for the eventual ACK from the requesting host that will complete the negotiation. If that ACK isn't timely in its arrival, the firewall sends the reset to the web server, killing that half-open session. Note, the SYNDefender options are set for the firewall as a whole and apply to any inbound requests, not to specific network addresses or ranges.

From the Firewall-1 Policy Editor GUI, select Policy | Properties | SYNDefender tab. The three options are None, SYN Gateway, and Passive SYN Gateway. Selecting None (the default) disables SYNDefender, selecting SYN Gateway enables the proxy mode, and selecting Passive enables the Watch mode. You can choose two further options at this point: Timeout and Maximum Sessions. *Timeout* specifies how long the firewall will wait for the ACK before sending the reset to the server. The default value is ten seconds. *Maximum Sessions* specifies the maximum number of pending sessions allowed from the external network. The default value is 5000. Remember, on a Solaris-based Firewall-1 installation, changing these values requires manually stopping and restarting the firewall services for the changes to take effect.

Firewall Network Designs

The need and benefits of implementing firewalls in the network should now be apparent. Which firewall is chosen is almost irrelevant but, again, it will most likely be a function of name recognition and corporate relationships. From an administrator's point of view, the functions of a firewall are more or less similar. The question now before us is "Where do we put them, now that we have them?"

Answering this question definitively requires more information, of course. One of the first follow-up questions should be "Well, how many do we have?"

Figures 12-1 and 12-2 give some idea of where and how to use a firewall. The use of two firewalls in Figure 12-2 is a matter of taste and isn't really necessary, but the level of security added by a second firewall is significant. Many government organizations use similar arrangements, with several layers of firewalls between the protected network and the untrusted one. Note, classified networks aren't protected in this way. Such networks aren't connected to public networks at all! Some facilities will simply have two desktop machines on the desk with two separate wall plates connecting the two machines to two completely separate networks. A bit extreme, perhaps, but certainly more secure.

In less-critical environments, firewalls can be used wherever a significant change exists in the security policy. Such resources as satellite offices, corporate HR, R&D networks—all these things could well require having their own firewalls to separate them from the other networks that surround them. Another element common to the two figures is a Demilitarized Zone (DMZ). What a *DMZ* allows for is a region of lowered security where certain resources are made available to the public. The DMZ usually separates the corporate network from the Internet, and web servers, FTP servers, and the like are generally placed there. Security policies usually allow web and application traffic to pass through to the DMZ, and, depending on the level of security, perhaps only that traffic would be allowed in. Note, the DMZ is a dead end, with only one way in and one way out, ideally. Many configurations employ dual-homed servers in the DMZ, with the public NIC for traffic ingressing from the Internet, and a private NIC for communicating with back-end database servers. As with any security configuration, added complexity isn't necessarily a good thing—compromising a dual-homed server could give a would-be hacker much greater access than a simple one-NIC box. In dual-home environments, a second firewall should be considered, placed between the web servers and the database servers to restrict, log, and control traffic between the DMZ and a protected network.

A *honey pot* is an area, usually distinct from a server farm or DMZ, where "dummy" machines are placed in hopes of inviting attack. While the hacker mucks about with the honey pot, sophisticated logging and tracking systems record all the activity systematically, and, in conjunction with an IDS, could be used to identify and isolate threats, and to track attack patterns. The data collected could perhaps track, identify, and prosecute offenders. A good honey pot is a completely configured box and will be, for all intents and purposes, a fully functioning system. The choice of creating a honey pot from a workstation or server is a matter of choice. The more "life-like" the honey pot, the more likely a hacker will delay over it, enabling the tracking and logging software sufficient time to gather required information. Whether honey pots are a good idea is still up in the air. Some believe creating such traps is a great way to invite attacks—especially when the ruse is revealed. Retributive attacks have been known to occur in response to honey pot installations.

Figure 12-3 shows overindulgence in the use of firewalls throughout a network. The purpose of this, of course, is to be illustrative rather than prescriptive. Firewall 1 is the standard implementation of a firewall. With three interfaces, it allows access from the Internet to both the DMZ and the corporate network. Firewall 2 could be used in implementations where the network off Firewall 1 is, in fact, a honey pot. In cases like this, a secondary firewall could be used to add a further layer of protection behind the relatively exposed honey pot—a layer that could provide a further high level of security for the web server farm and the corporate intranet that lies behind it. Additionally, Firewall 2 could be used to terminate VPN sessions with clients located outside the corporate network entirely.

Implementing a firewall at Firewall 3 would be useful in situations where an access router is aggregating several remote sites. A firewall here can provide security if the remote sites are less than fully trusted. Further, it could also be used to provide security on the backup path to the remote sites but, perhaps, this only makes sense during a failure of the primary and secondary links. Such an implementation could be configured so it only takes effect with respect to traffic transiting the backup interface heading to or from the Internet. This firewall's rules could and probably should be ignored when that link is down. Firewalls implemented in the operating systems of the routers for Firewall 6 and 7 would be along these lines. A firewall at Firewall 4 is relatively common where access to the server farm needs to be heavily controlled. High-speed firewalls can be implemented to alleviate the potential bottleneck that introducing a firewall might cause. Remember, vendors such as Cisco and NetScreen both offer gigabit throughput solutions, and Checkpoint isn't far behind in having such an offering. Firewall 5 is a more common implementation of an internal firewall—this is used when, for whatever reason, some segment of the internal network needs a separate security policy. R&D networks might be such because the materials being developed there might not be for the consumption of the general corporate staff. Implementing password access on the firewall might be a good way to keep illicit users from getting at the valuable stuff that lies within. Or, a firewall could be used simply to limit the exposure of the corporate network to whatever toxic experimentation might be occurring.

HIGH-AVAILABILITY CONTENT SECURITY SOLUTIONS

Implementing firewalls and ACLs in the network is definitely a good idea. Common wisdom has it, though, that as security increases, usability decreases. That is, the more secure your network, the less can be done on it, which makes sense. The most secure network of all is the one that's "off"—and you can't do much with that.

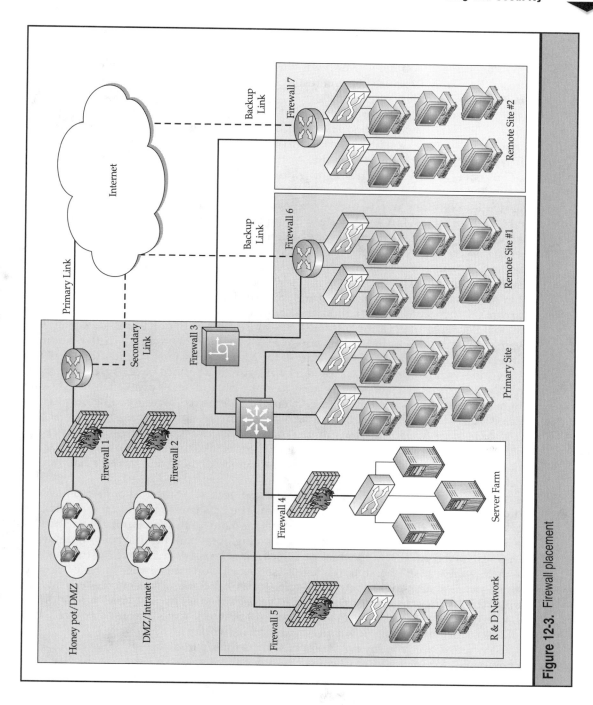

Figure 12-3. Firewall placement

Unfortunately, rendering a network off can usually be accomplished through the failure of a single key piece of hardware. A router or firewall failure can take the corporate network completely offline—or bring down a revenue-generating web site. Either way, failure is bad. Infrastructure gets interesting in trying to minimize, if not outright eliminate, this vulnerability.

High-availability (HA) solutions target the single point of failure in networks. In Figure 12-1, the failure of the Local Area Router will take the entirety of the corporate network offline. Moving up a level, the failure of the firewall or the Internet Router could do that as well, plus take down the web site. All three are classifiable as single points of failure.

The goal of an HA solution is to provide reliability and redundancy, so the failure of any single device no longer becomes fatal to the operation of the network. As you might expect, these solutions aren't exactly inexpensive (peace of mind never comes cheap) and can be quite complex. HA solutions can be implemented to cover nearly any kind of failure, including the loss of a router, firewall, Internet uplink, server (addressed in Chapter 10), or even power. While providing facilities redundancy, such as those for power or air conditioning, is probably best dealt with elsewhere, HA solutions for the Internet uplink are best dealt with now.

In most networks, connectivity to and from the web server farm is provided through the primary corporate network link, provisioned from a service provider like one of the Regional Bell Operating Companies (RBOC). More often than not, this is a T-carrier link, ranging in bandwidth from 128 Kbps up to 45 Mbps. More is obviously better, but more will certainly cost more. This is the heart of the argument against HA solutions—it's expensive, like I said. Most service providers will provide a Service Level Agreement (SLA) with their service, guaranteeing service to some absurd level of availability, usually somewhere north of 99 percent uptime. Of course, 1 percent downtime could be quite significant. A 30-day month has 720 hours. With 99 percent uptime, that gives you at least 712.8 hours of service during that month. That's 7.2 hours a month downtime allowed by that SLA—almost an entire business day. Good SLAs take this a step farther, to 99.9 percent uptime, and that's a world of difference—expect no more than about a half hour of downtime per month.

All this is great—except when the unexpected occurs. At the end of July 2001, Baltimore had a train derail in a tunnel downtown. The crash and resulting fire caused network outages and disruptions for several days for many of the companies in and around the area. Wouldn't you know it, the fiber carrying aggregated traffic up and down the East Coast all ran parallel to the track on which train derailed. The heat from the chemical fire melted the transit fiber and, while this isn't exactly an everyday occurrence, failures of this sort are distressingly common. Engineers with facilities in major cities can cite any number of city construction projects that have backhoed an uplink: leaky air conditioners, overflowing toilets, water main breaks—all network water hazards, any of which could be sufficient to bring down all or part of a network.

"So what?" I hear you saying. "Happens all the time, part of the job." True enough, but for companies relying on Internet connectivity for all, or at least a large part, of their revenue, temporary signal loss could mean thousands or millions of dollars in missed opportunities. Retail sites like Amazon.com and Buy.com, news sites like CNN.com and MSNBC.com, web portals Netscape.com and Yahoo.com, web search engines like Northernlight.com, Lycos.com, and Altavista.com—all these (and many, many more) are candidates for some sort of solution that eliminates or at least minimizes the capability for a random chance to ruin business for an hour, a day, or a week.

At a minimum, a network design that incorporates some kind of backup path for Internet traffic is going to be required. Depending on the level of business need, this can be as simple as an ISDN link configured to activate only on the loss of the default route through the primary link. Cable and DSL also fit this sort of emergency-link niche. As business needs dictate, more robust solutions can be implemented, perhaps something along the lines of a hot-standby T-1. Companies that have made investments in hosted solutions typically contract with the provider to provision a redundant link. A pair of fully redundant 10 Mbps Ethernet drops into the customer cage is possible and, with sophisticated protocols such as VRRP and HSRP, the failover can be made utterly transparent to the end user (see Chapter 10 for a more detailed discussion).

Figure 12-3 shows a potential solution that offers primary site backup via a secondary Internet feed and backup Internet access to the remote sites via an independent dial-up link. This type of solution provides some redundancy and promises continued Internet access for large portions of the network if anything goes awry in any one place.

Figure 12-4 shows a somewhat better solution, providing redundant routing options at the primary Internet access points. Using VRRP or HSRP, as discussed in Chapter 10, this type of solution provides protection if a connection to the Internet is lost or an Internet router itself is down. Often, a secondary link is unused and only becomes available during a failure; this scenario is known as *hot standby*. Some providers allow fully active "redundant" feeds, in which traffic is load balanced across the two active circuits. The purpose of the redundancy is that if a single link goes away, the load balancer (whatever it is) simply shunts all traffic to the live link.

Ideally, Internet connections of this sort will be provisioned through separate and distinct ISPs, that is, each link should be provided by different vendors. Reasoning for this type of redundancy follows the same lines as the arguments already raised—failures at a single ISP can be circumvented by a connection to a secondary ISP. At least, that's the hope. Of course, if the secondary ISP rents bandwidth from the primary and the primary is down . . . well, the secondary could be down as well, and so much for all that redundancy. So, caveat emptor, ensure your secondary connection is truly distinct.

The primary flaw in Figure 12-4 would be revealed with the loss of the firewall itself, of course. When that firewall goes down, all access to the DMZ and the corporate network could be lost. Figure 12-5 takes the redundancy down a level. By adding two firewalls, say, in a hot-standby situation where a single firewall stands idle unless an error occurs in the primary, the loss of a single firewall no longer becomes catastrophic. This also requires a modification to dual-home the web farm to support this configuration fully and the addition of a VLAN somewhere in the top part of the network to break a Layer 2 bridge loop. By doing these things, the HA solution now provides protection all the way through to the revenue-generating content servers. Figure 12-5 doesn't take this down to the corporate level, but doing so would follow the same sort of principles.

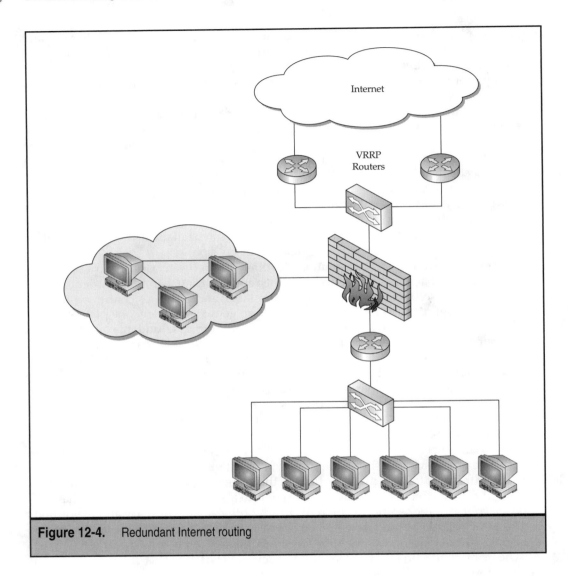

Figure 12-4. Redundant Internet routing

Figure 12-6 makes this a bit more interesting. A set of four Alteon Web switches has been added to provide more functionality. What these devices do is permit firewall load balancing, discussed in detail in the following. This allows not only for a redundant path if a firewall fails, but also for both (or more) firewalls to be used in parallel, simultaneously, and at full speed. The type of solution in Figure 12-6 is called a Bücher Box, after Eric Bücher, the Alteon Web Systems sales engineer who pioneered the design. Do you have a firewall that's acting as a bottleneck? A *Bücher Box* lets you continually add fire-

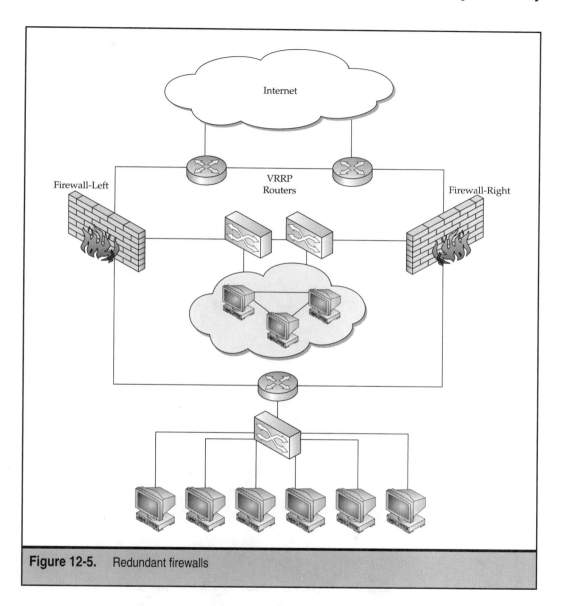

Figure 12-5. Redundant firewalls

walls until demand is again exceeded by availability. This network design, at least as deep as the web farm, is pretty much as bulletproof as it gets. Any single device can fail, and all traffic then flips to the opposite side and proceeds as normal. Any single device can be removed for upgrade, replacement, or repair, and network connectivity will be maintained. Multiple failures can occur, so long as they don't occur on opposing legs.

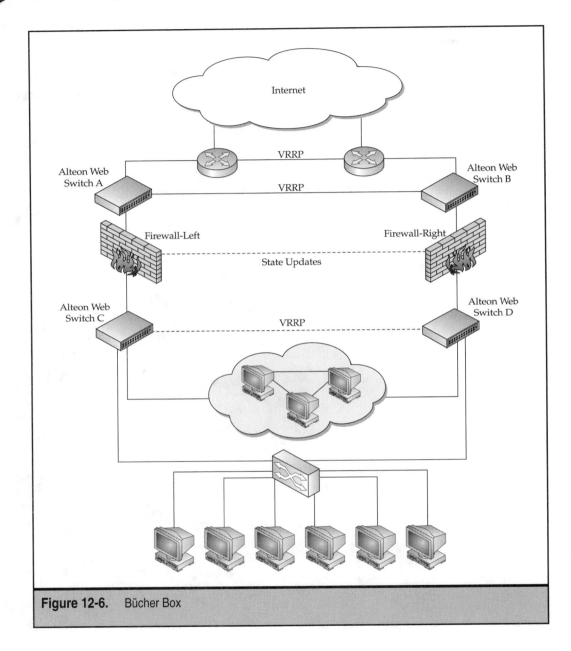

Figure 12-6. Bücher Box

For even more flexibility, get a firewall solution that supports at least five interfaces (and can dynamically route between them) and a load balancer that can handle weighted path metrics. Then, cross-connect each firewall to each of the load balancers above and below.

Finally, configure as normal, but add a step where the cross-connected paths are given high-cost metrics so they'll only be used during a failure. That done, you should be able to take out any two devices, even if they're on opposing paths! Sadly, most vendors can't support this because it would require support for a routing protocol on the firewall. Currently, only Nokia-based Checkpoint firewalls seem to be supporting this, though such super-HA solutions should be common soon.

State Updates and Clustering

Stateful firewalls maintain tables for tracking the communications passing through them to identify them better and match up legitimate responses with legitimate requests. Implementing more than one firewall in the same network, as in Figures 12-5 and 12-6, poses some difficulties. Two firewalls were installed for HA reasons—the trick now is to get the design to work that way. Specifically, traffic flowing through Firewall-Left must be shunted through Firewall-Right if a failure occurs on any of the following: Router 1, Alteon A, or Alteon C. Assuming the failover mechanism works, no problem should occur, except sessions currently in progress will most likely be lost. Firewall-Right might not have seen or authenticated the traffic from a host that had been serviced by Firewall-Left and, hence, might simply drop the next mid-session packet it sees.

Most firewalls now incorporate some sort of state update feature, also called *firewall clustering* or *synchronization*. This feature allows the communication of the session tables between two or more firewalls. These updates occur frequently and are very fast, kicking off somewhere in the neighborhood of 100 msec after a new session is established in the state table of the firewall. On a busy firewall, these updates could be quite a bit of traffic, so hardware vendors supporting this feature usually incorporate or require a dedicated port for a direct firewall-to-firewall connection, which is then dedicated to update traffic. In the case of a failure, transit traffic can then be instantly rerouted through to the remaining firewall(s), ideally, with no session loss, making the failure utterly transparent to the user. In practice, whatever delay is involved is still non-zero, so the potential for session loss is real. In a high-volume system, sessions could be established before an update is sent, which would then be lost in a failure. The counter argument is, of course, that the number of these dropped sessions will at least be minimal. Another side benefit is it's even easier to load-balance across an HA firewall pair that are exchanging these updates. In a typical scenario, load balancers take great pains to ensure that traffic flows are routed through only one of the firewalls in any set. This is done in both directions to maintain the state table in the firewall and to ensure that a particular traffic flow, already authenticated on one firewall, isn't then sent to another with no authentication records for that flow, where the flow will be killed. When state updates are added to the mix, the failover is much more graceful because the firewalls have information on all but the last session or two.

HA Firewalls and Firewall Clusters

Implementing the HA solution at the firewall level requires some commitment in equipment. Both the Cisco PIX firewall and the Checkpoint Firewall-1 High Availability Module require the specification of a standby device that sits idle, waiting for a failure on the primary device. As you can see, this can be quite expensive, requiring not only firewall technology but also twice as much hardware and software, with the inability to use them both at the same time!

The way this all works is as follows: for a Cisco PIX HA solution, you need to buy a standby PIX with the same software version, RAM, and Flash memory. Ensuring that the unit being used as backup is, in fact, a backup unit is important. Cisco sells devices that fill this particular role exclusively. Failing to get a failover unit, or using a failover unit as a standalone, won't work. Failover units deployed this way have a nasty tendency to re-boot themselves once a day, spitting out a complaint to the console on reboot. Anyway, to enable the Stateful Failover option previously discussed, you also need a full duplex Fast Ethernet or Gigabit Ethernet port free for the dedicated failover connection (FDDI won't work), in addition to the standard ingress and egress ports. Configuration will be performed only on the primary. The secondary will be synchronized with the primary at reboot, and thereafter as commands are entered on the primary.

Failover information, including status and power information, is exchanged between the two PIX devices via a special serial cable available from Cisco. By default, the two PIXes send out a special HA "hello" packet every 15 seconds (this is configurable, with the range being 3–15 seconds), and this will be sent out every interface, including the two direct con-nections (serial and Fast Ethernet). Missing two consecutive hellos will initiate the failover to the standby machine. Note, the total failover time could be almost 45 seconds before full functionality is restored. Of course, some interruption will occur to service.

On a Checkpoint Firewall-1, the operation is pretty much the same. A dedicated connec-tion carries the failover information, as well as the state-table synchronization data. One de-vice acts as a primary, with the secondary standing by in a hot-standby configuration, not passing data. Health checks are passed between the two devices, similar to the hellos sent by the PIXes and, when a fault is detected, the secondary will assume the role of the primary.

Configuration on the Checkpoint is done via the Properties option under the Policy tab in the Policy Editor. Once the window opens, click the High Availability tab. You need to specify the primary and secondary firewalls, and specify the IP address and MAC address the firewalls will share.

On failure, the secondary firewall (whether Cisco PIX or Checkpoint Firewall-1) as-sumes control of the shared IP address, as in the case of the Checkpoint, or that's config-ured on the primary, as in the case of the PIX. The MAC address will also get borrowed. The reason for this is simple transparency. As the primary fails, the secondary needs to step in as seamlessly as possible. Stateful updates are great and provide the promise that at least some sessions might not get broken. But, if the routers on either side don't know how to get through the firewall because they can't find it, then no amount of state updates are going to help. By preserving the IP and MAC of the primary, the secondary can step in and assume control, with no configuration changes necessary on upstream or downstream devices.

The trick is getting those devices to pay attention to the secondary at all. With an HA firewall solution, the firewalls need to be connected to a hub, both upstream and down. As packets come through the hub destined for the firewall, they're flooded out of every port on the hub. That two of these ports are connected to the firewall means both firewalls see all traffic destined for the firewall interfaces. If the primary goes down, no harm, no foul, the secondary simply starts accepting the packets. Of course, using a hub in a network infrastructure of any kind tends to be frowned on and, because we're working on a security solution, having every packet blasted every which way like a hub is required to do, well, that's somewhat frowned on. Replacing the hubs with routers won't necessarily work. Plugging each firewall into a different router interface requires each firewall to have separate network addresses, say, Net A and Net B. In the event of failure, we want traffic to go from one firewall to another—and the upstream and downstream devices only have the primary's IP address, on Net A, configured. So, if a failure occurs, the secondary assumes the IP of the primary, which is on a different network. In other words, a Net A address is now on Net B. The router won't handle this well, and the secondary won't ever see transit firewall traffic, because the router won't send Net A traffic out of its Net B interface.

So, replacing the hubs with switches seems like a great idea. The problem here is that switches tend to store MAC addresses and port numbers in memory for some period of time, usually upwards of five minutes. Switches do this so they can forward traffic to the appropriate MAC address without flooding it out of any port except the correct one. What this means is port 5 will get all the traffic destined for the MAC address of Firewall A, the primary firewall. In a failure, the secondary is standing by on port 6. The way either a Checkpoint or PIX device tells the switch that the failed-over IP address/MAC combo is to be found on a new port is relatively elegant—the backup sends a gratuitous ARP message from the directly connected interfaces. This is then recorded in the memory of the upstream and downstream switches, and all subsequent traffic to the firewall address will flow down port 6. Again, this is done to facilitate the failover from primary to secondary—without the gratuitous ARP message, the switch might wait several minutes (or longer) before flushing its ARP table and re-ARPing for the now-failed-over MAC.

This brings me to the point of this long-winded discussion: port security. Cisco switches support a feature that allows a network administrator to specify which devices are allowed to speak on specific switch-ports. This is done, of course, to prevent just any old device from being plugged in just any old place on the network. This is a good security measure but, in this circumstance, ensure that this feature is off.

Firewall Load Balancing

Firewall Load Balancing (FWLB) is a means to provide redundancy in the network to ensure that if one firewall or component goes down, you still have paths to allow for data to flow from the dirty side of the network to the clean side. In this respect, FWLB is similar to the previously discussed firewall clustering. The primary limitation of clustering is surmounted with FWLB, however. Recall that with clustered solutions, even ones with state-table updates, a significant investment in infrastructure exists in that not one, but two devices must be implemented to ensure redundancy. The problem is half your solution is idle at any given time—only one firewall is active. With FWLB, this need no longer be the case. A further side benefit of moving the HA up to the load balancer is alleviating latency because of an overloaded firewall. Using FWLB to load balance multiple firewalls allows for greater throughput and optimizing data flows to ensure that each session is treated optimally from a performance standpoint.

Hardware

To load balance the firewalls, at a minimum, a pair of load balancing devices are needed. This at least ensures redundancy on the firewalls, but creates a single point of failure in the load balancing devices themselves, which are implemented in such a way as to "sandwich" the firewalls—that is, one is upstream from the firewalls and another is downstream. What this means, of course, is if one of the load balancing devices is lost, all traffic will be blocked (see Figure 12-7).

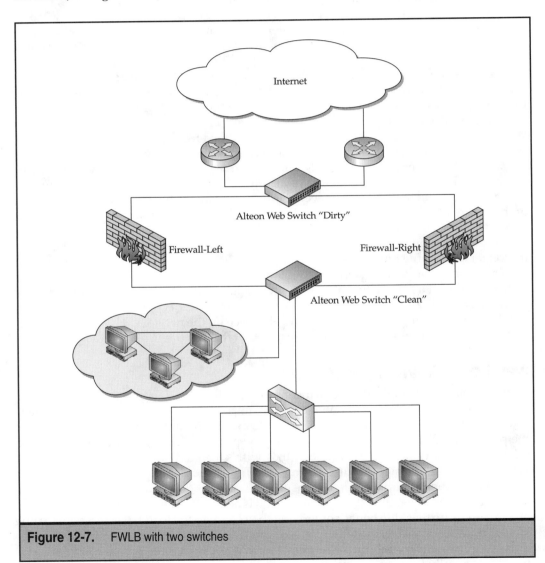

Figure 12-7. FWLB with two switches

Now, if full redundancy is the requirement, then two pairs of load balancing devices must be used. Two devices would be placed on the dirty side of the firewalls and two devices would be placed on the clean side. This is illustrated in Figure 12-6. This network design allows for the highest degree of flexibility for failure; however, it's also the most expensive to implement.

Another benefit when using FWLB is different types of firewalls can be used. For example, firewalls from Checkpoint and NetScreen can be load balanced in the same network. While this isn't common or recommended, the reasons for avoiding it are more support-related than technological difficulties. Supporting multiple firewall technologies tends to get expensive in terms of the skill set required to support them all. On a side note, an SE once explained to me that implementing two different firewall types can be a good thing—the tricks for hacking a firewall tend to be specific to the vendor implementation. Throw two different firewalls into an FWLB mix and the would-be hacker could be getting one or the other firewall, session by session. Interesting thought, but this does tend to double the amount of potential security holes, not lessen them, because you now have two sets of flaws that need to be watchdogged, not just one.

Getting back to the subject, different versions of the same type of firewall can be load balanced or even different size firewalls can be load balanced. Again, this isn't recommended because it adds another layer of complexity to already complex technology but, if needed, it's there.

The primary benefit with FWLB, however, is you can move away from Active-Standby configurations when implementing firewall redundancy. With FWLB, an Active-Active solution is possible, where all load-balanced firewalls are fully functioning. In case of a failure, traffic will simply be shunted away from the failed device toward the remaining devices and will typically do so much faster than a firewall cluster failover.

Firewall Load Balancing Basics

Once the decision has been made to implement Firewall Load Balancing, several items must be addressed for a successful implementation. This is aside from the basic choices, such as the type of firewalls and the FWLB devices.

We need to investigate three steps in executing FWLB: health checking, persistency, and network design.

Health Checking

Health checking is used to ensure the entire data path is functioning. The entire data path is from the dirty side switch, *all the way through a firewall,* to the clean side switch. It's possible to health check to the firewall; however, this only indicates that the data path from the switch to the firewall is operating. It doesn't guarantee that the path from the firewall to the opposite switch is up and running or that the firewall or other switch is processing traffic. In Figure 12-7, we have a simple network with a "Dirty" switch, a firewall, and a "Clean" switch. The Dirty switch will perform a health check to the Clean switch and, likewise, the Clean switch will health check to the Dirty switch.

Chapter 9 discusses load balancing and health checks in more detail.

Persistency

Typically, FWLB doesn't have the firewalls synchronizing their session tables because this wouldn't increase the total amount of sessions that can be used at any one time. In fact, this requires the firewalls to be implemented in an Active-Standby mode. Because no state-updates are being transmitted between the firewalls, the switches on the dirty and clean sides must send all the packets from a specific session through the same firewall. If they don't, the firewall receiving mid-session traffic will probably drop it. Alteon Web Switches can handle this in one of three ways: via hash, hash with NATing, or maintaining session information on the switch.

The first is by using an algorithm called *hash*. The switch looks at the Source IP (SIP) address and the Destination IP (DIP) address, and comes up with an index number that points to a specific firewall.

When the traffic returns, it would have the same information, order-reversed. The switch now runs the same calculation on the same information (the same SIP/DIP pair, order is ignored), and comes up with the same index number. Because the index numbers match, the packet will be sent through the same firewall.

If the firewall is NATing the packet, this wouldn't work. An incoming packet would have a different DIP prior to hitting the firewall than after the firewall. For example, a packet with SIP 42.180.100.15 and DIP of 200.10.134.88 hits a NATing firewall. When NATed, the DIP is replaced with a private address of 192.168.100.91. The problem lies in that the first hash was done on the SIP and DIP, where the SIP/DIP pair was 42.180.100.15/200.10.134.88, and the second hash was performed when the SIP/DIP pair was 42.180.100.15/192.168.100.91. These two pairs aren't identical, so they might not get the same indexes. Therefore, they might end up coming and going through different firewalls, and (deep breath) get dropped by the firewalls.

You can avoid this problem in three ways. One is to simply eliminate NAT on the firewall. Suggesting this to a firewall administrator is a great way to get incredulous stares. For most folks, NAT goes hand in hand with security. This is bunk.

The reason for using NAT is to extend the allotment of addresses beyond what is currently bought, rented, or borrowed from the pool an ISP doles out. This is all it does: extend an IP addressing scheme. That's it. If you're an enterprise, it lets you design and grow your network without having to lease large blocks of addresses, which can get expensive. If you're an ISP, NAT enables you to deal with overlapping addresses in your clients' networks. The argument that NAT "hides" machines from malicious activity is usually one proffered by someone who believes in security through obscurity. Don't buy into it.

So, if you want, you can choose not to NAT. Or, at least, not to NAT on the firewall. For those wedded to the technology, NAT can be performed on the dirty side switch, which is the second way to avoid the problem. Because NAT functions occur before load balancing functions, the SIP/DIP pairs will be identical on either side of the firewall and, therefore, pose no difficulties to load balancing.

The third method is to maintain a session table on the switch. If a packet is sent through Firewall Left from Switch A (referring to Figure 12-6), Switch A maintains that session information and updates Switch B with it over its dedicated HA link. On the clean side of the network, Switches C and D will track sessions similarly. Any subsequent packets associated with the tracked session are then sent to the correct firewall, regardless of who gets the packet first. Recall the previous discussion of firewall clustering. To get that to work, you needed some extra cabling on the firewalls to support a dedicated failover/state-update link. The same design should be followed here and should build on a VRRP-based solution, as discussed in Chapter 10.

To enable load balancer-based state update sharing between peer Alteon Web Switches (the two either above or below a firewall set), use the following commands. Note, this is a four-switch, firewall load-balanced design (see Figure 12-6).

```
>> Main# /cfg/slb/sync
-------------------------------------------------------------
[Config Synchronization Menu]
     peer    - Synch Peer Switch Menu
     filt    - Enable/disable syncing filter configuration
     ports   - Enable/disable syncing port configuration
     prios   - Enable/disable syncing VRRP priorities
     pips    - Enable/disable syncing proxy IP addresses
     bwm     - Enable/disable syncing BWM configuration
     state   - Enable/disable syncing persistent session state
     update  - Set stateful failover update period
     cur     - Display current Layer 4 sync configuration
>> Config Synchronization# state
Current synching stateful failover: disabled
Enter new synching stateful failover [d/e]: e
>> Config Synchronization# update
Current update period in seconds:        30
Enter new update period in seconds:      1
>> Config Synchronization# peer
Enter peer switch number: (1-2) 1
-------------------------------------------------------------
[Peer Switch 1 Menu]
     addr    - Set peer switch IP address
     ena     - Enable peer switch
     dis     - Disable peer switch
     del     - Delete peer switch
     cur     - Display current peer switch configuration
>> Peer Switch 1# addr
Current IP address: 0.0.0.0
Enter new IP address: 10.1.1.1
>> Peer Switch 1# en
```

```
Current status: disabled
New status:     enabled
>> Config Synchronization# apply
----------------------------------------------------------
Apply complete; don't forget to "save" updated configuration.
```

FWLB Network Design

The basic design to load balance two firewalls is to sandwich them between a pair of switches. The design discussed will be an internal network connecting to the Internet. Routable addresses on the internal network will be used to simplify the design.

Static Routes   The basic design is shown in Figure 12-8. A total of six networks are defined, four of which are used for FWLB. The other two are for ingress from the Internet and for egress into the local network. The networks used for FWLB can be used elsewhere in the network. They needn't be unique because they're used solely for health checking and won't appear in any router's routing tables anywhere in the network.

Two basic paths are being used. The first path is from Alteon Clean, to Firewall Left, to Alteon Dirty. The data path is from 192.168.1.0 to 192.168.3.0. The second data path is from Alteon Clean, to Firewall B, to Alteon Dirty. The data path is from 192.168.2.0 to 192.168.4.0.

Static Routes are defined on each switch. Static routes needn't be defined on the firewalls because the Clean switch is aware of the 192.168.1.0 and 192.168.2.0 networks (they're directly connected). The Clean switch doesn't know about the 192.168.3.0 and 192.168.4.0 networks. Firewall Left must only be aware of its directly connected networks: 192.168.1.0 and 192.168.3.0. Similarly, Firewall Right needs to be aware of the 192.168.2.0 and 192.168.4.0 networks. The firewalls needn't be aware of the networks connected to the other firewall.

The static routes on the Clean Alteon are defined as such: network 192.168.3.0 via 192.168.1.2 and network 192.168.4.0 via 192.168.2.2. On the switch, this might look like the following:

```
>> Main# /cfg/ip/route/add 192.168.3.0 255.255.255.0 192.168.1.2
>> Main# /cfg/ip/route/add 192.168.4.0 255.255.255.0 192.168.2.2
```

The static routes on the Dirty Alteon are defined as such: network 192.168.1.0 via 192.168.3.2 and network 192.168.2.0 via 192.168.4.2. On the switch, this might look like the following:

```
>> Main# /cfg/ip/route/add 192.168.1.0 255.255.255.0 192.168.3.2
>> Main# /cfg/ip/route/add 192.168.2.0 255.255.255.0 192.168.4.2
```

Notice the Clean switch doesn't have any routes to the Internet and the Dirty switch doesn't have any routes to the internal network. These routes simply aren't needed because

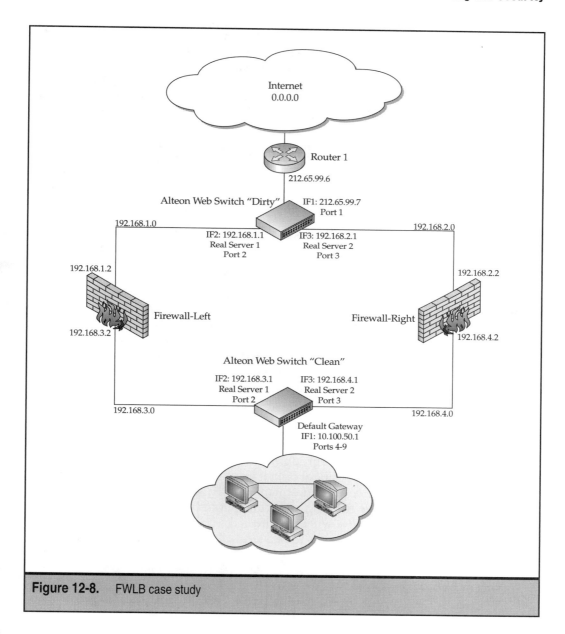

Figure 12-8.   FWLB case study

of the filters, discussed later. The Dirty Alteon does need to know how to send outbound packets to the Internet, so a default gateway must be defined.

```
>> Main# /cfg/ip/route/add 0.0.0.0 0.0.0.0 212.65.99.6
```

Real Servers   Once the data paths are specified, health checking needs to be defined. The Clean and Dirty switches will point to each other for the health checks. Starting with the Clean Alteon, two *Real Servers* are defined, and are used only for health checking and to set the next hop for transit traffic. The two Real Servers will be 192.168.3.1, set to Real Server 1, and 192.168.4.1, set to Real Server 2, which are the network interfaces on the Clean switch. On the Clean Alteon, we define the two interfaces on the Dirty Alteon. They are 192.168.1.1, set to Real 1, and 192.168.2.1, set to Real 2.

When the real servers are defined, it's important they're ordered so Real Servers on each side point to the same firewall. In the network described in Figure 12-8, the first Real Servers both go through the same firewall. If Real 1 on the Clean Alteon went through Firewall A, and Real 1 on the Dirty Alteon went through Firewall B, then the persistency could be lost and packets dropped.

Real Server Groups   Once the Real Servers have been defined, they need to be placed into a group, which is used in conjunction with the filters. The number of real servers in a group, which translates into the number of firewalls being load balanced, is only limited by the capacity of the switch.

Two types of health checks can be defined, ICMP and HTTP. ICMP is more than sufficient to test the data path. The health check sends a ping from the Clean switch to Real Server 1, and uses the data path that goes through Firewall A. A second ping is sent to Real Server 2, using the data path that goes through Firewall B. By sending these ICMP messages, both switches and firewalls are checked.

The next option that needs to be set is persistency. Configuring the load balancing metric on the two switches as the hash algorithm does this. This ensures packets are sent to the correct firewall.

Filters   The key to FWLB is the filtering. On routers, the normal operation of a filter is either to allow or deny packets. For FWLB, filters are used to redirect packets, with the destination of the redirection being a real server group.

The filters can be written as specific or broad. They can be based on source IP addresses, destination IP addresses, source ports, destination ports, packet type, or any combination of the previous. The filters we're going to deploy will be broad in scope, so any packets not destined for the local network will be redirected.

The first filter on each switch needs to be a local allow filter. This way, devices on the local segment can communicate with the switch. For the Dirty switch, the local allow filter would be configured in this manner:

```
SIP ANY
SMASK 0.0.0.0
DIP 212.65.99.7
DMASK 255.255.255.255
ACTION Allow
```

This allows external networks the capability to hit the Dirty switch. So long as packets are destined for this device, the switch can see them. If nothing else, this is nice to have if you need to test connectivity from the outside.

The next filter is the redirection filter for FWLB. It's configured as such:

```
SIP ANY
SMASK 0.0.0.0
DIP ANY
DMASK 0.0.0.0
ACTION Redirect
GROUP 1
```

This filter would send all traffic—other than local traffic—through the firewalls. The settings under the group option then are used to make the determination as to which firewall to send the traffic to. As mentioned earlier, hash should be set at that point, to ensure persistency.

For the Clean switch, the local allow filter would look something like the following:

```
SIP ANY
SMASK 0.0.0.0
DIP 10.100.50.1
DMASK 255.255.255.255
ACTION Allow
```

The next filter is the redirection filter for FWLB. It should have the following characteristics:

```
SIP ANY
SMASK 0.0.0.0
DIP ANY
DMASK 0.0.0.0
ACTION Redirect
GROUP 1
```

As before, this filter would send all traffic other than local traffic to the firewalls.

To complete this, the filters must be applied to the appropriate ports, so they'll be placed to fire on the appropriate traffic. On the Dirty switch, port 1 will have both the local allow and the redirection filters applied. On the Clean switch, ports 4–9 are used to connect the servers in the server farm directly, so all six ports would have both filters applied.

Notice how both filters have the same options. As you can see, this is a broad redirection filter. The switches could have been configured with more restrictive filters that would only pass certain traffic, such as port 80 or HTTP traffic. However, the logging features on the switches won't provide the same richness of detail on passed or dropped packets as the firewall software could generate.

Also note, no traffic generated from outside the "firewall sandwich" can reach the firewalls directly. The only devices that accept traffic from the outsides are the edge devices, the two switches themselves. From the point of the view of the Internet, or of clients on the local network, the pair of firewalls aren't present, aren't reachable, and, unless they kill some illicit traffic stream, aren't visible.

With the routes, Real Servers, Groups, and filters defined, FWLB has now been configured.

Scalability

With the increase of Internet traffic, the capability to scale the number of firewalls becomes more important. With one of the basic designs provided, it's easy to scale this design to implement additional firewalls.

To add additional firewalls, the following items will be added or changed in the config:

▼ New networks for each firewall. One new network per interface, per firewall.

■ New static routes for the opposite network segments.

■ Interfaces on each of the switches need to be added, one for each firewall.

■ New Real Servers of the opposite Alteon's interfaces are configured.

▲ The new Real Servers are added to the group.

In Figure 12-9, two new firewalls had been added. Notice the four new network segments added, two on the Clean switch and two on the Dirty switch. On the Clean switch, filtering is now being moved to port 1, to free up more ports on the switch for firewall connections. Server connections must be served by some other layer 2 fan out switch.

SUMMARY

Content Networking solutions should and will incorporate some degree of security. The sophistication of that security is a matter of need and a certain willingness to exercise the company checkbook. One of the goals of this chapter was to provide an introduction to a large and thorny field, and to keep an eye on what will be useful to the providers as they try to keep tabs on who gets to get to what. No matter what security solution is eventually employed, the lesson is that *something* ought to be implemented.

This chapter has reviewed some of the basics of security, as they apply to Content Delivery Networks. We've looked at filters and firewalls, primarily, and ended on a prolonged discussion of HA security solutions. For most networks, filters and firewalls cover the entirety of security needs. Virtual Private Networks are great, but are only relevant to remote access issues. In terms of Content Networking, this relegates to how you accesses the content you're managing. For the top-tier networks that require no downtime availability, some form of HA is a must. Companies such as CNN, Staples, Microsoft, Amazon, Buy.com—any Internet retailer that relies on the Internet for revenues—will need to look closely at an HA solution such as a FWLB configuration.

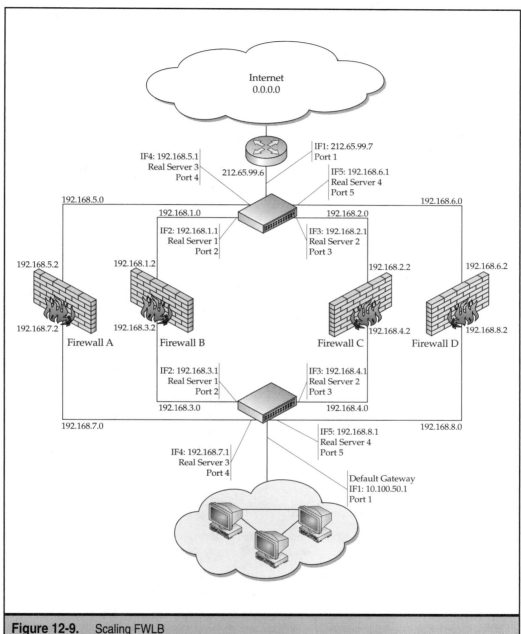

Figure 12-9.   Scaling FWLB

Security is now a fixture in most networks. Content Networks are no different in this regard. As more companies are making or breaking themselves on the Internet, more technologies will be developed to create, manage, and meet their needs. This chapter illuminates a few.

REVIEW QUESTIONS

1. **Can you completely eliminate the DoS threat to a web site?**

   No. The best you can do is deal with the attack closer to the source and "stop" the attack close to the ingress of the network.

2. **Are firewalls always necessary security devices?**

   No, firewalls aren't necessary for small, SOHO-type networks. Filtering would do fine to protect most smaller networks.

3. **Are filter sets on a router stateful?**

   No.

4. **What do SYNDefender and TCP Intercept prevent?**

   SYNDefender and TCP Intercept prevent excessive embryonic sessions with a server.

5. **Where would you place a firewall?**

   You would place a firewall at the ingress to a web server farm, a local area network, and/or network segments with heightened security needs, between two networks where one is untrusted by the other.

6. **What is the primary disadvantage to firewall clustering?**

   The primary disadvantage to firewall clustering is twice the hardware for no gain in throughput.

7. **When would NAT not be implemented on a firewall?**

   NAT won't be implemented on a firewall when those firewalls are being load balanced.

8. **Given an FWLB installation with two Checkpoint firewalls, can two NetScreen firewalls be added to increase throughput further?**

   Yes.

CHAPTER 13

Application Redirection

OBJECTIVES

▼ Discuss the differences between redirection and routing

■ Draw a distinction between forward and reverse, and transparent and proxy caching

■ Identify cases where Application Redirection would be appropriate

▲ Define and discuss WCR, DNS redirection, and SSL offloading

If nothing else, Content Networking is about intelligent traffic management. The goal is to increase use and availability, while minimizing delays and overhead. Application Redirection uniquely fits this role. Network designers often find it useful to redirect certain types of traffic or simply to route traffic differently, depending on its type. The emphasis is important to note: We're discussing routing traffic, not only by the protocol type, but also by the application type. A common example of where this is used is with transparent web cache servers, where HTTP packets are simply diverted to cleverly placed cache servers while other, noncached or noncacheable traffic is passed through to its destination, unmolested.

Redirection shouldn't be confused with server load balancing (SLB). While SLB can, and often does, play a role in Application Redirection, the difference is quite simple to state. With SLB, functionality is accomplished by means of implementing a virtual IP (VIP) address as the target a client hits to achieve load balancing. With Application Redirection, the IP address of the target is irrelevant—all traffic meeting certain requirements will be intercepted and acted on.

Redirection is also frequently confused with routing; however, the criteria used for redirection decisions come from higher layers in the OSI model than the layer used for routing decisions. The information used can be source and destination ports, HTTP header, or URI information. It requires devices that can make routing or switching decisions based on the application type indicated in the packet's protocol header—usually the *type* field in the TCP or the UDP header. This is a layer beyond the capability of most routers or layer 3 switches, and delves into areas of technology not as thoroughly standardized in RFCs as are the first three layers. While most would agree this functionality could be defined as layer 4 switching (layer 7, if URI information is used), disagreement still exists about what a layer 4 switch is or what it should do. Nevertheless, a number of vendors provide this functionality. Alteon Web Systems is commonly given credit for coining the term "Layer 4 Switching" and pioneering the technology. Manufacturers such as Foundry and Cisco are also heavy hitters in this market. Also, some multiprotocol routers could have layer 4 capability simply added to their feature set via a software upgrade. An example would be Cisco's Web Cache Communication Protocol (WCCP, which is a Web cache redirection application that can run on many of their routers (and some of their switches). As always, you get what you pay for. Hardware-based solutions, such as those you get from Nortel Networks, will generally and routinely outperform software-based solutions.

A number of uses exist for Application Redirection functionality:

▼   E-mail traffic could be diverted to different routes or for scanning

■   HTTP and HTTPS traffic could be sent to low-latency routes for faster response

■   FTP traffic could be sent to caching servers

■   DNS traffic could be captured and served regardless of how clients were configured

■   Caching of various types of traffic could be enhanced to boost performance

▲   SSL encryption/decryption processing could be offloaded from the servers

All these points relate to improving Content Delivery on the Internet but, clearly, the most widely used form of application redirection is in support of content caching and cache servers, via a process called Web cache redirection (WCR). To illustrate application redirection, we'll go into WCR at some length. This is partially because WCR is a common use of the technology, and also because it's possibly the most involved application. Therefore, WCR gives us the opportunity to explain many nuances not used in other applications. Other applications, such as DNS redirection and SSL offloading, are interesting in their own right and are dealt with separately.

WEB CACHING

When a Web page is sent to an Internet client browser, much of the data in the page probably doesn't change from one request to the next, or even from the previous day or previous month. Most World Wide Web traffic traversing an ISP's backbone (some estimates place that figure at upwards of 90 percent) is data that's both relatively unchanging and accessed repetitively by a lot of people. As an example, think about most WWW home pages you've seen. They contain company names, logos, and text information about the company, as well as its history, primary clients, and products. These parts of the page's information don't change often (or so we hope). On other pages, dated material might exist that does change periodically—hourly, daily, weekly, or monthly. A mixture of these elements is on typical Web pages, some of which might be static (unchanging) or dynamic (changing), and that might originate on different servers. Even the relatively static elements might have differing expirations: web authors can set expiration dates in HTML tags to determine how frequently particular elements must be refreshed by the origin server. On highly interactive pages, such as shopping cart applications, are data elements unique to that single client at that particular time, along with a mixture of more static items. So much of the data is relatively static (logos, advertisement banners, news articles, or movie times for a particular theater) that the operation of the network can be made much more efficient by storing that content at the edges of the network, rather than requiring that all requests go back to the originating servers. In many cases, this might be many thousands of miles away from the client initiating the request. Ideally, these caches would be placed at obvious aggregation points, such as POPs maintained by an ISP, a colocation facility, or something similar. Such Web caching can dramatically reduce backbone traffic, improve response times, and alleviate congestion, all of which helps speed network operations and reduce costs.

HTTP, HTTPS, FTP, and audio and video streaming traffic can all be delivered more quickly and more effectively when cached throughout the Internet, rather than always being served by the origin server. A vendor whose business involves software distribution over the Internet can vastly improve customer service by distributing that software on cache servers in various locations. Various companies, such as Akamai, make their money providing and managing just such a service.

Web Caching Applications

Web Caching can be found in two different flavors and in three different environments, though combinations are common and strongly encouraged. The first flavor is *subscriber-edge* caching. In an enterprise network, local caching of remote Internet content for local internal clients produces much faster response time for cacheable content, and reduces backbone congestion and WAN access costs. For an ISP, caching has the same goals of reducing backbone access costs and improving service. Caches would be located in a point of presence (POP) or super-POP (large-scale interconnection point), would likely serve many more clients than an enterprise system, and probably would be a larger system for that reason. The Content Distribution business, such as those exemplified by services provided by Akami, involves content generators paying carriers and/or ISPs to cache their content in various locations to better serve their geographically diverse customers. Another factor driving ISPs and carriers to update and add to their caching facilities is that an ISP is even more likely than an enterprise network to be sensitive to use-based costs, and many have, thus, enthusiastically embraced caching. Almost every ISP is either already currently using or planning to install web caching systems at its major POPs. Many are anticipating upgrading their caching facilities to enhance their revenue opportunities for Content Distribution revenue.

The second flavor of Web Caching is called *provider-edge* caching. Here, caching can be set up locally to a hosted Web site, whether that's in a colocation center (Integrated Data Center), in a POP, or at some enterprise's server farm. The most extreme form of this is what's done by default by a web browser. Provider edge caching is typically considered to begin at one level of abstraction from the single user. In any case, the goal is to reduce the load—in provider edge caching, the focus is on the Web servers. Because cache servers tend to be faster than Web servers, and are typically less expensive and harder to break, this can be effectively used to increase performance and further reduce the costs of delivering static content. For networks with both internal users and web servers, such as enterprise networks or POPs, cache servers could do caching for both directions.

By definition, most caching applications are considered *forward-caching*. This implies an application where a set of users (whether one or many) is accessing the Web—the content can come from anywhere in the world, from any web site. Caching for a web site is considered *reverse-caching*, where the users can be anywhere in the world, but the data source is specific and finite. For some networks with both internal users and web servers, such as enterprise networks or POPs, cache servers could do caching for both directions. Chapter 8 covers this in more detail.

Web Cache Redirection (WCR)

Web cache redirection (WCR) makes transparent cache servers more efficient by relieving them of the burden of handling all the noncacheable traffic on a network path. A router or switch, with layer 4 Application Redirection capability, could be inserted in the network between a fairly large group of users and the Internet backbone, and in the place where a transparent cache server would be most useful. One or more cache servers would, of course, be located nearby. The switch would be configured to redirect appropriate Web traffic (HTTP and/or HTTPS) to the set of cache servers while passing other traffic through. Besides efficiency, another goal realized is reliability—the switches or routers that perform the WCR function are generally more reliable devices than servers. Even better, with a switch or router in the data path rather than a server, the caching will automatically be bypassed if the cache servers go down. Additionally, a WCR device can support load balancing to multiple cache servers for added capacity and redundancy—more on that later. Ideally, a WCR device would perform multiple functions:

▼ Redirect only HTTP Get Requests for cacheable content to the cache servers

■ Pass all other traffic directly to the Internet, relieving the cache servers from having to forward other traffic to the Internet

■ Intelligently load balance across multiple cache servers, as necessary

▲ Perform health checks on the cache server(s), bypass individual caches if they're nonresponsive, and bypass the entire group if they're all nonresponsive

Infrastructure Requirements

A WCR switch should be inserted in the network between a fairly large group of users and the Internet backbone. Installations need to be well planned and coordinated. One or more transparent Web cache servers will be required, either dedicated hardware/software systems or general-purpose hardware running Web cache application software. With most layer 3–4 switches doing WCR, it's unnecessary to have routing functionality in the cache server, although this is a fairly common capability in transparent cache servers. Depending on the size of the system and number of connections, separate layer 2 switches might be required for extending port density.

Most switches can provide some traffic filtering, but cannot provide firewall-level protection to the cache servers. If the facility is vulnerable to attack, adding a firewall to the design might be desirable. Other than performance statistics, however, cache servers contain no content that isn't readily available from the origin servers, so they don't make likely targets for hackers. If filters have been added to this configuration to control traffic ingress from the Internet, HTTP traffic from the Internet must be permitted to get to the cache servers, so they can update pages. In some designs, the cache servers can access the Internet through a second port and network adapter, using the routing or bridging capability of the cache server, essentially going around the WCR device to access the Internet. With most WCR switches, this isn't necessary—client and Internet traffic can pass to and from the cache server on the same port.

Cache Redirection Traffic Flow

Figure 13-1 is a diagram of a simple, flat network with WCR. At the top is the router that serves as an Internet gateway for a small enterprise network—a firewall would probably also be there. The internal network uses the private address range 10.1.1.1/24. The cache servers are also connected to the WCR switch, through a layer 2 switch that might be needed if there were more servers—it's here only to show how the number of ports could be expanded. The WCR switch is connected between the client network and the clients. It functions as a simple layer 2 switch, except packets coming *from* the client network are subjected to a filtering process that redirects certain packets to the cache servers instead of passing them directly to the Internet. The following describes that filtering process in detail. No other ports need be subjected to any filtering, and no routing is turned on in the WCR switch.

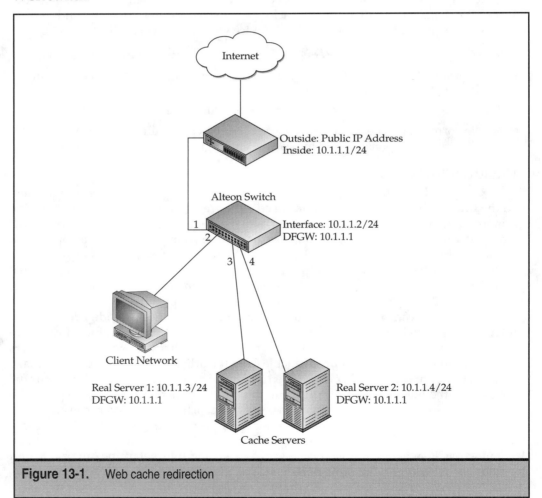

Figure 13-1.   Web cache redirection

As mentioned, the WCR switch is typically inserted in the network between a fairly large group of users and the Internet backbone. One or more transparent Web cache servers would be located nearby. Traffic from the cache servers to the Internet or to the clients is unimpeded, but the WCR switch filters incoming traffic from clients for the following parameters:

▼ **Protocol**   Anything but TCP would be passed through to the Internet unmolested (unless the switch is also doing routing or NATing).

▲ **Application**   The switch would examine the TCP destination port number in the TCP header. Anything but Port 80 (or 443, if HTTPS is being cached) in the destination port field would cause the packet to be again passed though to the Internet. Traffic not passed to the Internet would be redirected to the port or ports where the cache servers were connected. This would be the end of the redirection process for some WCR products, as it is for Cisco WCCP. Some switches, such as Alteon's, however, can examine the packet more deeply:

■ **HTTP/HTTPS Packet Type**   Is it a GET request? No need exists to send any HTTP or HTTPS traffic other than a GET request to a cache server, so other packet types, such as HTTP Posts, are passed on to the Internet.

■ **Cookie**   If the HTTP/HTTPS header contains a cookie, this implies a client is continuing a persistent connection to a specific server. This is required for applications like Shopping Cart. The client must connect to the same origin server again or the client data is lost—so don't send this to the cache server.

■ **Non-Cacheable File Type**   Is this a file type that's unlikely to be cached? If so, pass the packet on to the Internet. File types such as .cgi, .exe, and .asp indicate the client is requesting an application-generated dynamic page that won't be cached, so why send the request to cache? URLs can be examined up to 4,500 bytes deep for an expression that would indicate noncacheable content. These include, but aren't limited to: cgi, bin, shtml, cgi-bin, .asp, .cfm, .htx, and .exe, as well as the following symbols: !, =, %, &, and +. Any of these would indicate the probability of noncacheable content and cause the packet to be sent to the origin server. This expression list could be edited if, for example, a customer specifically wanted to cache .exe files for downloading. This intelligent redirection is only one of the advantages over other kinds of products.

Did you catch the subtle difference in that last requirement? The last feature is a bit beyond the layer 4 switching discussed earlier—it requires looking into the content of the GET request, and that would be called layer 7 switching. This trick requires a new layer of complexity in the switch called *delayed binding*. To look that far into the packet to make a switching decision, the switch itself acts as a proxy for the server by binding the client session to itself. When the client sends a SYN packet that meets the other requirements, the switch itself sends a SYN-ACK to the client and begins parsing the content. Alteon Web Switches have sophisticated L7 logic. The switches can look up to ten packets, or 4,500 bytes (whichever comes first), into the client's GET request to find the URL's file type and make a switching decision based on that. At this point, the switch then creates a session to the cache or the origin server and fetches the page for the client. After serving up the page, the switch breaks the session to the server. In HTTP 1.1, the client can request another page in the same client session. Otherwise, the client will reset the session to the switch.

Delayed Binding enables URL Parsing and is available on the newer Alteon Ace Director product line, where these models have sufficient memory that allows the implementation of delayed binding. Any switching device that supports layer 7 decisions must perform some similar process. Once the switch creates the second connection to the server chosen, it then acts as an intermediary, adjusting packet sequence numbers, and maintaining and tearing down the connections as required.

Cache Server Load Balancing

Load balancing for cache servers has both similarities to and differences from server load balancing (SLB). Server health checking is just as desirable with cache servers as it is in SLB, except finding a file to check might be more difficult (see the following). But there's a major difference in the purpose of the load balancing: web server load balancing is done primarily to improve the load capability, that is, to increase the number of sessions handled. As a result, the load-balancing metric most often recommended by those that support it is the Least Connections metric. This does require a layer 4 device, as layer 3 devices have no idea how many connections they carry to any given server. Cache servers tend to be quite a bit faster than web servers. One reason is cache servers don't have to run applications to generate dynamic content. As a result, the usual purpose of load-balancing cache servers isn't to expand the session capability, but to expand and accelerate the content being served. Adding redundancy in case of a server failure is a secondary, but usually a supported, feature. Cache server load-balancing metrics, for forward caching, are usually chosen to allow multiple cache servers to store different content on different servers—in other words, to avoid duplication of content on multiple servers. You can do this in two ways with Alteon Web switches.

Generally, all load-balancing switches support the address-hashing load-balancing metric. On a web server, clients can be all over the world, with widely varying IP addresses, but the server address usually remains constant, so web server load-balancing does address hashing on the source IP address. With forward cache servers, the target IP address might be any web server in the world, while the source IP address might be a narrow range—maybe a single subnet—on an enterprise network. For this reason, when doing WCR, WCR switches usually use the destination IP address for hashing. Cisco's WCCP also adopts this method. This results in the storing of different web site content on different servers, depending on the targeted origin server's IP address, irrespective of the client's address. This provides the best guarantee that content duplication on multiple servers will be minimized and, hence, that the caches will be used optimally.

Along these lines, the Alteon Web switch allows the WCR load-balancing metric to be set, alternatively, to URL hashing. In this approach, the URL itself is hashed into a number that represents one of the servers. This, again, tends to avoid content duplication, but now the cache server selection is based on the URL, not the IP address. Because this is a layer 7 function, only L7 switches can offer this function.

Note, should a cache server go down, it's dropped from the rotation in any event and the requests are then sent to another cache server in the rotation. Because this new server won't originally have the requested content (it was storing for a different destination), it must then retrieve all of it from the origin server. However, the system soon catches up. When a server is added to the rotation, a similar thing happens—it must retrieve content until it catches up. The content now assigned to it, which was on other servers, is no longer accessed and will soon be overwritten with active content. Either metric provides for redundancy, maximum distribution of content, and routine maintenance of servers. If all cache servers go down, all traffic is passed directly to the Internet.

Server Health Checking

Before beginning to configure a WCR device, some network issues need to be studied in some detail. One important issue is the server health-checking strategy to be used. While Web servers usually contain some kind of default file that can be checked with HTTP requests (often named default.htm), cache servers are designed to hold content that's obtained elsewhere, and some don't have a resident default file that can be accessed with HTTP requests. As a result, the health-checking strategy is highly dependent on the particular server type and the customer needs. Several alternative approaches will be discussed here. Getting clear information from the server vendor is critical.

▼ **Default HTTP file**   The simplest choice of all is on those servers with a file that's resident from installation, which is accessible from the HTTP request and not overly large. Often these are named default.htm, default.html, default.txt, or something similar. HTTP health checks that reference this filename are generally the best strategy and are simple to implement.

■ **Outside-sourced HTTP file**   Another strategy is to source a small static file from a Web server that's reliable and not expected to change. It could be a small text file on the customer's own Web server, it could be the .gif file that contains Yahoo!'s trademarked logo on the Yahoo! homepage—whatever, so long as it's a file unlikely to go away. If you select HTTP health checks and give the full URL for this file as the "content" for the health check, it will be sourced from the origin server once, and then health checked on the cache server afterwards. Drawbacks exist: if the selected origin server is down or the selected filename disappears from that server, the health checks will appear to fail for all the caches. Similarly, if the file chosen has an expiration date and the server goes down or the file disappears, your cache server will probably fail the first health check after the expiration.

■ **"No content" HTTP health check**   This is the next best strategy because it still tests the same server software entry point the client will expect to access. But, by configuring for HTTP health checks and setting content to "none", only the status response is generated and checked. The drawback to this is that it only checks the status response, rather than checking to see that a file can be retrieved, which can be considered an error on some servers. For example, this approach using Inktomi cache servers gives a correct status response and, hence, will be "up" from the perspective of the WCR switch, but it will flood the error log.

- ■ **Retrieving a file on another port**   Often servers will have a file that can be used, but it can only be accessed from another port. For example, Inktomi cache servers have a file named synthetic.txt, which is accessible only from the management port, 8083. To health check this file, you would set health checks to HTTP, content to synthetic.txt, and set the remote port to 8083 in the redirection filter. The drawback to this strategy is it doesn't check the same server software used by the clients.

- ▲ **TCP and ICMP**   These can also be used as a health-checking method. However, they check only that the protocol stack in the cache server is functioning instead of the web server software, and so are less than ideal for testing the integrity of a web server.

High Availability Switching

Another important issue is whether the customer needs or wants high availability (HA) switching for caching. While the loss of the origin server or the server caching content from that origin server can be catastrophic, it tends to be so only to a small segment of the transiting traffic. A Web switch, by contrast, is in the direct path to the Internet for all traffic and, as a single point of failure, its loss could be quite dramatic because all service might come to a halt. In such cases, prudence dictates a need to have a redundant switch configuration. To that end, using switches with Virtual Router Redundancy Protocol (VRRP) to achieve HA is advisable.

In a VRRP redundant switch configuration, there are two Alteon WCR switches. The clients are connected to both switches via a layer 2 switch. The key to understanding this topology is in the Alteon Hot-Standby VRRP option—except for switch updates on the interswitch link, only one switch at a time will be processing packets to or from the Internet, or to or from the cache servers.

Two virtual routers are configured: one is for the client subnet and the other is for the cache server subnet. Because they're grouped, these two virtual routers (VR) always switch together, so only one will be handling traffic among the Internet, the clients, and the cache servers. Each device is either *master* or *backup* for both VRs, and the master controls the IP address of each of the them. In VRRP, the MAC address given in response to an ARP to the VR's IP address isn't the MAC address of the particular switch, but a specific, special VRRP MAC address that contains the ID number of the VR. When the VRRP pair fails over, neither the IP address nor the MAC address of the Virtual Router changes, so the surrounding devices needn't learn any new address, and no learning delay occurs in the switching process. The master constantly reports the status of each active port to the backup. If the backup detects a failure, it assumes the role of master and forces the other to backup mode (if it is still online). In case of a failure of the interswitch link, the switches open other ports to interswitch communication and, if the backup does hear the updates, it will not then become master. If the backup fails to hear them through other ports, however, the backup becomes master. VRRP is covered in more detail in Chapter 10 and in RFC 2338.

All client traffic *not* sent to the cache servers is sent to the top layer 2 switch and to the Internet. The port where the clients are connected has the same cache redirection filters described previously. Note, the interswitch link and the two L2 switches could form loops in this network. Using VLANs is intended to avoid that, allowing this configuration to use the VRRP Active-Standby mode of operation. If a flat network is required, Alteon's VRRP extension of hot-standby mode—where the standby switch passes nothing except interswitch control packets—could be used with all the addresses in one subnet. VRRP is flexible, and other ways exist to architect a redundant switch topology. This one is given only as an example.

WCCP and WCR

Web Cache Communications Protocol (WCCP) is Cisco's answer to caching. WCCP consists of a software feature-set/upgrade that runs on many of its routers and switches, as well as on the cache server itself. In addition to Cisco's Cache Engine product line, some independent brand cache servers support WCCP. WCCP defines a protocol by which the cache servers and the switches or routers communicate the configuration and operational information necessary to support caching clusters. This protocol requires the cache servers to support WCCP, as well as the routers.

The original version of WCCP had some shortcomings, but the current Version 2 is much improved. It now does active server health checking, supports more applications (not only HTTP), provides multirouter support for fault tolerance, and more. Compared to using an L4 switch for WCR, Version 2 has both benefits and drawbacks, as might be expected. One major benefit is that Version 2 is somewhat self-configuring. Once a router or switch has been configured with WCCP, adding servers is fairly easy. The servers must also have WCCP software and be configured with the router/switch addresses, and they will self-register with the routers or switches in the WCCP cluster. There's no need to add them manually to the configuration on the routers or switches. However, Cisco does recommend creating a cache server access list for the routers/switches to limit the possibility of a hacker acting as a WCCP cache engine and grabbing some of the traffic.

The multirouter support could allow the cache engine cluster to provide caching for more than one subnet, where there are parallel routes to the Internet in forward caching. In reverse caching, this could also allow the same cache cluster to serve multiple web sites on different subnets. But the big advantage seems that it allows fault tolerance because multiple routers, say, in an HSRP/VRRP group, could access the same cache cluster. Of course, you'd also want multiple cache engines in the cluster. Layer 4 switches that support VRRP (RFC 2338) or HSRP (Cisco's proprietary Hot Standby Routing Protocol) could also provide fault-tolerant redundancy.

In terms of load balancing the cache servers, WCCP offers destination IP or source IP hashing, hashing all 32 bits into a number that represents one of the available servers. Destination IP address hashing is good for forward caching because it puts content from different web sites in different caches, based on the web site's IP address. This is intended to minimize content duplication and maximize content space. Only sites using round-robin DNS to load share, or some other DNS-based global load-balancing scheme, will have duplicated content in the cache. Source IP address hashing is offered for reverse caching, where only one DIP address, but many source addresses, might exist. While source IP address hashing causes distribution of content across the cache servers, it won't avoid content duplication because identical content requested by different sources will go to different cache servers. Some layer 4 switches, such as those from Nortel Networks, offer a modified DIP hashing, where the hash table isn't recomputed if a server is lost. Instead, added load is given to one of the remaining servers. This keeps the algorithm running, instead of risking lost packets during recomputation of the hash table.

Comparatively speaking, a switch designed for server load balancing can offer some advantages over WCCP in handling web caching. Server load balancing layer 4 and layer 4–7 switches are likely to offer a wider variety of health-checking choices, a wider variety of load-balancing choices, and, perhaps, more flexibility of configuration and operation. For example, a layer 4 switch can track connections, so it can distribute load based on the Least Connections method, which generally enhances response times, an important goal in reverse caching. WCCP does some layer 4 functions, but it doesn't do this because WCCP isn't truly a layer 4 device. Where maximizing content space is a goal, URL hashing, as offered only on L7 capable switches, works better than destination IP hashing in forward caching where sites have multiple IP addresses. URL hashing is the only practical way to avoid content duplication in reverse caching with multiple cache servers. Last, when Cisco mentions Reverse Proxy Caching, what it describes is reverse transparent caching. Supporting forward or reverse Proxy caching, where the packets are addressed to the cache instead of the web server, cannot be handled by redirection—packets not redirected to the cache servers have nowhere to go! Server Load Balancing must be used to support Proxy mode cache servers, and WCCP simply doesn't offer that capability.

The primary benefit to WCCP is platform ubiquity—you may well already have the gear in place (Cisco routers and switches), all you need is the software! WCR requires another piece of hardware, hence, might be significantly more costly. Still, you get what you pay for.

DNS REDIRECTION

Help desk costs for Internet service providers (ISPs) are skyrocketing. In fact, for many ISPs help desk costs rival, or even exceed, WAN bandwidth costs as the single biggest expense item.

As ISPs consolidate, larger numbers of subscribers come online, and the profile of the typical subscriber changes from technologically sophisticated to the technologically challenged. ISPs are faced with an uphill battle. This battle consists of automating end-user connectivity, regardless of geographic location, optimizing infrastructure performance, as well as the management and configuration of end user systems.

Many calls to ISP help desks have their roots in domain name services (DNS) problems. *DNS* is a distributed database service that provides the mapping between IP addresses and hostnames.

Proper network operation requires that subscribers' computers be configured with the correct DNS server address. A DNS server address that's misconfigured because the subscriber made a mistake entering it, the entry was accidentally changed, or any other reason results in the subscriber's losing Internet connectivity and, moments later, a call to the ISP's help desk.

Further, the need to configure subscribers' computers with the correct DNS server address can hamper an ISP's capability to implement DNS changes needed to keep up with subscriber demand. For example, an ISP might want to move from a centralized DNS server to a number of decentralized DNS servers to meet the needs of a growing user base.

Ideally, with decentralized DNS servers, subscribers would access the closest DNS server. Because DNS servers in a decentralized architecture have unique IP addresses, however, this isn't possible unless each subscriber reconfigures the DNS server address on their computer.

For any ISP, getting users to change the DNS server address on their computers can be an arduous and time-consuming task, fraught with potential problems. Still more difficult is dealing with the ensuing help desk calls that result from subscribers misconfiguring their DNS server addresses during such a change.

Although the Dynamic Host Control Protocol (DHCP) might alleviate some of these problems, ISPs would have to convert all their users to this automatic addressing solution.

DNS redirection, implemented on Web switches, can eliminate these problems. Web switches are a new and special class of LAN switch that front-ends individual servers or server farms, providing customized services that allow for increased scalability, availability, and better server efficiency. The capability to load balance or redirect server-bound traffic is one such value-added service.

By redirecting DNS traffic, all DNS requests are directed to the DNS server of the ISP's choosing, regardless of where the requests are addressed. If a subscriber's computer uses an erroneous DNS server address for any reason, it doesn't matter. DNS requests are still directed to the DNS server chosen by the ISP, and the subscriber's network connectivity is maintained—with no calls to the ISP's help desk.

Additionally, an ISP might want a subscriber to use a DNS server other than the one for which the subscriber's computer is configured, even if the configured address is correct for their local POP. A good example of this situation is mobile subscribers who have ventured beyond their home area when their ISP has implemented a distributed DNS architecture.

Without DNS redirection, DNS requests are sent to the user's home POP's DNS server, instead of to the DNS server for the POP into which they've dialed. Again, DNS redirection comes to the rescue because the DNS server address used by the subscriber is ignored, and DNS requests are directed to the DNS server designated by the ISP.

Finally, DNS redirection allows DNS requests to be dynamically spread over multiple DNS servers in a server farm. This scales processing power, reduces response time, and increases DNS availability.

Operation and Benefits

As shown in Figure 13-2, the Web switch sits in the data path between subscribers' computers and the Internet, generally in the POP of an ISP. The Web switch examines each packet, determining which are DNS requests. Using layer 2 or layer 3 switching, packets not identified as DNS requests are subsequently forwarded to their ultimate destination. DNS packets are intercepted and automatically redirected. For redirected packets, Web switches perform the required network address translations, and then send them to the DNS server specified by the ISP. This DNS server might be located locally, in the POP of the ISP, or at a remote location. The DNS server can also be a single device or a virtual DNS server created by a DNS server farm.

When multiple DNS servers are used in conjunction with DNS redirection, Web switches distribute DNS requests across the servers in the server farm based on a preconfigured algorithm. Choices for this algorithm are round-robin, least connections, hashing, and minimum misses.

The Web switch performs health checks on configured DNS servers, sending DNS requests only to DNS servers that have passed these health checks. Redundant Web switches can also be deployed to eliminate any single point of failure in the system, yielding the ultimate in uptime.

When deploying DNS redirection, a Web switch must be topologically situated so subscribers' DNS requests pass through it before going to the Internet. This allows for the interception and redirection of all DNS requests. If the network topology permits DNS requests to bypass the Web switch, they can be switched or routed around it, and won't be redirected to the desired DNS server.

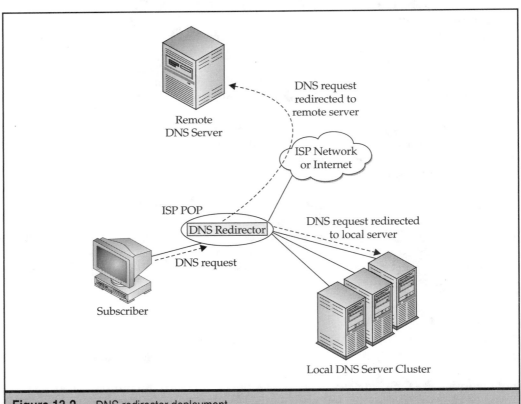

Figure 13-2. DNS redirector deployment

Fixing Misconfigured DNS Clients

When subscribers misconfigure the DNS server address in their computers, their DNS requests will either be sent to a system that isn't a DNS server or dropped. In either case, subscribers won't receive any responses to their DNS requests, and they'll be unable to obtain IP addresses for Internet hostnames, thereby losing Internet connectivity (see Figure 13-3).

With DNS redirection, the DNS server address configured in the subscriber's computer doesn't matter. The Web switch intercepts all DNS requests, regardless of the destination IP address, and sends these requests to the DNS server designated by the ISP.

The Web switch also manipulates the DNS responses, so they appear as though they came from the address configured for the subscriber's DNS server. Doing this, users' Internet connectivity is maintained, no matter how DNS server addresses have been configured on their computers.

Implementing a Distributed DNS Architecture

As subscriber bases grow, many ISPs that have implemented a centralized DNS server architecture see advantages in distributing the DNS function.

For a large subscriber base, a distributed architecture with many DNS servers—each located close to part of the subscriber population—offers faster, more efficient response than having a single centralized DNS server. Fast DNS responses are key to maintaining

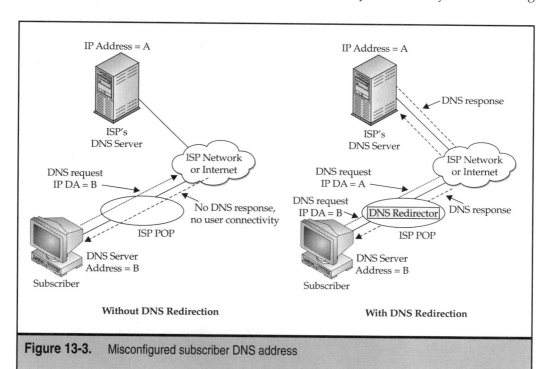

Figure 13-3. Misconfigured subscriber DNS address

high-application performance and subscriber satisfaction. Until the DNS function is completed, connectivity to the end system housing the application cannot take place. As a result, users must wait for DNS transactions to be completed until applications can be accessed.

Further, a distributed DNS architecture allows ISPs to manage their Internet traffic better. For example, many portals support mirror sites across the country or world. ISPs using distributed DNS servers can configure those servers to direct traffic to specific mirror sites located nearby.

But moving to a distributed DNS server architecture brings the ISP face-to-face with some harsh realities. If it cannot get subscribers to reconfigure the DNS server address on their computers, the move to a distributed DNS server architecture offers no benefits because subscribers will continue to send requests to the original, central DNS server (see Figure 13-4). Conversely, if the ISP gets its subscribers to change the DNS server address on their computers, a significant percentage of them will make mistakes, and the ISP is then faced with the misconfigured DNS server address problems previously described.

DNS redirection resolves this dilemma because the DNS server address configured in subscribers' computers doesn't matter. All DNS requests are intercepted by the Web switch and sent to the desired DNS server.

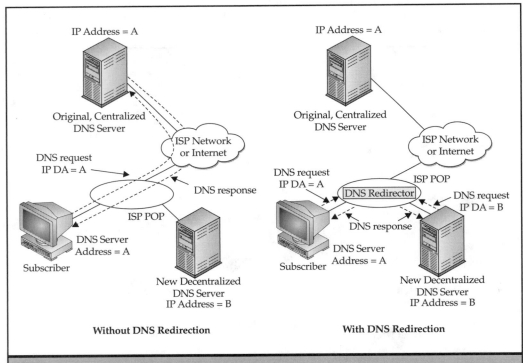

Figure 13-4.   Change in DNS server architecture

In fact, with DNS redirection, subscribers retain the benefit of keeping the address of the original, central DNS server configured in their computers.

If the DNS server, or all servers in the DNS server farm to which the Web switch sends DNS requests fail, the Web switch sends DNS requests to the host identified in the destination IP address specified by the subscriber's computer.

If this address is the original, central DNS server, then the DNS request will be directed to that server, providing a backup to the failed server or server farm.

Coping with Mobile Subscribers

In distributed DNS server environments where all subscribers have their local DNS server address properly configured on their computers, mobile subscribers present a significant challenge. For a mobile subscriber, the DNS server that is local to their home POP may not be local to the POP they dial into away from home. While it's desirable for a mobile subscriber to use the DNS server local to the POP into which they dial, that's not where their requests will go.

Instead, DNS requests will go to the subscriber's home POP's DNS server, slowing responses (see Figure 13-5). As previously noted, fast DNS responses are key to maintaining high-application performance and subscriber satisfaction.

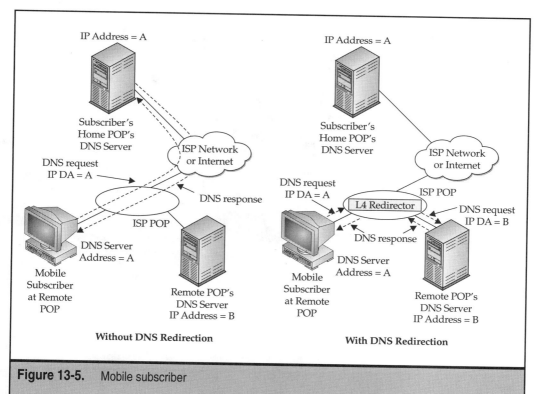

Figure 13-5.   Mobile subscriber

With DNS redirection, this problem is solved. A mobile subscriber's DNS requests are intercepted by a Web switch at each POP and can be automatically redirected to the closest DNS server. When subscribers uses a different POP, they'll use a different DNS server, if that's how the ISP has configured the DNS service.

What's at stake here isn't simply where DNS requests go, but also how other traffic is handled. As previously noted, portals can support mirror sites, and ISPs can configure distributed DNS servers to direct traffic to local mirror sites. Mobile subscribers away from their home POP, but using their home POP's DNS server, won't send traffic to the best mirror site for their current location. If this happens, application performance will suffer.

Using DNS redirection to send the subscriber's requests to the DNS server for the POP they're currently using eliminates this problem.

Increasing DNS Availability

Subscribers must be able to access a DNS server to resolve Internet hostnames to IP addresses. If subscribers can't access a DNS server, they can't access the Internet. Because of this, maintaining high-DNS server availability is key to maintaining high-subscriber satisfaction (see Figure 13-6).

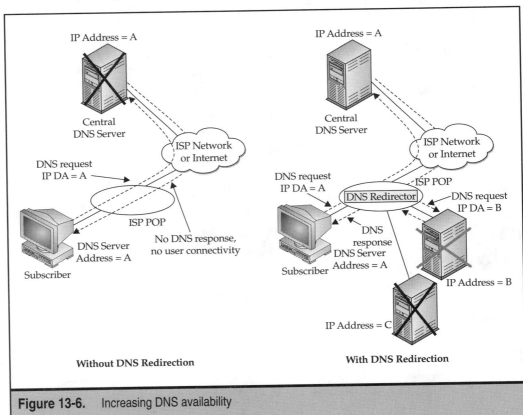

Figure 13-6. Increasing DNS availability

DNS redirection can increase DNS server availability. An ISP can deploy multiple DNS servers and configure Web switches to distribute DNS requests across the servers in the server farm.

The Web switch performs health checks on the DNS servers and sends DNS requests only to DNS servers that pass the health checks. For example, in Figure 5, if the DNS server with IP address C fails, as represented by the black X, all DNS requests go to the DNS server with IP address B.

The ISP can, optionally, configure the Web switch to send DNS requests to a backup server if any server in the server farm fails or if all the servers in the server farm fail. For example, in a distributed DNS architecture, one POP's DNS server(s) can both support local subscribers and act as backup for other POPs.

As a last resort, if the configured DNS server or all configured DNS servers in a server farm fail and no backup server is available or configured, the Web switch sends the DNS request to the specified host using the destination IP address used by the subscriber's computer. ISPs who want maximum availability should have their subscriber's computers to use the address of a central DNS server that can be used as a fail-safe if all other DNS servers fail. If they do fail, then the Web switch's last resort will result in subscribers' DNS requests being directed to the fail-safe DNS server.

This is shown in Figure 13-6, where both DNS servers in the local POP have failed (as represented by the black X and the gray X). In this case, DNS requests will be sent to the central server with IP address A.

DNS Server Health Monitoring

As earlier noted, DNS server availability is crucial to ensuring ISP subscribers have continuous network connectivity. To facilitate this goal, Web switches monitor the health of DNS servers and direct packets only to healthy DNS servers.

Request-Based Monitoring

Web switches monitor the health of DNS servers by sending requests to each DNS server in the server farm on a regular basis. These requests identify both failed servers and failed DNS services on a healthy server.

If DNS request-based testing indicates a failure, the Web switch places the DNS server in the Server Failed state. At this time, the Web switch stops redirecting DNS requests to the server, distributing them across the remaining healthy servers in the DNS server farm. If all servers in the DNS server farm are unavailable, and no backup server is configured and available, the Web switch sends DNS requests to the server to which the requests are addressed.

When a DNS server is no longer in the Server Failed state, the Web switch begins sending DNS requests to it. Once the Web switch receives a DNS response from server, it brings the previously failed DNS server back into service.

Physical Connectivity Monitoring

Web switches also monitor the physical link status of switch ports connected to DNS servers. If the physical link to a server goes down, the switch immediately places that server in the Server Failed state, taking the same actions as if the DNS server had failed request-based monitoring. When the Web switch detects that a failed physical link to a DNS server has been restored, it brings the server back into action in the same manner described earlier.

Overflow and Backup DNS

Web switches can also be configured to introduce overflow servers when any or all of the servers in a server farm hit their maximum connections threshold. They can also bring in backup servers when they detect that any or all of the servers in a server farm have suffered from a service or physical link failure.

Overflow Servers

As discussed previously, a maximum connections limit can be configured for a DNS server. When the number of active connections to a DNS server reaches the maximum connections limit, the Web switch won't send any additional connection requests to that server until its number of active connections falls below its maximum connections limit. Overflow servers can take over temporarily.

The idea behind overflow servers is a server that doesn't normally supply DNS to a particular POP can be configured to do so under special circumstances. Under normal circumstances, the Web switch won't forward any DNS requests to this server. If one or all of the DNS servers in the server farm hit their maximum connections limits, however, the Web switch introduces the overflow server into the load-balancing mix. When the load on the DNS server(s) falls to an appropriate level, the Web switch removes the overflow server from the load-balancing mix by ceasing to direct DNS requests to it.

Overflow servers can be configured to become active when an individual DNS server, or when all the DNS servers in the server farm, exceed their maximum connections' thresholds.

As it's called on to process connections from the Web switch, the overflow server continues to support its normal functions. The intent is to have the overflow server temporarily add capacity to the hunt group.

If an overflow server is recruited into service too frequently and for prolonged periods of time, it might signal a need to increase the permanent capacity of the server farm by adding more servers.

Backup Servers

Application, server, or link failure can cause Web switches to remove a server from the load-balancing mix.

Users can configure the Web switch to introduce a backup server into the load-balancing mix when any or all of the servers within a server farm fail.

In the case where the switch introduces the backup server into the load-balancing mix after the removal of a single server, the backup server is taken out of the mix when the Web switch determines the server is again operational.

In the case where the Web switch introduces the backup server into the mix after the removal of all servers in a server farm, the backup server is taken out of the load-balancing mix when the Web switch determines all servers in the server farm are once again operational.

As with overflow servers, taking a backup server out of the mix means the Web switch stops directing DNS requests to it.

High Availability DNS

Beyond DNS server health monitoring, even higher levels of application availability can be achieved by using hot standby Web switches.

Web switches can be used in pairs—with one active and the other in hot standby mode—to build network topologies with no system-wide single point of failure.

This means the Web switches aren't single points of failure and their use doesn't force a single point of failure at some other point in the network. Eliminating single points of failure increases application availability.

An example of a hot standby configuration is shown in Figure 13-7.

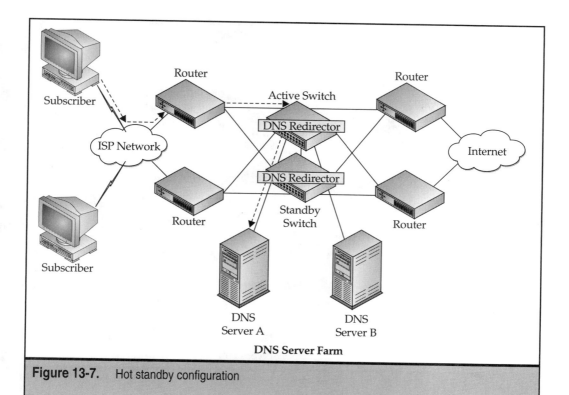

Figure 13-7.   Hot standby configuration

This topology supports use of active and standby Web switches, redundant network devices, and redundant, load-balancing DNS servers. Note, no traffic flows through the standby Web switch. For example, all traffic from client 1 to DNS server *A* flows through the active Web switch only, as shown by the arrows.

When implementing a hot standby configuration, one of the Web switches is designated as the active switch and the other as the standby switch.

A direct link, known as the *failover link,* is configured between the active Web switch and the standby Web switch. The failover link is used to send keep-alive messages between the active and standby Web switches. Data traffic crosses the failover link only if a port on the active switch has failed.

If the active Web switch detects a link failure, it communicates that information to the standby Web switch via the failover link. If the corresponding port on the standby Web switch is healthy, that port is activated.

For example, Figure 13-8 shows the case where the link from the active Web switch to DNS server *A* has failed. In this case, the port on the standby ACEDirector that connects to DNS server *A* becomes active. All traffic between client 1 and DNS server *A* now passes through the active Web switch, crosses the failover link, goes through the standby Web switch, and traverses the newly activated link, as shown in the figure.

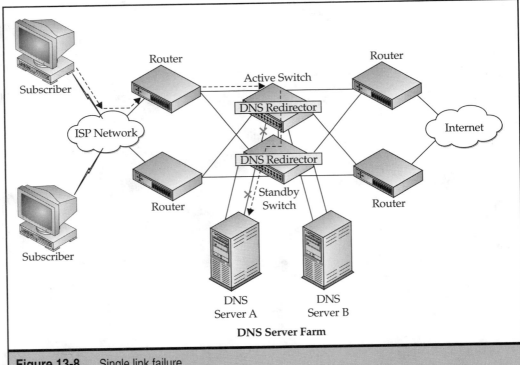

Figure 13-8.   Single link failure

Where an entire active Web switch fails, the standby Web switch becomes active, as shown in Figure 13-9. After the router on the upper left determines (using OSPF, for example) the originally active Web switch has failed and the standby has become active, traffic will again flow from client 1 to DNS server *A*, as the following shows.

As noted earlier, the failover link is used to send keep-alive messages between the active and standby Web switches. If a Web switch fails to receive keep-alive messages from its counterpart, this might be an indication the failover link has failed or its counterpart has failed.

Distinguishing between these two cases is important. If the failover link has failed, but both Web switches are healthy, this must be determined to avoid the "split brain" problem, where the original standby Web switch attempts to become active, while the original active Web switch is still active—a situation that could disrupt communications.

Conversely, if the standby Web switch stops receiving keep-alive messages because the original active Web switch has failed, it must determine this so it can become active. Distinguishing between the two cases is accomplished by combining physical layer and data-link layer health checks used on all Web switch ports along with specialized messaging.

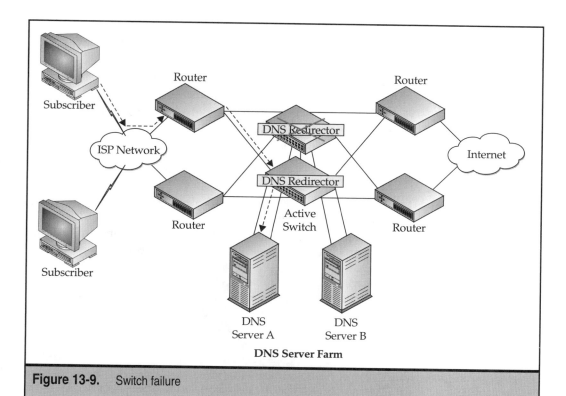

Figure 13-9.   Switch failure

SSL OFFLOADING

Offloading SSL encryption and decryption from the content servers is another important area for application redirection that works a little differently from the prior examples mentioned earlier in this chapter. In SSL, content must be encrypted before being sent to the client. Traffic from the client must be decrypted before it can be understood. Because web servers aren't optimized for the heavy number crunching involved in this process, this can severely impact the server's operating capacity. Web servers running industry standard software—Apache, Microsoft IIS, and Netscape/SmartPlanet are among the most common—typically suffer performance degradation of up to 80 percent when handling SSL traffic. This is largely because of the processor intensive tasks of key exchange and bulk decryption/encryption. Key exchange, as described in Chapter 5, typically relies on the multiplication of large numbers, especially with larger key sizes (that is, 1,024 bits and larger).

Special processors have been developed and put on to circuit cards that can be plugged into existing network servers to increase SSL performance. These generally use specialized chipsets to perform these processor-intensive tasks in hardware for efficiency and speed. Some drawbacks exist, though, to using this type of solution.

▼ **Scalability** Most servers have limited space in their motherboards to accommodate additional cards, making it difficult for the solution to scale by adding more cards as traffic needs increase.

■ **Performance** Even though a hardware accelerator card assists the web server in the key exchange process, bulk decryption still relies on the central CPU of the server. This creates a diminishing returns scenario in terms of performance.

▲ **Loss of intelligent web-switching decisions** Termination of SSL sessions directly on the server prevents the load balancer from accessing information in the TCP session, including URL, cookie, and host header information as all of that information is encrypted.

Intelligent web switching is particularly critical in e-commerce applications, where it's important for a user's session to be temporarily "bound" to a single server for the duration of a session. This technique, called *persistence*, enables a user to fill up a virtual shopping cart with items and proceed to a checkout or continue to browse the site without losing items stored in the cart during a given session. Currently, three ways exist of achieving persistence that the majority of load balancers support: Source IP, SSL session ID, and cookie. Cookie persistence is the best, for reasons described in the following.

Source IP persistence is easy to use; the source IP address is unencrypted. However, megaproxies on the Internet hide large numbers of users behind a few IP addresses. America Online users are the predominant example of this issue, although the same situation happens on a smaller scale with large corporations or smaller ISPs using NAT on their outbound firewalls. Using persistence based on the source IP addresses under these circumstances results in a domino effect—traffic gets directed to one server until it is saturated, and then proceeds to the next server until it, too, is overloaded.

SSL session ID persistence was popular for some time, but newer versions of many web browsers will time out the SSL session ID at fixed intervals or if the connection is idle. For example, Microsoft's Internet Explorer will time out an SSL session ID every two minutes. This makes the persistence last only as long as the browser doesn't time out the session ID, which, in the majority of cases, in a bit shorter than is ideal. If users take a short break, they lose their shopping carts!

Of the three techniques for achieving persistence, cookie-based persistence is by far the most effective. *Cookie persistence* works by having the web server insert a preconfigured cookie into the response to the client. Most load balancers can check for the presence of this cookie and either act on the value the server inserts or rewrite the cookie (or some part of it) with a value that identifies which server initiated the session. Subsequent requests from the same client will have the cookie in them, allowing the load balancer to send the request back to the same server. The one drawback to cookie persistence, however, is the information is inaccessible to the load balancer when SSL is used because that portion of the packet is encrypted. Therefore, it's beneficial from a persistence standpoint to offload the SSL traffic for decryption prior to making load-balancing decisions.

SSL redirection consists of two main networking components—a server load balancer that can do application redirection and an SSL offload appliance. Some manufacturers have incorporated both functions into a single device, but most of the industry hasn't adopted this approach. A purpose-built load balancer and separate SSL offload device offer more scalability because more SSL devices can be added as the need for SSL capacity grows in an application. In addition, combination devices usually use a centralized CPU approach, which hinders the performance of both the load balancing and SSL bulk decryption functions, each of which rely heavily on the central CPU.

The Alteon iSD-SSL is just such a device. This is a small, rack-mounted, high-performance SSL offload device occupying only a single rack mount slot (1U). An Alteon load-balancing switch, when configured with an iSD-SSL, will redirect all SSL client traffic to the iSD-SSL, which decrypts it and returns it to the switch, which then routes it to the server chosen by the load-balancing algorithm. Likewise, when the server sends SSL traffic, the switch redirects it to the iSD-SSL for encryption, and then routes the encrypted traffic to the user. Other vendors, such as Pivotal, also make SSL offload devices.

Figure 13-10 shows a simplified diagram of how such a device would connect. Through application redirection, the switch directs all incoming SSL traffic (TCP Port 443) to the iSD-SSL SSL Offload device (or bank of offload devices). The SSL device is configured with the certificate and private key of the corresponding virtual IP address of the load balancer, and completes the SSL transaction with the client. The SSL device then issues an HTTP request on a nonstandard TCP port that isn't encrypted back to the web server farm. The web servers themselves need to be configured to "listen" on an additional TCP port that's used strictly for communication between the SSL device and the web server farm.

This handles the decryption of incoming SSL traffic, but the traffic returning to the client must be reencrypted or the session will fail. An additional filter is configured on the load balancer to intercept traffic on the preconfigured TCP port and redirect it back to the SSL device for reencryption back to the client. HTTP traffic sent to the web site would

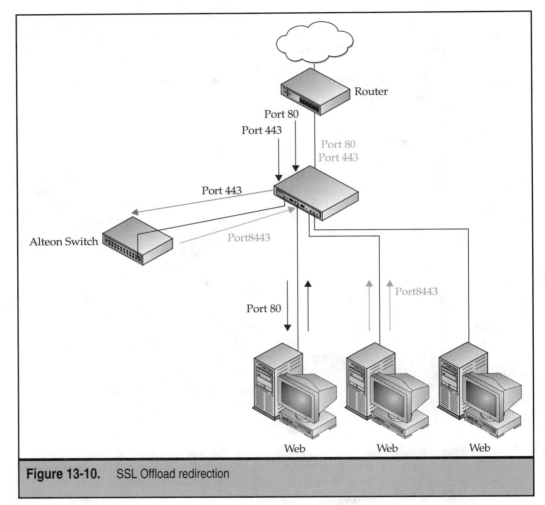

Figure 13-10.   SSL Offload redirection

bypass the SSL processing and go to the server load-balancing mechanism for that service. Traffic from the servers to the clients is handled the same way—redirected to the SSL offload device if SSL, sent straight out if HTTP.

With the server load-balancing mechanism now able to deal with unencrypted packets, cookie persistence can be used. Shopping carts can last as long as the web site administrator wants—he gets to set the cookie timeout period. While two minutes was the limit using SSLID with Microsoft Internet Explorer, now the time can be much longer. The popular web site eBay.com uses a 40-minute cookie timeout. Other shopping sites might use an hour, two hours, or more.

Caveats to SSL Redirection / Offload

When implementing SSL offloading, certain security issues must be noted. The following discusses the most common issues.

Unsecured Traffic Segments

The most common concern of most network architects is the presence of unsecured traffic segments in their network—primarily the segment from the SSL offload device to the web servers. This would never occur when the SSL session terminated on the servers themselves. This concern is usually addressed by implementing network security on the segments above the load balancer, providing protection to the unsecured segments. A hidden benefit to having these segments is the capability to install an intrusion-detection system onto the segment. Because a potential attack could be hidden in an SSL session, an additional level of intrusion detection can now be implemented in the network.

HIPAA Requirements

In 1996, the federal government approved the Health Insurance Portability and Account-ability Act. Portions of this act regulate, in detail, the transfer over networks (as well as other media) of sensitive patient information. Any sensitive medical information must conform to these guidelines, or the responsible provider could be subject to severe penal-ties. As SSL transactions are implemented in the medical billing and service provider field, HIPAA requirements must be taken into account in the final solution. In almost all cases, as long as the unsecured segments of the network are properly protected from pub-lic networks, SSL offloading solutions are still valid.

Managing Certificates and Keys

In all current implementations of SSL offload devices, the certificate and private key must be obtained in a nonencrypted format and installed on the device. Care must be taken to safeguard this information because the private key would allow a hacker to decipher messages intended for the secure site. In those applications where the client is also au-thenticated in the SSL transaction (as discussed in Chapter 5 under client certificates), care must be taken with the client's certificates and privates keys, which must reside on the SSL offload device. The public/private key pair involved in this transaction should be limited to the specifically intended business-to-business service. This issue would arise if a company tried to keep the number of private keys small for its internal clients and used the same certificate for several applications, including the business-to-business applica-tion. If the private key for that particular client were ever compromised, then security could be breached at any site where that client used that certificate/key.

High Availability and Failover Scenarios

An important consideration when implementing SSL offloading is that of high avail-ability. Depending on the manufacturer, some SSL offload devices allow the SSL traffic to failover to the server, allowing secure traffic to continue to the server, albeit more slowly, using the server for SSL tasks. The web and application servers must be config-ured to handle this traffic prior to SSL offload deployment. Another approach to high-SSL availability is to use several SSL offload devices in a pool and load balance them, using the methods outlined in Chapter 9. This allows for high site availability, as well as scalability.

OTHER APPLICATIONS

Another application that will likely become more important in the near future is the redirection and caching of streaming content. This would involve redirecting Real-Time Transport Protocol (RTP) and other protocols used for streaming audio/video content. HTTP encapsulation of streaming traffic is currently common and makes passing firewalls easier, but it limits the caching possibilities to being cached (or not cached, depending on the header information) with the other HTTP traffic on the Web cache. Separating out streaming traffic for special handling requires the use of the real streaming protocols, instead of HTTP encapsulation. And network managers will have to open their firewalls for these newer protocols for their customers to use them.

Application redirection capable switches can be used for FTP redirection to redirect FTP requests to servers where downloadable files are stored or cached. FTP redirection works much like web traffic redirection. Traffic types other than HTTP, HTTPS, FTP, RTSP, and SSL can also be redirected, but they're largely similar to, and often simpler than, WCR, so a detailed discussion of each probably wouldn't be useful. Basically, any TCP/IP application type (Destination Port Number) can be checked in the header and used to redirect the packet to a different location. WCR devices can typically support port mapping and/or address translation in this process.

Combinations

Application Redirection can be combined with other switching applications. One example would be to use the same switch to perform web server load balancing and WCR. Another combination might be Firewall Load Balancing combined with WCR. Or, even combining all three: Firewall Load Balancing, WCR, and Web Server Load Balancing. Such a combination would probably use different algorithms for load balancing the cache servers and the web servers: maximize content capacity for the cache servers and maximize performance for the web servers. However, when combining WCR and firewall load balancing, you must decide on which side of the firewalls to place the caches. Do you want, say, for a web server farm, to put your reverse cache servers outside the firewall or inside? Outside, the user traffic doesn't all have to pass through the firewall, but they are less secure and traffic is more difficult to monitor. Architectural limitations of one or the other location might exist, depending on the particular vendor's implementation, or even with product revisions. These tradeoffs are another subject altogether.

SUMMARY

Application Redirection is like the Swiss Army™ knife of network tools—it has a thousand uses. One of the most widely adopted is WCR, but many other, new uses exist, as has been outlined here. The capability to insert a device transparently into a network and split off—at wire speed—traffic flows based on layer 4–7 information will only become more useful as network applications become more and more creative—and more and more bandwidth-intensive.

WCR is a tool whose value cuts across the distinctions of enterprise and service provider. Subscriber edge caching, with WCR that supports it, will be useful to the enterprise client attempting to alleviate congestion on expensive WAN transit links, as well as to the service provider seeking to do the same. Provider edge caching will be useful to any service provider (especially the ASP) that is seeking to streamline the operations of its network operation centers (NOCs) or simply to optimize traffic flows feeding into a web site. Deciding between transparent versus proxy caching is usually a matter of taste—and it depends largely on the desire of the implementer either to stay out of client configurations or to become immersed in them. Either way, the level of service should be dramatically improved; however, WCR only makes sense for the transparent sort. The distinction between forward caches and reverse caches is somewhat novel. Forward caches are considered the norm, but experts are predicting this might well swing the other way as providers investigate more clever arrangements for content serving from their NOCs.

As an aside, it's worth noting that caching isn't Content Networking, even though Cacheflow, Inktomi, and Akamai might disagree with this, and given the sheer amount of marketing material they and other cache manufacturers generate along these lines, it's small wonder many buyers miss the forest for this one, particularly leafy, tree. Caveat emptor. One particularly high-profile element in a successful Content Networking solution is most definitely the cache, but the best way to use and expand a network with a cache is via a WCR device. This entire book is devoted to illuminating some of the other important, if not so . . . colorful . . . trees in that forest. Application Redirection is one such tree.

REVIEW QUESTIONS

1. **Name three uses for Application Redirection.**

    Three uses for Application Redirection are DNS, WCR, and SSL.

2. **Which would benefit the most from WCR: an ISP, an enterprise WAN, or a server data center?**

    All three (an ISP, an enterprise WAN, or a server data center) might benefit from WCR.

3. **What is the primary advantage of WCCP over WCR?**

    Ubiquity is the primary advantage of WCCP over WCR. You probably already have the hardware in place to implement WCCP.

4. **What is the difference between an overflow server and a backup server?**

   The difference between an overflow server and a backup server is an overflow server will offload processing for busy or overloaded servers, whereas a backup server is used if a failure occurs.

5. **What is the primary advantage to SSL offloading?**

   Speed is the primary advantage to SSL offloading. Web servers can process thousands of times more unencrypted sessions than encrypted sessions.

CHAPTER 14

Bandwidth Management

OBJECTIVES

▼ Provide an appropriate definition of bandwidth as it relates to computer networks

■ Discuss the era of "push" technology and early solutions to contain and control bandwidth utilization

■ Discuss and explore the business drivers, such as SLAs, behind the need for bandwidth management

■ Provide some practical applications for bandwidth management in e-commerce for both the ISP and ASP environments

■ Discuss the various techniques and methods presently deployed for bandwidth management

■ Explore the different vendors' approaches and solutions for bandwidth management

■ Present a case study of one vendor's implementation of bandwidth management, including configuration details

■ Discuss standardization initiatives with IETF to promote vendor interoperability (Diffserv)

▲ Summarize the different methods and vendor implementations of bandwidth management

Bandwidth, defined as the width of a band of electromagnetic frequencies, is used as an expression of how fast data flows through a given transmission path. Bandwidth is directly proportional to the amount of data transmitted or received per unit time. In computer networks, bandwidth is often measured in bits/second. A modem rated at 57,600 bits/sec has twice the bandwidth of a modem rated at 28,800 bits/sec. *T1,* which is a bandwidth of 1,536,000 bits/sec, is a common bandwidth base for connections to corporate data centers.

Corporations globally, in support of mission-critical applications on both the Internet and dedicated wide area networks (WAN) links, are increasingly using IP-based technologies. VPN (virtual private networks) technology has become popular within the last two years and has allowed corporations to gain competitive advantage while connecting branch offices, employees, business partners, and customers securely via the Internet. The onslaught of traffic can and has caused severe congestion and choke points on the more limited WAN-to-Internet connections. Bandwidth-hungry discretionary traffic often overwhelms business and mission-critical traffic on these links.

SLA AND THE BUSINESS CASE FOR MANAGING BANDWIDTH

Corporations today are increasingly reliant on WANs to deliver critical business information, so it's no wonder the WAN has developed into a key corporate asset. The performance of the WAN can positively or negatively impact a wide range of key mission-critical corporate processes for inventory, accounting, and sales information. As a result, corporations are demanding that carriers enable a process for WAN service-level management and, further, to enter into a service level agreement (SLA) with corporations that want to ensure their critical traffic is accorded a negotiated quality of access. Service-level guarantees also require carriers and service providers to provide some type of financial penalties if they fail to meet their contractual obligations. This has spurred carriers and service providers to design and engineer their networks to meet parameters that exceed SLAs offered to their customers. The following lists some of the parameters that are components of the SLA:

▼ **Network availability**   Percent uptime, i.e., 99.5 percent

■ **Average round-trip network delay**   Typically ranges from 100 to 300 milliseconds

■ **Effective throughput**   Typically 99 to 99.9999 of frames delivered

■ **Mean Time to Respond**   Typically four hours to respond to a trouble ticket

▲ **Mean Time to Repair**   Typically four hours to repair a problem

Managing bandwidth, therefore, is crucial to enable the carrier or service provider to meet or exceed the average round-trip delay and effective throughput parameters.

BEFORE THE BANDWIDTH MANAGEMENT ERA

The technology term *push* came from the notion that the server pushes content to the user, instead of the traditional method of the user visiting the server and requesting (pulling) information. In early 1997, push technology became popular because it enabled people to have news and information delivered directly to their desktops, instead of them having to go out to the Web and dig for it. Content aggregators, such as PointCast and Desktop Data, became a one-stop source of news and information. They would gather the content, format it, and push it to your desktop at scheduled times. These services were offered free, earning revenues by sneaking in advertisements with the content.

PointCast Floods Networks

Due to its popularity in the 1997 timeframe, PointCast became synonymous with push technology, although the company is now trying to shed that image. PointCast falls into a category of content aggregator. It gathers news and information from hundred of sources, formats it for consistent look and feel, and delivers it to the desktop. Unfortunately, PointCast also delivers news and information simultaneously to your co-workers who may be on the same local area network (LAN). The predictable result is congestion on a network. A single 30K news story sent to 100 people might mean 3MB of bandwidth is consumed. Sending hundreds of these news stories to subscribing desktops quickly became a source of congestion to the local networks.

Push Technology Solutions

As "push" technology vendors like Pointcast struggle to gain acceptance, they must address the bandwidth congestion problem quickly and decisively. Here are some of the solutions that were deployed by these vendors to improve access and reduce delays for the users.

Cache Managers

PointCast sells advertising piggybacked on top of the content it pushes to the desktops. It would have to transmit massive amounts of data to give advertisers a fair return on their investments and, as such, the company quickly knew this revenue model was reliant on a large, continuous data flow. One solution was to develop a *Cache Manager*, a system that would receive the content once, and then distribute it to subscriber desktops. The investment of a single PC, plus some IT configuration time, was worth the effort to preserve the precious WAN bandwidth. Of course, desktop PCs would need to be reconfigured so they were automatically directed to the Cache Manager.

Compression Tools

To contain the massive inflow of push data, a useful tool was to turn on the compression feature on the routers on the boundary of the WAN. This could effectively cut the bandwidth utilization to one-half or even one-fourth, depending on the compression algorithm in use. Compression can take place on the entire packet, header only, or payload only. While compression may be a viable bandwidth optimization feature, disadvantages exist. One obvious disadvantage of compression is that it is CPU-intensive and, thus, impacts the routing capability of the boundary routers. In addition, the lack of compression standards among vendors, requires deployment of the same vendor's equipment for both end routers or switches, to ensure interoperability and proper functionality.

Optimize Download Criteria

To conserve precious bandwidth, push companies are using filtering, or end-user selection of content. One company, Tibco, lets end-users pick which information they want to get from a single multicast. For example, users could set up their environments to receive entertainment news once a day, but receive their stock quotes in continuous streaming feeds.

PRACTICAL APPLICATIONS OF BANDWIDTH MANAGEMENT IN E-COMMERCE

Discussed next are some of the environments that have turned bandwidth management into both technical and competitive business advantages. It is worthwhile noting that measurable SLA (service level agreement) has now become a reality due to bandwidth management.

ISP Environment

The Internet Service Provider (ISP) is constantly challenged by a number of factors that make bandwidth a very scarce commodity indeed. An upgrade at the local loop, such as DSL, certainly creates a bandwidth disparity at the expense of the slower dial-up user. New Internet services such as Napster cause utilization, which was usually sporadic, to become constant, impacting everybody else. The promise of live Internet broadcasts of flashy shows like rock concerts or somewhat more sedate presidential debates adds even more demand on a dwindling supply. Bandwidth management allows the ISP to provide virtual pipes—to each of which is applied a bandwidth contract—for each of these types of users to distribute bandwidth fairly to all their users.

ASP Environment

The Application Service Provider (ASP) typically serves clients with a wide variety of bandwidth requirements. ASP operators need to offer their clients SLAs to ensure the best performance for their money or to avoid paying over-subscription penalties. A popular bandwidth management solution is to offer tiered service, that is, bronze, gold, and platinum, with platinum configured for the fastest, most reliable access. *Tiering* enables clients to start off by purchasing the bronze service and to scale up as their businesses increase and consume more bandwidth.

Enabling Service Providers to Aggregate Profitably

In a traditional access ISP point-of-presence infrastructure, different types of remote access servers share a single connection to the Internet. The ISP depends on the law of averages in provisioning shared resources to maximize their profit while trying to maintain customer satisfaction. But bandwidth isn't shared equitably. Fast DSL modem users can and do impact slower dial-up connections. On the Web server end of the infrastructure, a Web site experiencing congestion because of flash-crowd traffic can quickly and easily overwhelm other Web sites co-located in the same infrastructure. Bandwidth management lets providers enforce fairness, and, at the same time, offer flexible, usage-based services to increase revenue.

Increasing Security and Preventing DoS Attacks

Denial of Service (DoS) attacks can occur suddenly and cripple a Web infrastructure by swamping it with more requests than it could ever hope to fulfill. A sophisticated DoS attack is difficult to prevent and can appear as legal, legitimate traffic. Bandwidth management can diffuse DoS attacks by setting rate limits at traffic ingress points for such traffic as TCP SYN packets, PING packets, and so forth. Imposing limits also for traffic at egress ports destined for unknown ports is another way of thwarting, or at least ameliorating the effects of, attacks.

SOLUTIONS

Let's explore several different vendor implementations of bandwidth management. The following list shows those that are available as of this writing.

- ▼ Dedicated bandwidth management appliances
- ■ Bandwidth management integrated with routers and switches
- ■ Bandwidth management integrated with Web switches
- ▲ Bandwidth management integrated with firewalls

Dedicated Bandwidth Management Appliances

Purpose-built bandwidth management appliances were the first solutions to hit the market. Among the pioneers of this technology were Packeteer and Xedia. Here are the details of their implementations.

Packeteer PacketShaper

PacketShaper is an application-based bandwidth management solution from Packeteer. It automatically classifies network traffic based on application, protocol, subnet, URL, and other criteria. This allows the product to look at OSI model Layer 7 information in the packet to identify applications such as SAP, Oracle, Napster, Pointcast, and others. It allocates bandwidth based on policy, where an administrator can specify minimum and maximum bandwidth parameters on a per-session or per-application basis. PacketShaper allows partitioning of bandwidth into separate virtual channels, and then enforce policies on those partitions. The package provides detailed information on application performance and network efficiency, such as peak and average bandwidth utilization, response time divided into network and server delays, top web pages visited, top users, and top applications. PacketShaper also has excellent reporting capabilities, providing graphs, statistics, and SNMP MIBs. This enables the client to compare actual performance versus SLA agreements, to define performance standards, and to generate report on compliance.

Four models are available. The 1500 series platform is targeted for small sites, while the 2500 series platform handles large branch offices or midsize data centers. The 4500 and 6500 series platforms are targeted towards large data centers or ISPs.

TCP Rate Control   The TCP Rate Control feature of PacketShaper paces packets on both the inbound and outbound flows to prevent congestion. At the same time, this feature eliminates unnecessary packet discards and retransmission, and promotes a smooth, even flow rate to maximize throughput. It applies explicit rate-based flow control to both individual and classes of traffic flows. The TCP Rate Control feature doesn't rely on a queue and provides bidirectional bandwidth management for both inbound and outbound traffic.

Control of TCP Traffic at Transmitter   TCP Rate Control evenly distributes packet transmissions by controlling TCP acknowledgements to the transmitter, causing the sender to throttle back, avoiding packet discards when insufficient bandwidth exists. This, in effect, prevents congestion even before it occurs. TCP rate control yields evenly spaced packet transmissions and can increase network utilization up to 80 percent.

To illustrate how the TCP Rate Control feature of PacketShaper controls the end-to-end connection, Figure 14-1 shows the flow of traffic from transmitter to receiver with PacketShaper in the middle.

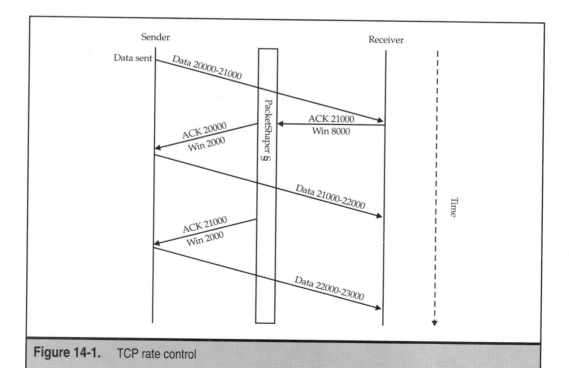

Figure 14-1.   TCP rate control

PacketShaper intervenes and paces the data transmission flows to deliver predictable service. Let's analyze how it accomplishes this step by step:

1. Data is sent from the transmitter to the receiver.

2. Receiver acknowledges receipt of the data and, at the same time, advertises a window size of 8,000 bytes.

3. PacketShaper intercepts and holds the ACK from the receiver and determines the data must be more evenly transmitted.

4. After the calculated delay, the ACK and the window size information (note, PacketShaper determines it must be 2,000, not 8,000 as originally instructed from the receiver) is sent to the transmitter, calculated to arrive at the transmitter, so it will send the next data immediately.

As previously demonstrated, PacketShaper changes the end-to-end TCP semantics from the middle of the connection. PacketShaper does a calculation of the round-trip timer (RTT), and then intercepts and holds the acknowledgement for the time required to smooth the traffic flow without incurring retransmission timeout (RTO). PacketShaper also calculates a new window size, which it sends to the transmitter that helps it determine when to send the next packet.

The end result is evenly spaced transmissions when PacketShaper takes control. Figure 14-2 shows the before-and-after result of this methodology.

Handling of Non-TCP Traffic   Approximately 275 types of application layer traffic can be identified or classified by PacketShaper. This powerful feature allows the product to provide granular bandwidth management capability. Once classified, Quality of Service (QoS) and bandwidth-allocation policies can be set to protect and control each traffic flow. The capability to set policies based on application is a big differentiator for PacketShaper, and is particularly critical when setting different policies for items such as Web browsing flows versus business-critical e-commerce transactions, such as SAP. The flexible policies of PacketShaper enable you to tune bandwidth allocation and response time. Bandwidth can be guaranteed or capped, protecting or restraining applications as appropriate. If a "bursty" application swells, it does this on its own virtual partition without infringing on other applications' bandwidth.

Xedia CBQ (Class-Based Queuing)

Xedia, acquired by Lucent in 1999, incorporates class-based queuing (CBQ) in its Access Point products for bandwidth management. CBQ is a traffic management algorithm usually deployed at the boundary of the WAN. CBQ was developed by the Network Research Group at Lawrence Berkeley National Laboratory and is now in the public domain as an open technology. Xedia offered one of the first commercial implementations of CBQ, which is now implemented into the Access Point 450 and 1000 products.

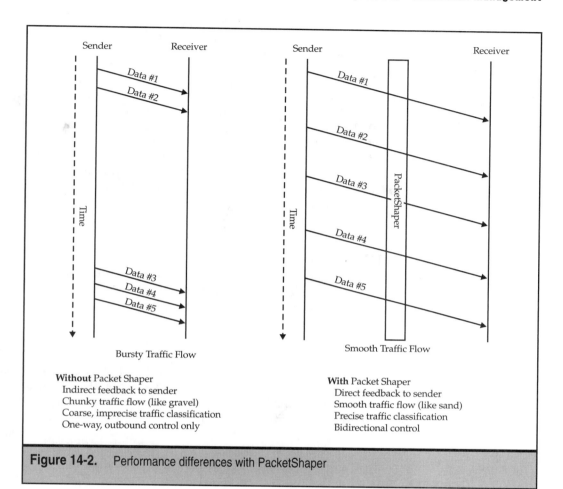

Figure 14-2. Performance differences with PacketShaper

Traffic Identification and Classification   The goal of CBQ is first to divide user traffic into a hierarchy of classes based on any combination of IP addresses, protocols, and types of applications. Each class is then rate-shaped to meet a defined bandwidth rate. One rate could be termed a "minimum commitment, best-effort" service level, while another could be termed a "premium, fully committed" service level. High-priority applications can then be given the premium rate that assigns an explicit amount of bandwidth to ensure their service requirements are met. Lowest priority applications can be given the best-effort service level. This class can be given a zero committed bandwidth, but with the capability to borrow from idle or unused bandwidth on a first-come, first-served basis.

CBQ Borrowing   Borrowing is a unique feature of CBQ, allowing traffic classes to utilize bandwidth not used by other classes when they need to burst above their guaranteed rate. Priority can be defined so those mission-critical applications get first access to unused bandwidth. On the other hand, low-priority applications or users can even be denied access by setting a bandwidth rate of zero, but with no borrowing allowed.

Handling of TCP and Non-TCP Protocols   CBQ operates at the IP network layer and provides the same benefits across any Layer 2 technologies. CBQ is equally effective with any IP protocol, that is, TCP and UDP, including increasingly prominent UDP-based multimedia applications, critical SNMP management traffic, and the often-undesirable bandwidth-hungry news feeds. CBQ also takes advantage of standard TCP/IP flow control mechanisms to control traffic on an end-to-end basis. It operates with any client or server TCP/IP stack variation.

Integration with Routers and LAN Switches

Integration of bandwidth management into existing devices such as routers and LAN switches provides a compelling argument for Web administrators in their pursuit of ease of administration and higher ROI (return on investment) for their web infrastructures. Here is the Cisco implementation of this design.

Cisco WRED

Congestion avoidance on routers is achieved mainly through dropping packets. Among the most commonly used techniques is Random Early Detection (RED). To accomplish congestion avoidance, RED controls the average queue size by indicating to the end hosts when they should temporarily slow down transmission of packets. RED works by randomly dropping packets prior to periods of high congestion, which tells the packet source to decrease its transmission rate. If TCP is the protocol in use, the transmission rate is decreased until all packets have arrived at their destination, which indicates the congestion is cleared. RED is used as a means of causing TCP to slow down transmission of packets. When enabled on a router interface, RED begins to drop packets when congestion occurs at a rate selected during the configuration process.

Weighted Random Early Detection (WRED), as the following explains, is the Cisco Systems implementation of RED for standard Cisco IOS platforms.

Weighted Random Early Detection   WRED combines the functionality and algorithm of RED with IP precedence to give preferential treatment to higher priority traffic. WRED selectively discards lower priority traffic when congestion is detected at the router interface. IP precedence is the mechanism used, that is, traffic with a lower precedence has a higher drop rate and is, therefore, more likely to be throttled back. On the other hand, traffic with a higher precedence is less likely to be dropped and, therefore, has a higher probability to be delivered. This causes differentiated performance characteristics for different classes of service. WRED begins to work when the router output interface begins to show signs of congestion. By dropping some packets early and not waiting until the queue is full, WRED avoids dropping large amounts of traffic all at once.

WRED is only effective when the bulk of the traffic is TCP-based. In the TCP protocol, dropped packets indicate congestion, so the packet source slows transmission. With other protocols, when packets are dropped, the source may continue to re-transmit at the same speed. Therefore, dropped packets don't reduce congestion. WRED gives a precedence value of 0, the lowest level of precedence, to non-IP traffic. This causes non-IP traffic to be dropped more than IP traffic. The behavior of WRED is it drops more packets from large users than small users. Packet sources generating the most traffic are more likely to experience slowdowns than sources generating little traffic.

Cisco has a distributed WRED (DWRED) implementation that uses the Versatile Interface Processor (VIP) to provide WRED functionality. This is in contrast to WRED, which uses the route-switch processor (RSP) to implement the WRED functionality. DWRED provides faster performance than the RSP-based WRED. DWRED, while providing faster performance than WRED, has some restrictions. DWRED is only available on a per-interface basis and cannot be configured on a sub-interface. In addition, DWRED is neither supported on Fast EtherChannel nor does it support the multicast RSVP protocol.

Supported Cisco Routers   WRED is supported on the following Cisco routers:

- ▼ Cisco 1600
- ■ Cisco 2500
- ■ Cisco 3600
- ■ Cisco 4000 (includes 4500 and 4700)
- ■ Cisco 7200
- ▲ Cisco 7500 with RSP

DWRED is supported on the following Cisco routers.

- ▼ Cisco 7000 series with RSP7000
- ▲ Cisco 7500 with VIP2-40 or greater

Please refer to the Cisco Web site (http://www.cisco.com) for the most current and complete list of supported Cisco routers.

Configuration Tasks   The configuration of WRED on a Cisco router involves the performance of the following tasks:

1. Enable WRED—use the following command in interface configuration mode.

```
router(config-if)#random-detect
```

This enables WRED. If you configure this command on a VIP interface, DWRED is enabled.

2. Change WRED parameters—use one of the following commands in interface configuration mode.

```
router(config-if)#random-detect exponential-weighting-constant
[exponent]
```

This specifies the weight factor used for calculating the average queue length.

```
router(config-if)#random-detect precedence [precedence]
[min-threshold]
[max-threshold] [mark-prob-denominator]
```

This sets the parameters for packets with a specific IP precedence. The minimum threshold for IP Precedence 0 corresponds to half the maximum threshold for the interface. Repeat this command for each level of precedence.

NOTE: When you enable WRED with only the random-detect command, the parameters are set to their default values. The weight factor is 9. For all precedences, the mark probability denominator is 10, and maximum threshold is based on the output buffering capacity and the transmission speed of the interface. The default minimum threshold depends on the precedence. The minimum threshold for precedence 0 corresponds to half of the maximum threshold. The value for the remaining precedences falls between half the maximum threshold and the maximum threshold at evenly spaced intervals. The default WRED parameter values are based on best available data. Cisco recommends you don't change the parameters from their default values unless you've determined your applications will benefit from the changed values.

Integration with Web Switches

"Web Switch" is the Alteon term for its server load balancing (SLB) appliance. Alteon pioneered server load balancing and at the height of its success garnered 50 percent worldwide market share for this technology.

Nortel BWM

The Nortel bandwidth management (BWM) solution is based on integration of the bandwidth management application in its Alteon Web switch platform.

Alteon Web Switch Bandwidth Management Integration   Neither the bandwidth management nor QoS solutions as previously described for routers and LAN switches offer the flexibility and precision necessary to manage the wide variety and combination of virtual services housed in today's Web data center infrastructure. At the same time, dedicated bandwidth management appliances lack the performance and scalability to keep pace with the growing traffic in today's Web data centers.

To bridge the gap, Alteon has introduced a bandwidth management service that provides Web data center operators' fine-grained control over bandwidth utilization. This service is integrated on a scalable Web switch platform with server load balancing (SLB), traffic redirection, access control, and content processing. This service is completely compatible with existing QoS mechanisms on routers and LAN switches.

Product Highlights Alteon bandwidth management solution simulates multiple virtual pipes within one or more real physical ports on the Web switch, up to either 256 or 1024 virtual pipes, depending on the switch model. Virtual pipes are synonymous with traffic classes. Each traffic class is defined by a broad range of policies, which include the following:

▼ Physical port

■ VLAN

■ Source/Destination IP address

■ TCP/UDP port number

■ URL

■ HTTP cookie

▲ Access control filters

Complex classification can also be defined for such things as source-destination flow, QoS class, HTTP cookie within a virtual service, and others.

Order of precedence can also be defined when handling packets that fit the criteria for multiple virtual pipes. By default, the order of precedence is according to virtual service, then filter, then VLAN, and finally, physical port.

Functional Description For each virtual pipe, the administrator applies a bandwidth policy that includes three data rates:

▼ **Committed Information Rate (CIR)** is the data rate the Web switch guarantees the virtual pipe. For a given sample period, the data rate will never be lower than this value.

■ **Soft Limit** is the data rate the Web switch constantly works to move traffic flow. The Web switch dynamically adjusts the frequency with which it forwards traffic from the virtual pipe according to the volume of traffic and the rate it's trying to simulate.

▲ **Hard Limit** is the data rate the Web switch considers the "cut off" rate, over which traffic is discarded. Set this rate to the maximum rate of the physical port to avoid traffic from being discarded.

The availability of the soft limit allows Web administrators to regulate traffic flow to the desired target rate, while allowing the system a degree of flexibility to respond to temporary bursts and congestions.

For each virtual pipe, the Web switch simulates a physical link by pacing packet transmission at a simulated rate, initially set to the soft limit. Packet buffers at each egress port are divided into a queue per virtual pipe. Different queues can have a different amount of buffer allocations (queue depth), as defined by the administrator.

If a queue is approaching its queue depth over time, the Web switch increases its simulated rate, up to the hard limit, to allow for temporary bursting. When the hard limit is reached, new packets won't be queued until the simulated rate drops; however, the rate won't drop below the CIR rate.

Each queue's transmission is regulated individually, until global congestion is experienced. When the global queue depth reaches a congestion threshold, the simulated rate at each queue is reduced according to its bandwidth policy. This scheduling scheme effectively allows each virtual pipe to borrow bandwidth up to its hard limit, if bandwidth is available.

Statistics are polled via SNMP interfaces or downloaded to a preconfigured e-mail address for history and accounting records.

An optional feature, IP Type of Service (ToS) tagging, enables administrators to mark the packets transmitted below and above the soft limit with different QoS settings. This enables upstream, QoS-capable switches and routers to prioritize packet delivery according to the target bandwidth rate set for each traffic class, without incurring additional tasks of tagging traffic themselves.

Configuration Tasks   Configure the Web switch first according to its server load balancing (SLB) requirements. Then configure the bandwidth management service parameters and sequence as follows:

1. Configure the policies (CIR, soft, hard limits).
2. Configure the contracts (virtual pipes) and bind to the desired policy.
3. Apply contracts to appropriate egress ports of the Web switch.
4. Turn on or enable bandwidth management service.

Integration with Firewall

Checkpoint is the undisputed market leader for firewalls in Web infrastructure today. To capitalize on its popularity, Checkpoint has been integrating additional functionality in its firewall products.

Checkpoint Floodgate-1

Checkpoint's bandwidth management solution is a product called Floodgate-1, a policy based QoS solution for Internet and dedicated WAN links. This solution allows the administrator to prioritize business critical traffic, such as ERP or e-commerce over less important or discretionary traffic, in effect aligning network resources with business goals.

Floodgate-1 is typically deployed as an integrated component of Checkpoint's Firewall-1 and VPN-1, running on the same hardware platform.

Policy-Based Bandwidth Management   Floodgate-1 management of inbound and outbound traffic flows at WAN and Internet access points is based on a bandwidth management policy, which consists of rules that assign bandwidth privileges to certain classes of packets. Each rule uses two fundamental criteria required for bandwidth management. The first of these is *Traffic Classification,* which sorts traffic according to the following criteria:

▼ Source

■ Destination

■ Application

■ Internet Service

■ Group of Internet Services

■ Group of Users

■ URL

■ Time of Day

▲ Traffic Direction

The second is *Bandwidth Control,* which specifies the primary control criteria used to assign privileges to more important traffic or limit less important traffic. The criteria are

▼ **Weighted Priorities**   Allocate bandwidth by assigning weights configured as an integer number. For example, HTTPS traffic might be given a weight of 20 and HTTP traffic a weight of 10. When congestion occurs, Floodgate-1 ensures that the data ratio of HTTPS over HTTP is 2:1.

■ **Guarantees**   Allocate minimum bandwidth to certain traffic flows identified as requiring specific service levels at all times. An example is *video conferencing,* a streaming media format, which requires a minimum amount of bandwidth to work.

▲ **Limits**   Restricts bandwidth for noncritical applications. An example might be to limit bandwidth allocation for certain push traffic such as Pointcast.

Core Elements: Stateful Inspection and IQ Engine   Floodgate-1 incorporates the Intelligent Queuing (IQ) Engine, an implementation of a hierarchical Weighted Fair Queuing (WFQ) algorithm that works in concert with Checkpoint's INSPECT Virtual Machine, which sits between the data link and the network layer, and provides enforcement of user-defined bandwidth management policies. The IQ Engine doesn't modify TCP packets to control transmission rate. Instead it controls bandwidth at the IP layer using precise per-flow packet scheduling to achieve accurate bandwidth shaping.

The INPECT Virtual Machine provides detailed packet information to the IQ Engine to classify incoming traffic properly. Then, each classified packet is placed into the correct queue and scheduled for transmission based on the user-defined management policy. The IQ Engine controls when the packet is put on the wire, thus precisely controlling the overall mix of traffic. For example, if HTTPS traffic is given a weight of 20 and HTTP traffic is given a weight of 10, this results in the IQ Engine, during a period of congestion, transmitting two HTTPS packets for each HTTP packet to maintain the 2:1 ratio.

Enterprise Traffic Management   Checkpoint has a three-tier traffic management architecture, which is designed to support scalability for an unlimited number of VPN links. A single policy can be edited from a remote GUI, stored on a centrally located management server, and then distributed to enforcement modules (firewalls) across the enterprise.

HOW BANDWIDTH MANAGEMENT WORKS— CASE STUDY OF THE NORTEL SOLUTION

Let's explore in detail the Nortel implementation of bandwidth management as integrated into its Web Switch appliance. The case study will provide conceptual network design drawing plus step-by-step configuration of the Web switch.

Overview

In Nortel's implementation of bandwidth management, Web site administrators allocate portions of available bandwidth for specific users or applications. Traffic is classified based on either user or application information, and then policies are configured to set lower and upper limits on the bandwidth allocation.

From a configuration standpoint, bandwidth contracts are created and used to limit individual traffic flows, with a limit of up to a maximum of 256 per switch. A contract has two components:

▼   Classification policy to group certain frames together

▲   Bandwidth policy to set usage limitations applied to those frames

Traffic Classification and Control

We need to identify and classify the traffic before we can set the bandwidth enforcement policy. In its simplest form, this is the methodology of the Nortel bandwidth management solution.

Traffic Classification at Ingress Port

Bandwidth classification is done on the ingress port (port where frames enter the switch), and is based on source port, VLAN, VIP (virtual IP address), service, filters, and so on.

Traffic Enforcement at Egress Port

Bandwidth management is done on the *egress* port (the port where frames exit the switch). Each frame goes into a buffer and is placed in a contract queue. Then, a calculation is made based on the configured rate of the bandwidth contract, the current egress rate of the port, and the buffer size set for the contract queue. This calculation is provided to the scheduler, which then organizes all the frames to be sent according to their time-based ordering and meters them out to the port.

Bandwidth Policies

Before we can enforce a policy, first, let's ask the fundamental question—what is a bandwidth policy?

Rate Limits

A bandwidth policy defines three limits, which the following lists describe.

CIR or Reserved Limit   This is the guaranteed rate bandwidth class. Ensure that when configuring bandwidth management contracts, the sum of all Committed Information Rates (CIRs) does not exceed the link speed of the egress port. Remember, this is networking, not airline booking. In a case where the link speed is exceeded, the Web switch performs a graceful degradation of all traffic on the associated port.

Soft Limit   This is the desired bandwidth rate, the rate the client is paying for on a regular basis. When output bandwidth is available, a bandwidth class is allowed to transmit at this speed.

Hard Limit   This is the never exceeded bandwidth rate. No bandwidth class is allowed to transmit above this rate. Clients are normally charged for traffic bursts between the soft and hard limits.

Bandwidth Policy Configuration

Here are the details for configuring bandwidth management on a Nortel Web switch.

Bandwidth Range/Interval   Each bandwidth policy, comprised of the reserved soft and hard limits, is assigned an index. Up to 64 policies can be defined. To allow for better granularities at slower configured rate, any value can be entered in Kbps by appending a *k* to the entered value. For example, 1 Mbps can be entered as 1 or 1, 024K.

The following table lists the granularity of policy limits:

Bandwidth Range	Interval	Bandwidth Range	Interval
250 Kbps to 5,000 Kbps	250 Kbps	50 Mbps to 150 Mbps	10 Mbps
1 Mbps to 20 Mbps	1 Mbps	150 Mbps to 500 Mbps	25 Mbps
20 Mbps to 50 Mbps	5 Mbps	500 Mbps to 1,000 Mbps	50 Mbps

A queue size is also associated with each policy, and is measured in kilobytes.

Classification Policies

Classification policies falls into the following distinct groups:

▼ Classification aimed at limiting traffic outbound from the server farm

■ Classification based on application or group of applications

▲ Combination of these two

Server Output Bandwidth Control

Frames associated with a bandwidth contract are classified using the following parameters. These classifications are aimed at limiting the traffic outbound from the server farm for bandwidth measurement and control.

- ▼ **Physical Port**   All frames from a specified physical port.
- ■ **VLAN**   All frames from a specified VLAN. Even if VLAN translation occurs, the bandwidth policy is based on the ingress VLAN.
- ■ **IP Source Address**   All frames from a specified Source IP address with subnet mask.
- ■ **IP Destination Address**   All frames from a specified Destination IP address with subnet mask.
- ▲ **Switch Virtual Services**   The following Layer 4 groupings are classified
  - ■ A single virtual server
  - ■ A group of virtual servers
  - ■ A virtual service for a particular virtual server

Select a particular port number, which specifies a virtual service, within a particular VIP.

Application Bandwidth Control

Through bandwidth classifications, you can limit the traffic based on particular applications or groups of applications. Classification can also be specified based on a filtering rule, including those listed here.

- ▼ **TCP Port Number**   All frames from a particular TCP port number (source or destination).
- ■ **UDP**   All UDP frames can be specified.
- ▲ **UDP Port Number**   All UDP frames from a particular UDP port number (source or destination).

Combinations

When combining classifications, you're limited to grouping them together into a contract. As an example, you can classify three different virtual servers associated with a contract by specifying the same contract index on each of the three VIP addresses. You can combine filters in this manner as well.

Precedence

If a frame qualifies for several classifications, you can specify the precedence for which the frame will be associated. If you don't configure precedence, the default ordering is as follows:

1. Virtual Server

2. Filter

3. VLAN

4. Source Port/Default Assignment

Restricting Bandwidth Usage

Data pacing is the mechanism for restricting bandwidth usage on the egress port. Here it is in detail.

Data Pacing

The mechanism used to keep the individual traffic flow regulated is termed *data pacing* and is based on the concept of a virtual clock and theoretical departure time (TDT). TDT is initially calculated based on the soft limit, which is the target rate. As long as bandwidth is available and the queue isn't filled up at a rate greater than the soft limit, the TDT for both incoming and outgoing frames will be met, and no borrowing or limitation is necessary.

If frames are arriving more quickly than the soft limit rate, however, and sufficient bandwidth still exists, then the rate is adjusted upwards based on the depth of the queue, until either the hard limit is reached or the queue depth is reduced. If the frames cannot be transmitted at the soft limit, the rate is adjusted downward until it can be transmitted or the CIR is reached. If the CIR is overcommitted among all the contracts, a graceful degradation occurs to reduce each CIR until the total bandwidth allocated fits within the total bandwidth available.

Frame Discard

When the queue is already full, then any frames attempting to be placed in the queue are discarded.

Bandwidth Statistics and History

To allow for accounting and billing, statistics regarding bandwidth management and utilization are maintained in the Web switch. The administrator can configure both the frequency and the count of the statistics. Statistics care kept in the individual Switch Processors (SP) and collected every second by the Management Processor (MP).

The MP also collects some global statistics, such as total octets, and a window of historical statistics. The historical statistics are kept at a configurable time per interval. When the history buffer is ready to overflow, it can, optionally, be e-mailed to a user. SMTP is used for this transfer.

Statistics Maintained

The total number of octets, octet discards, and times over the soft limit are kept for each contract. The history buffer maintains the average queue size for the time interval and the average rate per interval.

Configuring the History Buffer

A total memory block of 128 Kbytes is kept available for the history buffer. This block is specified in the /cfg/bwm/stats menu.

Statistics and MIBs

The MP maintains per-contract rate usage statistics. These can be obtained via a private MIB.

Third Party Bandwidth Management Billing Solution

Web administrators can now capture usage statistics into a third party software product for billing purposes. One such product is Netcountant from Apogee Networks.
     Here are some product features of Netcountant:

▼   Usage-based billing capability for content service types (hits, bytes, type of file, type of server)

■   Flexible new revenue models for content services

■   Simple "plug and play" format enables Web hosters to offer differentiated services they can bill for, based on:

   ■   **Type of Service**
       (such as secure e-commerce, streaming)

   ■   **Pre-specified content performance levels**
       (e.g., high availability servers vs. standard service)

   ■   **Class of User**
       (e.g., segment customers into service tiers)
       Each service can be billable at distinct rates for each customer, in shared server environments

■   Pricing models for any service based on bandwidth, bytes transferred, objects served (hits), with differentials for time-of-day

▲   Pricing models based on the response time or service level delivered by the Web hoster

Packet Coloring

Packet coloring refers to the technique of modifying the bits of an IP header to induce other devices such as routers to impose QoS policy on arriving packets.

ToS Bits and Burst Limit

Every time the soft limit rate is exceeded, packet coloring can optionally be accomplished that allows the writing of ToS bits in the IP header, so downstream routers can use this information to delay or discard these "out of profile" frames. Frames that are not out of profile can also be marked with a different, higher priority value. This feature can be enabled or disabled on a per contract basis.

Configuring Bandwidth Management

Configuring bandwidth management on the Alteon switch is done right after the configuration for Server Load Balancing (SLB). The following are SLB configuration tasks:

- ▼ Define an IP interface on the switch.
- ■ Define each real server. Assign an IP address to each real server.
- ■ Group the real servers.
- ■ Define a Virtual IP Address (VIP).
- ▲ Define the port configuration (see Figure 14-3).

Complete Configuration Commands

The following configuration exercise creates two bandwidth management contracts. Contract 1 uses Policy 1 and limits traffic egressing port 7 to 10 Mbps. Contract 2 uses Policy 2 and limits traffic egressing port 8 to 5 Mbps.

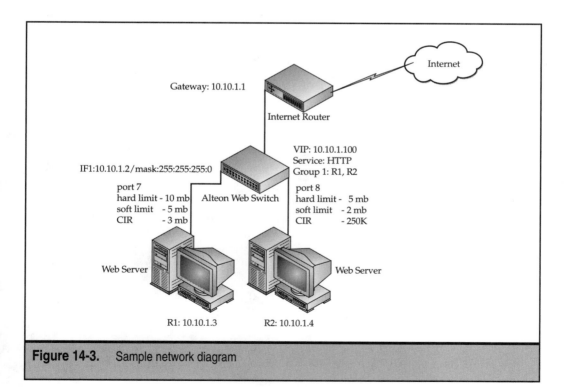

Figure 14-3.   Sample network diagram

The following are step-by-step procedures for configuring bandwidth management:

1. Configure a bandwidth management policy:

   `Main#` `/cfg/bwm/policy 1`

   This selects bandwidth management policy 1.

2. Set the *hard* (this is the never exceed rate), *soft* (this is the desired rate), and *reserved* (this is the CIR or committed information rate) rate limits for the policy. Value is in Mbps, and must be set between 256K–1,000M.

   `Policy 1#` `hard 10`

   This sets the hard limit to 10 Mbps.

   `Policy 1#` `soft 5`

   This sets the soft limit to 5 Mbps.

   `Policy 1#` `resv 3`

   This sets the CIR limit to 3 Mbps.

3. Configure a second bandwidth management policy:

   `/cfg/bwm/policy 2`

   This selects bandwidth management policy 2.

4. Set the hard, soft, and reserved rate limits for the policy:

   `Policy 2#` `hard 5`

   This sets the hard limit to 5 Mbps.

   `Policy 2#` `soft 2`

   This sets the soft limit to 2 Mbps.

   `Policy 2#` `resv 250k`

   This sets the CIR limit to 250 Kbps.

5. Configure a bandwidth management contract. Provide a name (optional):

   `/cfg/bwm/cont 1`

   This selects contract 1.

   `BW Contract 1#` `name gold_client`

   This sets a name for contract 1.

```
BW Contract 1# policy 1
```

This sets policy 1 for contract 1.

```
BW Contract 1# ena
```

Don't forget to enable contract 1.

6. Configure a second bandwidth management contract. Provide a name (optional):

```
/cfg/bwm/cont 2
```

This selects contract 2.

```
BW Contract 2# name silver_client
```

This sets the name for contract 2.

```
BW Contract 2# policy 2
```

This sets policy 2 for contract 2.

```
BW Contract 2# ena
```

Don't forget to enable contract 2.

7. Apply contracts to the appropriate ports:

```
/cfg/port 7
```

Select port 7.

```
Port 7# cont 1
```

Apply contract 1 to port 7.

```
/cfg/port 8
```

Select port 8.

```
Port 8# cont 2
```

Apply contract 2 to port 8.

8. Enforce and turn on the bandwidth management policy:

```
/cfg/bwm/force ena
```

This tells the switch to enforce the policy.

```
/cfg/bwm/on
```

This turns on bandwidth management processing.

9. Apply and save the configuration:

`apply`

This applies all the changes, and

`save`

saves the configuration.

STANDARDS

This section provides some information on the standardization initiatives that are ongoing with regards to bandwidth management as of this writing.

IETF Diff-Serv Working Group

The Diff-Serv Working Group is one group active in the pursuit of standardization with respect to implementing a QoS mechanism through the use and interpretation of certain bits in the IP header.

Differentiated Services Overview

A clear need exists for relatively simple and coarse methods for providing differentiated classes of service to Internet traffic to support various types of applications and specific business requirements. The differentiated-services approach to providing quality of service in networks employs a small, well-defined set of building blocks from which a variety of aggregate behaviors may be built.

The IETF Diff-Serv Working Group has standardized a small number of specific per-hop behaviors (PHBs), which the following describes, and recommended a particular bit pattern or code-point of the DS field (see the following) for each one, in RFC 2474, RFC 2597, and RFC 2598. No more PHBs will be standardized until all the current milestones of the Working Group have been satisfied and the existing standard PHBs have been promoted at least to Draft Standard status.

The Working Group has investigated the additional components necessary to support differentiated services, including such traffic conditioners as traffic shapers and packet markers, which could be used at the boundaries of networks. Many examples of these are in the technical literature.

The Working Group will define a general conceptual model for boundary devices, including traffic conditioning parameters, as well as configuration and monitoring data. A subset of this is expected to apply to all diffserv nodes. The group will also define a MIB and a PIB for diffserv nodes, and an encoding to identify PHBs in protocol messages. It will document issues involving diffserv through tunnels.

The Working Group will not work on the following:

▼ Mechanisms for the identification of individual traffic flows

■ New signaling mechanisms to support the marking of packets

■ End-to-end service definitions

▲ Service level agreements

IPV4 ToS Octet and IPV6 Traffic Class Octet

A small bit-pattern in each packet, in the IPv4 ToS octet or the IPv6 Traffic Class octet, is used to signal that a packet is to receive a particular forwarding treatment, or per-hop behavior (PHB), at each network node. A common understanding about the use and interpretation of this bit-pattern is required for interdomain use, multivendor interoperability, and consistent reasoning about expected aggregate behaviors in a network.

Standardized DS Field

The Working Group has standardized a common layout for a six-bit field of both octets, called the *DS field*. RFC 2474 and RFC 2475 define the architecture, and the general use of bits within the DS field (superseding theIPv4 ToS octet definitions of RFC 1349).

The PDB (per Domain Behavior) Format

The WG will develop a format for precisely describing various per-domain behaviors (PDBs). A *PDB* is a collection of packets with the same codepoint, thus receiving the same PHB, traversing from edge to edge of a single diffserv network or domain. Associated with each PDB are measurable, quantifiable characteristics that can be used to describe what happens to packets of that PDB as they cross the network, thus providing an external description of the edge-to-edge quality of service to be expected by packets of that PDB within that network. A PDB is formed at the edge of a network by selecting certain packets through use of classifiers and by imposing rules on those packets via traffic conditioners. The description of a PDB contains the specific edge rules and PHB type(s) and configurations that should be used to achieve specified externally visible characteristics.

In addition to defining a format for PDB descriptions, specific descriptions of PDBs that can be constructed using the standard PHBs will be developed and reviewed by a design team prior to informational or standards track publication.

Security Threats and Countermeasures

The group will continue to analyze related security threats, especially theft of service or denial of service attacks, and suggest countermeasures.

Goals and Milestones

Here are the current goals and milestones of the Working Group:

Done	Publish draft of format for BA descriptions
Done	Meet at Adelaide IETF to review tunnels draft, discuss initial PDB descriptions
Done	Solicit PDB descriptions
Jul 00	Finalize model and MIB drafts, submit to IESG
Done	Finalize tunnels draft, submit to IESG
Aug 00	Finalize PIB draft, submit to IESG
Done	Finalize PDB format draft, submit to IESG
Aug 00	Meet at Pittsburgh IETF to finalize initial PDB descriptions, submit to IESG
Dec 00	Meet at San Diego IETF to close any open issues, make WG dormant

Internet Drafts

The following reference materials are available to further assist the reader to gain valuable information. All are available at http://www.ietf.org/internet-drafts/.

- ▼ An Informal Management Model for Diffserv Routers
- ■ Management Information Base for the Differentiated Services Architecture
- ■ New Terminology for Diffserv
- ■ Differentiated Services Quality of Service Policy Information Base
- ■ Definition of Differentiated Services Per-Domain Behaviors and Rules for Their Specification
- ■ The "Virtual Wire" Per-Domain Behavior
- ■ A Bulk Handling Per-Domain Behavior for Differentiated Services
- ■ A Revised Expression of the Expedited Forwarding PHB
- ■ Per-Hop Behavior Identification Codes
- ■ An Assured Rate Per-Domain Behavior for Differentiated Services
  An Expedited Forwarding PHB
- ▲ Supplemental Information for the New Definition of the EF PHB

RFCs (Request for Comments)

Listed next are the relevant RFCs to date regarding Diff-Serv. All are available at http://www.ietf.org/rfc/.

- ▼ Definition of the Differentiated Services Field (DS Field) in the IPv4 and IPv6

- Headers (RFC 2474)
- An Architecture for Differentiated Services (RFC 2475)
- An Expedited Forwarding PHB (RFC 2598)
- Assured Forwarding PHB Group (RFC 2597)
- Per-Hop Behavior Identification Codes (RFC 2836)
- ▲ Differentiated Services and Tunnels (RFC 2983)

SUMMARY

Bandwidth management has evolved over the last few years into a critical technological tool for enterprise and ISP/ASPs to gain maximum return on investment spent to build Lan/WAN infrastructures at the data centers and service provider centers.

To summarize what has been described in this chapter, the existing bandwidth management methodologies employed to date are

- ▼ Class Based Queuing (CBQ)
- Weighted Random Early Detection (WRED)
- TCP Rate Control
- Policy-based BWM
- Contract-based BWM
- ▲ Filter-based BWM

Clearly no "one size fits all" solution exists for bandwidth management. Stand-alone appliances are added into the infrastructure and into the path of traffic. Solutions are integrated into existing routers and LAN switches, integrated into existing firewall modules, and, finally, integrated into existing Web load-balancing switches.

Pros and Cons

TCP Rate Control can make a case that if the majority of traffic is TCP/IP, then this is the best solution if the overall goal is to prevent dropped packets and retransmissions. Standalone appliances are cost-effective and can be installed into the infrastructure without having to reconfigure existing routers and LAN switches.

With infrastructures that are "Cisco shops," the implementation of WRED on the existing routers is cost-effective and maximizes existing investment. Likewise, the same argument can be made on the integration of bandwidth management on existing firewall devices.

Integration of bandwidth management on existing Web load balancing switches—especially the Nortel solution where hardware ASICs on the ingress and egress ports are utilized to achieve wire-speed bandwidth management—is a powerful argument for a solution that is cost effective, scalable, and high performance.

Standardization Roadmap

The author defers to the Differentiated Services (Diffserv) Working Group of IETF for guidelines into the standardization roadmap for bandwidth management.

The premise of Diffserv networks is that routers within the core of the network handle packets in different traffic streams by forwarding them using different per-hop behaviors or PHBs. The capability of these routers from different vendors to determine the PHBs, which is applied as indicated by a Diffserv code point (DSCP) in the IP header of the packet and, thus, how to treat that packet, determines the degree of interoperability among these vendors.

The desired implementation is that, as packets classified by means of IP-layer marking using the DS Field enter into a differentiated services-capable network, routers within that network can interpret and determine the per-hop forwarding behavior on nodes along the path, and, thus, interoperate.

Future Applications

The ultimate goal of bandwidth management that differentiated services will allow us is the creation of scalable end-to-end QoS in the Internet. This requires that we can identify and quantify behavior for a group of packets preserved when they are aggregated with other packets as they traverse the Internet. If this is a doable proposition, then enterprises and service providers can offer meaningful SLAs to their internal and external customers and enhance their profitability.

Applications can be written to track and measure SLAs, providing validation for increased IT budgets, as well as to promote different service offerings from service providers.

REVIEW QUESTIONS

1. **Define bandwidth.**

   Bandwidth, defined as the width of a band of electromagnetic frequencies, is used as an expression of how fast data flows through a given transmission path. In computer networks, bandwidth is often measured in bits/second.

2. **What impact did "push" technology have on bandwidth management?**

   The "push" technology resulted in flooded networks and congestion in local area networks as content aggregators such as Pointcast pushed massive information to their users. Network administrators realized that to contain and control this massive information deluge requires implementation of some form of bandwidth management.

3. **Name the three solutions adapted to contain bandwidth consumption for the push technology.**

   Cache Managers, Compression Tools, and Optimized download criteria.

4. **Provide at least three components or criteria measured for Service Level Agreement (SLA).**

   Any three of the following:
   Network availability—percent uptime, Average round-trip network delay, Effective throughput, Mean Time to Respond, Mean Time to Repair.

5. **Describe TCP Rate Control.**

   TCP Rate Control is a technique of bandwidth management that paces packets on both the inbound and outbound flows in a TCP session, and results in a smooth, even flow rate to maximize throughput.

6. **Is TCP Rate Control bidirectional or unidirectional bandwidth management?**

   TCP Rate Control provides bidirectional bandwidth management for both inbound and outbound traffic.

7. **Describe some benefits and features of TCP Rate Control.**

   Eliminates unnecessary packet discards and retransmission; promotes a smooth, even flow rate to maximize throughput; provides bidirectional bandwidth management.

8. **What does CBQ stands for? Is CBQ a proprietary implementation of bandwidth management?**

   CBQ is the acronym for Class-Based Queuing. No, CBQ is not a proprietary implementation of bandwidth management. It was developed by the Network Research Group at Lawrence Berkeley National Laboratory and is now in the public domain as an open technology.

9. **Describe some features and benefits of CBQ.**

   Opens technology, not proprietary; can classify traffic into a hierarchy of classes based on any combination of IP addresses, protocols, and types of applications; can configure different bandwidth rate, (premium rate, best-effort rate), and each application or application type can then be given the appropriate bandwidth rate; allows bandwidth borrowing, so traffic classes can utilize bandwidth not used by other traffic classes when they need to burst above their guaranteed rate.

10. **What is the difference between WRED and DWRED?**

WRED is Weighted Random Early Detection and is a Cisco implementation for bandwidth management. It combines the functionality and algorithm of RED with IP precedence to give preferential treatment to higher priority traffic.

DWRED is Distributed Weighted Random Early Detection, which is also a Cisco implementation for bandwidth management that uses the Versatile Interface Processor (VIP) to provide WRED functionality. This is in contrast to WRED, which uses the route-switch processor (RSP) to implement the WRED functionality. DWRED provides faster performance than the RSP-based WRED.

Index

E

G

H

I

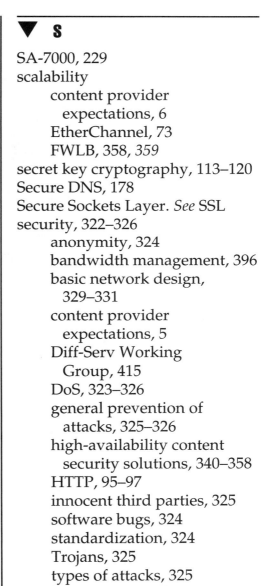

▼ **T**

INTERNATIONAL CONTACT INFORMATION

AUSTRALIA
McGraw-Hill Book Company Australia Pty. Ltd.
TEL +61-2-9417-9899
FAX +61-2-9417-5687
http://www.mcgraw-hill.com.au
books-it_sydney@mcgraw-hill.com

CANADA
McGraw-Hill Ryerson Ltd.
TEL +905-430-5000
FAX +905-430-5020
http://www.mcgrawhill.ca

**GREECE, MIDDLE EAST,
NORTHERN AFRICA**
McGraw-Hill Hellas
TEL +30-1-656-0990-3-4
FAX +30-1-654-5525

MEXICO (Also serving Latin America)
McGraw-Hill Interamericana Editores S.A. de C.V.
TEL +525-117-1583
FAX +525-117-1589
http://www.mcgraw-hill.com.mx
fernando_castellanos@mcgraw-hill.com

SINGAPORE (Serving Asia)
McGraw-Hill Book Company
TEL +65-863-1580
FAX +65-862-3354
http://www.mcgraw-hill.com.sg
mghasia@mcgraw-hill.com

SOUTH AFRICA
McGraw-Hill South Africa
TEL +27-11-622-7512
FAX +27-11-622-9045
robyn_swanepoel@mcgraw-hill.com

**UNITED KINGDOM & EUROPE
(Excluding Southern Europe)**
McGraw-Hill Education Europe
TEL +44-1-628-502500
FAX +44-1-628-770224
http://www.mcgraw-hill.co.uk
computing_neurope@mcgraw-hill.com

ALL OTHER INQUIRIES Contact:
Osborne/McGraw-Hill
TEL +1-510-549-6600
FAX +1-510-883-7600
http://www.osborne.com
omg_international@mcgraw-hill.com